WEB DATABASES WITH COLD FUSION 3

Web Databases with Cold Fusion 3

John Burke

McGraw-Hill
New York • San Francisco • Washington, D.C. • Auckland
Bogotá • Caracas • Lisbon • London • Madrid • Mexico City
Milan • Montreal • New Delhi • San Juan • Singapore
Sydney • Tokyo • Toronto

Library of Congress Cataloging-in-Publication Data

Burke, John (John M.)
    Web databases with Cold Fusion 3 / John Burke.
       p.   cm.
    Includes index.
    ISBN 0-07-913092-5
    1. Databases. 2. Cold fusion (Computer program) 3. Web sites.
I. Title.
QA76.9.D32B87   1997
005.75'8—dc21   97-44548
                                                                         CIP

McGraw-Hill

A Division of The McGraw·Hill Companies

1 2 3 4 5 6 7 8 9 0 DOC/DOC 9 0 2 1 0 9 8 7

P/N 008989-2
PART OF
ISBN 0-07-913092-5

The sponsoring editor for this book was Michael Sprague and the production supervisor was Sherri Souffrance. It was set in Century Schoolbook by Douglas & Gayle, Limited.

Printed and bound by R. R. Donnelley & Sons Company.

McGraw-Hill books are available at special quantity discounts to use as premiums and sales promotions, or for use in corporate training programs. For more information, please write to Director of Special Sales, McGraw-Hill, 11 West 19th Street, New York, NY 10011. Or contact your local bookstore.

 This book is printed on recycled, acid-free paper containing a minimum of 50% recycled de-inked fiber.

To my best friend and wife, Barbara.

CONTENTS

Contents

INTRODUCTION

You are about to begin an exciting experience in using databases on the Internet. This book will teach you how to "Webconnect" databases over the World Wide Web and how to create high-powered business applications using Windows 95 and Windows NT-based servers. Read this book to stay current with the information wave that is still building—the recent introduction of wireless Internet-connection companies such as Richochet and the development of broadcast satellite datalinks at up to 400K per second shows that digital connectivity is sweeping around the world! In the Far East, Singapore and Malaysia vie for information highway connections to the Orient. In Europe, new business nets open daily; in the former Soviet Union, digital technology is pouring in from Japan and Korea as new webs develop. This book shows you how to be a player in this world digital information revolution.

Who Needs to Read This Book

You need to read this book if you use PC databases, if you need quick and easy ways to Webconnect your favorite database to the World Wide Web, or if you need to learn how to install Windows NT and Internet Server software. Each author brings specific professional expertise to tasks in the specialized world of the Internet. Each chapter shows you how to quickly get software installed, get applications up and running, and how to start generating your own Web traffic. This book keeps you on the cutting edge of PC databases, servers, Cold Fusion Professional 3.0 software, and Microsoft operating systems and servers. It showcases the premier middleware CGI-Script writing software: Allaire's Cold Fusion Professional 3.0.

From the Authors

Bob Nielson, a professional commercial C programmer, writes chapters about Windows NT Versions 3.5 and 4.0 Workstation and Server pros and cons, Netscape Server, O'Reilly, Microsoft ITS servers, and Microsoft's new SQL Server—the up-and-coming database—and Cold Fusion Professional 3.0 installation and configuration.

Don Brenneman, a Visual Basic programmer and previously published author, presents a commercial level industrial-strength database Internet application featuring Cold Fusion 3.0 using multiple-pass SQL database queries, transaction control, HTML "cookies," and in-depth variables, functions, and arrays. His extended business application covers three full chapters of integrated Cold Fusion programming modules that are broken apart and annotated to show you at great depth how to harness the power of Cold Fusion Professional 3.0 to build your own commercial business applications. Don also writes a chapter covering new features in Cold Fusion 3 which includes arrays.

John Burke, a working Internet Web designer with Seagate Technologies, Inc., and previously of Varian Associates, Inc., and previous contributing author to *Running a Perfect Website*, 2nd Edition, writes chapters covering introductory and advanced HTML, Frames with embedded Cold Fusio,n and JavaScript mouse events, window creation, and data validation. He writes chapters on SQL (he studied under an IBM SQL dialect expert) and major PC databases such as Microsoft's Access, the easy-to-use database; Microsoft's Visual FoxPro, the fast, hierarchical database using Rushmore Technology; Borland's Visual dBASE, featuring easy connectivity to Borland's IntraBuilder as well as Cold Fusion Professional 3.0; Corel's Paradox, the multiuser PC database; Oracle's Personal Oracle 7, the miniframe-style PC database.

John also writes about Crystal Reports, bundled at no extra cost with Cold Fusion and which generates automated SQL code and allows easy image manipulation inside reports. Crystal Reports features a WYSIWYG report-building environment. Other topics covered include automated e-mail using Cold Fusion, CF Templates creation for reusable modular design and auto-generation of HTML pages.

This book is designed to be used like a PC database tool; you can use this book to quickly and easily build multitable databases, Webconnect databases and tables to servers using plug-n-play ODBC drivers, and use SQL to do *data mining* on tables for precise information retrieval.

Programming examples show how to solve business problems; database chapters show how to include text, image, and multimedia data and how to connect to Web servers. The multiuser database chapters show how to configure users and privileges, use unique keys, ensure data integrity, referential integrity, and database security. The text uses sequences of figures to carry the story visually and to show query results, database output, and coding examples.

A self-discovery process is employed throughout the book, with notes, warnings, and cautions added along the way. The book assumes no familiarity with software products but also contains sections written specif-

.ically for commercial-level computer professionals (see the three-chapter programming examples in Chapters 17–19). The book is divided into four parts: Introductory/Intermediate Level Database Programming, Advanced Database and Cold Fusion 3.0 Programming, A Multi-Chapter Cold Fusion 3 Programming Example, and HTML Language Extensions. This multi-author work gives you the insight and understandings of three working computer professionals from start to finish using these software products.

We, the authors, hope that you have a great time using this book to solve problems, explore issues, and build database and server knowledge just as we have had writing it. This book is designed to be a handy Web Development resource that covers all the major PC databases you've always wondered about but never got around to.

The Authors:

John Burke, Don Brennemann, and Bob Neilson

Web Overview

Public use of the Internet exploded in 1993 with the release of the Mosaic graphical browser. (Up until that point, you could send text over the Internet, but not as easily send graphics). Marc Andreesen, a University of Illinois student at Urbana, built Mosaic, a Web Browser that read hyperlinks, which could be used to navigate the Web, and could display graphics. The next step was to create browser plug-ins to make possible the use of multimedia, including movies and soundtracks.

The WWW with text and images was not much in the public news before 1994 because the supporting software was just being developed. The introduction of HYPERTEXT in Web documents made possible easy access to documents on servers on the other side of the world; users could very quickly find information even if the actual information was thousands of miles away. In 1996, Cold Fusion was introduced as an answer to the challenge of connecting databases to Web servers.

How It All Works

Cold Fusion uses a *CLIENT / SERVER* approach (client/server architecture is the technical term) to work its wonders. A *server* (a computer mounted with appropriate software) stores a database that a *client* (someone behind the steering wheel of a browser program on a remote computer) requests—using a *uniform resource locator* (URL) to make the request. The request is processed something like this:

Connection Speeds

Type of connections	Speed	Cost of connection	Provider
Dial-up	28.8/33.3K	$15-$50	AOL, MSN,ISP
ISDN	64K	$50-$250 plus install	PAC BELL
T1	1.56M	$100-$3000	PAC BELL
T3	44.7M	$50-$150K	PAC BELL

INTERNET FLOW DIAGRAM Browser on PC→ISP→ROUTER→ Internet→ISP→PC and loops back.

ISP—Independent Service Provider (or) a large service provider.

Servers can handle multiple simultaneous document or database requests. To get your Web page to a server, you must send out the computer address of your server (and Web index page) to a search engine. This enables you to publish your Web page when the search engine puts your computer address in its data bank. Your Web page is now ready to be accessed by someone using the same search engine over the WWW.

When a data request from a fill-in form comes in from a Web site visitor, the fill-in form can send a query to your server, where a Cold Fusion template (an automated CGI script) will retrieve database information, and generate a HTML document back to the Web site visitor. The whole process takes only moments. If you put your URL on 10 separate WWW search engines, you are then Web-accessible to visitors using those 10 different services. All that's left to do is to put up some banner advertising on several of those search engines, and watch the hits start coming.

HOW TO USE THE CD-ROM Each chapter on the CD-ROM contains examples with working code. Copy HTML documents, GIFs, JPGs, and Cold Fusion templates into the document directory of your Web server. Place database tables into the corresponding database storage areas as recommended in the database software product's literature, and then use Cold Fusion to connect the databases to the HTML fill-in forms as shown later in the book.

PART 1

Introductory/ Intermediate Level Database Programming

1

HTML Web Style Minicourse

- Creating HTML documents
- Developing a Web style
- Using Web utilities: LVIEW PRO and Paint Shop Pro
- Building interactive fill-in forms to connect to Web servers
- Creating a combination Check box-Select element **NEW!**
- Building nested tables in forms
- Using frames

Creating HTML Documents

You can use HTML to communicate on the World Wide Web (WWW). Most documents and images traveling back and forth across the Internet are written in a hybrid word processing/multi-media capable language called HTML (Hypertext Markup Language). This chapter shows how to use HTML formatting tags to create your documents, how to include images and sounds, and how to intelligently select elements for an HTML document style. If you already are an experienced HTML user, you'll benefit from this chapter's coverage on using forms with databases. Later in the book, a separate chapter covers using HTML frames. But to be completely fair, many Web sites do not use frames at all, but rather rely on an integrated text and image design to achieve a successful Web site.

To build an HTML document, use a word processor, the MS Windows Notepad editor, or a custom HTML editor to create HTML files. Files are saved in a *plain-text* format using an .HTML file extension. Several word processors (including Microsoft Word 97) have HTML converters built-in. But if you need greater control plus specialized features, download an HTML editor from the Internet. For basic Web page development I use HTML Assistant PRO version 3.0 from Brooklyn Software software, but there are many other excellent HTML editors being used.

NOTE   *HTML Assistant PRO Version 3.0 contains features such as find and replace across all files in a directory, find and replace for transforming upper-case tags to lowercase tags, color display of tags, and so on.*

HTML documents use markup tags to control text formatting, position graphical user elements (such as images), include sound files, and build interactive forms used as front-ends to databases on the Internet. Each HTML tag is made up of two elements, a beginning tag and an ending tag. Each tag consists of two brackets, < ... >, with a short word or abbreviated word inside. For example, an opening <HTML> tag is the first tag of an HTML document, and a closing </HTML> tag marks the end of an HTML document. All closing tags must contain a forward slash "/". HTML tags were developed by extending existing word processing tags. You can search the Internet using the word *Cougar* if you are interested in what the new HTML 4.0 standard will be like. If you want to technically investigate the current HTML 3.2 standard, search on the word HMTL 3. *(Wilbur)*.

▬ ▬

WEB JUMP   *To download a trial HTML editor, go to any Search engine, enter the words* **HTML editor**, *for example. You can find more than 60 HTML editors on Yahoo's Search engine at the following WWW address:*

```
http://www.yahoo.com/Computers_and_Internet/Software/Internet/
    World_Wide_Web/HTML_Editors/MS_Windows/
```

HTML Document Sections

The Head Section: The first section of an HTML document is the *Head section*, containing information about the document such as the title, creator, and date of creation. On the top line of the document put an opening <HTML> tag. (See Figure 1-1.) On the next line use a <HEAD> tag to open the Head section. On the next line use a comment tag, <!- ...->, to add title, author, and date of creation; for example, *<!—topframe.htm, created by J. Smith, 6/1/97->*. On the next line type the <TITLE> tag and then type on the same line; for example, *World Corp., Inc. World Headquarters*. Then type </TITLE> at the end of the line. The browser displays the title information prominently in the Browser's title bar above the Web page.

   The Body Section: The next HTML document section is the *Body section*. Use a <BODY> tag to open and add working tags. Then close with a </BODY> tag. The body contains the content of your document. The following example shows all the sections of an introductory HTML document. The document is closed with an </HTML> tag on the last line of the document.

   This document only has one line of output plus a title displayed in the title bar. Later in the chapter, documents will contain much more.

An Introductory
HTML Document

```
<HTML>
<HEAD>
<!—Topframe.htm, created by  M. Smith , 6/1/97 —>
<TITLE World Corp., Inc. World Headquarters </TITLE>
</HEAD>
<BODY>
Corporate Information goes here…
</BODY>
</HTML>
< — OUTPUT — >
Corporate Information goes here…
```

Developing Your Own Web Style

HTML documents employ different font sizes and colors to highlight important text and help the eye scan the Web page. Because reading text on a computer screen is 20 to 30 percent more difficult than reading identical material on paper, it is helpful to think about how much and what you are going to present to Web site visitors. Developing a clear, forceful interesting style is the key.

WEB JUMP   *View a Web Style Manual at this WWW address:*

`http://www.sun.com`

It is helpful to remember that a standard monitor displays approximately 20 to 26 lines of text. And in contrast to the printed page (where readers glance up to the top of the page to see the book title and headings to reorient themselves, when the Web page visitor scrolls down past your first page), the top of the browser page disappears. (Unless you are using frames, see Chapter 21, "Using Frames with Cold Fusion.") Therefore, design for *browser-sized pages*—that is, separate 20 to 26 line units that are separate visual entities. Set off each Web page with its own individual heading. To stop lines, use the paragraph tag <P> to begin new paragraphs (this creates a single empty line space) and use the line break tag <BR> to begin new lines with no line space.

Developing a Web Style

When moving from paper to Web page, consider only using a couple of type sizes. I have done hundreds of hours of work converting legacy documents to HTML documents and find that less is more. Using too many different font sizes in Web documents reduces clarity for readers. A number of Web stylists are now recommending to only use two font sizes throughout Web documents. To further improve readability, consider using one or more of the following paragraph header styles to help your readers scan your documents.

WEB PARAGRAPH STYLES   Style 1—Centered and **Bolded Text Title With The First Letter Of Each Word In CAPS** Followed By Two Line Spaces—Use this dramatic heading only at the top of major sections of your document. Usually, the wording of this heading matches the heading taken from your document's index of hypertext links. (How to build a hypertext links index is shown later in this chapter.)

Style 2—**Bolded text title alone on its own line**—A commonly used secondary heading for setting off one or two paragraphs of text.

Style 3—**Bolded text** (or *italicized text title*) **embedded in the paragraph**—This style is a more subtle way of embedding headings into the body of a paragraph. Consider putting an empty line after each paragraph to set off individual paragraphs.

If you use colored fonts, use a font tag to turn color on and off; for example, <font color=teal> *text is in color here* </font>. (Pick a user-friendly color other than red.) The title of your document can be italicized using the italics tag: <I> *italicized text here* </I>. A font tag, which increases the standard font size, can be used in the title: <font size=+1> *a larger font here* </font>. The font is increased one size only between the font tags.

CAUTION *Be careful to return text to default values after using custom font sizes and colors. If you forget an ending tag for font color or font size, all the rest of your documents will display the custom font.*

USING BOLDED PARAGRAPH HEADINGS The following code uses a centered title, a bolded paragraph heading, and a standard paragraph. The bolded paragraph heading is bolded.

```
<HTML>
<CENTER><I><FONT SIZE="+2" COLOR=teal>A Document
      Title</I></FONT></CENTER>
<! — Comment: The next line produces a bolded header
      line — >
<B>This Paragraph heading is bold</B><BR>
This is a one sentence paragraph featuring <br>
a hypertext link right here: <A HREF= "http://.sun.com" >
      Guide to Web Style" </A>.
</HTML>

< — SCREEN OUTPUT — >
                A Document Title
This Paragraph heading is bold
This is a one sentence paragraph featuring...
a hypertext link right here: Guide to Web Style" .
```

BUILDING HYPERTEXT LINKS Hypertext links are made up of four parts:

A HREF=   Opens the hypertext tag. (HREF stands for hypertext reference.)

"bigcorp.com"   The WWW address is placed inside double quotes.

Guide to Web Style   The hypertext title displayed in your document.

</A>   Closes the hypertext tag.

If you leave off the closing </A>, every line in your document will be blue and underlined.

CREATING BULLETED LISTS   You can easily create indented bulleted lists of hyperlinks. Use the <UL>...</UL> tag to create the bulleted list:

```
<UL>
    <LI> Hyperlink 1
    <LI> Hyperlink 2
    <LI> Hyperlink 3
<UL>
< — OUTPUT — >
Hyperlink 1
Hyperlink 2
Hyperlink 3
```

NESTED LISTS   Lists can be nested under the main list by inserting a second nested <UL> tag as shown here:

```
<UL>
    <LI>Topic 1
    <LI>Topic 2
    <LI>Topic 3
        <UL>
            <LI>Topic 3a
            <LI>Topic 3b
            <LI>Topic 3c
        </UL>
    </UL>
```

HTML creates a different style bullet for the *second level* nested list. When nesting tags inside other tags in HTML documents, it is a good practice to indent three spaces. This helps the reader to quickly understand the level of nesting when inspecting your HTML document. (And that reader could be you!)

The above HTML tags create the following nested list:

```
Topic 1
Topic 2
Topic 3
            Topic 3a
```

```
Topic 3b
Topic 3c
```

ORDERED LISTS: NUMBER AND LETTER SEQUENCES Numbered lists are created by using numbers or letters of the alphabet. The tag used for ordered lists (such as 1,2,3 or a,b,c) is <OL>...</OL>. Type in your desired heading right after the first <OL> tag and it will show up as a left-justified title in the ordered list.

The following HTML code creates a numbered list:

```
<HTML>
<OL>
A Numbered List Header
<LI> Open an unformatted text document
<LI> Create the Header
<LI> Create the Body
<LI> Close the document
</OL>
</HTML>


< —    OUTPUT  — >
A Numbered List Header
    1.   Open an unformatted text document
    2. Create the Header
    3.Create the Body
    4. Close the HTML document
```

In an HTML document, use the <OL> tag with <LI> tags to give the preceding output.

To correctly build lists containing alphabetic, roman number sequences, or symbols, see Table 1-1. The type= parameter is used to select roman numbers, smallcase, uppercase letters, etc., as shown below.

NOTE *Some browsers display small squares, disks, or circles differently than as shown in the Table 3.1. You should test how small squares, disks, or circles are displayed on the browser that your company has standardized on, or on several different browsers if you are going on the WWW. The following code creates an ordered list with uppercase roman numerals on Netscape Navigator.*

```
<HTML>
<OL>
How to Create HTML Documents
<LI type=I> Open an unformatted text document
<LI type=I> Create the Header
<LI type=I> Create the Body
<LI type=I> Close the HTML document
</OL>
```

Table 1-1

Symbols Used in
Lists

List Desired	Tag Used	Example
Numbers	<type=1>	1, 2, 3
Uppercase roman numerals	<type=I>	I, II, III, IV
Lowercase roman numerals	<type=I>	i, ii, iii, iv
Uppercase letters	<type=A>	A, B, C
Lowercase letters	<type=a>	a, b, c
Small square	<type=square>	■, ■, ■
Disk	<type=disk>	◯, ◯, ◯
Circle	<type=circle>	◯, ◯, ◯

```
</HTML>
< — OUTPUT — >
             How to Create HTML Documents
I.   Open an unformatted text document
II.   Create the Header
III.   Create the Body
IV.   Close the HTML document
```

DEFINITION LISTS To create a list without bullets or numbers, use the <DL> and <DT> tags as shown here:

```
<HTML>
<DL>
<DT>The Title
    <DD>The first indented item
    <DD>The second item
    <DD>The third item
</DT>
</DL>
</HTML>

< — OUTPUT — >
The Title
      The first indented item
      The second item
      The third item
```

CUSTOMIZED BULLETS If you want to create customized bullets to use as symbols for your lists, you can make small GIF images using a program such as Paint Shop Pro, LVIEW PRO, or PhotoShop, or you can purchase a commercial collection of GIF images. Use Paint Shop Pro to resize

GIF or *JPG* images. Paint Shop Pro can be downloaded from the Internet and is easy to learn.

USING PAINT SHOP PRO   Paint Shop Pro can import many different file formats. You can also create your own images in Paint Shop Pro or modify already existing symbols or images. After opening Paint Shop Pro, click the Open File List icon and then select the *GIF* or *JPG* image file you would like to modify. (This is assuming you have already located a GIF or JPG image you want to modify and use.) Paint Shop Pro displays the screen shown in Figure 1-1.

In Paint Shop Pro, if the displayed image is hard to see and you want to magnify it, click the left mouse anywhere inside the image to zoom larger, or the right mouse button to zoom smaller. The image resizes.

To change the image size in bytes, click the Image button, and then select the Resize button. The Resize dialog box appears, as shown in Figure 1-2. Click the Custom Size radio button.

The Resize dialog box displays two boxes containing numbers. These numbers represent the dimensions of the image in pixels. (For example, screen monitors measure space in pixels.) If the numbers of an image

Figure 1-1

The main screen in Paint Shop Pro

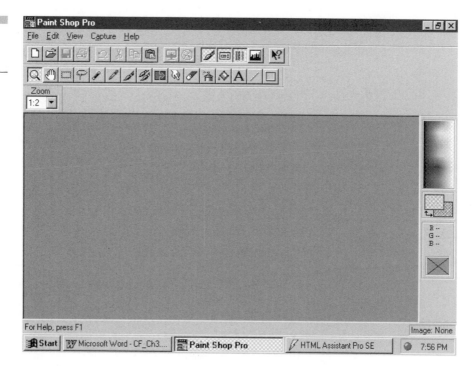

Figure 1-2
Using the Resize
dialog box

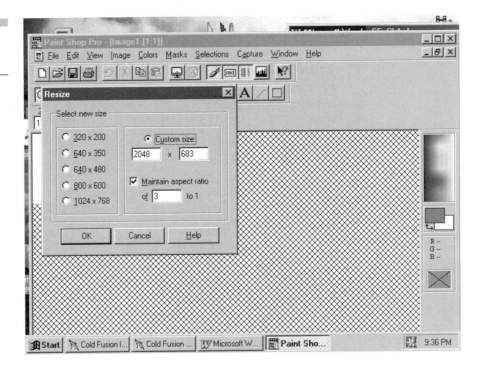

(which represent the image size) are 30 pixels by 7 pixels, and you want to resize this image upwards, click the cursor inside the 30 box and enter **40**. Then, click the cursor in the 7 box, and the box automatically updates itself to 9 pixels. Click OK. You have now proportionally enlarged the image. If you don't like the result, click the Edit button and press Undo.

By entering larger numbers, you can resize the image to 40-by-9 pixels, which in this case is a good size to match to standard size text (font size=10). Paint Shop Pro redraws the resized image on the screen. Save the redrawn image using an eight-character DOS filename with a .GIF file extension, (for example, mynew. gif).

Using LVIEW PRO Software

WEB JUMP   *To download an evaluation copy of LVIEW PRO, use this URL:*

`http://www.lview.com/`

Use LVIEW PRO to further fine-tune your GIF, JPG, or other image type. After you open a file in LVIEW PRO, you can easily click and drag your cursor to include the parts of an image you would like to retain; then you can easily click Edit and then Crop to edit out the extraneous parts of the image. After cropping, click Save to save the file. If you are not satisfied with the outcome, you can easily resize. You may also import and edit other types of images such as PCX images. And after cropping the image, you can save it as a GIF or JPG image.

The following Figure 1-3 shows how to insert GIFs in a Web page.

```
<HTML>
<IMG SRC="star.gif" ALIGN=TOP> My first list item<BR>
<IMG SRC="star.gif" ALIGN=TOP> My second list item<BR>
<IMG SRC="star.gif" ALIGN=TOP> My last list item
</HTML>
```

Image tags <IMG SRC> are made up of the following parts:

\<IMG SRC=	Opens the image source tag
"star.gif"	The title of the GIF file
ALIGN=TOP>	Image alignment can be TOP, MIDDLE, BOTTOM, LEFT, or RIGHT in comparison to the text image title.

Figure 1-3
Using GIF images in lists

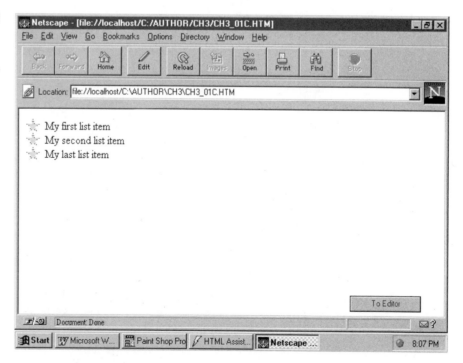

You may also use JPG image files—in many cases these are smaller and load faster than the corresponding GIF files. The next section describes how to incorporate these elements in fill-in forms, which you create for your HTML documents.

Introduction to Using Forms in HTML Documents

Your Web page is evaluated by visitors on the basis of its appearance. If you have not spent sufficient time in Web page design, your visitors may not stay long. The following section shows how to build fill-in forms, which later will be the front-end for database entry. Carefully examine how the following tables and forms are constructed.

Using Forms with Internet Databases

Web pages use fill-in forms to send information to server databases over the WWW. When form information is collected from the user and *submitted*, the browser creates data packets out of the form data and sends a URL with the attached data to the server. When the URL is received, the server starts a CGI script to process the information. At this point, if you have CGI software a CGI script processes the URL. If you use Cold Fusion, Cold Fusion uses its own internal CGI script to connect to databases or spreadsheets on the server.

After the database information is retrieved (if this is your goal), the CGI script can generate an HTML document and send it back to the end user's browser (the client). The transaction takes place quickly. The author has personally tested Cold Fusion-powered client-server databases between Internet sites separated by more than 1,500 miles. The data came up just as if it had come from a local LAN or WAN server. The next section shows you how to build user-friendly fill-in forms to Web connect to your Web server's databases, spreadsheets, e-mail documents, and legacy files.

BUILDING INTERACTIVE FORMS Most users have browsers that support the major graphical user elements (such as GIF and JPG images, radio buttons, text boxes, and check boxes). Therefore, this section will show you how to incorporate these tag-based elements in your HTML document.

Fill-in forms are always placed inside HTML documents. It is possible to place the opening form tag immediately in the Header section at the top of the document. (If you want to query some database information before the user gets to the form, then the opening form tag is placed after the database query. Forms contain three main elements:

- A *header* section, which includes a URL containing the http address of a particular Cold Fusion template.
- A *body* section, which contains input fields to be filled in.
- A *submit* button and a *reset* button, which control the action of the form.

Figure 1-4 shows HTML tags used to create a fill-in form.

```
          <HTML>
<TITLE>Quick Form </TITLE>
<h2>Quick Form</h2>
<HR>
<! — The form header contains a URL address of a Cold
     Fusion template processing
the form — >
<FORM ACTION= "http://127.0.0.1/HOTDOCS/AUTHOR/
     CHPT3_01.CFM" METHOD=POST>
Enter your first name: <INPUT NAME="firstname"> </P>
Enter your last name: <INPUT NAME="lastname"></P>
```

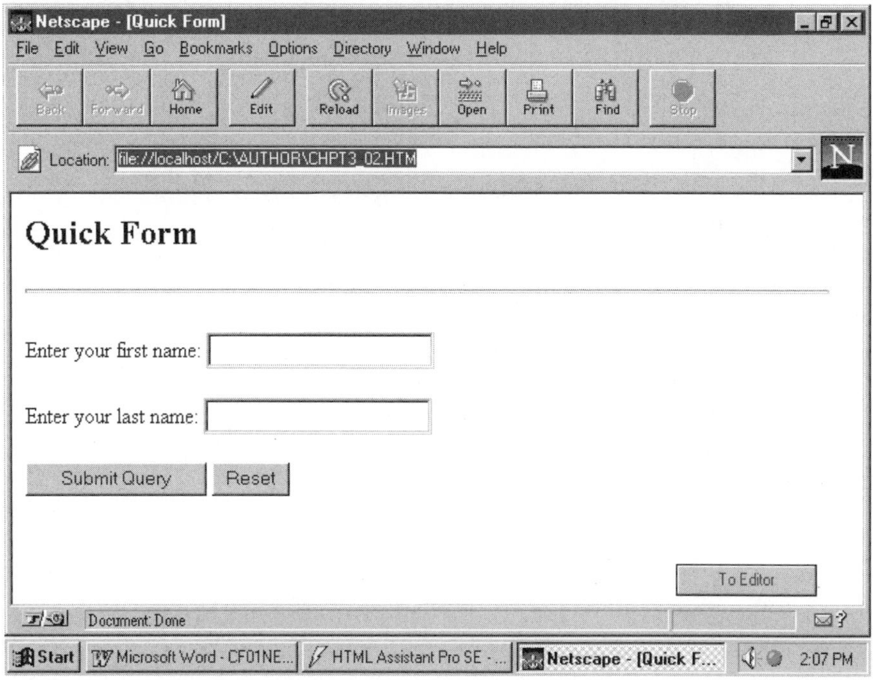

Figure 1-4
A quick fill-in form

```
<INPUT TYPE="Submit">
<INPUT TYPE="Reset"></P>
</FORM>
</HTML>
```

The Form header (<FORM ACTION…>) must contain a URL with the address of a Cold Fusion template; it must also end with METHOD=POST. The POST method allows all the form field data to be attached to the URL and sent to the server. When it arrives, the URL (with its included form data) starts Cold Fusion on the server, which processes the form data, queries the database, and sends a URL back to the client (end user).

In the next lines of the form—the Body section—various input field elements are used. For example, if you want to ask the end user to input their first name, you would create the input field name *firstname*. Similarly, you would create a *lastname* input field, and so on. At the very bottom of the form, after you have requested all the input field information you need from the end user, use a *Submit* button to cause the browser to process the data and encode the form information into a URL to be sent to the server. The *Reset* button allows the user to start over by clearing the input field data.

Table 1-2 lists available graphical user interface elements that can be used inside HTML fill-in forms.

USING FORMS WITH RADIO BUTTONS   Using graphical user interface elements allows the form to perform varied tasks. The form shown in Figure 1-5 uses radio buttons to present multiple choices to end users.

Table 1-2

Graphical User
Interface Elements
in Forms

Element	HTML Tag
Check box	<INPUT TYPE= "check box" NAME= fieldname1>choice#1
Radio	<INPUT TYPE= "radio" NAME=secondfieldname>choice#2
Text	<INPUT TYPE= "text" NAME= "yourtext">
Textarea	<TEXTAREA NAME= "paragraph1">
Select	<SELECT NAME= "credit_card_type">
	<OPTION>VISA
	<OPTION>MASTERCARD
	</SELECT>
Hidden	<INPUT TYPE= "Hidden" NAME= "name@email_address" VALUE= "email">

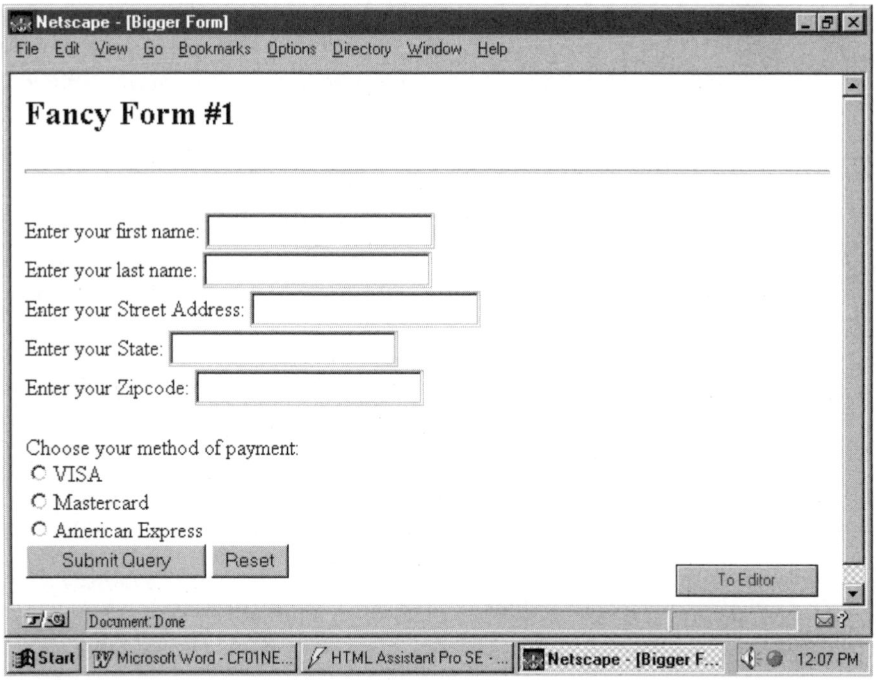

Figure 1-5

Using radio buttons
to present user
choices

```
Netscape - [Bigger Form]                                              _ 🗗 ✕
File  Edit  View  Go  Bookmarks  Options  Directory  Window  Help
```

Fancy Form #1

Enter your first name: [   ]

Enter your last name: [   ]

Enter your Street Address: [   ]

Enter your State: [   ]

Enter your Zipcode: [   ]

Choose your method of payment:
○ VISA
○ Mastercard
○ American Express

[Submit Query] [Reset]

[To Editor]

```
  Document: Done
```

```
Start  | Microsoft Word - CF01NE... | HTML Assistant Pro SE - ... | Netscape - [Bigger F... |    12:07 PM
```

USING RADIO BUTTONS

```
<HTML>
 <TITLE>Fancy form #1</TITLE>
 <h2>Fancy Form #1</h2>
 <HR>
 <! The form header contains an  URL which points to a
      Cold Fusion template. The Cold Fusion template on
      the server processes the form and then generates
      an HTML file back to the enduser >
<FORM ACTION= "http://127.0.1/AUTHOR/CHPT1_01.CFM"
  METHOD=POST>
  Enter your first name :<INPUT NAME="firstname"></BR>
  Enter your last name: <INPUT NAME="lastname"></BR>
  Enter Street Address: <INPUT NAME="address1"></BR>
  Enter your State:  <INPUT NAME="address2"></BR>
  Enter your Zipcode:<INPUT NAME="zip"><P>
  Choose your method of payment:<BR>
  <INPUT TYPE= "radio" NAME= "VISA">VISA</BR>
  <INPUT TYPE= "radio" NAME= "MASTERCARD">Mastercard</BR>
  <INPUT TYPE= "radio" NAME= "AM_EXPRESS">American
      Express</BR>
  <INPUT TYPE="Submit">
  <INPUT TYPE="Reset"></P>
  </FORM>
  </HTML>
```

As the form grows larger and more complex, spacing and alignment become increasingly important. The next section shows how to align form elements. (This form uses the *nonbreaking space* character   for quick spacing.)

The following example shows how to use the nonbreaking space   to align text input fields without using the table tag.

Nonbreaking spaces can be used almost anywhere in HTML forms to adjust hard-to-position graphical user interface elements. But try to use other elements (such as the center tag and align tag) to reduce the use of nonbreaking spaces.

```
<HTML>
        TITLE>Bigger  Form </TITLE>
        <h2>Fancy Form #1</h2>
        <HR>
        <! The form header contains a URL address to a Cold
    Fusion template used to process the form
            on the server>
            <FORM ACTION= "http://127.0.1/AUTHOR/
    CHPT1_01.CFM"   METHOD=POST>
Enter your first name : <INPUT NAME="firstname"></BR>
Enter your last name:  <INPUT NAME="lastname"></BR>
```

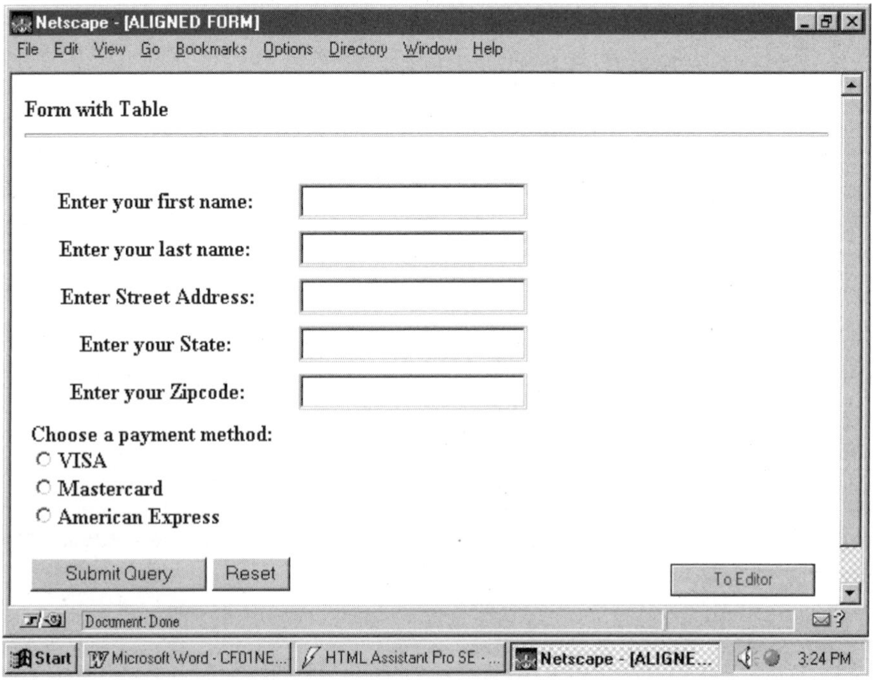

Figure 1-6
Formatting with non-breaking spaces

```
Enter Street Address: <INPUT NAME="address1"></BR>
Enter your State:       
    <INPUT
    NAME="address2"></BR>
Enter your Zipcode:   <INPUT NAME="zip"><P>
Choose your method of payment:<BR>
<INPUT TYPE= "radio" NAME= "VISA">VISA</BR>
<INPUT TYPE= "radio" NAME= "MASTERCARD">Mastercard</BR>
<INPUT TYPE= "radio" NAME= "AM_EXPRESS">American
    Express</BR>
<INPUT TYPE="Submit">
<INPUT TYPE="Reset"></P>
</FORM>
</HTML>
```

In addition to using nonbreaking spaces, slight alignment changes may be made by placing a single empty space before a nonbreaking space(s). (Different letter widths create these alignment problems.) Some browsers may ignore some tags (such as the <BR> tag) if they are used in formatting (for example, Microsoft Internet Explorer 3.0). This problem arises because the HTML language standard is supported differently by different browsers. The following Figure 1-7 shows how to use check boxes and select tags in fill-in forms to present choices to users.

Figure 1-7
Using check boxes
and select tags

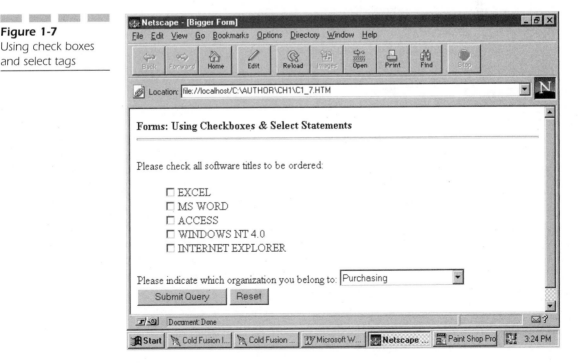

The following HTML code shows how to include check boxes and select tags into fill-in forms.

```
<HTML>
<TITLE>Bigger   Form </TITLE>
<B>Forms: Using Check boxes & Select
Statements</B>
<HR>
<!- The form header contains a URL which
     points to the Cold Fusion template used
     to process the form on the server ->
<FORM ACTION= "CHPT1_01.CFM"   METHOD=POST>
Please check all software titles to be
     ordered:
<UL>
<INPUT TYPE= "check box" NAME= "EXCEL">EXCEL</BR>
<INPUT TYPE= "check box" NAME= "MSWORD">MS WORD</BR>
<INPUT TYPE= "check box" NAME= "ACCESS">ACCESS</BR>
<INPUT TYPE= "check box" NAME= "NT4">WINDOWS NT 4.0</BR>
<INPUT TYPE= "check box" NAME= "INET_EXPLORER">INTERNET
     EXPLORER
</UL>
Please indicate which organization you belong to:
<SELECT NAME="org" SIZE=3>
<OPTION>Purchasing
<OPTION>Human Services
<OPTION SELECTED>Accounting
<OPTION>Shipping and Receiving
<OPTION>Administration
</SELECT>
<INPUT TYPE="Submit">
<INPUT TYPE="Reset"></P>
</FORM>
</HTML>
```

In this Select statement, the default item (in this case *Accounting*) is selected by using *OPTION SELECTED*. Usually the end user makes only one selection out of all the choices. But Select statements can also allow multiple selections to be made by using the keyword *multiple*: <SELECT NAME="org" MULTIPLE SIZE=3>. Additionally, when the *SIZE* attribute is used, it determines how many of the choices are displayed by the browser, (in this case three items: *Purchasing*, *Human Services*, and *Accounting*).

To make two or more selections, the user must hold down the Control key and click the mouse on a selection at the same time. Make sure that you give instructions to the user about multiple selection options.

The Select statement's choices are stored in a single variable (in our example, the *org* variable*)*. The script that processes the form will place a character (such as a dash or hash mark) between several values of the *org* variable when the script stores the selected values in the variable. A second way to use the Select tag is to use it in conjunction with the check-box. A powerful and compact tag consisting of a check box and select tag can be constructed by using these two elements on the same line. An example of using these two elements together is shown in Figure 1-8.

HOW TO CREATE THE CHECK BOX—SELECT ELEMENT   In the following code example, if the Select element is placed immediately after the Check box element, HTML will display both elements together on one line. To use the Select element as a help screen, omit the *name="…"* attribute. Notice how the two tags are used in the example that follows; the bolded code highlights the creation of this combined tag element.

```
<HTML>
(!—The table tag (next line) builds a table with a border
     4 pixels wide, creates a 410 pixel-wide form and
     makes 6 pixel-wide cell borders in the table
     (cellpadding option) —>
<table border=4 width=410 cellpadding=6>
<FORM>
<TR>
<TD><FONT SIZE=+1
```

Figure 1-8
The Check box-Select
dual element

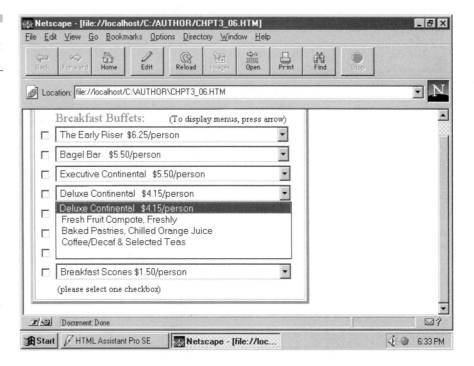

```
COLOR=RED>     Breakfast Buffets:
    </font>       
     <font size="-1">(To display  menus, press
    arrow)</font><BR>

<!--The Check box element is placed on the line above the
    Select element, but HTML combines them on the
        screen!>
  <b><INPUT type="check box" NAME="brkfast" VALUE="Early
    Riser"></b>
            <SELECT>
<OPTION SELECTED> The Early Riser  $6.25/person
            <OPTION>   Scrambled Eggs, Home
                Style Potatoes,    
            <OPTION>  Crisp Bacon Strips,
                Sausage Links,
            <OPTION>  Chilled Fruit Juice,
                Fresh Fruit Compote,
            <OPTION>  Fresh Baked Pastries,
                Coffee/Decaf
            <OPTION>  & Selected Teas
            <OPTION> 
  </SELECT><BR>
  <font size="-1">       
      (please select a check box)</font>
</TD>
</TR>
</FORM>
</TABLE>
```

When you use a combined Check box-Select element, more information is displayed on each screen and the end user has the option of either using or not using the pull-down help menus. Notice that the Select element does not function in its usual way, as an input choice, but is rather used to help create a series of pull-down help menus. You can also use the Select tag (again, omit the name field) to create help menus wherever needed on the form. If you use this special element combination, remember that it must be created inside a form tag, otherwise the element will not work. Also, do not forget to give the end user specific instructions on how to use the new-style pull-down menus. In the next chapter, a *Check box-Select* pull-down style menu is integrated into an easy-to-use automated e-mail program. (In the JavaScript chapter, (Chapter 21), an additional method of presenting pop-up help screens is shown.)

USING TABLES IN FORMS   The next section shows how to use tables inside forms. Multiple table creations can be tricky because tables must be carefully nested below the main table. HTML document authors who learn how to simultaneously employ three side-by-side tables have powerful formatting tools, which allow them to create many different kinds of visual presentations of information.

INSERTING TABLES INSIDE OF FORMS   The following example (Figure 1-9) shows how to create a single table *inside* a form. This step is useful because it allows special formatting to be done without using nonbreaking spaces. Notice the repeating <TR> and <TH> tag groups; each one of these tag groups begins a new line in the table.

Each *TR* tag begins a new line in the table. Each *th* (table header–bolded text) tag begins a new *invisible* box on that line. Each box can be made visible if an optional value *border=2* is added to the table tag (for example, <table border=2>). If you use *td* instead of *th*, the text is not bolded.

USING NESTED TABLES   Tables can be also nested inside the main table, as shown in Figure 1-10. You can change the width of the outer table by changing its numerical percentage; for example, *<table width=100%>* can be changed to *<table width=80%>*. In this case, the *"width=%"* feature only changes the main table. The nested table expands into the remaining unused space leftover by the first table. When you build the nested table, be sure to place it under a <TH> tag to work properly, as shown in 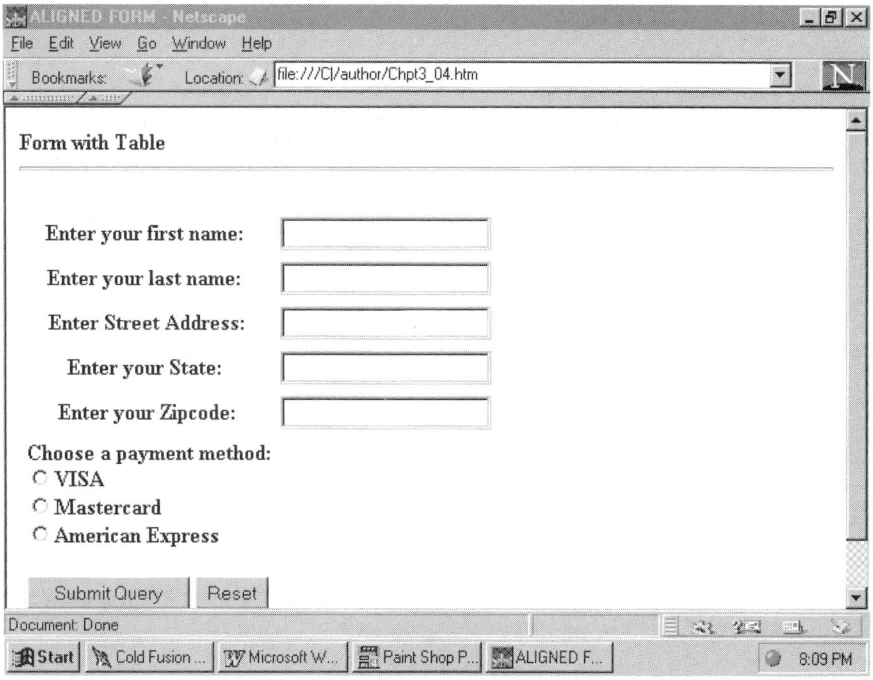

Figure 1-9
Form with inserted table

Code to Insert a
Table Inside a Form

```
<HTML>
<TITLE>ALIGNED FORM</TITLE>
<b>Form with Table</b>
<HR>
<TABLE>
<! COMMENT The form element is placed inside the table
      element>
<FORM ACTION= "CHPT3_01.CFM" METHOD=POST>
 <TR>
     <TH>Enter your first name: </TH>
     <TH><INPUT NAME="firstname"></TH>
 </TR>
 <TR>
     <TH>Enter your last name: </TH>
     <TH><INPUT NAME="lastname"></TH>
 </TR>
 <TR>
     <TH> Enter Street Address:</TH>
     <TH><INPUT NAME="address1"></TH>
 </TR>
 <TR>
       <TH>Enter your State: </TH>
       <TH><INPUT NAME="address2"></TH>
 </TR>
 <TR>
     <TH> Enter your Zipcode:</TH>
     <TH><INPUT NAME="zip"></TH>
</TR>
<TR ALIGN=LEFT>
  <TH>
  Choose a payment method:<BR>
<INPUT TYPE= "radio" NAME= "VISA">VISA</BR>
<INPUT TYPE= "radio" NAME= "MASTERCARD"> Mastercard</BR>
<INPUT TYPE= "radio" NAME= "AM_EXPRESS"> American
      Express<P>
<INPUT TYPE="Submit">
<INPUT TYPE="Reset"></P>
</TH>
</TR>
</FORM>
</TABLE>
</HTML>
```

the following example. Also, do not accidentally omit the final </*FORM*> tag or the final </*TABLE*> tag.

Another useful feature of nested tables is the capability to work more easily in either table, independent of the other. For example, in the main table, if you want to add a paragraph of explanatory text, you can just type it in. The text justifies to the left if you add *align=left* e.g. <*TH align=left*>

to the TH tag. The text also automatically word-wraps inside the first table as you type. In contrast, the inner *nested* table can be used to display radio buttons, check boxes, select tags, or other types of graphical user interface elements or images completely independent of the other table's text. Using an outer and inner table initially takes more initial effort. In the end, however, it gives much greater flexibility, especially if you need to revise your document later.

The following code shows how to nest a second table inside the main table:

```
<HTML>
<!—The following tag creates blue BODY text throughout the
       document>
<BODY   TEXT="#0000FF">
   <b>Using Nested Tables</b>
   <HR></P>
<TABLE WIDTH=80%>
   <TR>
   <TH align=left><BR> This left column area can be made
          attractive and interesting, by using background
          color and images.</TH>
                <TH>
          →<TABLE>
```

Figure 1-10
Creating nested tables

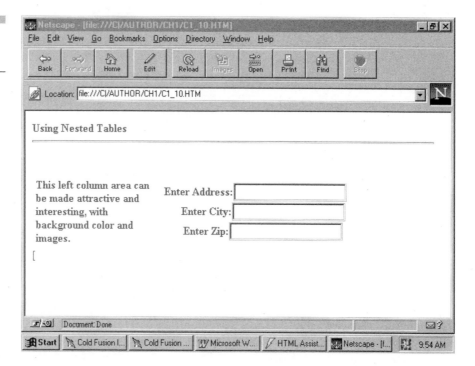

```
<FORM >
    <TR>
    <TH align=right><BR>Enter Address:<INPUT
        TYPE= "TEXT" NAME="address1"><BR>
            Enter City:<INPUT TYPE= "TEXT"
                NAME="address2"><BR>
                Enter Zip:<INPUT TYPE= "TEXT"
                    NAME="address3">
    </TH>
</FORM>
        </TR>
    </TABLE>
</TR>
</BODY>
</TABLE>
</HTML>
```

The arrow shows exactly where to place the inner nested table. *To nest a third table*, place it below the opening <TH> tag of the nested table. This third table can include additional field input choices, text, hyperlinks, or images. (See Figure 1-11.)

As you build Web pages, try to control urges to use large splashy GIF or JPG files. Corporate users (who have fast LAN or WAN connections) may tolerate waiting for 20 to 30 seconds for Web pages, but outside vis-

Figure 1-11

Creating multiple nested tables

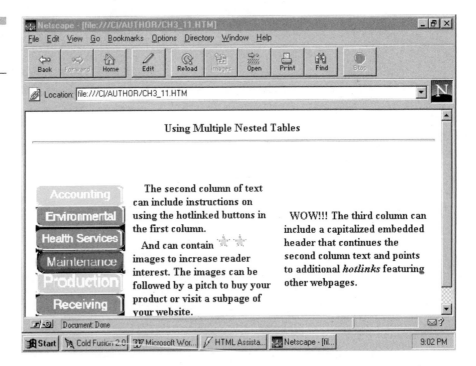

itors who dial over the WWW with slower Internet connections (such as 2400-baud connections) will quickly tire of image-generated long waits that add no final user benefit. A thoughtful alternate solution is to employ variation in font color and typeface (bold, italic, plain, caps, and combinations thereof) to emphasize text on your Web page. If you must cover your Web page with GIF or JPG files, at least consider only using thumbnail-size files that contain less than 3000 bytes. In this case, less is more.

MULTIPLE NESTED TABLES   To design competitive Web pages, you can use several more HTML formatting tricks. The first of these techniques involves vertically aligning a number of similarly shaped GIF image files. First create several equally sized GIF files, and then vertically align them (one on top of another) in the HTML code in the leftmost column of a multiple nested table Web page. (You can use <BR> tags after each image to create the stacked image look.)

You do not have to specify a table percentage for the first table, because the table will automatically be limited to the width in pixels of the widest GIF image making up this table. In the first nested table, specify a percentage; for example, use <TABLE WIDTH=40%> to make it easy for the eye to scan this second column.

NOTE   Use trial-and-error methods to get appropriate table widths. Because different monitor widths display tables differently, make your table design for a standard size monitor; you will please the most people. In the larger Internet community, probably more than 75% of all monitors are fourteen inches or smaller.

The third table can also contain text or images. To emphasize images or text even more, insert images into the text and use <BR> tags and non-breaking spaces between text and GIF images. This step will create dramatic white space around these images. You can also place hyperlinks inside text. (If you do this, limit your text to short paragraphs and terse sentences; it will emphasize the presence of the hypertext links.) The next screen shows one way to include both images and text.

In the Web page shown in Figure 1-11, the leftmost column (controlled by the first table) contains vertically stacked IMG SRC images (the user thinks *hot buttons*) which can be hotlinked to subpages or subsections of the main document. (It is better Web style to use a group of hyperlinks connecting to individual subpages rather than try to build a large, single-indexed Web page. Using this group of hyperlinks will help the main index document load much more rapidly.)

The middle table can contain important text messages and explanations. The third column is created by a third level of table nesting, which must be carefully placed. When you create the nested table, put the third <TABLE> tag immediately underneath the second table's <TR> tag. (See the proceeding extended code example.)

The closing </table> tag of the third innermost table must be placed immediately after its closing </TR> tag. When you use multiple nested tables, you can use a great deal of originality and develop visual interest, and the viewer can quickly read two narrower columns of text rather than scan a long line.

```
<HTML>
    <b><center>Using Multiple Nested Tables</center></b>
    <HR>
<!— The MAIN table uses 30% of the desktop, and can
     contain a stack of clickable images— >
<TABLE>
    <TR>
        <TH>
            <I><B>HyperLinks:</I></B><BR>
            <! — Each of the following GIF files can be
                 easily linked to a subpage document by
                 using a "http://www.anycorp.anydomain"
                 Interent address — >
            <IMG SRC="acct.gif"><BR>
            <IMG SRC="env.gif"><BR>
            <IMG SRC="health.gif"><BR>
            <IMG SRC="maint.gif"><BR>
            <IMG SRC="prod.gif"><BR>
            <IMG SRC="receiv.gif"></TH><BR>
        <TH>
            <TABLE width=30%>
                <TR>
                    →<TABLE>
                        <TR>
                            <TH align=left> 
                                   The second
                                column of text can
                                include instructions on
                                using the hotlinked
                                buttons in the first
                                column.
                            <BR>   And
                                can contain <IMG
                                SRC=star.gif>
                            <IMG SRC=star.gif> images
                                to increase reader
                                interest. The images
                                can be followed  by a
                                pitch to buy your
```

```
                                    product or visit a
                                    subpage of your
                                    website.</TH>
                          </TR>
                    </TABLE>
                       <TH align=left>   WOW!!!
                          The third column can include
                          a capitalized embedded header
                          that continues the second
                          column text and points to
                          additional <i>hotlinks</i>
                          featuring other webpages.
                       </TH>
                         </TR>
                 </TR>
              </TABLE>
        </TABLE>
        </HTML>
```

The arrow shows the beginning of the innermost (number three) nested table. It is placed under a <TR> tag of the second nested table.

NOTE   *Remember to visually indent your tags to show each level of subordination. Also, do not forget that each opening <TABLE>, <TR>, and <TH> tag must have a corresponding closing </TABLE>, </TR>, and </TH> tag.*

APPLYING FONT AND BACKGROUND COLOR   To change your Web page background color, the *BGCOLOR* attribute can be put inside a <BODY> tag. For example, <BODY BGCOLOR="#0000FF"> will produce a blue background color. (Please note that BGCOLOR is spelled without an *I*.) Some additional color possibilities are listed here:

ASCII Code	Color Produced
FFFFFF	White
FF00FF	Magenta
8C1717	Scarlet
0000FF	Blue
CC3299	Violet

To change text color within a portion of a document, use the <font> tag for maximum control. (For example, <font color=red> *your text is now red* <font>.) If you need to have document-wide scarlet text, use the following code: <BODY TEXT= "#8C1717">. Similarly, you can change your hypertext link color to Magenta: <BODY LINK="#FF00FF">, and your *already visited* link color to White: <BODY VLINK="#FFFFFF">. Notice the beginning and ending quotes around the six-letter color codes.

USING BACKGROUND GIFS AND JPGS   The background tag is used to display images behind text. Careful color coordination between text colors and background images is required to avoid garish or hard-to-read Web pages. If Web site visitors cannot read your Web page, they will quickly go to a page that they can read. When you use background GIF or JPG files, and you limit the file size to 2000 to 3000 bytes, your browser will fill up the Web page by repeating the GIF or JPG until the screen is filled. Use LVIEW PRO to crop and resize the GIF so that it will load quickly. An example of how to use a BODY BACKGROUND (the BODY tag can have other attributes as just described) is given here:

```
<BODY BACKGROUND="scenic.gif">
```

Using Frames

Frames are supported by Netscape Navigator and Internet Explorer and are a part of HTML version 3.2 (adopted in early 1997). Frames are empty *containers* used to display images and text in HTML documents. The following sections show how to build horizontal, vertical, and mixed frames.

BUILDING HORIZONTAL FRAMES   The basic frame splits the screen into two independent windows. With these windows, you can move back and forth with just a click of your mouse. In the following code line, the numbers "1*,2*" are used to create a small pane on top and a larger pane below:

```
<FRAMESET ROWS="1*,2*">
```

If you need a large top frame and a small bottom frame, use "3*,1*". You may also define frame sizes as percentages of each other (for example, <FRAMESET ROWS="70%, 30%">), or by absolute pixel values (for example, <FRAMESET ROWS= "450,150">). The next code line

```
<FRAME SRC="c1_1.htm">
```

inserts the HTML document, `c1_1.htm`, into the top frame.

To build vertical frames, use the FRAMESET COLS tag (for example, <FRAMESET COLS="40%,60%">). This code builds a first column using

An Example of a double-frame HTML Document.

```
<HTML>
<HEAD>
<TITLE>CERAMIC WORLDS</TITLE>
</HEAD>
<FRAMESET ROWS="1*,2*">
    < — The first SRC attribute names the URL to be loaded
        into the top frame — >
  <FRAME SRC="c1_1.htm">
    < — The second  SRC attribute names the object (or URL)
        to loaded into the bottom frame — >
  <FRAME SRC="teapot.GIF">
</FRAMESET>
</HTML>
```

Figure 1-12

HTML document divided into Two Frames

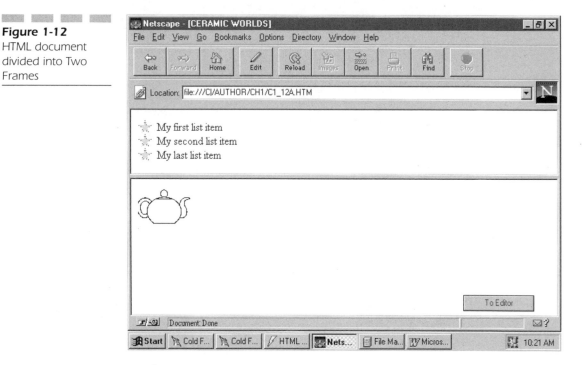

40% and a second column using 60% of the screen. The following example, Figure 1-13, shows how to integrate the FRAMESET COLS tag with the FRAMESET ROWS tag.

USING NESTED FRAMES The following code shows the top-level HTML file, which points to the other HTML documents shown in Figure 1-13. The FRAMESET COLS tag must be placed inside the FRAMESET

Figure 1-13
Nested Frame

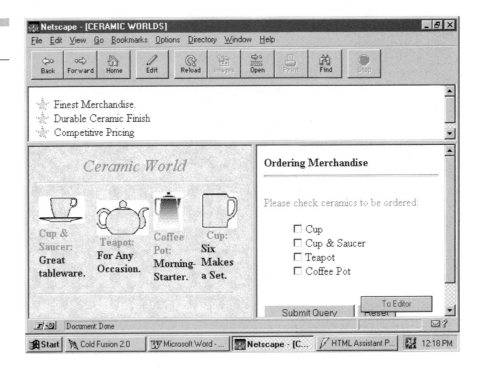

Figure 1-13
Nested Frame

ROWS tag. By using frames, you can build a fairly complex Web page using several basic HTML files, each having a separate function. The Web document, c1_15.htm, which displays GIF images, could be reformatted to present those images in a vertical stack for variety.

```
<HTML>
<HEAD>
<TITLE>CERAMIC WORLDS</TITLE>
</HEAD>
<FRAMESET ROWS="25%, 75%">
    <FRAME SRC="c1_16.htm">
    <FRAMESET COLS="53%,47%">
            <FRAME SRC=" c1_15.htm ">
            <FRAME SRC="c1_14.htm">
    </FRAMESET>
</FRAMESET>
</HTML>
```

The following table 1-3 describes describes the attributes that are used in Frame tags.

Table 1-3

Frame Attributes

Attribute	Example	Comments
SRC	SRC="mydoc.htm"	CF templates, image files, HTML docs.
NAME	NAME="myframe"	Useful to keep track of frames, OPTIONAL.
NORESIZE		
SCROLLING	Scrolling= "Yes, No, auto"	Displays a scroll bar if "yes", "auto" shows scroll bars if required by content.
MARGINWIDTH	MARGINWIDTH="1"	(numbers 1,2,3…), defines a width margin.
MARGINHEIGHT	MARGINHEIGHT="1"	(numbers 1,2,3…), defines a height margin.

CONCLUSION

This chapter shows how to build both individual tags and multiple HTML element combinations to create fill-in forms and tables within HTML documents. It also contains a section on Web style considerations. This chapter also presents an introduction to frames. For more additional material on how to use frames, see Chapter 21, "Using Frames with Cold Fusion." In Chapter 4, you will use your knowledge of HTML tags and elements to learn how to create automatically generated e-mail by using fill-in HTML forms.

Operating System Installation and Configuration

- Selecting an operating system
- Installing operating systems

Selecting an Operating System—
Preliminary Thoughts

Cold Fusion currently runs on the five most common versions of Microsoft's 32-bit operating systems—Windows 95, Windows NT Server versions 3.51 and 4.0, and Windows NT Workstation versions 3.51 and 4.0. If you already have one of these operation systems up and running and you know that the operating system you are running will support the information server you wish to use, you can probably skip this section. If you aren't yet running one of these operating systems and aren't quite sure which one is the right one for you, this section should provide some useful points to consider when choosing your operating system.

NOTE   The five operating systems just listed are referred to as 32-bit operating systems. The original personal computer (PC) was based on an 8-bit microprocessor, which meant that it was designed to handle data in 8-bit pieces (bytes). The microprocessors that ran the PC then advanced to 16-bit versions, and Microsoft developed the Windows operating environment to use these 16-bit systems. The 16-bit versions of Windows (most recently Windows 3.1 and Windows for Workgroups 3.11) can and do run programs in 32-bit enhanced mode, but much of Windows itself and all the MS-DOS functions that Windows uses run in 16-bit mode. A substantial fraction of the processor power is wasted switching between 16-bit mode and 32-bit mode. Programs that use the processor in 32-bit mode are easier to construct and run more efficiently on Intel (and clones from other vendors) microprocessors than programs that run in 16-bit mode.

Although 32-bit mode programs can run under the 16-bit versions of Windows (with a special set of extensions designed by Microsoft), they are handicapped by the fact that portions of Windows itself still must run in 16-bit mode. Windows NT and Windows 95 are true 32-bit operating systems. Windows NT also runs on DEC Alpha machines, which are 32-bit machines, because the design of this operating system effectively isolates the system itself and programs running on it from the hardware through what is called the Hardware Abstraction Layer. *Modern software, such as Cold Fusion, will not run on the Microsoft 16-bit operating systems.*

Windows 95 can be considered the *economy* model of the Microsoft line of 32-bit operating systems. Because Windows 95 is intended to be a single-user system, it can provide only a very limited Internet or intranet server function. You should choose Windows 95 only if you are providing service to a small intranet. Server software that runs on Windows 95 can be acquired from O'Reilly (Web site) and Netscape (FastTrack Server for Windows 95, among other vendors).

Windows NT is much better suited for use as an Internet or intranet server than is Windows 95 and, as you would expect, costs a bit more. Cold Fusion cannot be run on any version prior to 3.51, of either NT Server or NT Workstation. If you have not yet installed NT, install version 4.0. If you already have version 3.51 installed, you can either stay with that version or move to version 4.0. Most Internet information servers, database engines, and Cold Fusion will run on either version.

Upgrading to NT 4.0 from NT 3.51

Windows NT version 3.51, although a stable operating system, is fast becoming obsolete. If you are running 3.51 and are about to install an Internet server or Cold Fusion, seriously consider upgrading to NT 4.0. There never seems to be a good time to upgrade operating systems, particularly in an environment where your system is in constant use. You may find, however, the best time to upgrade your entire software environment is when you are about to install some major new software. Whichever version you decide to use, you will probably need to install a *Service Pack* (Microsoft-ese for *all the latest bug fixes and more)* after you have installed your operating system. NT 3.51 was up to Service Pack 5 and NT 4.0 was up to Service Pack 3 at the time this was being written. Beware, however, of downloading and installing the latest Service Pack from the Microsoft Web site (www.microsoft.com) before it has had some time in the field.

Windows NT is a very complicated piece of software, and each Service Pack usually creates about one bug for every ten that it fixes. Read the Cold Fusion installation information to determine if there is a Service Pack that is mandatory for the proper operation of Cold Fusion.

Selecting a Windows NT Version — Server versus Workstation

Either version of Windows NT comes in two flavors, Server and Workstation. What is the difference? Primarily two things: Optimization and licensing. Optimization in the Workstation has some restrictions built in that physically limit the number of clients that the Workstation can support at any one time when it is used as a server. Licensing is an issue because Microsoft restricts access to Workstation to no more than ten active connections, which translates into support for only three or four simultaneous accesses by any of the more common Web browsers. Your decision between Workstation and Server will then depend on the size of the user base that you wish to support. In anything but a small work group, Workstation will not be a practical choice.

NT Server costs a bit more than NT Workstation, but that additional cost is partially offset by the fact that Microsoft Internet Information Server, an efficient WWW, FTP, and gopher server is included at no extra charge. Workstation is a suitable choice for a small intranet, especially when you have already decided to use an information server other than Microsoft's.

Operating Systems — Installation

Installing Windows NT Server or Workstation Version 4.0.

Windows NT 4.0 can be installed from DOS (or 16-bit Windows), from any of the 32-bit Microsoft operating systems, or from the set of 3 setup floppy disks supplied by Microsoft. If you wish to install starting from the setup floppy disks, simply insert the disk labeled *Setup Boot Disk* and boot your system. If you are installing using this method, skip down to the "On Reboot" section.Everything from here to there is involved with creating your own set of three setup disks. You can install NT 4.0 without using any floppy disks, but only the experienced installer should tread that path.

If you have only the NT Server CD-ROM, and not the three setup floppy disks, you can still begin the installation from within any other Microsoft operating system. The NT Server CD-ROM contains (along with many compressed files) the executable files WINNT.EXE and WINNT32.EXE. Start WINNT.EXE if you are running DOS or Windows 3.1. Start WINNT32.EXE if you are running a 32-bit version of Windows. A brief overview of Windows NT Server 4.0 installation is given here. The installation of Windows NT Workstation 4.0 is almost identical, except that there will be no reference to client licensing or type of server (domain or standalone) involved. See "Additional Installation Help" at the end of this chapter for a more thorough, but still brief, description of this installation. The Windows NT Setup program does a good job of guiding you through the installation process, but some areas such as network setups can be extremely complicated and are well beyond the scope of this book. The following description will be an overview of an installation of NT Server 4.0 on a system that is already running a 32-bit version of Windows.

Run *drive*:\i386\WINNT32.EXE, where *drive* is the drive letter of your CD-ROM drive, either from the File Manager or using the Run option of the File menu from the Program Manager. Unless you have an unusual device installed on your computer, the default choices provided by the Setup program should be acceptable choices for your installation. The setup process is a multiphase affair. The first phase runs as an application on whatever system you are installing NT from. This phase copies the compressed system files from the CD-ROM and creates a set of three floppy disks that are used to boot a minimum NT system in the second phase of the installation.

NOTE I   *If Setup is in the process of creating the three floppy disks, or in copying files during this initial phase of the setup process, and you find that you wish to terminate the installation until a later time, you have few options. If you are installing from MS-DOS, you are probably best off to reboot. If you are installing from Windows 95, the natural action will be to close the installation window. When you do this, you will be warned that you should really stop the installation program first. Because the installation program won't let you stop it during this phase, if you really want to stop, you have to ignore this warning. The installation will stop and everything will appear to be okay, but if you later try to start the installation again without rebooting your system, you will find that the connection between the keyboard and the MS-DOS installation window is broken. At this point, you will probably have to reboot before restarting the installation.*

NOTE II   *It is possible to speed up the installation process by avoiding the creation and subsequent booting up from these three floppy disks. This is done by specifying the /b parameter on the WINNT or WINNT32 command line. We recommend that you use the default floppy disk method, for two reasons. First, it gives you a faster way to recover from a problem that corrupts your hard drive. Second, it avoids the problem of having Setup fail in its second phase, because the hard drive on which you wish to install NT is not one that is supported by a driver included on the NT installation CD-ROM.*

ON REBOOT Later in the installation process, you will be asked whether you wish to create an *emergency repair* floppy. Although the choice is yours, we recommend that you do. You should be aware that this Emergency Repair disk is *not* a bootable disk; it contains only a copy of the NT registry information. Label and retain the three floppy boot disks and the Emergency Repair floppy disk in case you later need to recover from a hard disk crash.

Setup will load each of the mass storage device drivers that is included on the NT installation disk, and each driver, in turn, will try to detect the presence of the device that it supports. If the system fails to detect one or more of your devices, you can add support for them manually—that is, if you have a vendor-supplied disk that contains an NT 4.0 driver for that device.

Setup will detect the presence of other copies of Windows NT on your computer. You will have the choice of upgrading (replacing) older copies or of leaving them intact and installing a separate new copy of NT. Choose which way you want to proceed based on your specific situation. Replacing the older version will result in most, if not all, of your installed applications being installed and ready to run on NT 4.0, which will save you the trouble of reinstalling them on the new system. Replacing your existing NT version, however, will leave you with no way to go back to that version if, for any reason, you find that you cannot use NT 4.0 (such as discovering that one or more of your favorite applications have not been upgraded to run on NT 4.0).

Setup will let you choose the drive and directory where you wish to install NT. If you are keeping an older copy of NT you *must* install the new version in a different directory from the older copy, and you *should* install it on a different drive if possible.

The Setup Wizard will help you install and configure Windows networking. There are many possibilities, depending on how your computer will access a network. You must, however, have TCP/IP support installed or your Web server and Cold Fusion will not run properly. For a brief discussion of what TCP/IP is and does for you, see the"TCP/IP" section at the end of the chapter.

When you have removed all floppy disks and rebooted the system for the third time, Windows NT Server installation is complete except for some housekeeping that you can do at any time, primarily setting up user accounts. Your system should be up and running and ready for the installation of your applications, including your Internet Information Server and Cold Fusion.

Microsoft Internet Information Server is included with Windows NT Server 4.0 and is installed along with NT unless you select otherwise. The installation of Windows NT Workstation version 4.0 is very similar to the installation of Windows NT Server version 4.0. One difference is that Microsoft Internet Information Server is not included and must be installed separately.

Installing Windows NT Server or Workstation version 3.51

The following brief overview of Windows NT Workstation also applies to the installation of Windows NT Server 3.51, except for a few details such as licensing and what type of server installation is desired. The differences between the installation of NT 3.51 and NT 4.0 are mostly self-explanatory, so the expanded discussion titled "Additional Installation Help" can be used for the NT 3.51 installation with a few minor changes. We have emphasized NT 4.0 because it is most likely the version of NT Server or Workstation that you will be installing, at least until NT 5.0 comes along.

Windows NT 3.51 can be installed from DOS or 16-bit Windows, from any of the 32-bit Microsoft operating systems, or from the set of three floppy disks supplied by Microsoft. If you wish to install from the setup floppy disks, simply insert the disk labeled "Setup Boot Disk" and boot your system. If you are installing using this method, skip down to the section titled "On Reboot". Everything from here to there is involved with creating your own set of three setup disks. You can install NT 3.51 without using any floppy disks, but only the experienced installer should tread that path.

The NT Workstation CD-ROM contains (along with many compressed files) the executable files WINNT.EXE and WINNT32.EXE. Start WINNT.EXE if you are running DOS, Windows 3.1, or Windows 95. Start WINNT32.EXE if you are running a previous version of Windows NT. A brief overview of Windows NT Workstation 3.51 installation is given here. The Windows NT Setup program does a good job of guiding you through the installation process, but some areas such as network setups can be extremely complicated and are well beyond the scope of this book. The following description will be an overview of an installation of NT Workstation on a system that is running Windows 95. Installation from DOS or Windows 3.1 will be the same except for the way that you start WINNT.EXE.

From Windows 95, click Start, click Run, and then click Browse. Navigate through the directories to My Computer\your CDROM drive\I386, and then double-click on WINNT.EXE. Add the /w option to the resulting command line and click OK. An MS-DOS box will appear. Press the keys on your keyboard as directed in the DOS box. Unless you have an unusual device installed on your computer, the default choices provided by the Setup program should be acceptable choices for your installation. The setup process is a multiphase affair. The first phase runs as an application on whatever system you are installing NT from—in this case, an MS-DOS box in Windows 95. This phase copies the compressed system files from the CD-ROM and creates a set of three floppy disks that are used to boot a minimum NT system in the second phase of the installation.

NOTE   *Have these three formatted, blank floppy disks available and labeled before you begin your installation. The safest method is to format them before you start. There is no graceful way to recover from an installation that fails because one of the floppy disks is found to be unformatted or to contain data. Make sure to check that each formatted disk has the entire disk available for use. The format program will remove bad clusters as part of the formatting, and then will complete normally. Make certain that the number of available bytes on each disk is the same as the total number of bytes on that disk. Setup expects that all sectors of each floppy will be available and will fail if it finds that a lesser amount of space is available. Setup failures at this point in the installation are impossible to recover from, without starting the installation over from scratch.*

It is possible to install Windows NT without creating these three floppy disks, but unless you are going to perform the installation over and over, it is best to use the floppy disk method. It doesn't take that much longer and it is the simplest way to proceed.

Label and insert each of the floppy disks as directed by Setup. When you complete this operation, Setup will copy files from your CD-ROM to a temporary directory on your boot drive. When this operation is complete, Setup will ask you to reboot. Leave the last of the floppy disks that were created in the drive when you reboot.

ON REBOOT   On reboot, the minimum system that was created on the three floppy disks will be loaded. Insert floppy disks as requested. At the end of loading the second floppy disk, you will be presented with a screen welcoming you to Setup, with choices of: `F1-learning more about Setup before you proceed`, `ENTER-continuing with the setup`, `R-performing a repair of a damaged system`, and `F3-quitting the installation`. Next you will be asked whether you want an express setup or a custom setup. The default choices in the express setup will be fine for most installations. Choose a custom setup if you know that you need something other than the default, or if you just want to see what choices are available. Insert the third floppy disk when requested.

Setup will load each of the mass storage device drivers that is included on the NT installation disk, and each driver, in turn, will try to detect the presence of the device that it supports. If the system fails to detect one or more of your devices, you can add support for them manually if you have a vendor-supplied disk that contains an NT 3.51 driver for that device.

Setup will detect the presence of other copies of Windows NT on your computer. You will have the choice of upgrading (replacing) older copies or of leaving them intact and installing a separate new copy of NT. Choose which way you want to proceed based on your specific situation. Replacing the older version will result in most if not all your installed applications being installed and ready to run on NT 3.51, which will save you the trouble of reinstalling them on the new system. If you have a previous version of NT, you will almost certainly want to upgrade it to NT 3.51.

Setup will let you choose the drive and directory where you wish to install NT. If you choose a drive that is not formatted, or wish to install on a disk that is not yet partitioned, Setup will run the appropriate utility to partition or format as you select.

When this section of Setup is complete, remove any floppy disk that is currently inserted and click on the button to reboot your system. The installed version of NT Workstation 3.51 will be loaded. You will be asked to enter your name, your company name, and then a name by which your computer is to be known on any network to which it is connected. You will also be requested to select the locale, which means the language that is to be used.

The next step is to configure your printer. If there are no printers attached or if you wish to defer printer installation until later, press ESC to bypass this step. Otherwise enter the information about your printer as required.

The next step is to select your networking choices. Your choice will depend on what network you are connected to and how you are connected to it. NT should detect any installed network cards unless your specific card has not been included in the NT library. If NT does not detect your card and you have an installation disk for NT 3.51 from the card vendor, follow the directions on your screen for the installation of hardware not detected by NT. See "Installing Network Cards Not Directly Supported by Windows NT" at the end of the chapter for help in the installation of network adapters that are not supported by Windows NT by default.

Choose the network protocols that you need, depending on what type of network you are connected to. Be sure to include TCP/IP support, because TCP/IP is required to connect to the Internet or your local intranet.

Select your Domain/Workgroup settings to be compatible with the network that you are going to connect to. Enter your administrator password and create any user accounts that you need. Perform any video setup as instructed by NT. Allow the system to create an Emergency Repair disk. A final reboot should load your running NT Workstation 3.51 system.

NOTE *If you chose to install NT Workstation 3.51 to an unformatted drive, and you chose NTFS as the file system for that drive, you may be surprised to learn that at this point in the installation, NT has formatted it as a FAT drive. Only after installation is complete is the drive converted to an NTFS drive. After this conversion, NT will automatically reboot again, so don't be startled by this extra reboot.*

Additional Installation Help

TCP/IP—THE MAGIC THAT MAKES THE INTERNET OR INTRANET WORK TCP/IP is an abbreviation for Transmission Control Protocol/Internet Protocol. There have been volumes written to describe, analyze, and criticize the various protocols that have been invented to enable electronic data communications. We leave it to the reader to acquire any or all of these volumes that go into these protocols in intense detail. Suffice it to say that there exists an International Standards Organization (ISO), which has developed a theoretical model for network communications that is called the Open Systems Interconnection (OSI) model. In this model, all the necessary hardware and software that it takes to convert a user message (an e-mail message, the components of a Web page, and so on) into the electronic signals that can be transferred between computers and back again is separated into seven distinct (or sometimes not so distinct) layers. The seven layers together are referred to as a *protocol stack*.

The seven layers of the OSI model protocol stack are: Physical (the wires or radio signals), Data Link, Network, Session, Transport, Presentation, and Application. I know of no actual working protocol in which these seven layers are actually distinct from one another, but the standard includes them, and indeed most implementations simply combine part or all of one or more layers into single software programs.

The most important of the seven layers from a networking point of view is, as you might guess, the Network layer. This is the layer of the protocol stack, which is responsible for routing packets of information between computers on a network. The IP part of TCI/IP is such a beast. It is the protocol that allows computers to communicate with one another on the Internet and on most intranets.

The function the IP performs can be clarified (for us novices at least) by using the analogy of the United States Post Office and its equivalent in other countries. If you want to send a letter using the post office, you have to know the address of the person to whom you wish to send it. In the electronic world of the Internet (or your company's intranet), to send a message you have to know the IP address of the recipient. Well, almost. IP addresses have the form *n.n.n.n*, where each *n* is a decimal number from 0 to 255. You, as a computer user, certainly don't want to remember an address in that format, so there are mechanisms in the layers above the IP protocol layer that translate addresses that are more human-friendly (such as www.allaire.com) into one of those n.n.n.n computer-friendly addresses.

That's really about all that IP accomplishes. Of course, there are at times many layers of complexity. If your computer is part of a local group or *domain*, then each computer in that group will have an n.n.n.n address assigned to it, either temporarily or permanently, and intercomputer communication will be very simple. If, however, you are connected to a large intranet or the Internet, there may be several levels of addressing that have to be negotiated. The post office equivalent would be like mailing something to an office building, sorting it by departments, and then within each department sorting it and delivering it to the actual person.

In fact, if you wish to use your computer to communicate across the Internet, be prepared. Your computer has a very limited knowledge of which user and domain name maps to which IP address. Every such computer, however, does know the IP address of at least one Domain Name Server (DNS). It is the particular task of the DNS to know either how to map the name and domain you specify into an IP address or to know how to communicate with another DNS to find this information.

There is one importance reason for understanding IP, at least to this very simple level. At times during the installation and administration of your operating system and the various components that combine to make your server accessible to your clients that you will come across one of those pesky *n.n.n.n* IP addresses. If you install Microsoft Internet Information Server, for example, you should know that it automatically assigns that IP address 127.0.0.1 to itself. Other programs that you install will have to know this if they are to communicate properly with IIS.

INSTALLING WINDOWS NT SERVER VERSION 4.0—ADDITIONAL NOTES Windows NT Server can be installed from DOS or 16-bit Windows or from any of the 32-bit Microsoft operating systems.

The NT Server CD-ROM contains (along with many compressed files) the executable files WINNT.EXE and WINNT32.EXE. Start WINNT.EXE if you are running DOS or Windows 3.1; start WINNT32.EXE if you are running a 32-bit Windows. It is possible to install multiple copies of Windows NT on your PC, as will be discussed soon in more detail. It is indeed possible to install Windows NT along with other operating systems on your PC, but that is beyond the scope of this book. In the example which follows, the installation is shown starting from an existing version of Windows NT Workstation version 3.51.

Start the installation by running drive:\i386\WINNT32.EXE, where *drive:* is the drive letter of your CD-ROM drive. Setup will ask you to enter the location of your Windows NT 4.0 source files; it will also have filled in what it thinks is the correct location. Setup's guess is usually correct (see Figure 2-1).

USING THE WINDOWS NT SOURCE LOCATION DIALOG BOX
Click the Options button to bring up the Options dialog box. You have two options, and both should be checked by default. Leave both of these boxes checked unless you are absolutely sure that you know the effect of not doing so.

There are 2 parts to the Windows NT installation. The first part, which you are now in, runs Windows NT Setup from within whatever operating system you are running, in this case NT Workstation 3.51. The main purpose of this portion of the installation is to copy the Windows NT system files to a temporary directory on your local hard disk and to create a simplified, bootable version of the Windows NT Server 4.0.

When the Create Boot Floppy Disks option is selected (the first option), the bootable system is created on a set of three floppy disks that you provide during this first phase of the NT installation. If this option is not checked, Setup assumes that you already have that set of three floppy disks and skips this initial step.

The just described "three floppy" option must not be confused with the *Floppyless* installation option. It is possible to install without creating or

Figure 2-1
Windows NT Source
Location Dialog Box

Windows NT 4.00 Upgrade/Installation

MICROSOFT.
WINDOWS NT.

Location of Windows NT 4.0 Files:

J:\i386

Continue   Options...   Exit   Help

booting from floppy disks. This method of installation is selected by passing the parameter /b to Setup (WINNT32.EXE /b). When this parameter is present, the simplified bootable system is created on the hard drive on which you are installing Windows NT, instead of the three floppy disks. The *Boot Floppy* installation method takes a few minutes longer, because you must create and then boot the floppy disks. You should use the Boot Floppy option unless you are positive that the hard drive on which you are installing Windows NT is supported by one of the drivers that are included in the simplified bootable system that Setup creates. If one of these drivers does not support your hard drive, your installation will fail when Setup tries to reboot, and you will get an error message stating that your specified boot device is not accessible. Booting the new system via floppy disks guarantees that the second phase of the Windows NT installation will proceed normally.

When you are satisfied with the options selection, and the location of your Windows NT Source files is specified correctly, click the Continue button. Setup will begin copying the NT source files to your hard drive, and it will ask you to insert a formatted, blank high-density disk into your floppy drive. Setup creates the three boot floppy disks in reverse order so that when they have all been created, the disk that is left in the floppy drive is the actual Setup Boot Disk. Label and insert these floppy disks as requested by Setup.

NOTE *Have these three formatted, blank floppy disks available and labeled before you begin your installation. The safest method is to format them before you start. There is no graceful way to recover from an installation that fails because one of the floppies is found to be unformatted or to contain data. Make sure to check that each formatted disk has the entire disk available for use. The format program will remove bad clusters from potential use as part of the formatting, and will complete normally. Make certain that the number of available bytes on each disk is the same as the total number of bytes on that disk. Setup expects that all sectors of each floppy will be available and will fail if it finds that a lesser amount of space is available. Setup failures at this point in the installation are not easy to recover from without starting the installation over from scratch.*

When Setup has copied the source files to your hard drive and has created the three floppy disks, it will present the dialog box shown in Figure 2-2. Setup has completed the first phase of the installation and is ready to proceed to the second phase. You should make sure that all other Win-

Figure 2-2
Windows NT Setup
Restart dialog box

dows applications are now closed. Leave the last floppy that was created in your floppy drive. Click the Restart Computer button.

The system will reboot and load the minimum system that was created on the floppy disks. Insert disks as requested by Setup. Setup will eventually present the *Welcome to Setup* screen. At this point, you may choose to proceed with a normal installation or try to recover a damaged installation. Label and retain the three-floppy set of disks in case you later need to recover from a failure that corrupts NT. You will also need to create and retain an emergency repair disk when the time comes (discussed later in this section). Press Enter to continue with NT Setup.

HINT *The emergency repair floppy is* not *a bootable disk; it contains only a copy of the NT registry information. The NT registry contains all the system configuration information. You can recover the system without the three-floppy set by starting an installation from scratch. Saving the set of floppy disks just saves you the time of recreating them when you perform the recovery.*

The next decision you must make is whether you want Setup to attempt to auto-detect your mass storage controllers and devices. You should usually allow Setup to do this. Microsoft warns that the system may hang up if you have a controller installed that NT does not know about, but I have yet to encounter a controller that will cause this problem. Press Enter to continue with the installation.

INSTALLING MASS STORAGE CONTROLLERS NOT DIRECTLY SUPPORTED BY WINDOWS NT After asking you to insert the third installation floppy, Setup will load, in turn, each of the device drivers that are included with NT. As each driver is loaded, Setup will attempt to find a corresponding controller or storage device. Each controller or device that is located is added to the list box of known controllers and devices. When this process is completed, Setup should display a list of all controllers and devices in your computer. You will not see any SCSI devices listed that your SCSI controllers control, but you should see the SCSI controllers, non-SCSI disks, and CD-ROMs that are hooked directly to the system bus.

If one or more of your controllers and devices do not show up in the list, NT has not included a driver for them. You must provide NT with a device driver for these controllers and devices if NT is to recognize them. Press S, insert the vendor-supplied floppy on which the device driver resides, and Setup will incorporate that driver into NT. The missing controller or device should now have been added to the list.

NOTE   *There is no standardized directory structure that all hardware vendors follow when creating installation disks for their products. Setup requires a file named oemsetup.inf, which contains the installation information for a specific device, to be made available before the program can install devices that are not supported directly by the operating system. You should check the contents of the vendor-supplied disk before you start the installation to find out where the oemsetup.inf file is located. It will usually be in the root directory, but if it is in a subdirectory, you will have to provide the complete path when Setup asks for it.*

When all your controllers and devices are included in the list box, press Enter to continue. Insert floppy disks as prompted by Setup, if you have removed the third NT installation disk. The next pause is for you to read and acknowledge the Microsoft license agreement. Page down until you come to the end of the agreement, and then press F8 to accept it. Setup will search your hard drive for existing copies of NT. If any are found, you are given the option of upgrading (replacing) the current system or of installing a fresh copy. If you choose the latter, you will create a *dual boot* system in which you can select (at boot time) which version you wish to run. You can, in fact, have more than two copies of NT installed on your computer at the same time. NT maintains a hidden file in the root directory of your boot drive named BOOT.INI. This is a text file that contains entries for each of the NT systems that you have installed; it points to the disk, partition, and drive on which each NT is installed.

NOTE   *Each installation of NT will create two entries in the BOOT.INI file, so you will see two entries for each installation on the boot selection menu. Newer entries are added at the top of the list. The two entries in each set are identical, except that the second entry indicates [VGA MODE]. This option is there in case you later manage to get your video card configured in a mode that*

NT cannot use, and therefore creates a screen full of garbage. You can reboot using the VGA Mode selection; everything will be the same except that the video driver will revert to standard character VGA mode, which should be supported by all video cards. You will probably never need this option, but if you ever do it can be a lifesaver. It is very hard to find buttons and dialog boxes from memory on a screen full of garbage.

If you do have a previous copy of NT installed, you need to decide whether you want to keep that copy intact. Your decision will be based on several things: how much confidence you have that the new installation will be up and running quickly, how many applications you have that would have to be reinstalled on a fresh NT installation, how much total disk space you have, how soon your users will be pounding on your door if the system is not back in operation soon, and so on. If you want to keep your existing installation and create a separate new installation, you *should* create the new installation on a different partition or drive from the previous installation. You *must* at least place the new NT in a different directory. The following information assumes that either you do not have a previous NT version installed or that you wish to preserve your old version and install a separate new version.

There is one further detail that you should understand concerning multiple-boot NT installations. NT places three important files in the root directory of your boot drive (usually C:), no matter where you install NT. These files are BOOT.INI, which NT uses to find the NT installation drive and directory, NTDETECT.COM, which is used before NT is loaded to explore the hardware environment, and NTLDR, which is the module that actually loads NT. Because each version of NT includes these three files, only one version of each can exist in the root directory. (Software such as System Commander, by V Communications, allows you to get around this restriction.) The version of NTDETECT.COM and NTLDR that you end up with will be the version from the last NT system that you installed. These modules seem to be compatible between NT 3.51 and NT 4.0, but there is no guarantee that this will always be the case.

Setup will now present its best guess of what type of computer, display, keyboard and pointing device exists in your system. You can change any of these selections if they are wrong, but only with configurations that NT knows about. Chances are good that Setup will present the correct configuration. When you are satisfied, move the cursor to the *No Changes* line and press Enter.

Setup will now allow you to decide which drive you wish NT to be installed on. Select the drive you desire and press Enter. Setup will format the drive if it has not been previously formatted. The drive may be formatted either as a FAT drive or as an NTFS drive. FAT drives are compatible with DOS, 16-bit Windows, and Windows 95. Only Windows NT can use NTFS drives; they will appear as unformatted drives to other operating systems (notably DOS or Windows 3.1). If you must share data with a system other than Windows NT, you must use FAT drives. The only exception to this rule is that Windows NT does support the HPFS file system of OS/2, so you could format your drives as HPFS drives if you only need to share them with OS/2. There are several advantages to NTFS over FAT drives, the primary one being the increased level of data security.

NOTE   The temptation is to let NT install on drive C, but a little thought at this point can pay dividends later on. If your C drive is large, say 2GB or more, you can safely install NT. If, however, your C drive is 1GB or less, and you have other drives that have sufficient space available, there is good reason to install NT on a drive other than C. The reason is that many of the applications that you will later install either default to or are forced to your boot drive, which is usually C. Additionally, many applications create their data directory structures on the C drive. Many programs by default choose the C drive, and NT runs quite well from any hard drive, so you can skip some down-the-road disk space headaches by installing NT somewhere other than on the C drive.

CONTINUING WITH NT SETUP   After the drive has been selected and formatted, Setup asks you which directory NT should be installed in. The default of \WINNT is fine unless you are installing a new version of NT on the same drive as a previous version that is already installed in the \WINNT directory. (NT version 3.51 installs by default to \WINNT35, so this should not be a conflict.) If a previous version of NT has been installed in \WINNT on the drive you wish to use, you must change to a different directory if you wish to maintain your previous installation intact. Setup now asks whether you wish it to perform an *exhaustive secondary examination* (more commonly known as a *surface scan*) of the disks. If you press Enter, Setup will perform this examination, which can take many minutes. If you press Esc, Setup will not perform this examination.

Setup now copies more files from the temporary directory to the installation directory; it also creates a bootable NT in the new installation directory. This phase of the installation is finished, and Setup asks you to reboot again. Make sure that you have removed all floppy disks and bootable CD-ROMs before you reboot. BOOT.INI has been altered to include entries for the new version of NT. When you reboot, this choice will be selected automatically.

RUNNING THE NT SETUP WIZARD—THE FIRST SECTION   On reboot, Setup moves some more files around and then initiates the Setup Wizard, which guides you through the next (and last) phase of the installation. This wizard has three sections. The first section gathers information about the hardware and the installation options. This information includes the following.

- The CD-key value. This is found on the back of your CD case.
- The name by which your computer is to be known on any network to which it is attached. You can give your computer any name that will be unique on your network.
- The type of server installation that you are creating. You may set it up as a primary domain controller, a backup domain controller, or a stand-alone server.
- A password to be used for the Administrator account. This password can be anything you wish, but be sure to write it down somewhere; without it you cannot log on to the system or create user accounts.
- Whether you want to create an Emergency Repair disk. You should create one of these, to save yourself time and trouble if you ever have to recover from a crash that corrupts NT.

RUNNING THE NT SETUP WIZARD—THE SECOND SECTION The second section of the Setup Wizard installs and configures Windows networking. There are so many possible combinations that we cannot possibly cover all of them here. Your choices will depend on what network hardware is installed, what type of network you will be connecting to, which protocols you wish to support, and many other factors. If your computer is to be part of a Microsoft network, you will probably want to configure the NetBios API running over the NetBEUI transport protocol. If it is to be part of a Novell network, you will want SPX/IPX support. The configuration that must be included in order for your Internet Information Server and Cold Fusion to function is the TCP/IP protocol.

One of the first questions you will be asked is what type(s) of network connections you will have. You can choose *wired* or *Remote* (via modem) or both. In the *Network Services* list you will probably want to set up *Simple TCP/IP services* in addition to the system defaults. Click Select From List, and then click Simple TCP/IP Services.

NOTE *If you are setting up NT server 4.0 on a machine that will communicate over a modem, Setup will assume that the modem will be used for incoming calls only. If you wish to set up the system to allow you to dial out as well, you will have to wait until Setup is completed. After NT installation is complete and NT is running normally, start the Start / Settings / Control Panel / Network applet, select the Services tab, and then select Remote Access Services. Click Properties and then click Configure. Under Port Usage, select Dial Out Only or Dial Out and Receive Calls.*

Setup will now present you with a dialog box in which you can indicate whether you want Microsoft Internet Information Server to be installed. The default is yes, which will be selected when the box is displayed. If you do not wish to install this product, remove the check from the box.

Setup will detect any network cards that you have installed, unless that card is one that is not known to NT. If this is the case, you can manually install the driver for your network card if you have a floppy from the vendor that contains the device driver. If you specified that your computer would access a network over a modem, then the modem installer will be activated to install and configure your modem. If the modem is not one for which NT currently includes a driver, you can manually install your modem if you have a driver provided by the modem manufacturer.

When you have successfully navigated your way through the thicket of network choices, review the network bindings to be sure that the proper services and protocols are bound to the correct network devices. Pay particular attention to the order in which services or protocols are bound to your devices if your system has more than one network device. For example, if you have a network card and access to a network through a modem, and if a service or protocol is bound to both devices, the system will try to access the network using the binding that is listed first. You can move the bindings up or down to ensure that the correct device is accessed preferentially.

After all network installation has been completed, you will be presented with a world map and given a chance to specify your time zone and the current date and time. Next, Setup will try to detect your display adapter type and let you set up the resolution and colors. When you have completed these tasks, Setup copies some remaining files to the installation directory, sets up security options on all system files, and saves the configuration in the registry. If you chose to create an emergency repair disk, one is now created. This disk contains a copy of the configuration that was just saved in the registry.

Remove all floppies and reboot the system one last time. Windows NT Server 4.0 installation is now complete except for some housekeeping that you can do at any time, primarily setting up user accounts. Your system should be up and running and ready for the installation of your applications, including your Internet Information Server if you choose to install it at this time.

CONCLUSION

This chapter has included a basic description of Microsoft Windows NT Server and Workstation, versions 3.5.1 and 4.0, including a discussion of what should be considered in choosing the operating system version that you should run. The installation of each version of the Microsoft Windows NT operation system has also been covered.

CHAPTER 3

Application Installation and Configuration

- Understanding Web Servers
- Installing Microsoft's Internet Information Server
- Installing Netscape's Information Server
- Installing O'Reilly's WebSite Professional
- Installing and Using Microsoft SQL Server
- SQL Enterprise Manager
- Installing Cold Fusion

Web Servers

There are several Web servers available, each with a unique combination of cost, features, support, and performance. Your decision as to which server you wish to purchase, install, and use will be effected by such considerations as the size of the network that you will be supporting, the operating system that you have chosen, and the cost of the server. Three popular servers are Microsoft Internet Information Server (IIS), Enterprise Server from Netscape Communications, and WebSite Professional from O'Reilly. A second tier of Web servers includes offerings from Process Software, Spry, and Internet Factory. Freeware Web servers are also available. This chapter covers the installation of Microsoft's IIS, Netscape's Enterprise Server, and O'Reilly's WebSite Professional server.

Installing Microsoft's Internet Information Server

Microsoft Internet Information Server (IIS) comes bundled with Windows NT Server version 4.0. Unless you take the specific action to *not* install it, it will be installed along with NT Server 4.0. If you choose to not install IIS along with NT Server 4.0, an icon is created on your desktop to facilitate installation of IIS later. The following information describes installation of IIS *after* NT Server 4.0 has been installed, but most of the installation is the same when IIS is installed along with NT Server 4.0.

Start the IIS installation by clicking the Install Internet Information icon. Enter the path to the Windows NT Server installation CD-ROM and click OK. Click OK again to acknowledge the copyright warning. Check the boxes in the next dialog box to include the services that you desire in the installation. The default selection of everything except the HTML version of the Internet Service Manager is probably a good choice for most installations. IIS will be installed by default in a subdirectory named *inetsrv* in the \system32 subdirectory of the directory in which NT Server 4.0 is installed, so if you have installed NT in its default directory, IIS will install in *drive*:\WINNT\system32\inetsrv, where *drive* is the drive on which NT has been installed (see Figure 3-1). You may change this if you wish.

The next displayed dialog box lets you specify the home directory for the WWW, FTP, and Gopher services of IIS. You will usually want to ac-

Figure 3-1
Microsoft IIS Program
Directory Structure

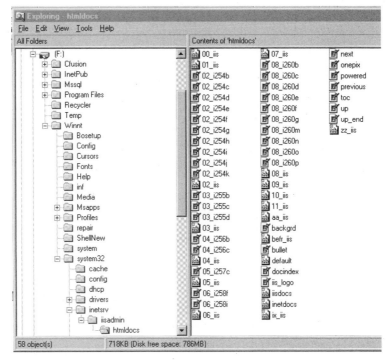

cept the default directories, since these directories are where most administrators expect to find the home directories.

Installation will continue with few interruptions from this point. You may get a warning message indicating that you have not configured a domain name and that Gopher services will be unreliable without one. If you did not install NT Server 4.0 as a domain controller, you will not have a specified domain name. You may use the Network Control Panel Applet to create a domain name later.

The next dialog box asks you to choose one or more OBDC drivers from a list of available OBDC drivers. If you have just installed NT Server 4.0 the only entry in the list will be for SQL Server. Select this driver. You can add other drivers later. IIS installation should complete without further intervention from you.

It is important to note the directories that IIS uses as home directories for its services, especially the one used for WWW service, because you will need to know this directory at various times in the installation and use of Cold Fusion. Unless you specify otherwise, IIS will use InetPub\wwwroot as its WWW home directory on the drive on which IIS was installed (see Figure 3-2). You should also know that IIS sets its IP address to 127.0.0.1.

Figure 3-2
Microsoft IIS
Document Directory
Structure

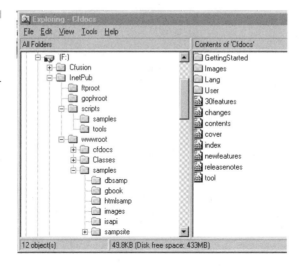

Installing Netscape's Enterprise Server

The Netscape Enterprise Server can be downloaded from the Netscape Web site or purchased on CD-ROM. The file that is downloaded from the Web is a self-extracting executable. The following section describes how to install Netscape's Enterprise Server on a server.

PREPARING FOR INSTALLATION   Netscape suggests that you do the following to prepare for the installation of Netscape Enterprise Server:

- Make sure that DNS is running. (This is not necessary for server installation.)
- Create an alias for the server. (This can only be done if you have DNS running.)
- Create a user account for the server and a group for all Netscape SuiteSpot servers.
- Choose unique port numbers for the Administration server and the Web server. (Most Web servers use port 80 and Setup will choose a random port number for the Administration server later in the installation process.)
- Install Netscape Navigator 3.0 (or later) or Netscape Navigator Gold. (A browser is required to complete the installation.)
- If you want to use the Netscape Enterprise Server's SNMP monitoring capabilities, make sure that SNMP is properly set up on your system before installing the server.

STARTING INSTALLATION   If you have obtained Netscape's Enterprise Server from the WWW, save the self-extracting executable file in a temporary directory, and then execute that file to unpack it and start the setup program. If you purchased the software on CD-ROM, execute the SETUP.EXE file in the CD-ROM root directory. The Welcome screen will appear. Click Next to continue. The Software License Agreement screen will appear. Read the license agreement. If you agree with the conditions, click Accept and you will proceed.

CHOOSE DESTINATION LOCATION   The default location for the server files is \Netscape\SuiteSpot on the C drive. There should be no need to change the default directory, but you may want to change the drive on which the server is installed. A Browse button is provided if you want to change either the drive or the directory. Netscape requires all Netscape 3.0 servers to be installed in the same directory if you have more than one, and the Browse button is deactivated if Setup detects that this is not the first Netscape server that is being installed. Click Next when you are satisfied with the destination location.

SERVER UPGRADE   This screen will only appear if you have a 2.x Netscape server installed. Use it to choose between migrating your 2.x server settings or creating new settings for your 3.0 server. Click Next to continue.

INTERNATIONAL   The following three screens will only appear if you are installing the international version of the server. Use the Choose Interface Language screen to select a language, and then click Next. Use the Global Default Search screen to choose the default language to be used for text searches, and then click Next. Use the Search/Index Engines screen to choose all the search engines you want to install.

ADMINISTRATION SERVER LDAP CONFIGURATION   The Lightweight Directory Access Protocol (LDAP) is a protocol for accessing online directory services. If you wish to use LDAP, check the box and specify the server name, server port, and distinguished name on the LDAP server. If you don't know what LDAP is or whether you want to use it, leave the box blank. Click Next to continue.

ADMINISTRATION SERVER AUTHENTICATION   Enter the user name to be used for administration server access, or accept the default of *admin*. Enter the Administration server password twice. Remember this password or you will not be able to access the server administration functions. Click Next to continue.

ADMINISTRATION SERVER PORT SELECTION   The Administration server runs on a unique port. The Setup program will provide a random port number between 1025 and 65535. Unless you have a good reason to change this default, accept it as is. The URL for administration access is displayed; it consists of the server name and this port number. Remember this URL. Click Next to continue.

ENTERPRISE SERVER CONFIGURATION   The default path to the root document directory is displayed (see Figure 3-3). You can accept this default or browse for a different one. Unless you have a good reason, accept the default; it is where administrators are used to finding server documents. The default port number is also displayed. Most servers use the default port 80. You should, too, unless you understand all the ramifications of changing to a different port. Click Next to continue.

SERVER CONFIGURATION SUMMARY   Review the choices you have made and click Next if you are satisfied. Installation of the server files will proceed. When the installation has completed, the Netscape Enterprise Server 3.0 screen appears. You can choose whether to view the Readme file or to connect to the server home page. This default home page contains information about features of the current release. Also, after the server is in-

Figure 3-3
Netscape Enterprise
Server Document
Directory Structure

stalled, you can access the administrative functions by specifying the administration URL remembered from an earlier step. You will have to enter the administration user name and password to access these functions.

Installing O'Reilly's WebSite Professional

O'Reilly's WebSite Professional comes with complete hard copy documentation. The *Getting Started* booklet contains complete installation instructions. The following is provided as a brief overview of WebSite installation. Insert the WebSite CD-ROM and execute SETUP.EXE from the \disk1 subdirectory. Click Next on the Welcome to WebSite Pro Setup screen. Enter the required information on the Registration screen and click Next. Click Next again on the Registration Confirmation screen.

CHOOSE DESTINATION LOCATION   Choose the default drive and directory, or click Browse to change to another drive or directory. Then click Next.

SELECT COMPONENTS   You do not need to install the Spyglass Enhanced Mosaic Browser if you already have another Web browser installed. Install Hot Dog Standard HTML Editor if you don't already have an HTML editor installed. Do not install Cold Fusion Standard Development Platform. This is an older version of Cold Fusion. You will be installing version 3.0 of Cold Fusion later. Click Next.

EXISTING WEB   Choose the default Web root directory and index document or enter the path to an existing Web root and the name of an existing index document. Click Next.

SERVER RUN MODE   The WebSite Professional server can run either as an application or as a service. O'Reilly suggests that you install it as an application the first time so that you can more easily control the server. When you have completed testing the server and are ready to make it accessible for users, you will want to install it to run as a Windows NT service so that it can run unattended. Select the desired Run mode and click Next.

HOST'S DOMAIN NAME   Enter your host's domain name. This step is not needed for local testing, but it is required if you want to access the server from another computer on your network. Click Next.

ADMINISTRATOR'S E-MAIL ADDRESS   Enter the e-mail address of someone (usually the system administrator) who is to receive messages from the server. Click Next.

MISCELLANEOUS OTHER INFORMATION   Installation will now continue as the program copies files, sets up directories, and so on. If you elected to install the older version of Cold Fusion, and the installation program detects that there is already a version of Cold Fusion installed, a dialog box will appear asking whether you want to replace that version. You should probably click No.

If you are installing WebSite Professional as a service, a screen will appear, telling you how to start the service. Click Next. A screen appears, describing the usage of the Windows NT Performance Monitor. Click Next. A screen appears, describing cryptographic support issues. Click Next. The WebSite Pro Setup Complete screen appears. You have the options of reading the Readme file and of starting the server. The short Readme file will tell you how to access the WebSite Pro online documentation. Click Finish.

The WebSite documentation, accessible at http://localhost/wsdocs, is complete and well written. You should explore it if you are new to using a Web server.

You will receive a security warning when you start the server until you either disable enhanced security or obtain a public key certificate.

Microsoft SQL Server

Microsoft's SQL Server will support an Enterprise-wide complex of data servers. This software is a high-end multithread server product that can handle databases containing more than 100 gigabytes of information.

Preparing for Installation

Create a SQLAdmins group and a user account within that group for use by the SQL executive. Make this account a member of the Administrators group. Check the Password Never Expires box. From the Policies menu select User Rights (see Figure 3-4). Check the Show Advanced User Rights box. Add the following User Rights to the SQLAdmins group: Act as part of the operating system, Increase quotas, Log on as a service, and Replace a process level token. This account will be needed later in the setup process.

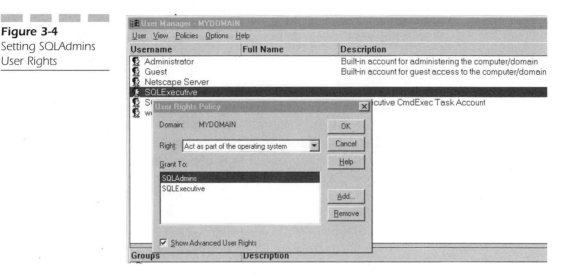

Figure 3-4
Setting SQLAdmins
User Rights

Installing Microsoft SQL Server

If you have acquired Microsoft SQL Server as a component of Microsoft BackOffice, start the BackOffice Setup program, select Microsoft SQL Server 6.5, and click OK. If you have downloaded Microsoft SQL Server from the Internet, run the file that you downloaded (sqlx86.exe for Intel processors) with the /D option, which creates the proper subdirectory structure. If you have acquired Microsoft SQL Server as a single product, run the Setup file from the CD-ROM.

WELCOME The first dialog box to appear will be the Welcome dialog box. Click Help or press F1 to access Microsoft's setup help. Read the Server Names section under Prerequisites for an explanation of restrictions that SQL Server places on the network name you have given your computer. Check the Procedures For section of the help screen for additional information on SQL Server installation, configuration, and operation; this section also includes a discussion of security options and account assignments. Anyone new to Microsoft SQL Server should take the time to at least scan the information provided in this help file. Click Continue to proceed.

NAME AND ORGANIZATION A dialog box appears in which you must enter your name and organization. A product ID is recommended but not required. Click Continue when you have entered this information. You are then asked to verify that you have entered the correct information and given a chance to go back and correct any errors. Click Continue when you are satisfied with your entries.

OPTIONS   The next dialog box allows you to select an install option. On an initial installation only three options will be available. The option that is selected by default, Install SQL Server and Utilities, is the one you want. Click Continue.

LICENSING   The next dialog box involves the licensing mode, of which there are two. These modes are explained briefly in the dialog box. You must purchase the licenses that you need from Microsoft. As the help for this dialog box says, if you are in doubt, select the Per Server licensing mode. You can later switch from Per Server to Per Seat if you find that you need to do that; you cannot switch in the other direction. Contact Microsoft for further information on licenses. When you click Continue, you are presented with another dialog box asking you to agree to the terms of the licensing mode that you have selected. Check the I Agree That box and click OK to proceed.

INSTALLATION PATH   Setup will be busy with some background operations for a few seconds, and then it will present a dialog box for the SQL Server Installation Path. Setup will have selected, by default, your C drive and the directory \Mssql. You should have no need to change the directory, but you can if you want to. You should be a bit more concerned about the installation drive, because SQL Server will use up 60MB or more. Installing SQL Server on a drive other than C will still require several megabytes of memory on the C drive. Click Continue when you are satisfied with the installation path.

MASTER DEVICE   The next dialog box contains information about the creation of the MASTER device. The default drive is the one that you have selected for installation of SQL Server. The default directory is the \Data subdirectory in the \Mssql directory. You can change these if you wish. The third entry in this dialog box is the size of the MASTER device. The default is 25MB. This size is okay because you can increase it later if needed. Click Continue to proceed.

BOOKS ONLINE   The next dialog box concerns the Books Online documentation for SQL Server. You have three options: Install on Hard Disk, Install to Run from CD, and Do not Install. You should install this documentation on your hard disk, because it only requires 15M and contains useful information. Select the option you desire, and then click Continue to proceed. The Microsoft SQL Server directory structure is shown in Figure 3-5.

Figure 3-5
Microsoft SQL Server
Directory Structure

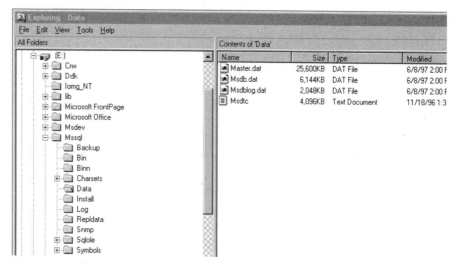

INSTALLATION OPTIONS   Next you must choose some installation options. Click Sets to see which character sets are supported. The default ISO Character Set is the one you want unless you specifically know which other character set you need. Click Orders to display your options for a sort order. The default is *Dictionary Order, Case Insensitive.* Select this order unless you are absolutely certain that you want another order. You should be careful in selecting your character set and sort; if you later decide to change, you will have to rebuild your entire database. The default network support is Named Pipes. It is okay to select additional network support if you are sure that you will need it, but do not deselect Named Pipes during installation; the installation procedure uses the default Named Pipes. You can and probably will want to check the option *Auto Start SQL Server at Boot Time.* You can also check the option to *Auto Start SQL Executive at Boot Time.* Click Continue when you are satisfied with your selections.

LOG ON ACCOUNT   The next dialog box concerns the SQL Executive Log On Account. You can choose to have the Executive log on by using a specific Windows NT account or you can log on by using the Local-System account. The default is to log on using the Windows NT Administrator account. Change this default to the account that you created earlier in the SQLAdmins group. If you did not create that account, you can choose to have the Executive log in by using the LocalSystem account now and by creating a separate administrative account later. Click Continue to proceed.

THE LONG INSTALLATION WAIT   Setup has now acquired the information that it needs to proceed with the installation and will present you with a message box indicating the progress of the file copy operation as it proceeds. This takes a while; there are many files. When the copying is complete, Setup will continue with the installation. During this process there will be a message box in the upper-left corner of your screen indicating what is being done. This may take several minutes. Don't despair as long as the sand is dropping inside the Q; Setup has a lot of work to do. Setup will inform you when it is done and provide a button for you to click to return to Windows NT.

AUTOMATIC INSTALLATION OF SERVICE PACK   When SQL Server installation is completed, service pack installation should continue automatically. You will be presented with another Welcome dialog box. Click Continue to proceed. After a few minutes, Setup will request your SA password. Leave the password blank; this is the default password that has been set up for the SA account. Click Continue to proceed. Setup will immediately get busy doing things without giving you a clue as to what is happening. Be patient. After several minutes, Setup will either report that it has been successful or that it has failed.

STARTING SQL SERVER   SQL Server does not automatically start at the end of installation. If you checked the boxes for starting the server and the executive at boot time earlier in the installation, SQL Server will start the next time you boot your system. If you wish to access the server without rebooting, you will have to start it manually. To do this, click Start, select Programs, select Microsoft SQL Server 6.5, and then click on SQL Service Manager. A traffic signal icon appears (see Figure 3-6). If the light is red (Stop), indicating that the SQL Server is not running, double-click the green light (Start/Continue) and the Server will start.

SQL ENTERPRISE MANAGER   SQL Enterprise Manager is a tool for managing all SQL Servers on a network. Before your server can be managed using this tool, it must be registered. Click Start, select Programs, select Microsoft SQL Server 6.5, and then click SQL Enterprise Manager. The Register Server dialog box appears. Select Use Trusted Connection in the Login Information section. Click the Servers button. The Select Server dialog box should appear as shown in Figure 3-7, with your server listed in the Active Servers list box.

Select your server if there are multiple servers listed. Click OK. Your server will now appear in the Server list box. Click Register. Your Server will be registered with the SQL Enterprise Manager. Click Close. Your

Figure 3-6
Microsoft SQL Server
Service Manager
Control

Figure 3-7
SQL Enterprise Manager Registration—
Server Selection

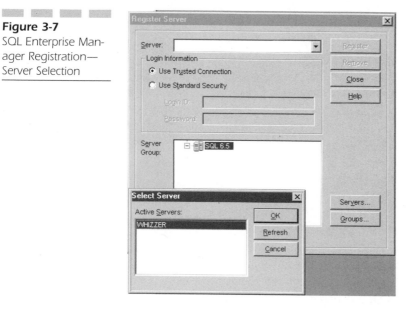

Server should now appear as a member of the SQL 6.5 group in the Server Manager list (see Figure 3-8). You may now use the SQL Enterprise Manager to administer your server.

Cold Fusion

Cold Fusion Professional 3.0 serves as "middleware" between the enduser and the database server by taking the place of CGI Script written in PERL, C/C++, or Visual Basic. HTML tags, Cold Fusion tags, and SQL statements are used to connect the enduser's HTML browser to your choice of Web server.

Figure 3-8
SQL Enterprise Manager—Server Management

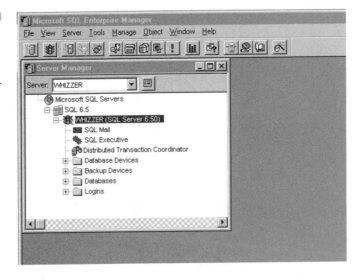

Installing Cold Fusion

Cold Fusion comes as a single SETUP.EXE file. Execute this file to begin Cold Fusion installation. The first message box that appears welcomes you to Cold Fusion Setup. Click Next to proceed. The following description applies to Cold Fusion version 3.0.

LICENSE AGREEMENT   This message box describes the Cold Fusion license agreement. When you have read through this information and are ready to accept the license terms and proceed, click Yes.

SELECT DESTINATION LOCATION   This dialog box allows you to select the drive and directory where Cold Fusion will be installed. The default drive is your C drive, the default directory is \Cfusion. You should not need to change these unless you wish to place Cold Fusion on a different drive for space considerations. Click Next when you are satisfied with the installation path.

SELECT INSTALLATION OPTIONS   This dialog box allows you to select which Cold Fusion components you wish to install. The default is all components. You should accept this default unless you have a specific reason for not installing a particular component. Click Next when you are ready to continue.

SELECT WEB SERVER This dialog box allows you to select the Web server to which you want to hook up Cold Fusion. If you have a Web server installed, the Cold Fusion setup program will have located and selected it for you. If your Web server does not appear in the list box, you will have to manually search for it. Click Next when you have selected the correct Web server.

SELECT WEB SERVER DOCUMENT DIRECTORY This dialog box allows you to select the Web Server document directory. This is the home directory that you selected when you set up your Web server. The Cold Fusion setup program will have located this directory for any Web server that it detected in the preceding step. It should appear in the dialog box and should be selected. Click Next when you have selected the correct Web Server document directory.

SELECT ADMINISTRATOR PASSWORD Cold Fusion 3.0 administration requires an administrator password by default. You can later remove this requirement if you have established some other form of restricted access to Cold Fusion Administration. Specify and confirm your password, and then click Next.

SELECT PROGRAM FOLDER This dialog box allows you to specify the program group into which the Cold Fusion icons will be placed. Leave the default or choose another. Click Next to proceed.

START COPYING FILES Setup will present a summary of the choices that you have made. Review them to be certain that you have entered the correct information, and then click Next. Setup will copy the necessary files and set up the Cold Fusion directory structure. When this is complete, an informational message will appear telling you that Cold Fusion Setup is about to set up the OBDC drivers. Click OK to let Setup continue.

When the OBDC drivers have been set up, the installation of Cold Fusion is complete. Click Finish. Setup will exit and bring up your default browser, directing it to the Cold Fusion Release Notes page.

COLD FUSION DIRECTORY STRUCTURE Cold Fusion templates must be placed in this directory or one of its subdirectories so that Cold Fusion can access them without having their complete path specified in the HTML documents (see Figure 3-9). You can place Cold Fusion templates in any directory you choose if you always use a complete path to access them.

Figure 3-9
Cold Fusion Directory
Structure

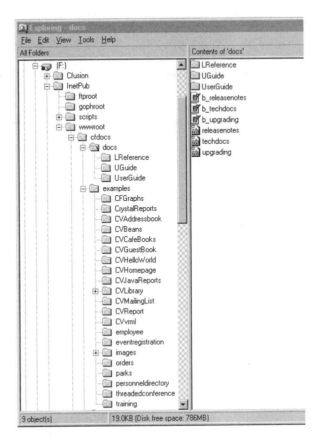

COLD FUSION ADMINISTRATION Start the Cold Fusion Administrator by clicking Start, selecting Programs, selecting Cold Fusion Professional 3.0, and then clicking Cold Fusion Administrator. Your default Web browser will start and bring up the Cold Fusion Administration home page. Enter your administrator password and click Submit.

The administrator sections are listed. Most of them are self-explanatory. The first section that you should visit is the Data Sources section (see Figures 3-10 and 3-11). All databases that have been included as samples and any databases that you have already created should be listed in this section. Double-click each database and the configuration screen for that database access appears. Make sure that the access user name and password are correctly specified. Any SQL Server databases should have the Use Trusted Connection box checked. Be sure to click Update if you make any changes to any configuration.

Figure 3-10
Cold Fusion
Administrator Data
Source Configuration

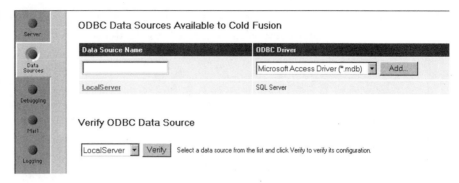

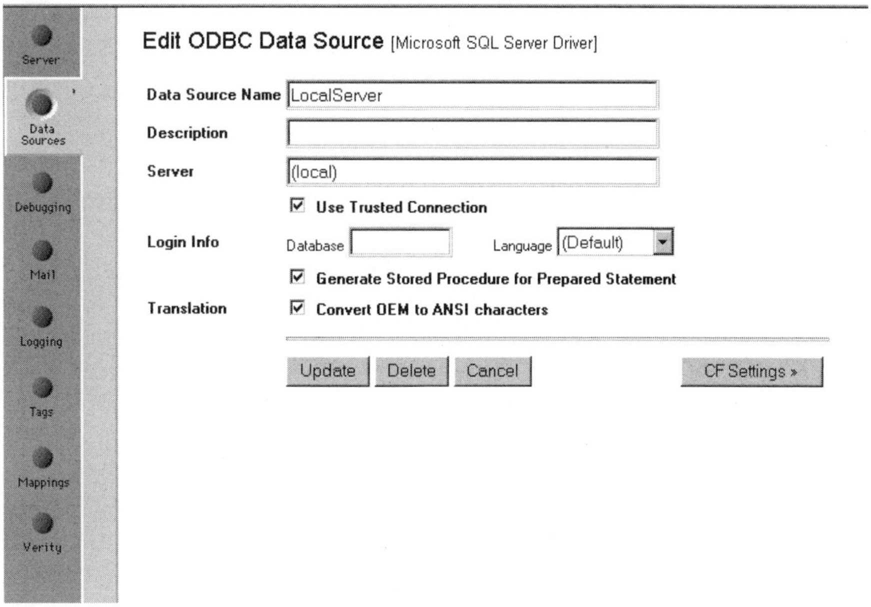

Figure 3-11
Cold Fusion Adminis-
trator Data Sources

You can verify access to each of the databases by selecting that database in the list next to the Verify button and then clicking Verify. A message will appear indicating success or failure.

The Debugging section allows you to specify one or more IP addresses for which debugging will be active. This allows you to turn debug on for your own IP address if you are testing Cold Fusion templates, while not cluttering up the log files with debug information from other user accesses.

The Mail section allows you to enter your mail server name or IP address. The server port should be 25 unless you know that your mail server uses a different port. You cannot use the mail features of Cold Fusion until you have mail configured. You can test the configuration by sending a sample message to an address that you specify.

CONCLUSION

This chapter has covered the installation of three Internet Information Servers: Microsoft Internet Information Server, Netscape Enterprise Server, and O'Reilly WebSite Professional. It also has covered installation of Microsoft SQL Server and the installation of Allaire's Cold Fusion.

4

Interactive E-mail

- Introducing interactive e-mail
- Configuring SMTP Mail for Windows 95 and Windows NT 4.0
- Building mail templates using HTML tags and CFML tags
- Using databases with Interactive e-mail

Introducing Cold Fusion's Auto-Generated E-mail

You can quickly and easily generate e-mail and send it over the Internet by using Cold Fusion. Web business activity can be conducted without your personal involvement or immediate attention. Until recently, it was difficult to generate automated e-mail; you needed to create a mail-processing CGI Script using PERL, C/C++, Delphi, or Visual Basic. But with Cold Fusion, you use an HTML fill-in form and a Cold Fusion template with some specific Cold Fusion e-mail tags. Cold Fusion uses its own built-in CGI Script to generate and *send the mail.*

On the client side, to trigger automated e-mail, visitors to your Web page fill-in and submit an HTML form. This form contains the hidden URL address of a Cold Fusion mail template used by the server to process the form. (To create mail templates, see the section titled, "Building Mail Templates" later in the chapter). After the end user submits the form, the browser sends the URL with attached form information to the server. Upon receiving the URL, Cold Fusion processes the form data and generates a return e-mail.

Using mail templates opens up interesting possibilities. For example, e-mail can include queried information from databases. You can use Microsoft's Access or FoxPro, Borland's dBASE, Oracle's Personal Oracle 7, Corel's PARADOX database, or Microsoft's EXCEL spreadsheet to retrieve information to be sent via mail to clients.

During mail processing, Cold Fusion spools (sends) mail to disk, and then processes the mail in the background. This technique acts as a safety feature. If mail processing is interrupted by power loss or server malfunction, unsent mail is not lost, because the spooling software keeps track of it. When system stability is re-established, e-mail is posted. Although a single mail message is processed immediately, larger groups of messages are processed in the background by Cold Fusion (using timesharing if you are doing other things also) and can take several minutes to send.

Setting up Cold Fusion's Simple Mail Transfer Protocol (SMTP) e-mail is not difficult. An active connection to the Internet is required, and then you use the Cold Fusion Administrator to set specific mail tab settings. The next section shows how to configure the Mail tab in the Cold Fusion Administrator.

Configuring the Cold Fusion Mail Tab

If you are using Windows 95, start Cold Fusion Professional 3.0 from the Windows 95 Start Menu, and then select the Cold Fusion Administrator.

Cold Fusion displays a password entry box. Enter your CF Administrator password, and then click the MAIL tab in the left frame (see Figure 4-1).

Using the Cold Fusion Administrator Mail Tab

Use the *MAIL* tab (mail configuration screen) to set up your SMTP Mail Server. If you don't know the name of your mail server, in most cases the name is created by substituting the first word of your e-mail address and putting in its place the word *mail*. (For example, if your e-mail address is *johnb@aol.com*, the corresponding SMTP Server name would be *mail.aol.com*. Click **Apply** after you have filled in the form. Cold Fusion will try out your settings.

NOTE *When you are creating the mail-server-address, replace the @ sign with a period. Set the SMTP server to Server Port = "25" if the box is blank. The Time-out and Logging settings (which track mail error messages) can be left at default settings at this time.*

Figure 4-1
Cold Fusion
Adminstrator:
Mail Tab

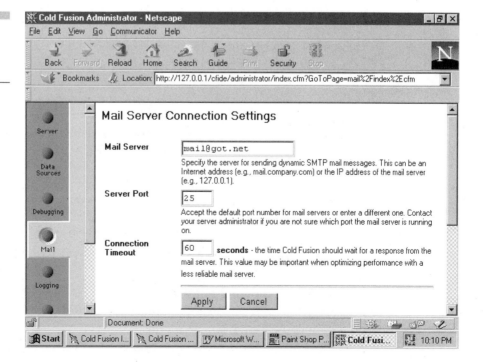

If you are using NT 4.0, you can start the Cold Fusion Administrator by clicking Start (no icon is formed during installation). Then select Programs, Cold Fusion Professional 3.0, and Cold Fusion Administrator and click. Select the Mail tab.

When you have completed *configuring* the Mail tab, press the OK button. Next, delect the Server tab, and then Stop and Restart the Cold Fusion application to make sure all configuration changes are recognized.

Verifying (Testing) SMTP Mail

To use SMTP Mail, you must be actively connected to the Internet. If you are up-and-running, press the *Verify* button. If everything is configured correctly, Cold Fusion returns a message box with the message `verification completed without error. Check your mail for a message.` Click Go Back to return to the previous screen. Cold Fusion is now correctly configured to send mail through your Internet/Intranet Mail Server. To exit the Mail tab, click *x* in the top-right corner of Netscape to exit the Cold Fusion Administrator or go to any other tab.

NOTE *If you press the Verify button without being up-and-running, Cold Fusion will attempt to start up your browser software, and it will bring up your Internet connection logon and prompt you for the password. You may get a message box with the message* `Error occurred while attempting to connect to mail server` *if you do not have a live POP mail connection.*

If Cold Fusion fails to connect to your browser, it will try to connect to your basic machine address: 127.0.0.1. You must have your server software (for example, O'Reilly Website 1.1) up-and-running for this connection to be successful. See Chapter 2 for information on selection and installation of server software, or see Chapter 3 for information on Windows NT if you have any questions about server software or Windows NT. You can run Cold Fusion over a closed-loop network on one machine (shown in the next section) if you wish.

Creating a Front-end Fill-in HTML Form

An HTML fill-in form is used as the front-end for *auto-mailings*. The next section shows how to create that HTML fill-in form used by the CF mail template residing on the server (see Figure 4-2).

Figure 4-2

HTML fill-in form

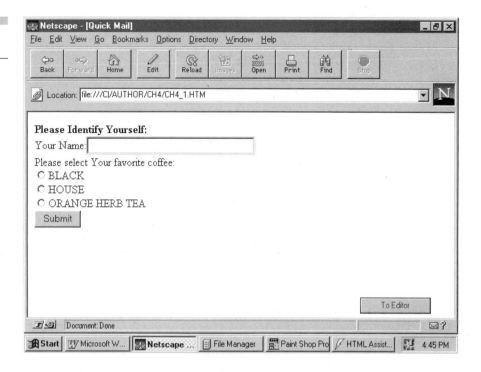

Look closely at the following HTML fill-in form. The only additional element is that the Form tag now contains a reference to a Cold Fusion mail template, (mailtiny.cfm).

```
mail1.htm front-end HTML form
<HTML>
<TITLE>Quick Mail </TITLE>
<FORM ACTION="mailtiny.cfm" METHOD=POST>
<B>Please Identify Yourself:</B><BR>
Your Name:<INPUT TYPE="TEXT" NAME="yourname" size="30"
      maxlength="30"><BR>
Please select Your favorite coffee:<br>
<INPUT TYPE="radio" NAME="beverage" VALUE="BLACK">BLACK<BR>
<INPUT TYPE="radio" NAME="beverage" VALUE="DECAF">HOUSE<BR>
<INPUT TYPE="radio" NAME="beverage" VALUE="ORANGE TEA">
      ORANGE HERB TEA<BR>
<INPUT TYPE= "SUBMIT" VALUE="Submit">
</FORM>
</HTML>


<< - Output from Cold Fusion-generated e-mail -  >>

(mail header information):
X-From_: johnb@got.net Thu Feb 20 14:58:02 1997
X-Delivered: at request of johnb on you
```

```
Date: Thu, 20 Feb 1997 14:58:02 -0800
X-Real-To: <johnb@got.net>
From: johnb@got.net
To: johnb@got.net
Subject: Beverages

          Your Name:Charles Smith
          Favorite Coffee: ORANGE TEA
```

The <FORM> tag must include the mail template's URL address on the server. (In this case, all that is needed is the name of the mail template.) Cold Fusion finds the template because it is in the \Cfdocs subdirectory on the C drive. If you have Cold Fusion templates in a customized subdirectory, you will have to add additional drive pathname information. The "Action=template" form points to the specific mail template file residing on your server. After you create the fill-in form, save it to your server's Cold Fusion HTML document directory.

You can look and see where Cold Fusion has placed other HTML documents during installation to see where you should put your HTML documents. Cold Fusion will normally *see* your server software and place the HTML documents directory where the server software can automatically *find* it. The HTML form document starts up the Cold Fusion mail template. How to build Cold Fusion mail templates is shown in the next section.

BUILDING CF MAIL TEMPLATES   This section highlights the major parts of a Cold Fusion mail template.

Section 1—The *HTML tag* section—If you are sitting at your server while testing your server's SMTP e-mail capability, use this section of the mail template to send a confirming screen message back to your server:

```
"Your E-mail has been sent".
```

Section 2—The *CFMAIL tag* section—This section contains the CF-MAIL tag. Within the CFMAIL tag is a FROM attribute, which identifies the Sender (a TO attribute, which identifies the Recipient) and a SUBJECT attribute (optional).

Section 3—The *Form-Field* section—This section displays the contents of the *Input Fields* form. (It also can be used to display information retrieved from a database. (Querying databases is covered in the section "Using Databases with Interactive E-mail" found later in the chapter.) This section also contains the closing </CFMAIL> tag.

In a CF mail template the initial HTML section makes up roughly the first half of the template, the <CFMAIL> tag makes up the second half. Notice in the following example that each field name (used in the HTML fill-in form) includes the prefix *form* as well as the field name used in the form.

AN EXAMPLE OF A COLD FUSION MAIL TEMPLATE — "MAILTINY.CFM"

```
<!—Mailtiny.cfm, a quick Cold Fusion Mail Template —>
<HTML>
<HEAD>
<TITLE> Automated Order Form </TITLE>
</HEAD>
<BODY>
<B>Your E-mail has been sent!</B>
</BODY>
</HTML>

   <CFMAIL
          FROM="johnb@got.net"
          TO="johnb@got.net"
          SUBJECT="Beverages"
   >
          Your Name: #Form.yourname#
          Favorite Coffee: #Form.beverage#

   </CFMAIL>
```

In the <CFMAIL> tag, the closing > character of the <CFMAIL> tag separated by the TO, FROM, and SUBJECT attributes, and is placed flush left on a new line. (This helps you visually see where the tag closes.) Without placing this *greater than* character after the CFMAIL tag attributes, the template will not run. Also, put the final </CF MAIL> tag on the last line of the template.

USING YOUR LOCAL MACHINE ADDRESS TO TEST COLD FUSION E-MAIL
You can test e-mail templates using your own server. This is a fast and convenient way to test mail templates before you put them up on your enterprise-wide intranet or the World Wide Web. Your own server has the following machine URL address:

`<http://127.0.0.1/mailtiny.cfm>`

This address is made up of two parts:

127.0.0.1—the machine address of your server

mailtiny.cfm—the name of the CF Template

To test the mail template, put the mail template and the HTML document containing the fill-in form inside the HTML documents directory of your server. If you can't find the right directory to use, use the FIND FILES Windows 95/NT command to search for *.cfm* and see where Cold Fusion installed the sample template files; then put the document file and the mail template file in that directory. Later, when you are more familiar with templates you can build a path to a document/template directory of your choice. Right now, lets keep it as easy as possible.

USING SMTP MAIL   In contrast to HTML's *loose* use of tags in HTML documents (incorrectly written tags are ignored), Cold Fusion mail template tags and corresponding HTML document tags must be more carefully written. Creating mail tags in a Cold Fusion template is just like writing HTML document tags. But, be aware that tags must be processed by two programs: the browser software and the Cold Fusion *engine* containing CGI Script. And CGI scripts are picky, even Cold Fusion's. The following list of Common Mail Template Tag-Writing Problems has been compiled to help you write templates that work the first time.

COMMON MAIL TEMPLATE TAG-WRITING PROBLEMS
PROBLEM: *A field name doesn't work in the Cold Fusion mail template.*

Field names are case-sensitive when used by both HTML documents and Cold Fusion mail templates. (CGI code is case-sensitive.) So even if you initially write an HTML tag correctly and then write a Cold Fusion mail template tag, you can still get an error message if uppercase is used in one file and lowercase in the other. *Suggestion*: To maintain consistency, put HTML *input field* names and corresponding mail template *form-field* names in either all lowercase or all uppercase. To reduce typing errors, print out your HTML document and then use the printout as a guide for entering mail template fields. Or, open both the HTML document and the template in separate windows and cut-and-paste between documents.

TYPICAL ERROR MESSAGE: `Form.Lastname not found.` This message means that a case-sensitivity problem or a field name misspelling has occurred during the building of the HTML document or creation of the template.

PROBLEM: *Missing right or left brackets.*

If you leave out the "<" or ">" tag character in a template, it can stop further processing. Check the mail template text example to see where to place these characters. HTML documents will still run with missing end tags; templates may or may not, depending what's left out. For best results don't skip ending tags.

ACCESSING MAIL TEMPLATES ON REMOTE SERVERS To use mail templates on a remote server, change the URL address (in the HTML document's form tag to a full http pathname-style URL:

```
<FORM ACTION="http://www.mycompany.com.mailtiny.cfm"
    METHOD=POST>.
```

The first part of this address `http://www.mycompany.com` is the Internet address for your company. The second part of the address `mailtiny.cfm` is your company's Web server pathname. Every Web server has a default server documents directory. Cold Fusion will create an HTML document subdirectory and use it, so you don't need to put in the entire directory path. Otherwise, if you were using Windows 95 and the O'Rielly Web server, you would have to include *C:\website\htdocs\mailtiny*. But, in actuality, all you have to include is the name of the mailtiny.cfm file. In this example, *website* is the O'Rielly Server top directory, and *hotdocs* is the HTML directory. Put the HTML documents and mail templates together in the same documents subdirectory (for example, *C:\website\htdocs*).

USING NT 4.0 The equivalent default template and document directory on NT 4.0 is *C:\InetPub\wwwroot*. In the MS Internet Server, you can specify what the *home* subdirectory should be. By default, it is *drive:'InetPub\wwwroot*, where drive is the drive on which the IS is installed, which is the drive on which NT 4.0 Server is installed. You can change this default through the IS Administrator. Then you can put your .htm and .cfm files in the *home* subdirectory (or any of its subdirectories) and it will work, provided you have the permissions set correctly. See Chapter 2, "Operating System Installation and Configuration," for complete details.

The CFMAIL tag has many attributes that can be added or omitted depending on your needs. These attributes and what they do is found in the following list:

CFMAIL Tag Attribute List

Required Attributes—(mandatory *fill-ins*)

1. TO   Recipient's e-mail address

2. FROM   Sender's e-mail address

Optional Attributes—(optional *fill-ins*)

3. SUBJECT   Mail Subject

4. CC   Additional e-mail addresses to copy e-mail messages to.

5. QUERY   The name of a CFQUERY, which allows you to retrieve information from a database table(s) to include in your e-mail

6. MAXROWS   Specifies the maximum number of mail messages to be sent

7. MIMEATTACH   Attaches a different file type to your e-mail (e.g.; a word-processing or spreadsheet file)

8. TYPE   Allows HTML tags to be used to format an e-mail message

9. GROUP   Uses a QUERY to specify the column in the database used to group sets of records together within a single e-mail. For example, if you are sending out a set of late payment notices, you might want to group on a database expression evaluating to *accounts_over_thirty_days.*

NOTE   *If you are not sure where to put template and form files on your Web server, use the Windows95/NT FIND command to find the default location for* *.cfm *files. Then copy your files into that subdirectory. After you are more familiar with Cold Fusion, you can make your own Web server subdirectories and paths for templates and HTML form files.*

Creating Interactive Forms—A Conference Center Early Notification System

The following automated e-mail program is one module in an online Conference Center, which can help track potential Conference Web site visitors. This program helps the Conference Center give prospective *conferees* needed information about up-and-coming conferences during evening hours and holidays when the Conference Center would otherwise be closed. After the Web page is visited, the e-mail part of the program generates an e-mail back to Registration Personnel from visitors.

BUILDING A FRONT-END HTML FILL-IN FORM   The form's Header section contains a four-column table. Column one is empty, column two is reserved for the conference logo (a JPG image created with LVIEW PRO and Arts & Letters Apprentice), column three is also empty, and column four is used for the title. Each column uses width in pixels or column width percentages. When making multicolumn tables, combine art with live testing to determine each column's width in pixels or numerical percentages.

Readability can be increased by using balanced length fields and careful spacing. (Web pages are approximately 25 percent harder to read than equivalent paper documents.) The submitted form information is processed by Cold Fusion's mail template, which generates an e-mail to the Conference Registration e-mail address. (The next section shows how to build the mail template.)

The following HTML code creates the form shown in Figure 4-3:

```
ch4_2.htm document

<!- c4_2.htm, uses c4_4.cfm - >
<TITLE>Early Interest Notification Form</TITLE>
<TABLE>
<TD WIDTH=10>
<TD><IMG SRC=camp1.jpg ALIGN=LEFT><TD>
<TD WIDTH=5%>
<TD>
<B><FONT SIZE=+1 COLOR=BLUE>Information Request
       Form</B></FONT>
<HR WIDTH=74% ALIGN=LEFT>
</TD>
</TABLE>
<FORM ACTION="ch4_4.cfm" METHOD=POST>

<B>Please Select Interest Group:</B>
<SELECT NAME="group1">
               <OPTION SELECTED>  Junior High
```

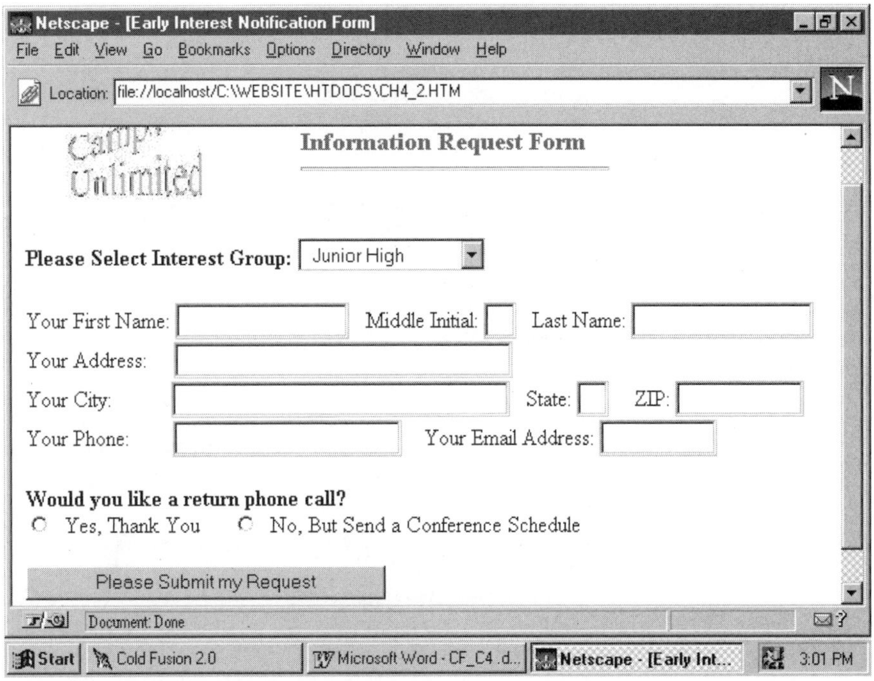

Figure 4-3
Interactive Early Notice Registration form

```
                <OPTION> High School
                <OPTION> College
                <OPTION> Singles
                <OPTION> Young Married
                <OPTION> Senior Focus
                <OPTION> Professionals
        </SELECT>  

        <P>
        Your First Name: <INPUT TYPE="TEXT" NAME="firstname"
             size="15" maxlength="20">  
        Middle Initial: <INPUT TYPE="TEXT" NAME="middle1" size="2"
             maxlength="2">  
        Last Name: <INPUT TYPE="TEXT" NAME="lname" size="16"
             maxlength="20"><BR>

        Your Address:    
        <INPUT TYPE="TEXT" NAME="address1" size="30"
             maxlength="30"><BR>
        Your City:       
                
        <INPUT TYPE="TEXT" NAME="address2" size="30"
             maxlength="30">  

        State: <INPUT TYPE="TEXT" NAME="address3" size="2"
        maxlength="2">    

        ZIP: <INPUT TYPE="TEXT" NAME="zip" size="11"
             maxlength="11"><BR>
        Your Phone:       
        <INPUT TYPE="TEXT" NAME="phone" size="20"
             maxlength="30">   
        Your E-mail Address:
        <INPUT TYPE="TEXT" NAME="email1" size="10"
             maxlength="30"><P>

        <B>Would you like a return phone call?</B><br>
        <INPUT TYPE="radio" NAME="contact1" VALUE="YES"> 
              Yes, Thank You     
        <INPUT TYPE="radio" NAME="contact2" VALUE="YES"> 
              No, But Send a Conference Schedule<P>
        <INPUT TYPE= "SUBMIT" VALUE="Please Submit my Request">
        </FORM>
        </HTML>
```

The opening Form tag is in bold text and contains the call to the mail template on the server:

```
<FORM ACTION="c4_4.cfm" METHOD=POST>
```

The Document title contains font size and color changes to *font size=14 and font color=blue*. If closing Font tags are omitted, the remainder of the document will have blue font and font size=14. Some fields are followed by nonbreaking spaces for visual balance. This form is also significantly enhanced with the use of the moderately sized colored logo:

```
<TD><IMG SRC=camp1.jpg ALIGN=LEFT><TD>
```

In the following code, the mail template is shown:

Early Registration Notice mail template

```
<HTML>
<! —ch4_4.cfm — >
Your E-mail is sent.
</HTML>
<CFMAIL

FROM="johnb@got.net"
  TO="johnb@got.net"
    SUBJECT="Early Interest Registration"
 >

    *** CONFEREE INFORMATION ***

    Interest Group: #Form.group1#
         First Name: #Form.firstname#
    Middle Initial: #Form.middle1#
         Last Name: #Form.lname#
    Street Address: #Form.address1#
                      City: #Form.address2#
                     State: #Form.address3#
                       ZIP: #Form.zip#
         Your Phone: #Form.phone#
                    E-mail: #Form.email#
    Please telephone: #Form.contact1#
      Send Schedule: #Form.contact2#


</CFMAIL>
```

Notice that the comment line uses an exclamation point followed by three dashes. This combination of exclamation point and three dashes is specific to Cold Fusion and tells CF to ignore and not execute the commented text that follows.

HTML tags do not work *inside* <CFMAIL> tags. (They can be placed everywhere else in the template.) Emphasize important text by using capitals and ASCII characters such as asterisks (***) on both sides of titles.

The *Early Registration Notice* mail template produces the following e-mail output.

(received and printed
using Eudora
Pro v. 2)

```
< - CF MAIL OUTPUT   - >
X-From_: johnb@got.net Wed Feb  5 16:56:11 1997
X-Delivered: at request of johnb on you
Date: Wed, 5 Feb 1997 16:56:10 -0800
X-Real-To: <johnb@got.net>
From: johnb@got.net
To: johnb@got.net
Subject: Early Interest Registration

  ***   CONFEREE INFORMATION ***

    Interest Group:   Junior High
        First Name:   Bill
    Middle Initial:   B
         Last Name:   Blythe
   Street Address:    100 Main
                        City:   Chicago
                       State:   IL
                         ZIP:   00000
      Your Phone:     111-222-3333
                      E-mail:   billb@mynet.com

  Please telephone: YES
    Send Schedule: YES
```

MAIL TEMPLATE TIPS:

1. The initial <CFMAIL> tag includes FROM, TO, and SUBJECT between the opening character (<) and closing character (>).

2. The FROM, TO, and SUBJECT attributes are followed by an *equals sign* (=) not a *colon* (:) as in a pen and pencil memo. Also, do not spell FROM as *FR* (also as commonly used in paper memos).

3. Form fields begin and end with a hashmark (#), *not* with quotes.

4. Form fields will not work if you accidentally omit the prefix *Form* when putting these fields into a template. (For example, the template field *#phone1#* is not correct, but *#Form.phone1#* is correct.)

5. There is an intermittent *bug* in Netscape Navigator Browser; sometimes an initially loaded HTML file stays active in the browser even though you are attempting to reload and use a newer, modified version of that same HTML file. To check if the edited version is active, select the browser's *VIEW* tab, and then select *Source* to make sure that your changes in the new version are present in the browser. Select Reload, or select Netscapes Options, Network, Preferences and then click the Cache tab. Under the Cache tab, you can clear the disk and memory caches, and then Netscape will load

fresh HTML forms each time instead of renewing from cache memory. If you are still not getting results, close the file in browser, and then close Navigator. Restart Navigator and then reload the file again. If that doesn't work, close all programs and do a restart of Windows 95. You have just become another Windows 95 cache victim. (This problem seems particularly aggravated when Windows 95 is connected to a network drive. Always test files in a live environment before believing that all is well).

6. HTML tags are ignored if written inside the CFMAIL tag. Use uppercase letters to emphasize text or use other ASCII characters (such as asterisks, dashes, vertical lines, and so on) to set off titles and highlight important text.

Using FROM: and TO: in Mail Templates

When a user inputs an e-mail address, that e-mail address can be used to generate a return letter. (It is not considered fair play to take and use the e-mail address of a Web site visitor without asking for it formally with an e-mail text input field.) If you own a company and decide to do that sort of thing internally on your company's Intranet, that's different; just make sure you warn your employees first. Noone likes to have their e-mail address automatically collected and used without permission, and why set yourself up to be *flamed* or *spammed* by an irritated person who suddenly starts receiving unwanted mail from your automated mailing list.

To send a return e-mail based on an inputted form field containing an e-mail address, use the following code in a CFMAIL tag:

```
<CFMAIL
    FROM= "#Form.EmailAddress#"
    TO= "yourcompany@bigbiz.com"
    SUBJECT= "Customer Request"
>
*** Please follow up on this website-generated customer
    request.  ***
Name:    #Form.Firstname#   #Form.Lastname#
Subject:  #Form.Subject#

#Form.Requesttext#

</CFMAIL>
```

USING HIDDEN FIELDS IN FORMS The FROM e-mail address must be in a "#Form.EmailAddress#" style, and it must begin and end with quotes and hashmarks. The hashmark symbol (#) tells the program to input the literal value received from the document's E-mail Address field.

In contrast, notice the use of quotes with the TO e-mail address. In this case, the literal value is entered by the user on the mail template. But it could have been taken from a *hidden input field* in the form. Notice the following hidden input field example:

```
<INPUT TYPE= "HIDDEN" NAME= "email"
     VALUE="anyname@mybiz.com">
```

When a hidden input field is used in a fill-in form, the entered e-mail address can later be used in a mail template, as shown in the following example:

```
<CFMAIL
    FROM= "#Form.EmailAddress#"
                     TO= "#Form.Email#"
        SUBJECT= "Customer Request"
>
Please follow up on this website-generated customer
    request from:

Name:     #Form.Firstname#   #Form.Lastname#
Subject:   #Form.Subject#

#Form.Requesttext#

</CFMAIL>
```

This feature is useful if you want to relay e-mail to a number of e-mail addresses in your company. The next section shows how to include information retrieved from databases into your auto-generated e-mail.

Using Databases with Interactive E-mail

When including database information in e-mail, a fill-in HTML form serves as the front-end to the mail template. When building the mail template, you use Structured Query Language (SQL) to retrieve information from the database. SQL is a fairly straightforward language to use. (See the two SQL chapters 12 and 13 later in the book for more detail.) The following section shows how to build the fill-in form that is used by the mail template (see Figure 4-4), and includes the necessary SQL statements.

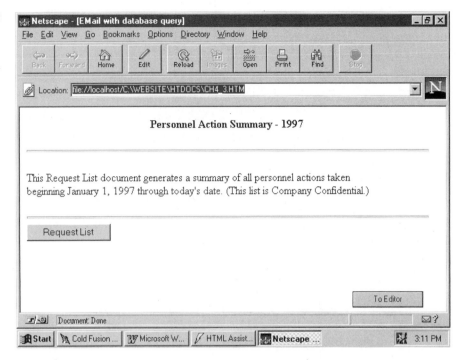

Building Front-end Forms to a Mail Template

The following code shows the front-end fill-in form, which starts up a mail
template, which queries a database.

```
c4_4a.htm document
<HTML>
<! —c4_4a.htm, uses c4_4a.cfm — >
<TITLE>E-mail with database query</TITLE>
<CENTER><B>Personnel Action Summary - 1997</B> </CENTER>
<FORM ACTION="c4_4a.cfm" METHOD=POST>
<HR><BR>
This Request List document generates a summary of all
      personnel actions taken <BR>beginning January 1, 1997
      through today's date. (This list is Company
      Confidential.)<P>
<HR>
<INPUT TYPE= "SUBMIT" VALUE="Request List">
</FORM>
</HTML>
```

The next section shows how to create the mail template, which performs
a query on the database table *Personnel_Actions* (created in Access). Within

the CFMAIL tag, notice that the word *QUERY* is placed immediately after the CFMAIL tag. The QUERY retrieves the database information and the CFOUTPUT tag includes the literals of the database fields into the e-mail that is generated and sent to the recipient. Also, each field name included in the e-mail must be surrounded by hashmarks. Hashmarks are used in the template as field delimiters.

Mail templates incorporating database queries follow the same coding format as standard mail templates except that the second section includes SQL. The following overview breaks apart the major pieces of a mail template, which includes a database query.

Mail Template Queries a Database

The template may be thought of as consisting of several sections. (In the example that follows the template has been split into four sections for discussion purposes.)

Section 1—The HTML tag section—This section contains an HTML tag section, which executes and then sends back a message to the sender that the e-mail was processed without any problems.

Section 2—The CFQUERY tag section—This section contains a CFQUERY tag with SQL instructions used to retrieve database information.

Section 3—The CFMAIL tag section—This section includes a reference to the CFQUERY name and the TO, FROM, and SUBJECT attributes.

Section 4—The CFOUTPUT tag section—This section displays retrieved field information from the database, information that was retrieved by the CFQUERY. Notice that each field name is surrounded by hashmarks; the hashmarks cause the literal field values to be incorporated in the e-mail.

USING CF MAIL TEMPLATES   Several new things are found in the database-retrieval e-mail template. Each database query must be given a name; in this example, the name *Actions*. The CFMAIL tag must include the entire phrase *QUERY= "Actions"*. The *DATASOURCE= "Personnel"* is a Cold Fusion data source name given to the Mail1.mdb database; you must use the Cold Fusion Administrator to give the database its own Cold Fusion name. The *"Select * FROM Mail1"* statement is an SQL command, which retrieves the contents of all the fields in the "Mail1" table. (But the Select statement does not display the results.) Rather, the CFOUTPUT tag is used to display in the e-mail the contents of the retrieved database fields. Thus, information retrieval and information display are handled by completely separate commands within the mail template.

CF Mail Template—
Personnel Action
Summary 1997

```
<HTML>
<!-c4_4a.cfm, uses c4_3.htm->
<TITLE> Personnel Action Summary - 1997 </TITLE>
<BODY>
<B>Your E-mail has been sent!</B>
</BODY>
</HTML>

<CFQUERY NAME="Actions" DATASOURCE="NewPersonnel">
SELECT * FROM Mail1
</CFQUERY>

   <CFMAIL QUERY="Actions"
                  TO="johnb@got.net"
             FROM="johnb@got.net"
        SUBJECT="1997 - Personnel Actions"
   >
THIS IS A LIST OF 1997 PERSONNEL ACTIONS.
                                          ..
<CFOUTPUT>
#Firstname# #Lastname# - #Action#
</CFOUTPUT>
                                          ..
Please call Human Resources at EXT. 9999 if you have
further questions.
Gerald Jones,
Human Resources
Gerald_Jones@megacorp.com
   </CFMAIL>
```

The Access table that contains the database information is shown in Figure 4-5. The fields are: ID, Firstname, Lastname, and Action.

The resultant e-mail from the form data and the database query produces a list of new hires, transfers, and separations. Additional fields could easily be added to the following straightforward example:

Automatically
generated e-mail
incorporating
database query

```
< - CF OUTPUT - >
X-From_: johnb@got.net Fri Feb  7 21:28:02 1997
X-Delivered: at request of johnb on you
Date: Fri, 7 Feb 1997 21:28:01 -0800
X-Real-To: <johnb@got.net>
From: johnb@got.net
To: johnb@got.net
Subject: 1997 - Personnel Actions
```

Continues

Continued

```
THIS IS A LIST OF 1997 PERSONNEL ACTIONS

Mary Benders - New Hire
Richard Smith - New Hire
Ben Daniels - Transfer
Sue Errol - Separation
Donald Forrest - New Hire

Please call Human Resources at EXT. 9999 if you have
further questions.
Gerald Jones,
Human Resources
Gerald_Jones@megacorp.com
```

Figure 4-5
ACCESS table "Mail1"

USING SMTP MAIL   Cold Fusion uses SMTP to work over the Internet. This mail protocol is extensively described in RFC 821, Request For Comment, by J. Postel, available on the Web at **ftp://nic/rfc/rfc821.txt**. Postel states *"SMTP is independent of the particular transmission subsystem and requires only a reliable ordered data stream channel."* SMTP mail can be initiated by any client and responded to by any SMTP-running server.

CONCLUSION

This chapter has shown how to set up Cold Fusion Auto-generated e-mail for both Windows 95 and Windows NT, how to query a database, and how to add the queried data to an E-mail. See Chapter 12, "Using SQL," and Chapter 13, "Using Advanced SQL," to learn how to use more complex SQL database queries in Cold Fusion auto-generated e-mail.

5

Introducing Microsoft Access 97

- Building a Microsoft Access database
- Storing binary objects in tables
- Using the Access Form Wizard
- Connecting a database to Cold Fusion using the CF Administrator
- Verifying Cold Fusion and database connections
- Using Cold Fusion CFINSERT and CFQUERY tags with Access tables

Using Microsoft Access

Databases are easy to build using Access special features such as Table Wizards, Cuecards, and Context-Sensitive Help. Small to large database projects are easily accomplished using Microsoft Access 97. When Access (a plug-n-play software product) is installed, you can begin designing databases. To start Access 97 from Windows 95, click the Office icon and select Microsoft Access from the pull-down menu. This displays the screen shown in Figure 5-1.

Click New File. A window showing a blank database icon is created. Double-click the blank database icon. The default database name is db1.mdb. Type `Personnel.mdb` in the File Name box and then click OK. Access renames the db1.mdb database to Personnel.mdb. When using Access 97, databases are made up of a group of related tables. Each table contains fields that can contain numbers, text, and objects such as GIF and JPG image files. The following Figure 5-2 shows how to begin creating the Personnel.mdb table.

To create an individual table, click New. Access displays the *New Table* panel. Highlight *Table Wizard* and click to open a new table. The Table Wizard will prompt you through each step needed to build an Access *table*.

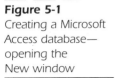

Figure 5-1
Creating a Microsoft Access database—opening the New window

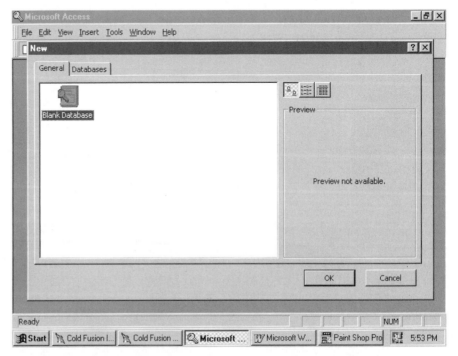

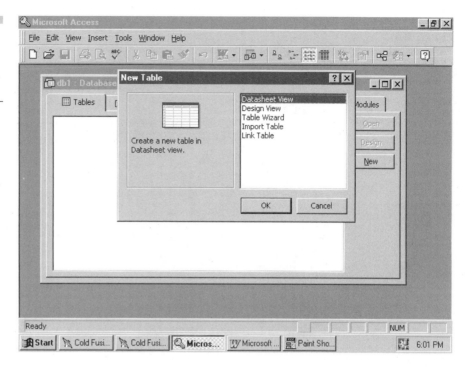

Figure 5-2
Creating the
Personnel.mdb table
using the New Table
dialog box

Designing—The Personnel Table

When you are creating a first Access database and are at the beginning of the design process, you can take mental notes and immediately begin using the Access' Table Wizard, or you can use a paper and pencil or whiteboard and dry-erase pens to draw database and table relationships. Whatever method you use is a personal choice, but the goal of creating a compact and useful database must be kept in sight at all times. The Personnel Table will be designed to contain related fields; for example, first name, last name, telephone, e-mail address, and so on.

You can expand your table design process to include visual information (such as digital photographs—not difficult to make by using a digital camera or a scanner—or graphics of departmental *trees*). These file types are generated by using Microsoft EXCEL or a word processor and then turned into a JPG or GIF file by using LVIEW PRO or Paint Shop Pro graphics software. (For more information and help, refer to Chapter 1.) And, information (such as telephone numbers and e-mail addresses) with special data masks will be included. Each of these information types can be easily stored in Access tables. In the following Figure 5-3, the sample Table

Figure 5-3
Table Wizard

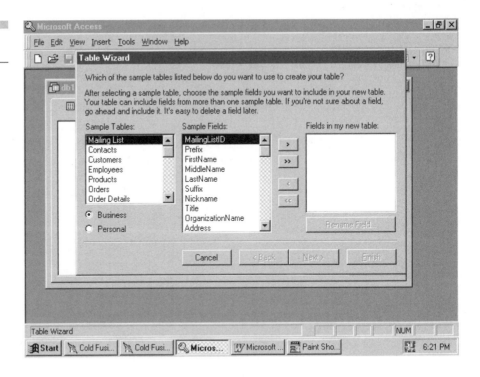

Mailing List has been selected. Each sample table contains fields that may be used to create your first table.

USING THE TABLE WIZARD   Select the Table Wizard. After it starts, in the leftmost column select the table called Contacts. Access displays a prospective set of field names in Column 2. Click Employees, and another set of field names appears. When you build tables, you can point and click to choose field names from any of these displayed field sets. Also, fields are preformatted to contain different types of information; for example, monetary fields are already configured to contain two decimal points—for dollars and cents. Therefore, if you aren't sure about how to build a new field requiring special formatting, you can rename an existing field that has the format that you need, and you can use it for the new field.

ENTERING FIELDS IN THE TABLE   To add fields when using the Table Wizard, use the column that includes the greater than character (>). To move a field into the table, highlight the Organization field and then click the greater than character (>) to its right. **Organization** immediately appears in the **Fields in my new table** box. Repeat the process with the Firstname and Lastname fields.

EDITING FIELD NAMES   Repeat the process with the Suffix field, but after it moves to the **Fields in my new table** box, notice that the word **Suffix** also appears in a separate small box located below the **Fields in my new table** box. Using the cursor, highlight the word **Suffix** and enter a new field name: **Extension**. Click on any blank space or field name in the **Fields in my new table** box. Access now displays the new Extension field in the **Fields in my new table** box. You have just modified a field name. In the same way, highlight the word **Prefix**, put it into the **Fields in my new table** box, and modify it to make the field **email1**.

Click the Next button near the bottom of the panel. Access asks, **What do you want to name your new table?** (It has the default name of **Mailing List**.) Change the word **Mailing List** to the word **Personnel**. Click Next and let Access select the key field. Key fields are used to uniquely identify each record stored in the table. This can be a unique identification number, such as a social security number or a serial number. Access asks, **Enter data directly into the field**. Click Finish to indicate *Yes*. You can also choose your own key field, described later in the chapter in the "Designing a Relational Database" section. The following Figure 5-4 shows an open but empty Personnel table.

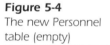

Figure 5-4
The new Personnel
table (empty)

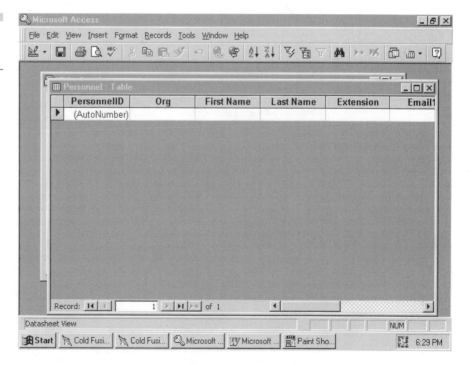

ENTERING DATA IN THE TABLE Use the Tab key to move the blinking cursor from the Counter field (an index field) to the First Name field. Enter **Bill** into the First Name field. Press the Tab key to skip to the next field, the Last Name field, and enter **Burdick.** Enter the following values in the same way into the next three fields: **1112, Bill_ Burdick@design.com,** and **manager.** Press the Tab key to skip to the next line, tab past the Counter field, and continue entering field information. Your table should look like Figure 5-5.

The Table Wizard eliminates some busy work, but some modifications to the fields are still needed. For example, default text fields are 50 characters in length, but this is unnecessarily large for fields such as First Name, Last Name, and Org. To change field type, click the word **text** in the Data Type column as shown in Figure 5-6.

The Design panel allows you to modify field length as well as other field characteristics. When you are in the Design panel and want to open the field definition tab, click the word **Text** in the Data Type column. For example, click Text next to the First Name field name, and Access displays a small *button* tab. Click the button tab. Highlight *50* in the field size box and change 50 to **20.** The final result should look like Figure 5-7.

Notice that the field size has been reduced to 15 characters. If a mask was going to be applied, it would be displayed here. If you do not know

Figure 5-5
Populated
Personnel table

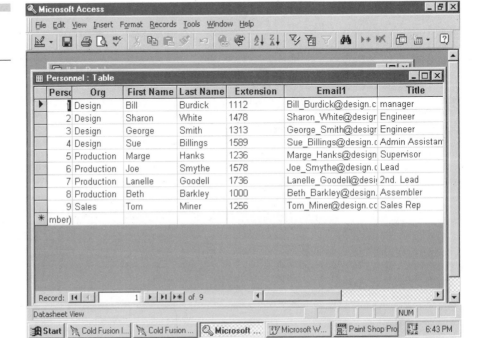

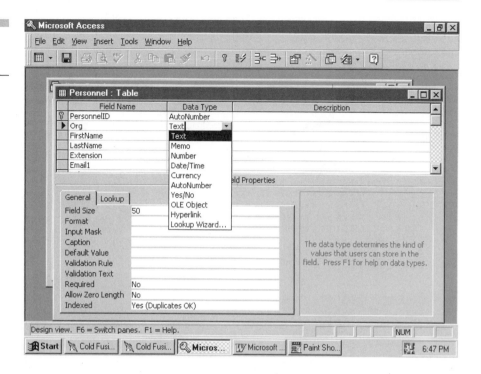

Figure 5-6
Modifying table
field structure

how to create a mask, create a sample table, and enter some sample fields
that contain masks you want to use in your table. Open the table to the
Design mode and see how the Access sample table has built the mask.

MODIFYING FIELD DEFINITIONS IN THE PERSONNEL TABLE

In the same way, change the field lengths for the Org, Last Name, and Title
fields to 20 characters long, the field lengths for the Ext. field to 4 characters long, and the E-mail field to 30 characters long. Also change the field
definition parameter of the Last Name field to **Required, Yes** so that a staff
person's last name must always be entered. Notice the field definition called
caption. This is the displayed title of the field used when you open the table.
To display as many fields as possible on the monitor, use short titles; for example, First Name can become Fname, Last Name, Lname. Changing the
title of the field does not change the actual field name.

USING NUMBER FIELDS AND VALIDATION RULES

To create a
number field, click on the default word text and click the button tab that
appears. Click the word *number* displayed by the pop-up menu. Notice
that the field size says **Double**. This refers to the size of the number that
Access can store in this field (a very large number). Also, notice the Validation Rule category. This allows entered numerical data to be tested

Figure 5-7
Field length changes

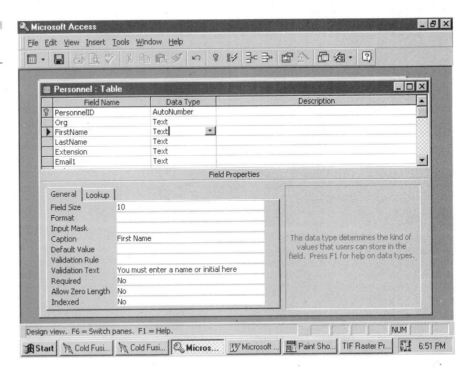

against a specified range of values; if the number falls outside the defined range, it will not be allowed to be inputted.

A Validation Rule could be: *all positive numbers allowed greater than 0 but less than 1500*. In Access, this would be represented algebraically as >0< 1500 in the Validation Rule option and used, for example, in a Part Number field for a group of parts that have unique part numbers between 1–1500. Validation Rules help data-entry staff to avoid errors. Similarly, if you are building a parts database and do not want unit prices for hammers to be entered as $1000.00, use a Validation Rule to require that the entered price be greater than $1.00 but less than $35.00—>$1.00<$40.00. (Yes, there are hammers costing $39.95 on the market, especially if being sold by government contractors!)

USING VALIDATION TEXTS   In the same way, validation text can be displayed indicating what is an appropriate input value. A typical input text could be **Please use two letter abbreviations for States**. Similarly, the Input Mask setting forces data to be entered in a specific format. For example, when entering telephone numbers, you may require that entries contain both an area code as well as a seven-digit number. For example, the input mask for a telephone number would be: "!\(999") "000\-0000".

An "Input Mask" could also force numerical entries to contain two digits; for example, for monetary amounts. To learn about input masks, use the context-sensitive help or investigate how Access builds the mask by looking at a Sample table field.

Using Fields Containing GIF/JPG Images

Storing images in Table fields is fairly straightforward. Access tables can contain one or more image-containing fields. But, these binary image fields are limited to storing images, not text. Two commonly used file extensions are .GIF and .JPG. (Interestingly, if GIF files are resaved as JPG files, the resulting JPG usually contains fewer bytes than the original GIF file.) Another good reason for choosing the JPG file format for image storage is that Access will display the actual JPG image in an Access on-screen form, whereas GIF images are displayed only as an icons in Access forms; you don't see the real image. However, if you store a GIF file in an Access table, whether it was displayed as an icon or an image in an Access form, an HTML browser *will* display the GIF file as an actual image on-screen. Additionally, photographs with graduated color patterns display more clearly with JPG format, whereas GIF formats more adequately display line drawings and schematics with sharp black and white contrasts.

Therefore, if you don't mind being unable to display GIF images in Access forms, store GIF files in Access tables as icons; your HTML browser will display the GIF as an image, not an icon.

NOTE: *Access uses OLE fields to imbed binary objects such as images (GIF and JPG files) and to link to outside programs. Cold Fusion supports stored binary files, but does not support OLE links to outside applications. Many database applications have separate fields for binary objects and OLE fields, but this is not true in Access.*

CREATING OLE FIELDS When creating a table, you may create an OLE field to store objects. For example, in the Personnel table to create a field such as Images, the default field type, *text*, must be modified. The Text Images field type can be transformed into an OLE field used to imbed JPG or GIF images. After opening the table, click Design from the Create–Open–Design panel. When the Design tab opens, it shows that the

Figure 5-8
Transforming a text
field into an Ole field

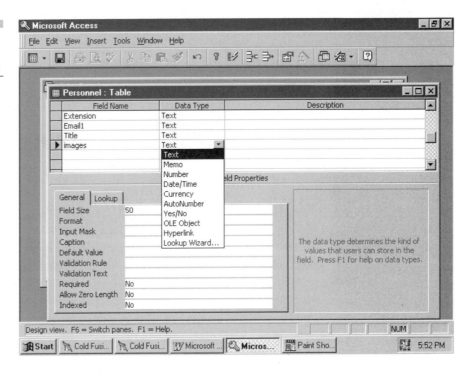

default field type is *text*. Figure 5-8 shows the "images" field that can be transformed into an OLE field type.

To change the default Text field definition to an OLE Object field, click the tab in the Data Type box. Access displays a pop-up menu. Highlight OLE Object, near the bottom of the menu. Access changes the field type to OLE Object. (Figure 5-9 shows a selected OLE Object field definition.)

IMBEDDING IMAGES INTO OLE (ALSO BINARY) FIELDS Click the *x* in the upper-right corner of the Design tab to close the Design tab. A message appears, asking you to **Save changes to Table Newtable**. Click Yes. Now the OLE field definition is saved. The next step is to insert a GIF or JPG image file into the empty OLE Object field. To begin, highlight the empty OLE image field.

NOTE: *If you have not yet created a JPG file, refer to Chapter 1, "Using Paint Shop Pro and LVIEW PRO," to learn how to create GIF and JPG files. Alternatively, you can use a digital camera or a scanner to scan in black and white or colored photographs to generate GIF or JPG files. The following Figure 5-10 shows how to begin inserting a binary object into a OLE field.*

Figure 5-9
Selecting an OLE
Object field definition

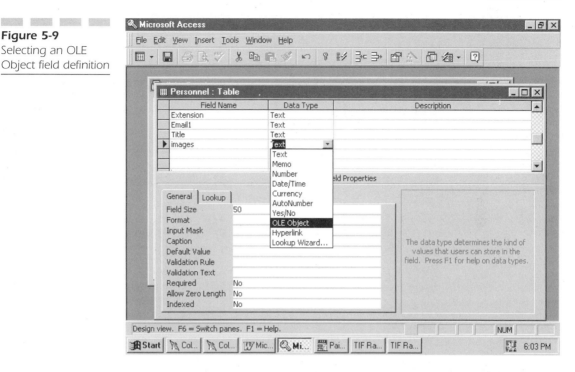

Figure 5-10
Inserting a binary
image

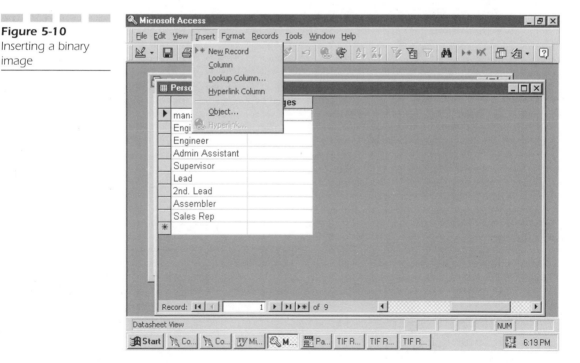

Open the table containing the new, empty OLE (binary image) field, and then activate the field by clicking it. On the main Access menu, click Insert, and then click Object found on the pop-up menu. Access displays a selection box containing various file types. Select Hijack Image, and Access displays a DOS directory tree. Go to a directory containing a GIF file and select the file you want to insert. Access displays both the file and pathname that you have selected. Click on the filename that will be displayed. When the filename appears, close the program, and Access displays the image file in the Images field. You store other types of formats in the OLE object field also. Figure 5-11 shows the results of storing a JPG graphic file in an OLE Object field.

PRINTING OUT TABLE DEFINITIONS After you have created and saved a table, you can print out the Table Definition from the main menu. First, open the table. Then click Analyze and select Documenter. Click options and then select the table you want to print a definition for—select **Properties** in the Include for Table choices and select **Names, Data Types and Sizes** in the Include for Fields choices to get a one-page summary printout. Access displays a preview page. Click OK and then click Print

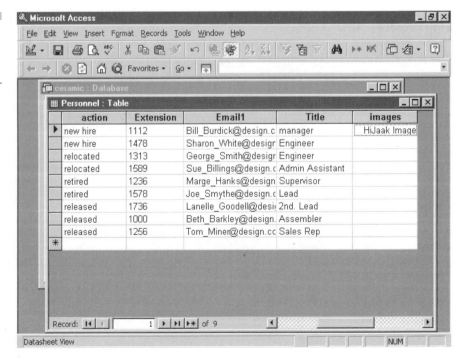

Figure 5-11
Stored binary objects in an Access OLE field

on the Toolbar. Access prints out a Table Definition including a field list with parameters such as field name, length, type, and date and time of file creation.

Building Access Forms

Access has an easy-to-use form generator. Anyone who has spent time using databases has probably worked with at least one cryptic, difficult-to-use form generator. In contrast, Access uses a Form Wizard that leads you step-by-step through the entire process. To employ the Form Wizard, you must first have an existing table.

USING THE ACCESS FORM WIZARD From the database menu, click the Form tab and then click New. Point to the Form Wizard. Click the spin arrow, and Access displays the names of the tables from which you can build a form. Highlight a table name and click OK. On the next screen, highlight the fields you want and then click the greater than symbol (>)symbol to place the desired field into the form. Click Next. Access asks, **What Layout do you want for your form?** Click the various radio buttons to display available styles and then select Columnar. On the next screen, select the Standard Style to avoid a colored background. Click Next. Access asks, **What title do you want for your form?** Access displays the title *Personnel*, the same name for the form that is used for the table. Click Finish. Access displays the completed columnar form and displays all fields as well as the Images field containing the Hijack image. You can scroll through the data by using the scrollbar at the bottom of the form.

You have now built the columnar form. This form will be used to display your GIF and JPG images. If you need information presented in a form over the Internet, you can build an HTML output screen with Cold Fusion or use the Crystal Reports software. (See Chapters 15 and 16 for information covering the Crystal Reports Report Writer.)

SAVING AND CLOSING FORMS Click the *x* in the corner of the displayed form. Access automatically closes and saves the form and returns you to the main screen.

CLOSING ACCESS TABLES When you have finished all field changes, click the *x* in the upper-right corner of the table to save all changes and exit the Changes tab. Click *x* in the top-right corner of Access to save your work and exit Access.

Designing a Relational Database
(A Set of Related Tables)

Relational databases are designed to avoid needless duplication of information and to organize database work. The relational model assumes that database information can be organized and related to other similar sets of information by using key fields across two or more tables. A key field (such as a part number or a social security number) can be placed in different tables and serve as a relational link between the tables. When a group of tables each contains a key field, the groundwork has been laid for creating a relational database. The relational database model will allow you to quickly open and retrieve needed information from several related tables by using Structured Query Language (SQL).

When designing a database containing related tables, think carefully about choosing key fields. Key fields are used as the connecting links between tables. For example, if a customer is given a unique number, this *custnum* (customer number) can be used in the customer's table as a key field to link the customer's table to a separate customer transaction's table. (This type of relationship is called a *one-to-many* relationship—that is, one customer record can have many individual transaction records (for example, created at different times) related to it. Then, a database query that *pulls up* customer address information from one table can also be used to open the customer purchases table by date, using the key field of *custnum*.

USING KEY FIELDS   Key fields use a literal value to retrieve all the records in a second table found in the same key field matching that literal value. To be able to do this, the key field must be given a specific value and be included in each record of both tables. The relational model makes sense because if one table is available for entering all information, for each transaction, current customer address information would need to be added, for example, each time a sale was made to the customer. This would require quite a big table, and the data entry person would be forced to spend much unneeded input time adding this information to the transaction record.

Companies such as VISA and MASTERCARD would have unacceptably slow validation times for credit card purchases because of all the duplicated data within the database. Also, each customer would be required to rein-put basic customer information before the transaction could be completed. Using key fields allows several tables to be related to one another.

For the database designer or developer building relational databases, each time several tables must be opened simultaneously to retrieve or process records, a query must be written to open and retrieve that information. Fortunately, using SQL makes query-writing much easier because it uses a high-level, English-like set of commands.

BUILDING AND RELATING KEY FIELDS When building tables with related data, it is useful to think about the active *subject* of the table and the repetitive connections that link the various bits of information. For example, if you are creating a customer-contact table, you need to include customer information such as first name, last name, street address, telephone(s) numbers, fax number, e-mail address—they occur only once per customer. If the name *John Smith* is entered respectively into the First Name and Last Name fields, in most cases a *John Smith* will also have only one mailing address. But in case Mr. Smith has two addresses or two phone numbers or two fax numbers, add a *general text* field to the table, which can be used for comments. This method is better than having double address, phone and fax number fields, which most of the time stand vacant but still take up database space. And, if many of your customers have double phone numbers or addresses, an additional field can always be added, or you can build another relational table for these additional addresses. This solution doesn't solve the problem of uniquely identifying John Smith from 100 other Smiths, (see the next paragraph for a solution to the identification problem), but at least you have a place to put his second phone number or address.

To solve the problem of unique identification, choose a key for the customer contact table (such as a unique identifying number like a customer's social security number, or a unique assigned consecutive number) to keep the innumerable Smiths of the world separated from each other in your database. Otherwise, you may end up having to use a multiple-field key such as firstname/lastname/address to keep Bob Smith of 1st Avenue, San Francisco, CA, separate from Bob Smith of 10th Avenue, San Francisco, CA, and that means more complex programming. Database programs can be programmed to automatically assign this key number and to even test to see if a unique key number has already been assigned.

NOTE: *Products are now offered world-wide over the Internet by businesses willing to take on the challenge of multiple currencies, uncharted markets, and multilingual communication challenges. Some areas in foreign countries have*

very few Web sites; if your commercial Web site is placed on a local net, it may receive a great number of hits just because it is only one of very few Web sites offering that product in that area.

The Relational Database Model

The following explanation shows how to begin creating a relational database (a group of related tables) that can be used to support some of the needs of an online business.

BUILDING TABLE RELATIONSHIPS When building a group of tables, during the building of the second table, the Table Wizard will ask `Is your new table related to any other tables in your database?` You can choose the default, **yes**, and allow Access to create the relationship, or you can choose **no** and do it yourself. If you choose **yes**, clicking the Change button will bring up a Relationship panel. You can then choose a one-to-many relationship between the tables, or you can choose no relationship. Access visually shows the new relationship. After the file is built, you can examine relationships from the main menu. Click File, Toolbars, and then Relationships. A Relationships button appears, allowing you to examine and change field relationships.

ONLINE IMPORT-EXPORT BUSINESS A second key to a successful business is a carefully chosen product line. By being able to display a business' product line over the Internet, an Internet business has a powerful tool to help prospective customers make ordering and purchasing decisions right on the spot. Credit card transactions can be used to facilitate payment. The international market is growing very rapidly, countries are busy setting up regional hubs for Internet connections, the author is currently corresponding over the Internet with individuals in Malasia, the former Soviet Union, and Slovakia. And where e-mail goes, Web sites can be put up.

In support of this process, a currently debated issue is whether Web sites should offer alternate language Web pages. If you offer a specialty product in another country from a home base using the appropriate language, if a potential customer can dial you up and read in their own language about your product, you may have an international sale!

The following Pottery Studio Business example shows how to use the relational model to build a three-table relational database. Also, the example shows how to connect a front-end HTML fill-in form to the Customers

Table 5-1

Pottery Studio
Database with
Related Tables

Fields	Field Description
	The Product Table
Modelnum	Model number (Key field)
ShipWeight	In pounds
Size	Total circumference in inches (important for international carriers)
AvailColor	Available colors
Glazetype	Available glaze finish
Price	Net price (tax not included)
ProdPicture	Image field containing product photograph
QuantityonHand	Number of pieces in inventory
	Customer Table
First Name	
Last Name	
OrgName	(Business name)
Address	
City	
State	
Postal Code	
Country	
PhoneNumber	
email1	
contact1	

table in the Pottery Studio database. (An even more extensive business model is shown in Chapters 16 and 17, after SQL and Cold Fusion programming techniques have been developed.)

HOW ORDERS MOVE THROUGH THE DATABASE Initially, the Internet Web site visitor brings up your Web site, which displays an attractive company name and logo. Your opening Web page contains unique,

Orders Table

OrderID	Key field
CustomerID	Key field
Orderdate	
Shipname	
ShipAddress	
ShipCity	
ShipState	
ShipRegion	
ShipCountry	
ShipPostalCode	
ShipDate	
ShipVia	
FreightCharge	

interesting, or distinctive company information. Your site displays product images or business locations (maps), greetings, and hyperlinks to product Web pages, which attract immediate attention.

NOTE: *When creating the tables making up this database, you may want to check the field Masks, check the field lengths, and check the required conditions on fields to make sure they meet your needs. For example, choosing a phone number field mask too quickly may not allow international telephone numbers to be correctly inserted into the database.*

The hyperlinked products page(s) can display thumbnail-sized product photos or graphics (see Figures 5-12 and 5-13) with short descriptions containing product information. It is helpful if the prospective customer can order displayed products from the same Web page; if they need to check product features, they do not have to load a second Web page. (Check out Chapter 20, "Introducing JavaScript", for classy ways to keep a customer on the same Web page while you show off your images on pop-up pages.) If they have to reload the main page several times, you may jeopardize the placing of the order, because Web connections can easily break, especially when dealing with overseas WWW connections.

Figure 5-12

Front-end fill-in form used to append records into a database

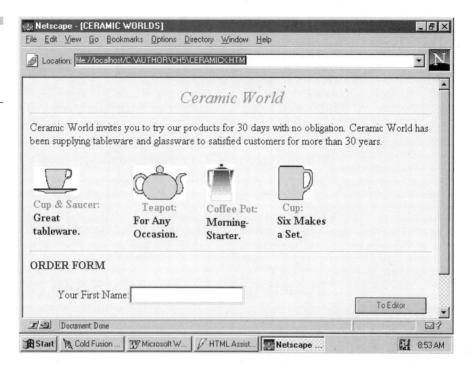

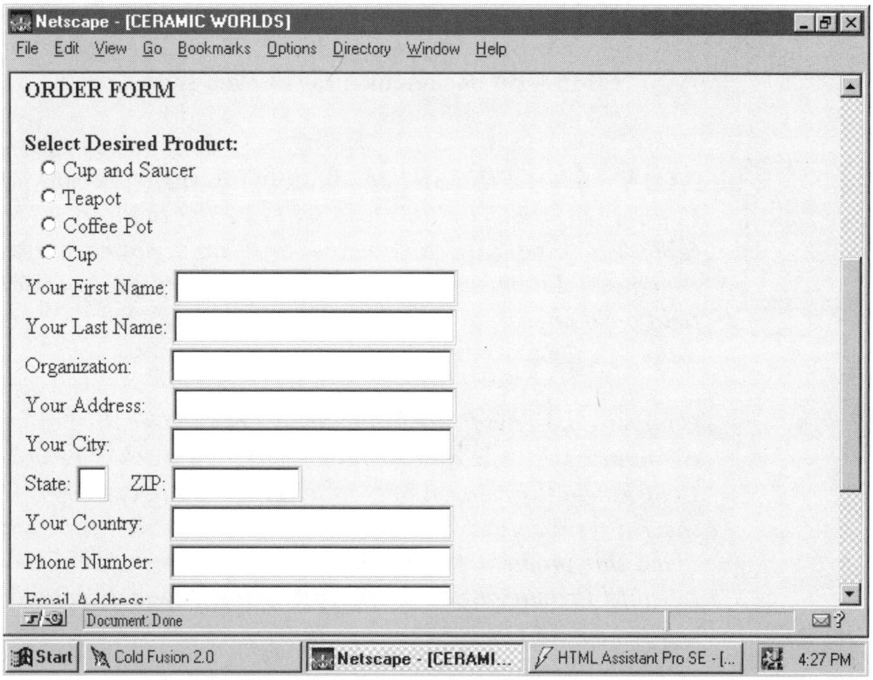

Figure 5-13

Form appending records into a database

To quickly check your form, connect the fill-in form to a Cold Fusion mail template. (For help, refer to Chapter 4, "Interactive E-mail," and the section called "Building CF E-mail Templates.") You can start up the business when you can create a Cold Fusion-generated e-mail. Automated e-mail gets results! But at some point, you will want to store customer information and order information in a database, especially if you need to store multiple transactions for a customer when your Web page starts getting a lot of hits. After the form is working, you will create a Cold Fusion database template to append records to the database table. (See the next section.) Also, the last part of the database template will be used to generate a reply to the customer indicating that the order is approved and in-process. You will find using a database a better process than answering international e-mails at 3 a.m. to give quick turnaround to customer orders.

Inserting Form Data into Tables

Figure 5-13 shows the template that inserts the contents of a single field *firstname* from the `ceramicx.htm` form into the Access table—`Customers`. This procedure is a two-step process. First, use the Cold Fusion Administrator to recognize (the Cold Fusion term is "verify") the database and its associated ODBC Driver. (This verification process builds an internal path to the Access database in the directory of your choice.) Second, put the Cold Fusion table insert template and the HTML fill-in form document into the Web server documents subdirectory.

NOTE: The CFINSERT tag blindly inserts fields containing form information into the table. Cold Fusion will attempt to insert all the form fields into the table. This procedure can create a problem if you have used the Table Wizard to design the database, because the Table Wizard automatically makes the first field a Counter data type field, and your first form field can't fit into a Counter data type field.

Counter data type fields are used to store consecutive numbers beginning with the numbers 1, 2, 3, and so on, to help keep track of records. When you do a Cold Fusion Insert, you may damage the database when Cold Fusion tries to insert literal values from the first form field into the Counter data type field. To avoid this problem, follow the instructions given in the next section titled "How to Build Primary Keys." These instructions show how to avoid creating a field containing a Counter data type.

How to Build Primary Keys

When using the Table Wizard, the second panel displays the question **What do you want to do?** with two radio button choices: **Let Microsoft Access Set a Primary Key for Me**, or **No, I'll Set the Primary Key Myself**. Select **No, I'll Set the Primary Key Myself**. Then, on the next panel, answer the question, **What kind of data do you want the primary key to contain?** Select the **Numbers and/or Letters I Enter When I Add New records** radio button. This choice will avoid a Counter data type field from being created in your first field; it will also allow you to designate your own key fields.

If you have set the primary key yourself, the first field of the table will be fully usable. And when you use a Cold Fusion template to insert fields of a fill-in form into the database, they will be inserted without causing problems with the table. Using the CFINSERT and the CFQUERY tags allow records to be appended to the end of your Access table. The following section shows how to use each of these tags to add fill-in form data from HTML documents to Access tables.

Connecting an Access Database to Cold Fusion

Before you can use the CFINSERT tag, you must connect Cold Fusion to the database. You do that by giving a DATASOURCE name to your database, and then *verifying* the database. This step connects the database to Cold Fusion across your server. The DATASOURCE name is the ODBC DATASOURCE name for your Access database. You create and assign this Cold Fusion name by using the Cold Fusion Administrator panel. (See the following section, "Using the Add a Data Source" panel to connect to a database.")

USING THE ADD A DATA SOURCE PANEL TO CONNECT TO A DATABASE Open the Cold Fusion Administrator by using the Windows 95 Start panel. Click the Data Sources tab. Cold Fusion displays the Data Source panel shown in Figure 5-14 (notice that the Data Source entry box is empty), start the process of adding (Web connecting) a new database to Cold Fusion by pressing the Add button. (Microsoft Access database software comes up automatically, so you don't need to choose it; if you were using Oracle Personal Edition, you would have to choose it.) Your status bar message will say **Connect: host 127.0.0.1 contacted,**

Figure 5-14
ODBC Data Sources
Available to Cold
Fusion

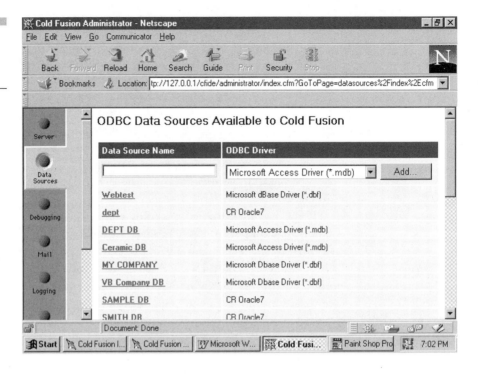

waiting for reply. The displayed Web page is about 4K and should come up in just a couple of seconds if you have a server connection.

NOTE: If you are running from a remote location across a server, you will not be connecting to a server host as 127.0.0.1—that address is a special address that represents your own machine address when you are running the server as a closed loop system. Nevertheless, even if you are using your own server, at this time you must have a Web server installed and up-and-running. See Chapter 3 if you have any questions about installing a Web server or TCP/IP.

In the Data Source Name box, type in `Ceramic DB`. Ceramic DB will be the name that you use to refer to your database when building this Cold Fusion template. You may leave the Description field empty; it is not required to be filled in. Also notice the phrase `Microsoft Access Driver (*.mdb)`, located immediately to the right of the Create ODBC Data Source title. This phrase means that your Data Source name will be connected to the MS Access ODBC Driver. This display is a little bit of serendipity; normally you would have to select the correct ODBC driver on the previous Web page, into Cold Fusion defaults to the MS Access ODBC driver.

Figure 5-15
The Create ODBC
Data Source
fill-in form

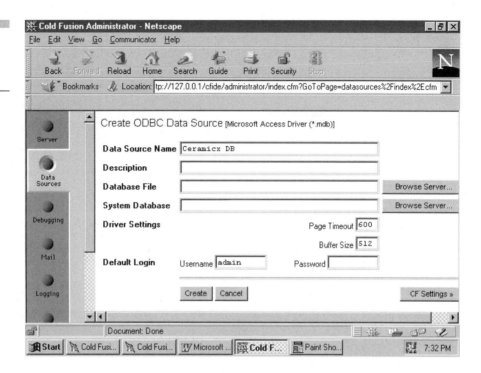

The next step is to click the top Browse Server button. The JAVA program starts up and displays *across the server network* all the available databases on your server (all the drives can be accessed as shown in Figure 5-16).

Again, you will see on the status bar, a message reading: `Connect: host 127.0.0.1 contacted, waiting for reply.` All the server drives will be displayed. Scroll down to the \Access subdirectory and then double-click Access to display the available Access databases. Highlight `Ceramic.mdb`, and then click OK. Click the Spin button, located next to the Verify ODBC Data Source button at the bottom of the CF Administrator page. Then select Ceramic DB from the pop-up list of databases. Now click the Verify ODBC Data Source button. Cold Fusion connects the database and gives you this message: `The connection to the DataSource was verified successfully.` If you have any trouble, select the Coffee Valley CF-supplied database and *verify* it to observe the process. If you have an old version of Access, the new Cold Fusion Access ODBC Driver may not connect to it properly, and you may have to upgrade your version of the Microsoft Access database before being able to verify the database.

After the database is connected to the ODBC Driver, (verified) you can proceed to the next step, which is to create a Cold Fusion template that can be used to retrieve information from the database.

Figure 5-16
Select File on
the Server

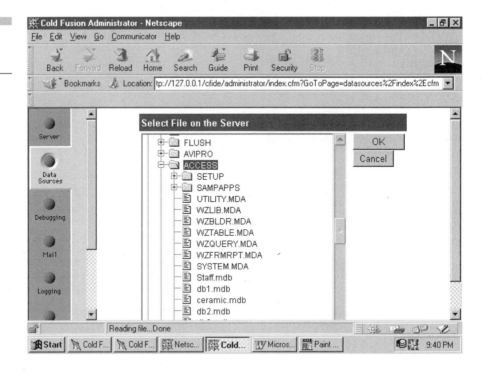

BUILDING A COLD FUSION TEMPLATE WITH A CFINSERT TAG

The CFINSERT tag is made up of two parts: the data source designation and the table name. Here is the first part of a CFINSERT tag example:

```
<CFINSERT DATASOURCE="Ceramic DB" TABLENAME="Ceramic1">
```

When building this tag, use the actual name of the Access table in the TABLENAME= "Customers" element. The remainder of the template uses HTML tags to send a message back to the client.

SOME COMMON ERROR MESSAGES   If you do not correctly recognize or connect the database to the Access ODBC Driver, when you attempt to use the template containing the CFINSERT tag, you will get an error message such as **Driver not capable…** or **ODBC Driver not found**. The best way to avoid these messages is to first use the Cold Fusion Administrator to select the database file and connect the ODBC Driver, making sure you *verify* the connection.

Field names in the database and the HTML fill-in form (see Figure 5-17) can be case-sensitive. If you are using the Access Expert when you are creating the Access table, the first table field is created as a Counter

Figure 5-17
Front-end HTML
fill-in form

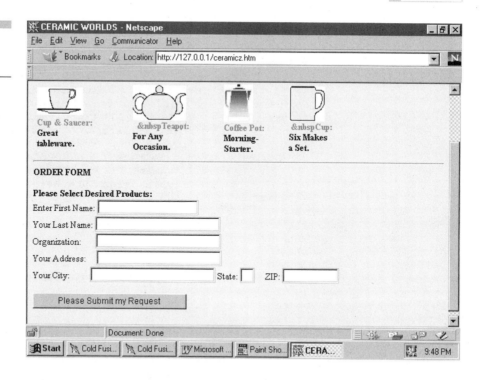

data type; if you use the CFINSERT tag against a Counter data type, it may not work correctly. If you encounter problems, check the database for the Counter data type; if you have this type of field, build your database without using Counter data type fields by not letting Microsoft Access automatically create the Counter field.

The CFQUERY Tag—General Form

If you use a CFQUERY tag, you can use a more flexible table design. You can use a Counter field in your table without difficulty. The CFQUERY tag inserts only the fields you specify in the tag into the table. The CFQUERY tag has the following form:

```
INSERT INTO tablename (columnames)
    VALUES (values)
```

BUILDING A TEMPLATE USING A CFQUERY TAG   The following template shows a working CFQUERY tag; the remainder of the code generates an HTML message back to the end user. This template contains a CFQUERY that uses the Ceramic1 table and the Ceramicz.htm fill-in form.

```
c5_13z.-cfm Template
<! — c5_13z.cfm TEMPLATE FILE, inserts ceramicz.htm form
      data INTO ceramic1.mdb, ceramicz Table —>
<CFQUERY NAME="AddOrd1" DATASOURCE="Ceramic DB">
    INSERT INTO Ceramic1 (Firstname, Lastname, Orgname,
        Address, City, State, Postalcode)
      VALUES ('#Form.FirstName#', '#Form.Lastname#',
            '#Form.Orgname#', '#Form.Address#',
            '#Form.City#', '#Form.State#', '#Postalcode#')
 </CFQUERY>
<HTML>
<HEAD>
<TITLE>CERAMIC WORLD</TITLE>
</HEAD>
<BODY>
<CENTER><H2>Thank you for visiting Ceramic World</H2>
      <CENTER>
<HR>
<P>
Visit CERAMIC WORLD for all of your tableware and glassware
      needs.
Our site is constantly growing to serve you better!
</P>
<HR>
</BODY>
</HTML>
```

When creating the CFQUERY tag, you must give a unique name to the CFQUERY (in this case *AddOrderInfo*.) Each CFQUERY contained within the same template file must have a unique name. The DATA-SOURCE is named using the CF Administrator. The phrase `INSERT INTO Ceramic1` uses the actual table name `Ceramic1`. Each inserted form field is named inside the parentheses; for example, `Firstname`, `Lastname`, `Orgname`, and so on.

NOTE: *When using Cold Fusion 3, do not use Cold Fusion reserved words. For instance, you cannot use the same name for a data source and for a query; it won't work. Also, notice that the database name and the table name are similar but not identical. The VALUES parameter indicates that inserted fields are from an HTML fill-in form and that literal field values will be entered into the respective table fields.*

TESTING THE APPLICATION When testing this program, open your browser and type `http://127.0.0.1/ceramic.htm` at the URL. Then search for the URL. When the ceramic.htm form displays, it will require you to fill out the form and then submit it. If you have previously *verified* the Ceramic DB database, the Cold Fusion engine will process the form data and write it into the Ceramic DB database. If you leave the Ceramic Access database open, Cold Fusion will have a sharing violation; you must close the database to use it on the network.

Also found in the VALUES statement are single quotes '...' used around each form field name. Single quotes are necessary for all literal strings of alphanumeric characters. The hashmarks (found inside the single quotes) help substitute the literal values of the form fields into the Ceramic Table's fields. When building the CFQUERY tag, notice the position of the closing greater than character (>). Without proper placement of this tag, you get an error message. Be careful of field names; if you use caps twice in the LastName field of the template, you must also use a field name LastName, not Lastname.

NOTE: *When testing the Microsoft Access tables in Windows 95 by using your local network machine address (for example,* http://127.0.0.1/ceramic.htm, *when a database insertion is done), the database and table may be left open by Cold Fusion. This problem may be a program bug. The network user ADMIN remains connected to the Access table. You may have to do a CF Administrator restart to be able to reenter the database and table.*

CONCLUSION

This introduction to the Access Database Software shows some basic ways to use Access with HTML fill-in forms across a webserver. Successive chapters will show many additional ways that Access databases and other database software can be used to implement databases over the Internet.

Introducing Borland's Visual dBASE

- Building Tables Using the Table Expert
- Working with Indexes, Using the Command Window
- Creating Command Files & Visual dBASE Programs
- Connecting VISUAL dBASE to Servers
- Using CF CFQUERY TAG to Retrieve Server-based Data

Introducing Visual dBASE

Visual dBASE allows databases to be used over the Internet with Cold Fusion. Visual dBASE stores and displays binary objects such as images, sound files as well as numerical and text data. In this chapter you learn how to create tables containing text, images, and audio files. Cold Fusion is used as middleware to connect Visual dBASE to the Internet. Several database examples show how to display products visually as well as demonstrate them using audio files.

Using Visual dBASE

Visual dBASE quickly installs as a plug-n-play application to the **c: \VISUALDB** directory and is fully icon driven. Figure 6-1 shows the main control panel, with an empty Command panel on the right side. (You can enter individual database commands or groups of commands in the Command panel for quick results.) The blinking cursor rests on the word Untitled, click Untitled to begin designing your first table. Visual dBASE

Figure 6-1
Visual dBASE—
main panel

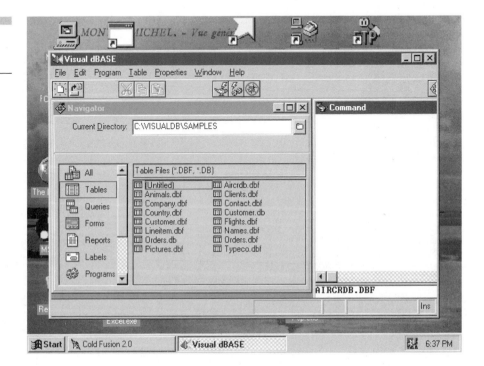

brings up the Expert/Designer panel that allows you to use sample templates or design tables from scratch. Click the Expert button for help in designing your first table.

Building Tables Using the Table Expert

The Expert displays three side-by-side command boxes: Sample tables, From sample tables, and For new table. This is where you add fields to your new table. In the Sample tables box, highlight Company info. Visual dBASE displays a list of fields in the Fields box, beginning with **COMPANY_N**. The "greater-than" arrow is used to move fields into the For new table box. Your screen should look like Figure 6-2.

Adding Table Fields

Use the double "greater-than" symbol to move all the fields from the sample table into the For new table box. Use the single "less-than" symbol to move back a single field called **TYPE** from the For new table box to the From sample table box. At this point, if you want to add other fields from

Figure 6-2
Table panel—
Step 1 of 2

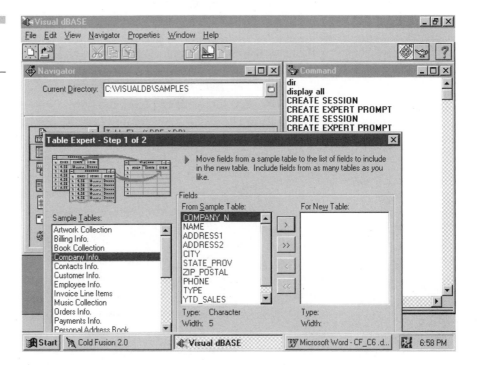

different sample tables, highlight the table you would like to use, (for example Contacts info.) and dBASE will display its sample fields. Then, move the fields you want into the For new table box.

To place a new field in a specific position in the For new table box, first click on the existing field in the For new table that you want the new field to follow. Then, in the From sample table box, highlight the field you want to move and use the greater-than symbol to transfer the field to the For new table box. For example, to position the FAX field after the PHONE field in the For new table box, highlight the PHONE field before moving FAX. dBASE inserts the FAX field immediately after the PHONE field.

If you need to reposition a field, highlight the field, then use the less-than symbol to remove it from the For new table box. Click the cursor on the existing field you want the moved field to follow. Then in the From sample table box, highlight the field you want to move and use the greater-than symbol to transfer the field to the For new table box. Click the Next button at the bottom of the page to go to the next table creation step, Modifying the table structure.

Modifying the Table Structure

Visual dBASE makes modifying table structures extremely simple through the usage of dialog boxes and drop down menus. Figure 6-3 shows the Table structure modification box.

If, for example, you want to change a field name, highlight the field name and type the change.

To create a new field in the field name list: highlight the field name one row above where you want to insert the new field, and click Structure, Insert field from the drop down menu. Type in the new name of the field, for example, **EMAIL1**.

To change the width of a field: move to the Width column (the default width is 10) and type **30**. The field width for the new EMAIL1 field is changed to 30 characters.

To remove a field: highlight a field, then click Structure, Delete current field from the drop down menu.

To index a field, for example, the COMPANY_N field, highlight the word **None** in the INDEX field, dBASE displays a button. Click the button and select the word **Ascending**, dBASE displays the word **Ascending**. The table's records will now be indexed by the field COMPANY_N in ascending order. (The natural order of records does not change, only

Figure 6-3

Table Structure modification panel

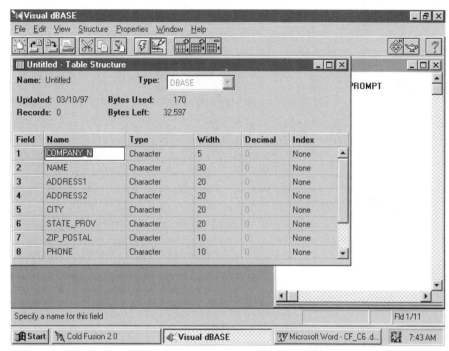

the indexed order.) Figure 6-3 shows the Table structure modification panel.

To save table structure changes: click Structure, Manage indexes. dBASE displays the question, `Company has been modified. Save Changes? Yes No.` Select the Yes button.

WORKING WITH INDEXES Large tables can contain thousands of records. As the number of records increases, system overhead becomes a significant factor. In a table of 100 records, whether a company is named Wittanauer, Inc. or Aardvark Systems it can be accessed equally rapidly. But when a table has 25,000 records, if the database must physically read every record during its search for Wittanauer, users may find the delay unacceptably long. To speed up searches, use an index. The index is a separate file containing internal record pointers that reference individual records in the table. The table records are left in their natural input order and the index is used to find a given record. Because the index file is very small, records are found much more rapidly.

In the Company database, the COMPANY_N field has been indexed. You can create other indexed fields as needed from fields such as NAME or STATE_PROV. When indexing tables, ascending order is the default, although in some cases a descending order is more useful. For example, a sales manager might want to use the descending order of largest to smallest accounts. If a sales total field was used, its descending index would then list the biggest accounts first down to the smallest and (probably) more inactive accounts. To define index attribute, click Structure, Manage indexes, Edit. Figure 6-4 shows the Define index box.

Indexes can also include expressions which introduce conditions to the index. For example, an index can be created which lists companies located only in states where the firm has most of its business, such as New York or California. Using specific indexes can speed up locating records for tables that contain large numbers of records.

To avoid displaying duplicate record entries, click the radio button Include unique key values only. Indexes may also be renamed, for example, the index currently called COMPANY_N could be renamed to COMP1 by highlighting the Index name box and typing in **COMP1**. (One naming convention for index files is to "rev" the index by "1" each time a new index is created, for example, COMP1,COMP2,COMP3 and so on.) Click OK and Visual dBASE displays **COMP1** as the index name. Click OK again to save the changes.

Figure 6-4
The Define Index box

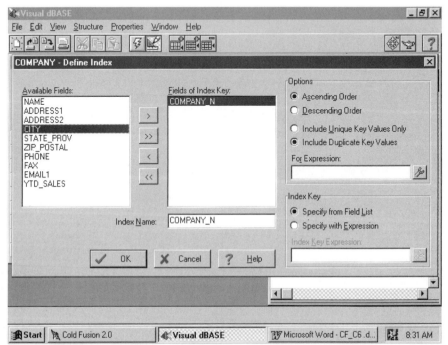

USING MULTIPLE FIELD INDEXES   Another use for an index field is to create a special primary key field used for organizing the table. For example, if individual tableware products were being offered for sale, a "product" category field could be added to the table that contained entries like glassware, ceramics, wood utensils, metalware, etc. See Table 6-1 for Sample index field data.

If the table is then indexed using the Category field, and has a secondary index set to ascending price, each product for sale can be viewed by product category and by ascending price. To create this index use the following index formula: **PRODUCT + PRICE**, (the plus symbol shows that two indexes are used together).

Entering Table Data

To save the structure and begin entering data, click the "lightning-bolt" icon on the speedbar. Then, click Table, Add Records from the drop down menu. You may now begin adding records. Let's make a field length adjustment, the COMPANY_N field is too small, click the "pencil" design icon to change the structure of the database. Change the width to **30** and save, then once again click the add data icon to continue adding data. Figure 6-5 shows the data entry screen.

Using the Command Window

The Command Window is one of the more powerful features of Visual dBASE. Individual commands can be entered to manipulate the database and its tables, and even the contents of individual fields. This functionality is available without having to use mouse clicks or menus.

Table 6-1

Double index sample data

ITEM	PRICE	CATEGORY
Bowl	$20.00	Glassware
Cup and Saucer	$ 4.00	Glassware
Vase	$15.00	Glassware
Lamp	$50.00	Ceramic
Ornament	$25.00	Ceramic
Fountain	$90.00	Ceramic

Figure 6-5

Adding records to
the Company Table

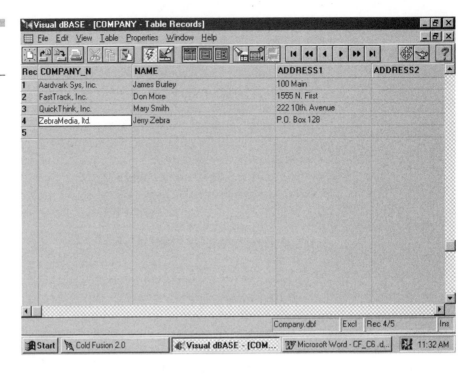

Open the Command window by clicking the "oil lamp" icon. A history list of recently used commands is displayed. If you highlight a recently used command, you can use it again, this saves typing. The command window's Input pane and Results pane can be resized by dragging and dropping with the mouse. When the Command window is opened, if you cannot see the Results pane, use your mouse to click on the bottom border of the Input pane and drag it upwards toward the top of the screen to expand the Results pane display area. Figure 6-6 shows the Command window.

In Figure 6-6 the two commands Goto and Display Record are used to locate and display records as shown in the following example. Type **goto 30**, press Return, and then type **display**. Visual dBASE displays the contents of record 30. In the following examples, other customizable commands are shown being used inside the Command window. Table 6-2 shows some example commands that can be issued from within the command window.

These examples show some of the ways that tables can be manipulated using the Command window.

The next section shows how to begin building program files that can execute one or more individual commands and can contain conditional logic. Program files can include frequently used commands that automate

Figure 6-6

Using the Command window

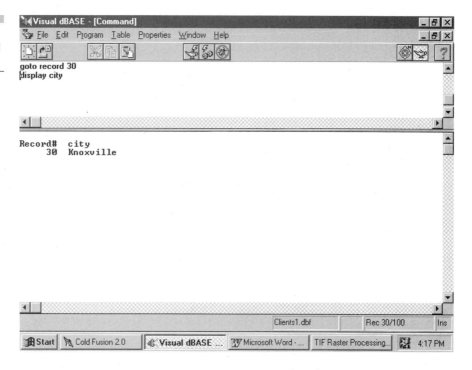

Table 6-2

Using the Command window

Command	Result
Replace Examples:	
`replace all client_id with "Jones"`	Replaces all client_id field entries with "Jones".
`replace next 10 client_id with ""`	Replaces the next 10 records with a blank, from the current record number (use, for example, **goto record 10**) to locate a given record.
`replace all client_id with "Jones" for client_id="harry"`	client_id field entries named "harry" are replaced with "Jones".
`replace all startbal with startbal*1.1`	Multiplies all startbal field entries by a factor of 1.1.
Delete Examples:	
`delete all for startbal > 50`	Marks all records for deletion which contain a start balance greater than $50.

Continues

Table 6-2

Continued

Command	Result
Delete Examples:	
`delete all for recno> 30`	Deletes record numbers greater than 30.
`delete all for recno > 30 .and. delete all for recno < 100`	Deletes a range of records between records 30-100.
File Manipulation Examples:	
`Copy all to temp`	Copies all records to a new table called **temp**. Used for creating a temp table for "what-if" calculations.
`delete table temp.dbf`	Deletes temp.dbf table. (This table can be deleted from Navigator using the DEL key.
Browse Examples:	
`browse fields name, ytd_sales`	Selected table fields can be displayed for quick record inspection and modification.

a programming task, create an input form, design a user interface or create modules and programs which can be shared with colleagues or marketed as commercial database programs. The sample programs provided with Visual dBASE contain extended programming examples.

CREATING A VISUAL dBASE PROGRAM The Program editor is used to create Visual dBASE programs. To open the Program editor enter the following commands: File, New, Program. Visual dBASE displays the Program editor window. Enter commands directly into the Program Editor as shown in the following example.

Save your first program file by entering the following commands: File, Save As, prog1.prg. Visual dBASE stores your program in the sample program collection.

All program files should contain an initial comment line (beginning with an asterisk) that provides the name of the file, its date of creation and the file creator. Other information can also be included such as the function of the program, what table(s) it uses, and so on. After the comment(s) line, use the second line to open the table **company.dbf** as shown in Figure 6-7.

The third line uses a browse command to display the selected fields: **orders**, **company_n**, **ytd_sales**, **and notes**. Even this short program file can save you many keystrokes if you regularly need to open up the

Figure 6-7

Creating a Program
File

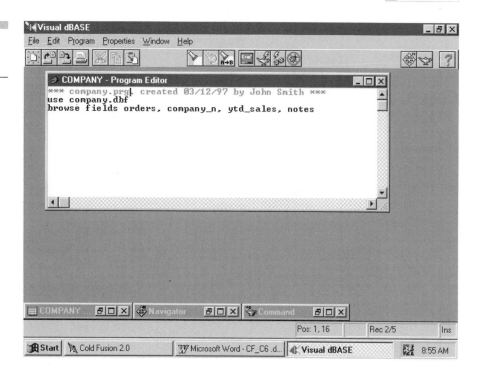

company file to search for specific customers, their ytd_sales information
and notes. And, you may also easily modify this command file to display
other fields as desired. How to run this command file program is shown
in the following section.

Running Visual dBASE Programs

Open Navigator, click the Programs (blue cogwheel) icon. Double click the
program you want to run, in this case, company.prg. The program displays
selected fields of the company.dbf table in the main window. (After this
short program displays the selected fields, it closes itself, returning control to you, but leaving the table open.) You may then browse or modify
the data of the company.dbf table. Obviously, using this short program is
much faster than having to open the table and remember the names you
want to type and then typing out the entire browse command, making
sure to correctly spell the field names. More complex programs can be
written that with the push of a button, you can open a database, display
an input screen with options, check entered data for acceptable data
ranges, display all entered data changes and close and save the table.

SAVING WORK AND CLOSING THE TABLE   To close the table, click File, Save record and Close. To exit Visual dBASE, click the 'X' in the top right hand corner.

Using Visual dBASE with HTML and Cold Fusion

One possible way to increase sales interest is to display products on-line to potential customers. The following code creates product interest by using JPG GIF (image) files and WAV (sound) files to display products. Visual dBASE supports storing both image and sound files, so this task is not especially difficult. The following section shows how to create JPG and WAV files using tools available on the World Wide Web, and how to store and display these different file types using Visual dBASE.

The following fill-in form shows how a fictitious company called Acoustics, Inc., a small instrument building firm specializing in stringed instruments, can create "out-of-town" sales interest by displaying products over the Internet.

DESIGNING A MULTIMEDIA FORM   The creation of an HTML form containing both GIF files, and sound files, requires image creation and sound recording. Image creation using Paint Shop Pro and LVIEW Pro is covered in Chapter 1. WAV file creation requires a sound source such as a microphone or tape player physically plugged into a sound card input and use of a program like WinDAT (Windows Digital Audio Transport) supplied with Windows 95, or other recording software available on the Internet.

The audio file is not hard to create, since the WinDAT software interface has been created with controls that look like those for a cassette recorder. A short examination of WinDAT controls will show that you must first click on the red record button, then click on the "greater than" arrow to start actual recording. Make sure your microphone is plugged into the sound board. The WinDAT software has a pre-startup time delay of several seconds before actual recording begins. Press the stop button to close the recording session. You must then save the file. The only difficult part of using this software is using the microphone for recording. You must keep the sound source close to the microphone, watch out for ambient noise and maintain an even volume from the sound source to have a properly recorded audio file.

Once the WAV file is recorded, copy the WAV file into the same directory as the HTML document that will use it. WAV files tend to be large —a twenty second WAV file can be more than 200K and can take 1 to 2 minutes or more to load over the Internet. Therefore, keep WAV sound files as short as possible, not everyone has a high-speed (for example ISDN or T-1) connection.

In order to play audio files, you need to set up Netscape Navigator to spawn an external viewer. This external program will decode and play the audio file through your system's speakers. If you have Internet Explorer 3.0 or higher, it automatically spawns mplayer.exe. It is a good idea to put directions in your HTML file on how to set up mplayer.exe.

ADDING THE PLUG-INS TO NETSCAPE NAVIGATOR   Netscape Navigator readily accepts many different plug-ins that extend its capabilities. To download audio software plug-ins visit **www.netscape.com**. The Netscape site offers numerous free multi-media plug-ins which can be downloaded and then installed on your particular operating system.

EMBEDDING WAV FILES INTO HTML DOCUMENTS   To test mplayer.exe, log onto the Internet and open an HTML document that contains an embedded WAV file. The following hyperlink reference tag shows how to embed a WAV file as part of an HMTL document. Notice that a standard HTML hypertext tag is used, but the audio file itself contains a WAV file extension. The WAV file reference can be placed anywhere in the HTML document. Figure 6-8 shows a typical usage of WAV files in an HTML document.

Embedded WAV File example:

```
<A HREF=myaudio.wav>My first Audio File</A>
```

The acoustic.htm HTML document file code contains both GIF images and WAV audio files, and is shown in the following example.

The HTML code shows how to embed GIF images and WAV sound files. The featured WAV files use close-miked, live recorded guitars controlled by the WinDAT software. The resulting Web page allows the buyer to both see a visual image of the product as well as hear a WAV file featuring the actual played instrument. To further enhance this product offering, digital images could be used to display snapshot pictures of instruments with serial numbers listed below each image and with stereo audio files recorded on each of those same instruments using Real Audio software. Or you could hire a guitarist and create an AVI file of the guitarist playing

Figure 6-8

HTML form with
WAV sound files and
GIF image files

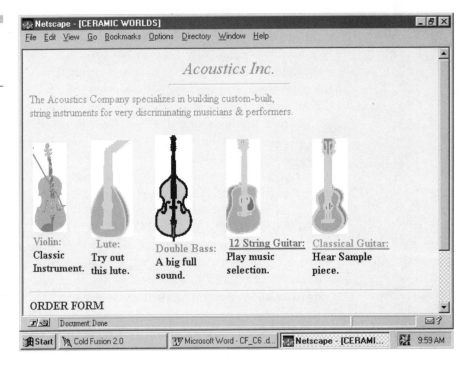

the instrument and place the AVI file in the database. Currently, Internet bandwidth constraints advise against the use of anything but very short AVI files.

The following section shows how to store GIF images and WAV sound files in Visual dBASE fields.

USING VISUAL dBASE FIELDS TO STORE IMAGES AND SOUNDS Open the table, click the Modify table structure icon (pencil icon). On the menu bar, click Structure, Insert field. Visual dBASE displays an unnamed field. Name the field (in this case use the word **IMAGES**, click Character, click the resulting button tab. Visual dBASE displays field type choice, click Binary. Your results should look like Figure 6-9. To save the binary field, click Properties on the menu bar. Click Yes to save the modified structure. Visual dBASE displays the empty binary field as eight small dots.

To add an image or sound, double click the empty binary field, an Empty binary field message box appears. The Empty binary field dialog box is displayed. Choose Image viewer and click OK. The Image viewer is displayed. On the menu bar, choose File, Insert. Specify the name and

```
<HTML>
<HEAD>
<TITLE>CERAMIC WORLDS</TITLE>
</HEAD>
<!- Acoustic.htm —>
<BODY BACKGROUND="redbackg.jpg" BGCOLOR="#FFFF80"
     TEXT="#00000" LINK="#0000FF" VLINK="#FF00FF"
     ALINK="#0000FF" LEFTMARGIN="100" TOPMARGIN="5">
<center><font size="+2" color="red"><i>Acoustics
     Inc.</i></font></font></center>
<HR width=30%>
<font color=teal>The Acoustics Company specializes in
     building custom-built, <BR>string instruments for
     very discriminating musicians & performers.</font>
<TABLE>
    <TR>
    <TH align=left><IMG
    SRC="violin.gif">   <BR><font
    color="red">Violin: <BR><font color="black">Classic
    <BR>Instrument.</font></font>   </TH>
    <TH align=left><IMG SRC="lute.gif"><BR>
<font color="red">  Lute: <BR><font
    color="black">Try out<BR>this lute.
          </font></font>
    </TH>
<TH align=left><IMG SRC="dblbass.gif"><BR>
<font color="red">Double Bass:  <BR> <font
    color="black">A big full<BR>sound. </font></font>
    </TH>
<TH align=left><IMG SRC="guitar.gif"><BR>
<font color="red"> <A HREF=twlvguit.wav>12 String
    Guitar:</A> <BR><font color="black">Play
    music    <BR>selection.  
      </font></font>   </TH>
<TH align=left><IMG
    SRC="ukelele.gif">   <BR>
<font color="red"><A HREF=clasguit.wav>Classical
    Guitar:</A><BR><font color="black">Hear Sample
       <BR>piece.</font></font> </TH><BR>
    </TR>
</TABLE>
<HR>
<B>ORDER FORM</B>
<FORM ACTION="c6_7.cfm" METHOD=POST>
<B>Please Select Desired Products:</B>
Product you desire: <INPUT TYPE="TEXT" NAME="Order"
     size="20"><BR>
<INPUT TYPE= "SUBMIT" VALUE="Please Submit my Request">
</FORM>
</BODY>
</HTML>
```

Figure 6-9
Creating a Binary
field

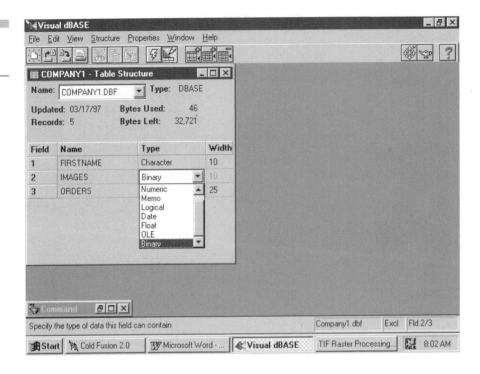

Figure 6-9
Creating a Binary
field

location of the image in any of the graphic formats to store in the field. Several file types are displayed, to store GIF or JPG, select the GIF or JPG file from the file directory. The file is stored as a small colored icon. Visual dBASE doesn't display GIF or JPG images, but will display many other binary field types. GIF and JPG files can be retrieved from Visual dBASE using Cold Fusion and displayed on a web browser.

To store WAV files, double click the empty binary field, choose the sound player option, click File, Insert. Select the desired file from the directory tree and close. Visual dBASE displays a musical clef icon in the binary field to show where the sound binary is stored. To play back the stored audio file click the musical clef icon.

NOTE: *Set up Netscape Navigator to play WAV files with mplayer.exe. However, Navigator may not be able to "find" mplayer.exe if you are trying to play a WAV file locally from the root directory on your server, resulting in a* **Not able to find mplayer.exe** *error message. This problem occurs only with locally accessed files, and does not happen when using Netscape Navigator over the Internet.*

Inserting HTML Form Data Into Tables

Form data can be easily inserted into a Visual dBASE table by using a Cold Fusion template. The contents of the field Order from acoustic.htm can be inserted into the Company table. This is a two step process. First, use the Cold Fusion administrator to link to the Visual dBASE table. Second, put the Cold Fusion insert template and the HTML document containing the fill-in form into your webserver's document subdirectory. Cold Fusion then uses the Template instructions to insert data from the fill-in form into the table.

In order to be able to connect the table to Cold Fusion, you must give a DATASOURCE name to the Visual dBASE database. The DATA-SOURCE name is how Cold Fusion references your database. You create and assign this Cold Fusion name by using the Cold Fusion administrator panel. See the following section, "Adding a Data Source."

USING THE CF ADMINISTRATOR TO ADD A DATA SOURCE

Click the Cold Fusion administrator in the Windows 95 Start menu. Cold Fusion displays the Data sources panel, as shown in Figure 6-10. Click the Add Button. Cold Fusion displays the Create ODBC data source panel. Click the top Browse Button. Cold Fusion starts up a Java applet and displays your top drive directory. In Windows 95, double click the "C" root directory and the drive directory where you have installed Visual Basic, click the **visualdb** subdirectory, then highlight, for example, the **company.dbf** Visual dBASE database file, click OK. Cold Fusion redisplays the Create ODBC data source panel.

Type in the Data source name **My Company DB**, then click the Create button at the bottom of the screen. Cold Fusion takes you back to the opening Data source page, and lists your Data source (**My Company DB**) with the other hypertext Data source links. At the bottom of the page the **Verify ODBC Datasource** text has a "spin" button. Click the Spin button and highlight **My Company DB**, then click the Verify button. If you have done everything correctly, Cold Fusion will verify the ODBC database connection by giving you the following message: **The connection to the data source was verified successfully**. Then click the Go back button to return to the Add data source panel. You may now exit from this panel or close the System administrator. The following Figure 6-11 shows a correctly selected database in the Verify ODBC database input box.

Figure 6-10
Add a data source
panel.

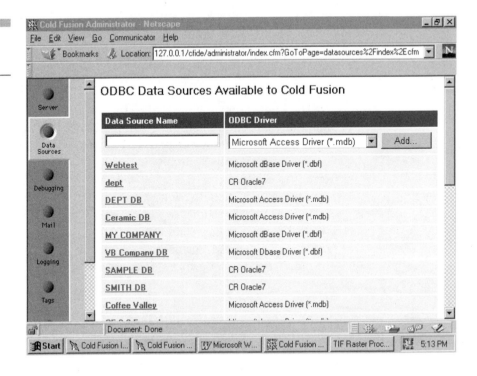

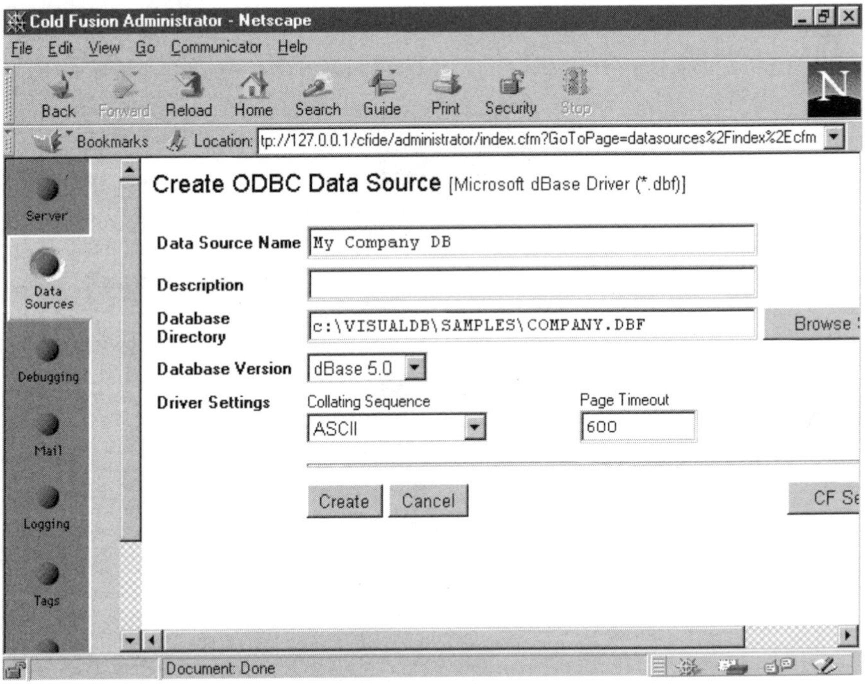

Figure 6-11
ODBC dBASE setup
panel

BUILDING THE CFQUERY TAG The CFQUERY Tag used in the Cold Fusion insert template file is made up two major parts: the data-source name and the table name. Here is a CFINSERT tag example:

```
<CFQUERY     DATASOURCE="MY COMPANY" TABLENAME="Company1">
```

When building this tag, use the actual dBASE table name in the TABLENAME=Company1 element. Also, make sure that the field names used in the fill-in form, template and Table are identical. HTML document field names become case sensitive when used across a network by Cold Fusion. (They must be interpreted by Cold Fusion's CGI Script, and CGI Scripts are case sensitive.)

Following the CFQUERY tag, the remaining template tags are used to send a message back to the client. The field name Orders is placed in parentheses after INSERT.

Notice on the VALUES line how the form input value is delimited by parentheses, single quotes and hashmarks. Figure 6-12 shows a typical HTML document that might be generated back to the enduser.

TEMPLATE ERROR MESSAGES If you do not correctly recognize or connect the database to the Visual dBASE ODBC Driver, when you at-

Figure 6-12
HTML document generated back to enduser

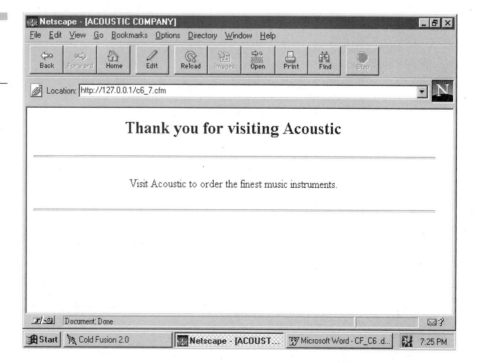

tempt to use the template containing the CFQUERY tag you will get an error message such as **Driver not capable**, **ODBC driver not found** or **Column not found** in database. The best way to avoid these messages is to double check that field names are identical in case and spelling against the field names used in the database.

You may insert a single form field into a database containing a number of fields, but check field lengths in both the table and the fill-in form in order to prevent data loss. For example, if a fill-in Form field width is 30 characters and the table field width is 20 characters, data more than 20 characters will be lost during the insert.

NOTE: *The CFQUERY tag allows the use of a very flexible table design, allowing you to include "counter" data type fields in your table without problems. CFQUERY will selectively insert form field contents into your table's fields, skipping past counter type fields. The CFQUERY tag has the following form:*

```
INSERT INTO tablename (columnames)
      VALUES (values)
```

When creating the CFQUERY tag, you must give a unique name to the CFQUERY (in this case "AddOrder".) Each CFQUERY must have its own unique name. Form field(s) are inserted inside single quotes and parentheses, for example, '#Form.Orders#'. Be careful to not accidentally use Cold Fusion "reserved words" such as template instructions like "loop", "counter" etc.) as field names, you will get error messages. The VALUES parameter indicates that inserted fields are from an HTML fill-in form, and that literal field values will be entered into the respective table fields.

Also found in the VALUES statement are single quotes '...' used around each form field name. Single quotes are necessary for all literal strings of alphanumeric characters. The hashmarks (found inside the single quotes) substitute literal form field values into the table's fields. When building the CFQUERY tag, notice the position of the closing ">". Without proper placement of this tag, you will get an error message.

When "inserting" fill-in form fields into a database, the CFQUERY tag allows you to selectively choose fields to insert. Maintain the same listed order of fields in the CFQUERY tag as found in the fill-in form and the target database.

Figure 6-13 shows the front-end fill-in form used by the Cold Fusion template.

Figure 6-13

Fill-in form fields

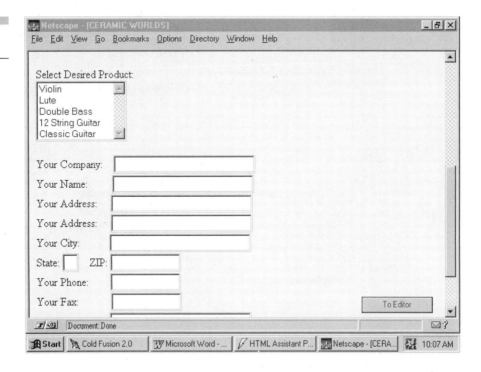

Before running the template containing the CFQUERY tag, give the query a unique name and check the database table to make sure it contains all of the fields specified in the CFQUERY, and double check the spellings of field names in the Fill-in form, Table and Cold Fusion template. The CFQUERY tag is shown in bolded text. The following CFQUERY example shows how to create a Cold Fusion template that will insert multiple HTML form fields into a database.

Myindex.html

```
<HTML>
<HEAD>
<META HTTP-EQUIV="Content-Type" CONTENT="text/html;
     charset=windows-1252">
<TITLE>My index</TITLE>
<X-SAS-WINDOW   TOP=26 BOTTOM=33!4 LEFT=28 RIGHT=558></HEAD>
<BODY LINK="#0000ff" VLINK="#800080">
<P><A HREF="time.cfm">Register</A> This registration screen
     sets time zone, then changes the scheduled time for
     the news. </P>
</HTML>
```

CFQUERY TAG EXAMPLE—MULTIPLE FIELD INSERTION The database table also contains a Notes field. Notice that there isn't a Notes field in the fill-in form or the corresponding CFQUERY Insert tag. The Notes field is maintained separately by the database administrator or the owner of the database, and contains sales comments about various customers.

CONCLUSION

This introduction to Visual dBASE shows you how to build tables, manipulate data and how to store multimedia files in Visual dBASE tables. It also shows how to build HTML fill-in forms and construct Cold Fusion templates using the CFQUERY tag. Please refer to the SQL chapters to learn how to do more complex queries against Visual dBASE database tables.

Introducing Personal Oracle 7

- Using the Personal Oracle Navigator
- Creating projects containing tables and users
- Granting table privileges to users
- Using front-end HTML documents/CF templates to retrieve Oracle data
- Generating HTML documents using retrieved Oracle data

Personal Oracle 7 for Windows 95 is fully upward scaleable database software that contains many of the same powerful features found in the company's mainframe Oracle database software. The author's personal recommendation is that Oracle should not be used for incidental database work; it is designed for extensive multiuser, relational database applications. Using the Personal Oracle Navigator makes developing projects and tables a less challenging task. Connecting Personal Oracle 7 to a server using Cold Fusion is more involved than connecting single user PC-based database software. This is not because any particular step is more complex; it is because Oracle's built-in multiuser capability increases the number of preliminary steps needed to get Oracle up and running on a server. For example, Oracle requires that each table have an owner with a certain level of privileges. Also, when you connect an HTML document to an ORACLE table, the table owner must be identified.

This chapter covers each of these issues carefully, and then presents working examples of how to use HTML documents with Cold Fusion to query tables and generate dynamic HTML documents containing the queried data back to the end user. Let's get started!

Installing and Using Personal Oracle 7

Personal Oracle 7 is a plug-n-play Windows 95 software product. During installation, Personal Oracle 7 creates a folder in the Windows 95 Start Folder called *Personal Oracle 7 for Windows*. When installation is complete, select this Folder and open Oracle by clicking the entry called *Personal Oracle 7 Navigator*. You must use the Oracle Start Database command to mount the *Sample* database, and when the database is up-and-running, Oracle adds a blue disk icon in the bottom-right corner of your screen in Windows 95. The first panel displayed is the Personal Oracle Navigator panel shown in Figure 7-1.

The Sample database can serve as a work area in which a project(s) can be constructed (each project can contain one or more related tables). In this introductory chapter, the Sample database which comes with the Oracle software will be used to create a project with associated tables. After you become familiar with Oracle, you can move forward to create your own database and tables, a more complex task which is outside of the scope of this introductory chapter. Oracle assumes that you will use the Sample database to both examine the Sample database application as well as create your practice tables in that database.

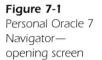

Figure 7-1
Personal Oracle 7
Navigator—
opening screen

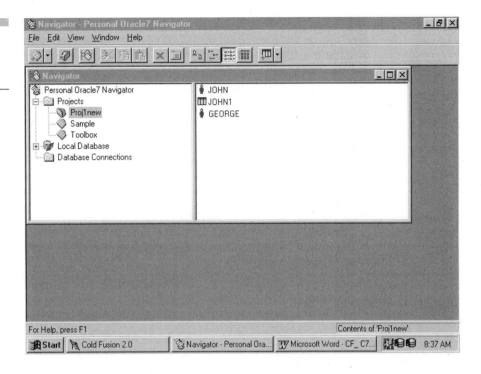

Installation Hints

Oracle recommends having at least 40Mb of disk space available for installation. Oracle also recommends not using disk compression with its data files. Also, when naming files, you must use eight character filenames (DOS-style) with extensions containing only three characters. Oracle states that they currently do not support the extended name, UNC—the Universal Naming Convention for filenames and directory paths. Oracle uses 12Mb to 16Mb of virtual memory during operation, and virtual memory is mapped to free space on the hard drive.

Using the Personal Oracle 7 Navigator

The Navigator Toolbar contains nine active tool buttons and six grayed-out tool buttons. To activate the greyed-out tools, a project with at least one table must be created and then opened. The Sample relational database contains a number of related tables showing how a database can be used by a model company. Oracle is a relatively complex product (compared with single-user PC database software products), so if this is your first time using Oracle, go through the following section "Getting Started", which gives a short tour of the Sample database.

To view individual tables in the Sample database, click the Local database icon. Oracle displays a list of the different objects (including Table, View, Index, and so on), making up the database as shown in Figure 7-2.

Select Table, and Oracle displays (in the right window) a list of the tables in the Sample database. To examine an individual table, click, for example, the DEPT Table icon to display the columns of the Department Table: DEPTNO, DNAME, and LOC. To close the table, click the x in the top-right corner of the table window. After you have looked at the DEPT table, open the EMP table. If you spend a moment and compare the DEPT table to the EMP table, you will notice that both contain a common field, DEPTNO. This common field is used as a key field to relate the two tables to each other. The advantages of using key fields is discussed in the "Using the New Table Wizard" section.

In the Display panel, notice that each table has a user name associated with it. Oracle requires that each table have an *owner*—a user who can create, modify, and control the table. Other users can be granted "privileges" by the owner to connect to the table and be given privileges to add

Figure 7-2
Personal Oracle
Navigator—Local
Database panel

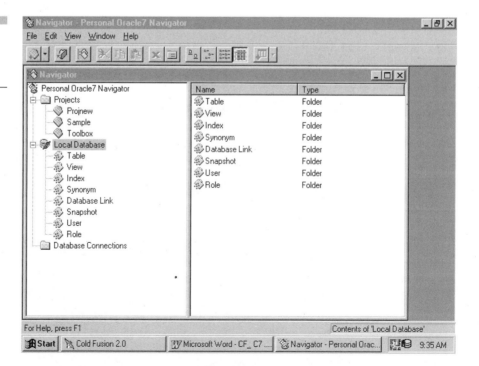

data or even modify the table structure. (This is not an issue with single-user database software products, but the Oracle default privilege level is set to *read-only*.) In contrast to this method of granting privileges to users, other familiar PC database products are set up to only have one user—the person who opens the database product immediately has privilege to be the system administrator, who can create and maintain the PC database. In single-user database products, there is no extensive functionality to create other users or grant privileges to other users. That is not to say that other PC database products do not have the ability to create access passwords on tables or make tables read-only.

USING VIEWS A view is a *named query* that allows you to see a table(s) data snapshot, which contains preselected columns and table(s). When you are in the Sample database and want to see a sample View, click the View icon in the left window. The display shows selected columns across several tables, allowing you to examine data in a convenient manner. (If the tables did not contain key fields, this view would not be possible.) Views can be created by using a query to select columns from one or more tables. To examine the sample query, which produces the view, click View. Then click the name *Sales* and select the Properties button on the Toolbar. Oracle displays the Sales panel as shown in Figure 7-3.

Figure 7-3
Properties panel
for the Sales view

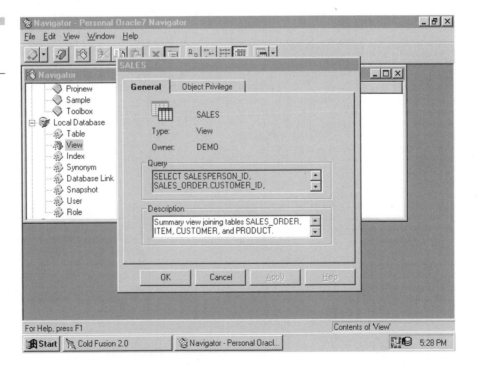

The Query message box shows the SQL code required to create the query that selects the columns and specific column values used in the Sales View. You can use the down arrow of the Query message box to display the *off the page* SQL making up the Sales query. After views are created, they are named and saved. Then the views can be used whenever needed.

USING INDEXES   Indexes use an index file that allows data to be organized without requiring that the table actually be sorted and put into an ascending or descending alphabetic order—a sorting process, which can take quite a while if a table has thousands of records. To see how Oracle labels indexes and primary key indexes, click the Index icon under the Local Database icon. Oracle displays two types of indexes: PK_ indexes are *primary key* indexes and I_ indexes. Each Index has an owner. Oracle tables may contain more than a million records, so it is important to sort the database *offline* when customers are not using it.

USING ONLINE HELP   Oracle Navigator Online help is context-sensitive, if you have questions regarding a particular operation, keyword or button, press the *F1* key on your keyboard. Also, while using Help, you may select or type in a keyword to bring up menu cards. These menu cards will guide you through the majority of the different operations used to manipulate the database and tables. Use the Contents tab in Help to display a list of basic operations by categories, many of which also have step-by-step cue cards. You may also print out help topics, which is recommended for complex operations.

It is beyond the scope of this introductory chapter to discuss the creation of a new database; you use SQL operations, which use the initial command Create Database, and then proceed forward using SQL data definitions. This level of detail is nicely covered in several Oracle Press' books offered by McGraw-Hill. This chapter shows you how to create projects, tables, and users within the Sample database using the Personal Oracle Navigator, and then connect these tables using Cold Fusion to a server. Oracle recommends that you not delete the sample tables, views, and indexes found within the Sample database until you have examined their structure and understand how they are used and created.

BUILDING A PROJECT WITH TABLES AND USERS   A project is a workspace area containing related tables. Creating a new project is easy. From the Navigator main toolbar menu, click the New project button—

the down arrow icon, second from the leftmost button. Oracle creates and displays `Proj1.zpj`. Click Save or enter a new name up to eight characters, using a .zpj file extension. When you have saved the project, Oracle displays a project panel with the default label `Proj1.jpj`, or with the custom project name you created and saved.

CREATING USERS   On the toolbar, click the rightmost down arrow button. Oracle displays various menu options including New user. Click New user. Oracle displays the New user panel. Enter, for example, `Smith` in the Name box. And in the Password box and the Confirm password box, enter `smith1`. You may use any user name or password you want, but no matter what name or password you use, write down the user name and password in an obvious place, such as the inside cover of your Oracle Manual, or some well-known and easily remembered location. To modify the tables belonging to Smith you will have to use the password, so you don't want to forget it. Each time a user is created, you must assign a password, therefore you may want to create a *little black book* of users and passwords.

CREATING DIFFERENT PRIVILEGE LEVELS FOR USERS   Oracle also allows you to create users with different levels of privileges. For example, if you are designing a financial accounting system, you can create a group of users with read/write privileges for the Accounts Payable tables, and then you can grant all Accounts Payable financial personnel that level of privilege. A second group of users could be created who have read/write privileges in the Accounts Receivable tables—that type of privilege could be granted to Accounts Receivable financial personnel. A third class of users could be created who have both read/write privileges on the Accounts Payable tables and the Accounts Receivable tables—that level of privilege could be assigned to departmental level supervisors or the head accountant. By creating and granting different levels of user access privilege to the various groups of employees, you help create a system of financial checks and balances; an AP clerk will not be able to easily create an AP billing and then move into the AR ledger to issue a pay voucher to an offsite dummy company.

The second task is to create a table. You may want to create users first, because when you create a new table, during the process you must select a user to be the table owner. (Oracle displays a list of prospective users.) It may be more convenient to create the user first, create the new table, and then assign the now existing user to the table. (You can, of course, create the user at the same time.)

Using the New Table Wizard

Click the New objects button, (the rightmost button on the toolbar menu). Oracle displays the New table panel. Click OK. Oracle displays the New table Wizard. The default radio button choice is New table. Click OK. Oracle mounts the Sample database and displays the following messages: `Starting up database` and `Checking Security`. If you are not connected to an Internet connection, Oracle brings up your Internet logon screen with name and password fill-in boxes. (If you really don't want to log on to the Internet, wait a few moments for Oracle to process its background files. Then Oracle will allow you to continue whether you are logged in or not.) The tables that you will create in the next sections will be a part of the already existing Sample database.

After the database is mounted, the first Table Wizard screen is displayed, as shown in Figure 7-4. Oracle asks, `What do you want the name of the new table to be?` Enter the name `Company`. Oracle asks, `The owner of the table is`? Using the arrow, click open the pop-down menu and choose the new user just created: `Smith`. (This user will become the table owner and will have full read/write privileges against the Company

Figure 7-4
Table Wizard screen
—Page 1 of 7

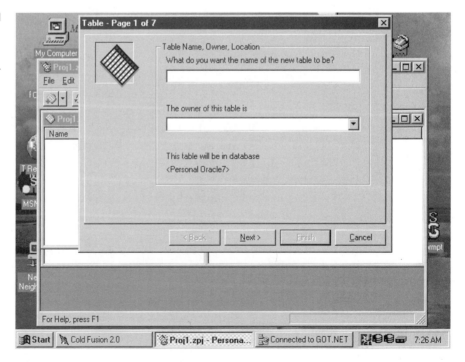

table.) Click Next and Oracle displays Page 2 of 7, the Column definition panel.

BUILDING COLUMN DEFINITIONS   The Column definition panel displays the Column name box; enter `Company` in this box. The Column type box has a default value of `VARCHAR2`, (which allows alphanumeric characters to be entered). Do not change the Column type. In the Size box, enter `20`. The Scale box can be left at *0* in this table, because this table will not use decimal numbers. Click New after entering this information about the Company field. Use the values found in Table 7-1 to create the remaining fields. Click Next when you have finished inserting values.

USING THE SCALE OPTION   Scale determines how many digits to the right or left of the decimal place rounding will occur. For example, a positive scale = 4rounds off a decimal number at four decimal places to the right. When you are presented with the unrelated question, `Does this column have default value, if any?` you may leave the answer blank. None of the fields in this table will require default values. A default numerical value could be *0*.

DEFINING COLUMN CONDITIONS   The Table Wizard, Page 3 of 7, displays the *Null, Unique* panel. The first question is, `Can the Column value be null?` Leave at the default value, `Yes`. Allowing Nulls means that you are allowing the column to contain a Null if no value has been entered. This is not the same as leaving the field with a *0* value. Conditional logic applied against a Null field evaluates to an indeterminate result. Conditional logic applied against a field containing *0* can evaluate

Table 7-1

Company table column definitions

Field	Size	Full Field Name
Company	20	Company
fname	15	First name
lname	15	Last name
addr1	20	Address
city	20	City
state	2	State
Zip	9	Zip
email	30	Email

to, for example, **Yes** (this field contains a value of zero) or **No** (this field does not contain a value of zero). When values are added to a field containing Null, the Null value is replaced with the inserted value.

The second question is, **Does the Column Value have to be unique?** If you are using this Column as a unique key (such as a value like a social security number), click **Yes**; otherwise, leave with the default value **No**. At the bottom of the panel, you can use the greater than and less than keys to scroll through your columns to make desired changes. When you are finished adding columns, click Next. Oracle displays a password box. Enter Smith's password **smith1** and click OK. Each time an outside process opens this table, it will have to send the values: user is **smith** and the password is **smith1**. (You can use the Cold Fusion Administrator data sources panel to add these user and password values to the database so that you will not have to supply them each time you open Cold Fusion to access the database table.)

The Table Wizard displays Page 4 of 7, Foreign key, check condition. Oracle asks, **Does this column have a foreign key?** A foreign key can be specified by selecting a table and a column from the table. (A foreign key is the name given to a primary key when it is used in a second table, when you are looking at the second table from the perspective of the first table.) At this stage, there is not yet a second table available, therefore, leave this box blank. If a second table is created, which also has the Company column, that column would be a foreign key in the second table, and the common Company column found in the two tables could be used to relate the two tables to each other if it contains unique values. (Because Oracle will not allow you to insert duplicate values in unique key tables, be very careful what you use for a primary and foreign key field.)

NOTE: *In the Sample database, the DEPT table and the EMP table have a common column, DEPTNO. If you are in the DEPT table and want to also open the EMP table to lookup related data, the DEPTNO column in the EMP table can be used as a foreign key to look up that data. The common column is used to relate the first table to the second table.*

CREATING PRIMARY KEYS The Ordered columns panel, Page 6 of 7, allows you to change the position of columns in the table by highlighting the column you wish to move and then clicking the Up or Down button to move the column. You can delete columns by highlighting a column and clicking the Delete button. Use the Back button at the bottom of the page to go back to any previous page in the Table Wizard to change column names, add new columns, or change column definitions as desired.

The End of table creation panel asks, **Do you want to enter data now?** If you are finished with your table design, click the Finish button at the bottom of the panel to save your table definition and bring up the data-entry panel to enter data.

Granting User Privileges

User privileges are activities against a table(s) of the database that the user has been granted permission to do. Users may be granted read-only privileges in one table, whereas in another table the user may be granted the privilege of both adding data or changing the structure of the table. The system administrator or the table owner can also grant **other** users privileges against the table. Figure 7-5 shows the panel used to grant user privileges.

USING THE USER PRIVILEGES PANEL   To bring up the User privileges panel, click the Properties button on the main menu. Click the Object privilege tab, and then enter the user password (in this case, **smith1**).

Figure 7-5

Password dialog box

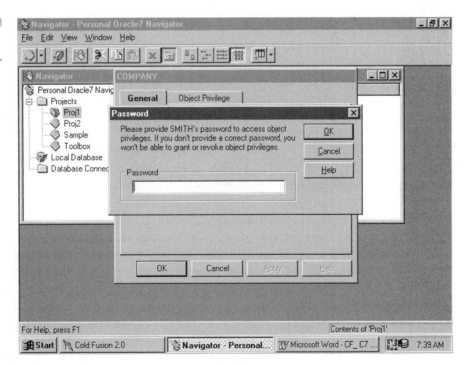

Click OK. Oracle now displays the Privilege for input box. Click the Privilege for down arrow, and Oracle displays a list of users, which includes Scott. Highlight Scott, and in the remaining (privileges) box, Oracle displays privileges that you can grant to the user Smith: `alter`, `delete`, `index`, `insert`, `references`, `select`, `update`.

ENTERING TABLE DATA   Using the Navigator main panel, double-click the word `Company` (the table name) or the small Table icon next to the word `Company`. Oracle displays an input screen. Right-click your mouse and click Insert after. Oracle displays an empty row. Input data by clicking into empty fields and entering these values: `New, Mary, Jones, 200 North, San Francisco, CA, 90000, Mary.Jones@new.com`. Use the Tab key to move between columns while inputting data.

When entering data into your table, think before entering abbreviations that are not customarily used in standard English. Some years ago, database space on hard disk drives was very precious, and so programmers came up with elaborate tables of abbreviation to save scarce disk space. Times have changed, drive sets can be purchased which can contain up to terabytes of information, and there is no longer any good reason to unnecessarily use cryptic abbreviations or replace standard English words with shorter numerical equivalents. And the same is true for column names. Don't be misled, though. You should still try to use brief data entries.

To add a new row, right-click your mouse, a popup menu displays, click Insert after, and then input data into the new blank row. When you have finished inputting all rows of data, commit the data to the table by right-clicking the mouse, this displays a popup menu. Then click Commit Insert. Oracle saves the data to the table. If you have mandatory entry columns, Oracle will not allow you to complete the Commit insert step until you have entered data in all mandatory data columns. An example of a mandatory data column would be the Company column. If you close the table before doing the Commit insert step, new uncommitted rows will be dropped.

To delete a row, highlight the row to be deleted, right-click the mouse, this displays a popup menu, and then choose the Delete row command. If you open a new row, but decide to not enter data, right-click the mouse, click Refresh, and then Oracle removes the empty row and redisplays your table data without the empty row.

SETTING UP A TEST ENVIRONMENT USING ORACLE   In the Server name text box, enter 2, which is the Oracle designation for the local server. This step allows you to use a feedback loop on your server to test HTML files and Cold Fusion templates against the Oracle database. Click OK.

In the Username text box, enter **SMITH**, enter **SMITH1** in both the Password and Confirm text boxes, and then click the OK button to save. The main Administrator panel redisplays. Click the Verify button to test your database connection. Cold Fusion displays a **Connection Verified** message. Because Oracle is a multiuser database, verification fails without the use of a valid username and/or password, and server ID. The following section contains Installation Error Messages which Oracle 7 may display during installation. A short comment after the error message explains the error message.

ORACLE 7 ODBC INSTALLATION ERROR MESSAGES:

```
Error Message: [Intersolv] [ODBC Oracle driver][ORACLE]
        ORA-12154: TNS: could not resolve service name.
        Comment: The server is incorrectly named.
Error Message: [Intersolv] [ODBC Oracle driver][ORACLE]
        ORA-01017: TNS: invalid user/password; logon denied.
        Comment: If you forgot to install a user and pass-
        word, return to Settings and add a user and password.
```

Connecting Personal Oracle Edition 7 to a Server with Cold Fusion

Understanding the Oracle Server Environment: To connect Personal Oracle Edition 7 (or the Oracle Workgroup Server) to a server, you must first have an Oracle database up-and-running. If you attempt to use the Cold Fusion Administrator to install the Oracle 7 ODBC Driver without having an Oracle database up-and-running, you will be interrupted by a request to mount the database. Therefore, make sure that your server (perhaps O'Reilly, Netscape, or Microsoft) is already mounted. Then start up the Oracle database. When the database is mounted and you are ready to begin the process of connecting Personal Oracle 7 to Cold Fusion, click the Start icon of the Cold Fusion administrator. The Oracle 7 ODBC Driver installation process begins.

Because Oracle is a multiuser database, during installation of the Oracle 7 ODBC Driver for a particular table, you must take an additional step; you must specify a user and a password for the table sometime during installation. This step is shown in the next section. (Oracle 7 ships with several already configured users and passwords, one of which can be initially used for this purpose.) The following section shows the installation of the Oracle 7 ODBC Driver using the Cold Fusion administrator. This installation requires that the database is up-and-running. If you need to refresh your knowledge of how to mount the database, refer to the section "Installing and Using Personal Oracle 7" found at the beginning of this chapter.

USING THE ORACLE 7 ODBC DRIVER (USING THE COLD FUSION ADMINISTRATOR PANEL)   Click the Cold Fusion administrator in the Windows 95 Start menu. Open the Cold Fusion administrator, and the Data sources panel is displayed. Click **Smith DB**. The Cold Fusion administrator panel appears, as shown in Figure 7-6.

Cold Fusion displays the Update CF Data source info panel. Notice the user name **Smith** and the password **Smith1** (shown by asterisks, not as Smith1). Click Update. Cold Fusion returns you to the opening Data panel tab. Click Verify to check your connection. If you do not have an instance of the database mounted, Oracle will start up the database and network connection to verify your connection. If you do not want to connect to the Internet, you can wait several seconds and then Oracle will connect to your local server.

Oracle recognizes the local (127.0.0.1) server as 2:.

Figure 7-6
The Data Sources tab

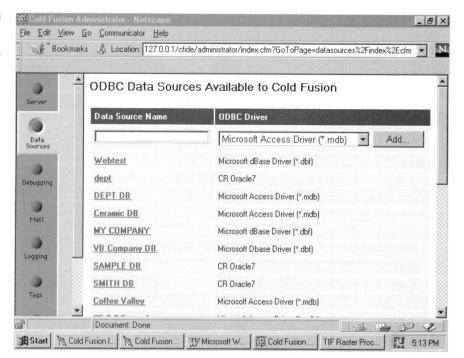

Figure 7-7
The Update CF Data
Source Info panel

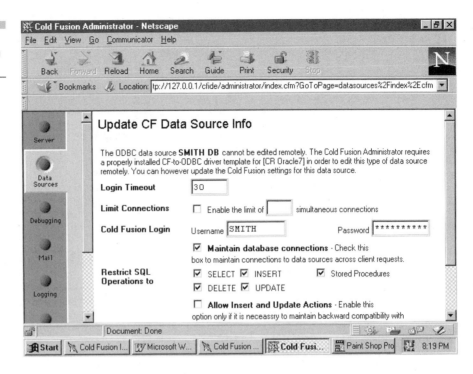

Building a Front-End HTML Document to Connect to the Company Table

Use an HTML form to start up the Cold Fusion engine on the server. Cold Fusion uses tag-based instructions found in a Cold Fusion template to retrieve the Oracle Company table data (in the NewProj project). Cold Fusion opens a path to the table by using the Oracle 7 ODBC Driver (see the following Note) to connect to the Oracle Company table. Then, after Cold Fusion successfully queries the Company table using the SQL found in the Cold Fusion template, a dynamic HTML page is generated back to the end user containing the results of the queried Sample table. Figure 7-8 shows the HTML document used to start up the Cold Fusion template file stored on the server.

NOTE: *It is important to know that the Microsoft or Visigenic Oracle ODBC Driver identifies each Oracle table by the username and password values inputted from the Settings text input box during the Oracle-side of the Oracle 7 ODBC Driver setup. Most popular PC database products do not require this username/password identification, because they are not designed to support*

multiple users. The Oracle 7 ODBC Driver does not automatically assign a default user for Oracle tables; you must name the user and the password.

During Oracle table creation, a table owner is assigned to each table. Therefore, each table always has a username and password associated with it for security purposes, but the Oracle 7 ODBC Driver requires a username and password to connect to a given table. During creation, tables are not given an automatic default user designation of the System Administrator as in many other PC products. The end result is that Cold Fusion will fail to open the table if you have not properly configured the Oracle ODBC Driver with the table username and password during the Oracle 7 ODBC Driver setup.

HTML DOCUMENT USED TO START UP COLD FUSION ON THE SERVER

```
c7_6a.htm
<HTML>
<HEAD>
<TITLE>Oracle "Connect" Test</TITLE>
</HEAD>
<BODY BGCOLOR="#FFFF80">
```

Figure 7-8
HTML document generated from Company table

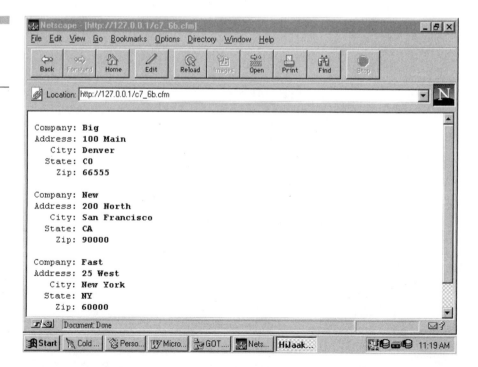

```
<center><font size="+2" color="red"><i>Oracle "Connect"
     Test Form</i></font></font></center>
<HR>
<B>Database "Connect" Test</B>
<FORM ACTION="c7_6a.cfm" METHOD=POST>
<INPUT TYPE= "SUBMIT" VALUE="Please Submit my Request">
</FORM>
</BODY>
</HTML>
```

This code shows the Form tag used to start up Cold Fusion on the server. The Form Action tag passes control to the Cold Fusion template named **c7_6a.cfm**, which resides on the server, and Cold Fusion uses the Oracle 7 ODBC Driver to open and query the selected Oracle table using SQL instructions found in the following CF template. The results from querying the Oracle table are incorporated into a Cold Fusion dynamically generated HTML document, which is sent back to the client's screen. Refer to Figure 7-8 to see the results of querying the Oracle Company table.

COLD FUSION TEMPLATE USED TO QUERY THE COMPANY TABLE

```
<! — c7_6a.cfm TEMPLATE FILE, queries the "Company" Oracle
     Table. —>
<CFQUERY NAME="OracleNewSearch" DATASOURCE="SMITH DB">
  SELECT * FROM COMPANY
</CFQUERY>
<BODY>
<CFOUTPUT QUERY="OracleNewSearch">
#Company# <BR>
</CFOUTPUT>
<HR>
</BODY>
</HTML>
```

This template uses the CFQUERY tag to select the entire contents of the Company file. Each CFQUERY must be given its own name—in this case, **OraclenewSearch**. The SQL statement **Select * from Company** retrieves data from all the columns making up the Company table. The CFOUTPUT tag displays the contents of the Company column to the screen as part of a dynamically generated HTML document displayed on the client's screen. This template file has been limited to a single column to help you in the process of getting your first Oracle table query up-and-running. The next template example includes a more complex CFOUTPUT tag, which is fully formatted. Chapters 15 and 16 will show you how to use the Crystal Reports Report generator to generate highly formatted accounting-style reports.

The CFOUTPUT tag allows you to insert HTML code; for example, a Break tag, <BR>, inside the CFOUTPUT tag. The <BR> tag formats the output of the Company column into three separate lines of output instead of writing all three Company names to the same line. The next example shows how to use the CFOUTPUT tag to display data from several fields.

COLD FUSION TEMPLATE USING SPECIAL FORMATTING

```
<! — c7_6b.cfm TEMPLATE FILE, queries the "Company" Oracle
        Table. —>
<CFQUERY NAME="OracleNewSearch" DATASOURCE="SMITH DB">
  SELECT * FROM COMPANY
</CFQUERY>
<BODY>
<CFOUTPUT QUERY="OracleNewSearch">

<PRE>
Company: <B>#Company#</B>
Address: <B>#addr1#</B>
   City: <B>#city#</B>
  State: <B>#state#</B>
    Zip: <B>#Zip#</B>
</PRE>

</CFOUTPUT>
<HR>
</BODY>
</HTML>
```

This code shows the <PRE> tag used to format individual columns. Using the <PRE> tag eliminates using Break tags, <BR>, at the end of each line. And an empty line is inserted after each record. The use of bold tags, <B>...</B>, helps the data stand out on the page.

CONCLUSION

This chapter introduces important features of Personal Oracle 7, shows how to connect Oracle to the Internet, and develops some output formatting techniques. In Chapters 12 and 13 covering SQL, you will learn additional uses of SQL to retrieve data from several tables simultaneously, how to loop through records using conditional logic, and how to manipulate multiple tables to retrieve specific records.

Introducing Paradox Version 7 for Windows

- Building a Paradox Database
- Creating Primary Keys and writing Referential Integrity Rules
- Storing Objects in Binary Fields
- Connecting a Database to Cold Fusion using the CF Administrator
- Verifying (the connection) between Cold Fusion and a Database
- Using Cold Fusion CFQUERY tags with Paradox Tables

Using Paradox for Windows on the Internet

Paradox version 7 for Windows is a powerful relational database that can be used to create easy-to-use, server-based, database business solutions. Paradox's Experts and Coaches contain helpful cue cards that explain how to set up Paradox databases and tables. In this chapter, you will learn how to create databases, tables and forms, and how to quickly Web-connect Paradox tables to HTML documents by using Cold Fusion. Paradox is a very user-friendly product. Paradox for Windows installs to the **C:\Pdoxwin** directory. After installation, just click the Paradox for Windows icon to begin using Paradox. The screen in Figure 8-1 appears.

When Paradox first opens up, you may choose to use the Coaches or bring up a Windows menu bar containing the following selections: File, View, Project, Properties, Tools, Window, and Help. Highlighting any of the main functions displays its status in the bottom status bar. Below the button bar is the Project Viewer, a control center used for manipulating database objects such as All, Tables, Forms, Queries, SQL, Reports, Scripts, and Libraries. We will look at the central features of Paradox by starting with quickly building some Paradox tables.

Figure 8-1

Paradox for Windows
main panel

To create your first table, click File, click New, and then click Table. The default file type is Paradox 7.0. Click OK to accept it. Paradox displays the Create Paradox for Windows 7.0 Table (Untitled) screen, as shown in Figure 8-2.. Use this screen to define table fields.

NOTE: *When thinking about designing a database, it may be most practical to begin by listing your information needs—paper or electronic reports, data-entry forms, related tables, or other elements before actually building the database and tables. You could use a white board or blank sheets of paper to* sketch *out reports and entry screens. The creators of the Paradox database suggest that as you determine needs, you should make a list of the data fields required to store the required information. Think about common groups of fields, where each of these groupings can be organized into a table. Use individual table names as headers and list all fields that you want to include underneath each table name.*

In this example, a table named **Company** will be created, and the first field will also be called **Company** (this is legal in Paradox). To begin, click the Borrow button to reuse a structure from a sample table. Highlight the

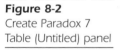

Figure 8-2
Create Paradox 7
Table (Untitled) panel

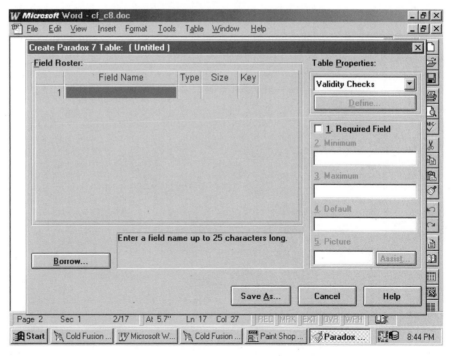

Customer DB table and click OK. Paradox displays a group of fields that can be easily modified to fit the sample table named `Company`. Type over the Name field and name it `Company`. Each field must be named, given a field type, a size, and the field indexed if desired. Use the Tab key or right-arrow key to move over to the next field parameter to be filled in—the Type field. Right-click your mouse to bring up a drop-down list of field types. (Paradox displays options using right mouse clicks.) Select the Alpha field, which will only contain Company names. (The Alpha field type also allows numbers and other ASCII characters.) Tab over and enter `25` in the Size field. Tab to the Key field and click once. You have now indexed the field. An asterisk (`*`) appears in the field, indicating that this field is now indexed.

Indexing creates a separate index file that can be rapidly searched during table lookups. Create the fields shown in the Company table field structure. Add the following data to the Company field after you have created these fields: `Inframail`, `George`, `Smith`, `250 Main`, `Chicago`, `IL`, `70000`, and `gsmith@Inframail.com`. Save your table by clicking Save as and entering a filename—in this example, `company.db`.

RESTRUCTURING TABLES   You may think of additional fields after you have saved the table. To *restructure* the table, click the Restructure icon (the wrench icon). Paradox displays the Field roster panel. To add a field, go to the bottom field definition—in this case, `email`—and press the down-arrow key on the keyboard. Paradox adds a new blank field. Type in a name, and then add the required parameters to the field. To move this or any other field to a different place in the table structure, click the cursor into the leftmost field column, drag and drop the field to a new lo-

Table 8-1

Company table:
fields

Field Name	Type	Size
Company	alpha	25
fname	alpha	10
lname	alpha	15
addr1	alpha	20
city	alpha	20
state	alpha	2
zip	alpha	9
email	alpha	30

cation. You will notice that when you click and hold down the cursor, Paradox displays the field in a light-outlined box. When you see this box you may drag that field up or down in the structure to a new location.

To delete a field, click the Restructure icon, highlight the field to be deleted, and then press the CNT and Del key simultaneously. Paradox asks, **Do you really want to delete the ___ field?** Click OK.

ADDING AND EDITING TABLE DATA   To add data to the table, click View, Edit data, or the Edit data icon. Paradox displays an empty record. To save your edits or new data, click the lower *x* in the top-right corner of the table data-entry/edit panel (not the *x* that opens and closes Paradox).

CREATING PRIMARY KEY   Paradox uses the first field of the table for primary key fields. Creating a primary key gives each record in the table a unique identifier. Paradox automatically assigns sequential numbers (1, 2, 3, and so on) to each record. But you can also use a unique number such as a social security number to uniquely identify records. When an existing primary key field is used as a unique key in a second table, it is known as a foreign key. Foreign keys are used to relate two tables. If you create a Company name field in a Customers table (primary key) and also create a Company name field (the Foreign key) in an Orders table, you will be able to relate the two tables using the common key field.

If you use SQL to query two related tables, data from both of the tables can be easily retrieved. In fact, one of the reasons SQL was created was to make data retrieval from several tables an easier process. In addition, these Primary key fields can be used to enforce Referential Integrity Rules.

REFERENTIAL INTEGRITY RULES   Referential integrity requires that a field value entered in one table (the child table) must match an existing value in corresponding fields of a second table (the parent table). For example, if a Customer table (the parent) is linked to the Orders table (the child), referential integrity rules can be used to ensure that no order in the (child) Orders table exists that does not have a (parent) Customer record associated with it. Using referential integrity ensures that an order record cannot exist alone without a customer record. And in real life, your accounting department will be spared the trouble of having to guess how to match up orphan customer orders with (missing) customer files during the billing cycle.

DEFINING REFERENTIAL INTEGRITY RULES   Use the following steps to define Referential Integrity Rules:

1. Use the Create Paradox table dialogue box to display the table structure.

2. Click the Table properties list box arrow. Paradox displays a drop-down list.

3. Choose Referential integrity. You must already have a primary key defined in your table.

4. Click the Define button. Paradox displays a list of tables. Select a table and then click OK.

The Referential integrity panel has `Cascade` as a default. This means that if data in a field under referential integrity in either the parent or child table is changed, the same field in the other table will be changed bi-directionally. Thus, if the child table field information changes, the parent table field information changes and vice versa. You cannot enforce referential integrity on Binary Large Object (BLOB) fields, auto-increment, logical, or bytes fields. Referential Integrity Rules are maintained in the .VAL file for all tables.

In Paradox, the default is Cascade. With Cascade "on" when you are using referential integrity, the child table will be updated when a value changes in the parent table. For example, when the company name is changed in the parent table, it also changes in the child table. If you don't want Cascade on, you can tell Paradox to *prohibit updates*. This is useful if you have legacy information, which is being used as the standard to which all other information must exactly conform. If you add referential integrity to a full table already containing records, Paradox moves existing child records with no parent record into the temporary *Keyviol* table. You can change the records in Keyviol to comply with the key requirements and then use the Paradox Add utility option to move them back into the appropriate table.

USING VALIDITY CHECKS   Paradox also allows you to define specific ranges of values for data-entry fields. Choose View and then choose Edit to be able to change data properties. Then, in the Table properties list box, click Data. The default condition is Validity checks. If you place a checkmark in the Required fields box, this field can never be left blank. If the field is a currency-type field, you might want to limit the dollar amount that could be entered into the field. For example, the prices that could be entered for hammers might be limited to >\$5.00 < \$60.00.

USING COACHES, EXPERTS, AND ONLINE CONTEXT-SENSITIVE HELP   Paradox Coaches and Experts cover 11 commonly used features such as building tables, forms, reports, and so on. The Online Context-sensitive help can be accessed during any command. Use the Coaches and Experts to work through the examples for building reports and using Paradox SQL, which are not covered in this introduction to Paradox. However, in order to use Reports and SQL over the Internet see Chapter 11 on using SQL with Cold Fusion and Chapter 15 on using the Crystal Reports Report Generator, because Reports created in Paradox and SQL created in Paradox cannot easily be used over the Internet.

STORING SOUND FILES IN BINARY FIELDS   To create a Binary field to store sound files (.WAV extension), click the Restructure icon. Paradox displays the Field roster panel. To add a field, go to the bottom of the field definitions—in this case, **email**—and click the down arrow. Paradox adds a new blank field at the bottom of the form. Enter **Sounds** for the field title, tab over to field Type, and right-click the mouse. Paradox displays a drop-down list. Select *Binary*. Paradox displays a **B** in the field Type. Click the Save button to save new field changes. Binary fields do not have a size parameter, and they cannot be key fields. Paradox doesn't display the contents of Binary fields. Binary fields can be used to store many different field types including sound (.WAV) files used on the WWW.

USING GRAPHICS IN TABLES   The Graphic field type can be used to store images such as GIF or JPG. To create a Graphic type field, click the Restructure icon. To add a field, go to the bottom of the field definitions, and click the down arrow. Paradox adds a blank field. Enter **Images** for the field type, tab over to Field types, open the list box, and click Graphic. Save the changes. A Binary field is shown in Figure 8-3.

To put a GIF or JPG image file into an empty Graphic field, click View, and select Edit data. The Paste from option is activated under the Edit command. Select Edit and then select Paste from. Click the arrow next to the Drive (or Alias) list box, and select a stored GIF image from your hard drive. After you have pasted the GIF image, if you highlight its field, part of the image shows. However, after you paste a GIF image, Paradox converts it to a .BMP file format. If you want to retain the GIF file extension, use the Binary field method shown in the next paragraph.

To put a .WAV file into an empty Binary field, click View, and select Edit data. Then select Edit and Paste from. Click the arrow next to the Drive (or Alias) list box to select a stored GIF image from your hard drive. After you have pasted the GIF image, the Binary field displays **<Binary Value>** (before this procedure, it displays **Binary Blank**). In Binary fields, pictures or sounds can be accessed by using the Paradox ObjectPAL language or an HTML browser.

Figure 8-3

A binary (sound-containing) field

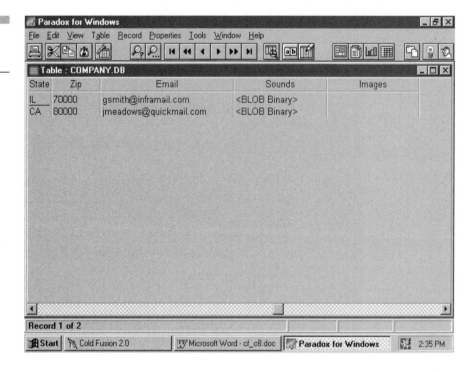

Creating Paradox Forms

Paradox contains a powerful forms generator containing six default form layouts. To use the Form expert for form creation, click the Forms icon, and then right-click to open a popup menu displaying the Form expert. Click the Form expert button (see Figure 8-4).

Select one of the default form layouts (such as #1), and click the Next button to go to the Step 2 of 8 panel. Now select a table to use. Click the Next button. The Step 5 of 8 panel shows the inclusion of all fields. You can also remove a form field. The Step 7 of 8 panel has a default screen output device. Go to the Step 8 panel and select a frame style. The Form New window displays the created form. Paradox asks, **The form you specified is complete. Do you wish to run this form?** Click No. The empty form is shown in Figure 8-5. You may now make design changes to the form.

To make form layout changes, click and drag a field to a different place on the form, and release the mouse to make the move permanent. Use the A tool button to create text to use, click the A button, and then move the cursor to a spot on the form and start typing. After you finish typing, click the text you just created. Paradox creates a dotted line box

Figure 8-4
The New Form
dialog box

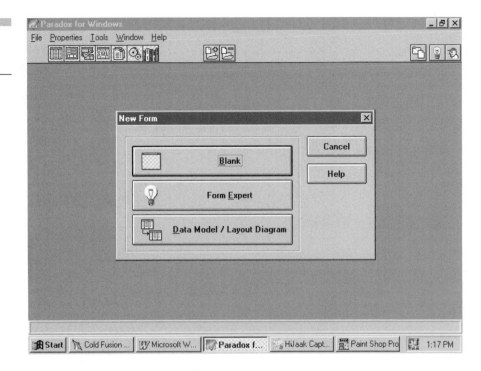

around it. Delete the text box with the Delete key or drag the text box wherever it is needed. Right-click the text box. Paradox displays an option list including Font. Select Font and then select a larger font size; for example, 14.

The design toolbar contains standard drawing tools such as straight lines, circles, ellipses, and rectangles. After you have finished designing, you can *Run* the form by selecting the lightning bolt icon. Paradox displays the underlying table data inside the form.

To save the form, click the Design button. This step activates the grayed-out File save command on the menu bar that is not available when the form is displaying data from the underlying table. Click File and then click Save. Name the form and then click OK.

Retrieving Server-Based Table Data Using an HTML Form

If you want to use a browser to retrieve data from a Paradox database residing on a server, you will need to do several things. First, create a table

Figure 8-5
Form Design
New window

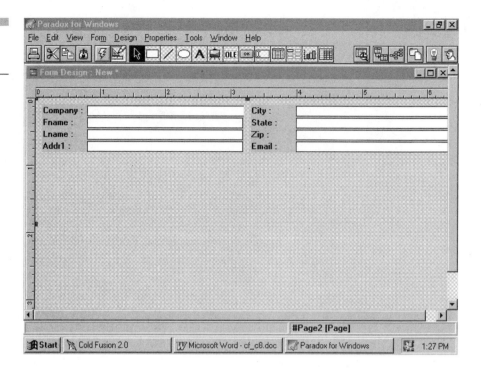

in which to store data. Then, create an HTML fill-in form to collect the data, and send it to the server. When the data arrives at the server, Cold Fusion processes the HTML Form data, then uses a Cold Fusion template to open and retrieve the Paradox table data, and then generates a dynamic HTML document back to the end user. To do this, Cold Fusion uses a Paradox ODBC Driver to connect to the database.

Installing a Paradox ODBC Driver

Cold Fusion contains various Paradox ODBC Drivers, representing the various versions of Paradox, which are used to connect Paradox tables to Cold Fusion. To install the ODBC Driver, click the Cold Fusion icon (displayed by clicking Start) and select the Cold Fusion Administrator as shown in Figure 8-6.

Click the CF Administrator in the Windows 95 Start menu. Enter your password. Cold Fusion displays the Server panel. Select the Data Sources panel. Click the Spin button and highlight the Microsoft Paradox Driver. Click the Add button. Cold Fusion displays the Create ODBC data source panel. Select the database version of your program. Click the top Browse button.

Figure 8-6
ODBC Data Sources
Available to Cold
Fusion "Add a Data
Source panel" popup
window.

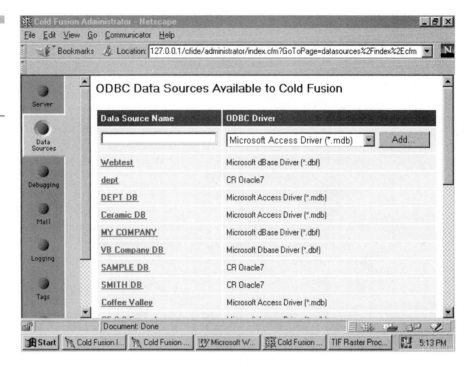

Creating the Cold Fusion Data Source

CF starts up a Java Applet and displays your top drive directory. In Windows 95, double-click the C root directory and the drive directory where you have installed Paradox. Select a Paradox subdirectory containing databases, and select one that interests you; for example, the company.db Paradox database file. Click OK. CF redisplays the Create ODBC data source page.

Type in the Data source name **My Company DB**. (Notice that Cold Fusion has filled in some path information to your database table.) Then click the Create button at the bottom of the screen. CF takes you back to the opening Data source page, and lists your Data source (**My Company DB**) with the other hypertext Data source links. At the bottom of the page the **Verify ODBC Data source** text has a Spin button. Now you need to verify your ODBC Driver connection.

VERIFYING THE PARADOX ODBC DRIVER CONNECTION To test or *verify* the new Paradox ODBC Driver connection to Paradox DB, click the Verify button. If you have done everything correctly, Cold Fusion will verify the ODBC database connection by giving you the following message: **The connection to the data source was verified successfully.** Then click the Go back button to return to the Add data source panel. You may now exit from this panel or close the System administrator. (The ODBC Driver manager was used to connect the Paradox ODBC Driver 5.X with the selected Paradox database.) The next step is to create an HTML form to collect data from the end user.

NOTE: **Some Common ODBC Driver Error Messages:** *If you do not correctly connect the database to the Paradox ODBC Driver, when you later attempt to use the Cold Fusion template, an error message will be displayed such as* **Driver not capable** *or* **ODBC Driver not found.** *The best way to avoid these messages is to verify the ODBC Driver connection before creating the HTML fill-in form.*

Building an HTML Document Containing a Form

The HTML document file is built with a Form tag. The form header contains a URL specifying the address of a Cold Fusion template. (The URL and Form data is sent by the browser to the remote server. The Form data template URL starts up Cold Fusion on the server. Cold Fusion uses Cold Fusion Markup Language (CFML) tags and SQL instructions in the template to query the Paradox table and then dynamically generate an HTML document back to the end user containing the database query results. The following HTML document shows how to build the HTML Document form tag. Use the Form method, = POST; Cold Fusion only supports the POST method.

FRONT-END HTML DOCUMENT FORM

```
<HTML>
<TITLE>Paradox Table Retrieval Test </TITLE>
</Center> <B>Paradox Data Retrieval Test </B></Center>
<HR>
<FORM ACTION="ch8_1.cfm" METHOD=POST>
<INPUT TYPE= "SUBMIT" VALUE="Submit a Data Request ">
</FORM>
<HR>
</HTML>
```

Figure 8-7

Paradox for Windows
Connect Test
(contains form)

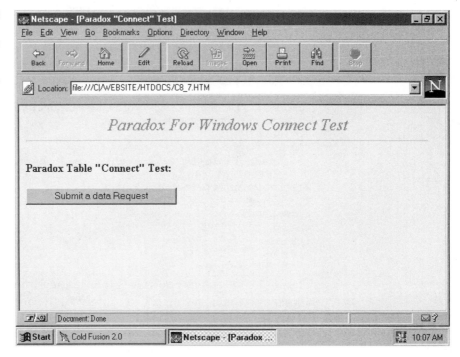

The Front-End HTML document in Figure 8-7 contains instructions inside the Form tag. These instructions start up the CF template on the server.

CREATING COLD FUSION TEMPLATES Cold Fusion templates contain SQL, HTML tags, and Cold Fusion CFML tags used to generate dynamic HTML documents back to the end user. The following c8_1.cfm template contains a CFQUERY tag, which specifies the correct data source and selects the Company table data by using the following SQL: **SELECT * FROM COMPANY**. The CFOUTPUT tag uses the CFQUERY results to generate information back to the end user's screen.

The hashmarks around field names (such as **#Company#**) cause Cold Fusion to display the contents of the Company field to the end user's screen. The Break tag, **
, after the **#Company# field causes each table record to be displayed on a separate line. To avoid ODBC Driver Manager error messages, make sure that the Paradox ODBC path is set to the correct database directory as well as subdirectory. If you receive the error message, **Collating error messages**, you may have set an incorrect directory path to a table. The correct pathname is listed on the Paradox Opening explorer main panel. The following listing shows how to build a CF Template containing a CFQUERY Tag used to retrieve data from a Paradox Table.

LISTING: COLD FUSION TEMPLATE WITH CFQUERY TAG

```
<! — c8_1.cfm TEMPLATE FILE, retrieves data from "Company"
      Table. —>
<CFQUERY NAME="ParadoxSearch" DATASOURCE="Paradox DB">
   SELECT * FROM COMPANY
</CFQUERY>
<BODY>
<! — Each field to be outputted must be specified in the
      CFOUTPUT tag — >
<CFOUTPUT QUERY="ParadoxSearch">
#Company# <BR>
</CFOUTPUT>
<HR>
</BODY>
</HTML>
```

The c8_1.cfm template retrieves information from the Company table and produces the following HTML output to the end user's screen.

```
<— Results from Cold Fusion Template Database Query -
      Fastlake Computer
      Questmaker Co.
      Omnibus Systems
```

To nicely format output from several queried fields , the CFOUTPUT QUERY tag can be used to format and display multiple Company table fields by adding a **<PRE>…</PRE>** tag. Each field must be specified to use the **<PRE>** tag correctly. The following CF Template Code Fragment shows how to include a **<PRE>** Tag inside a **<CFOUTPUT QUERY>** Tag.

<PRE> TAG EXAMPLE

```
<CFOUTPUT QUERY="ParadoxSearch">
<PRE>
<B>Company    </B>: #Company#
<B>First Name</B>: #fname#
<B>Last Name </B>: #lname#
<B>E-mail         </B>: #email#
</PRE>
</CFOUTPUT>
```

NOTE: *You may need to have formatted reports with displayed pictures from the database. You should use the Crystal Report Report Writer to create highly formatted GAAP-style reports or other complex report formats. How to use The Crystal Report Writer is covered in Chapters 15 and 16.*

INSERTING HTML FORMS DATA INTO TABLES   After collecting data from HTML forms, use the CFINSERT tag to insert this data into the Paradox table residing on a remote server. The Paradox database must be identified to Cold Fusion. If you have not installed the Paradox ODBC Driver, refer to the previous section called "Installing a Paradox ODBC Driver." Then, create the HTML fill-in form document and the Cold Fusion Insert template, and then place both of them together in the Web server's document subdirectory. Test the HTML form connection to the database by using the URL local address (127.0.0.1) of your Web server to do a loopback test; for example, the complete URL is: (http://127.0.0.1//mydoc.html). For this test to be successful, put both the HTML document containing the form and the Cold Fusion template in the Web server's document directory. This directory is located where Cold Fusion installed its sample HTML document files. Now put the files to be tested in the same place. (You can create your own "HTML document and CFML template directory" and build a path to that directory after you become more experienced with using Cold Fusion. The method described above is recommended because it simplifies the process for the new Cold Fusion user.)

Figure 8-8
Formatted company table output

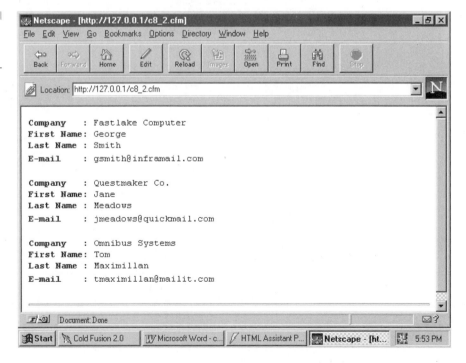

NOTE: *The Cold Fusion CFINSERT tag inserts Form field data into table fields. Paradox, however, uses the first field of a table as a counter data field. The first HTML form field from which you are collecting data is not a Counter data type field. Counter data type fields are used to store consecutive numbers beginning with the numbers 1,2,3 and so on, in order to uniquely identify each record. If you use the CFINSERT tag, you will have problems inserting fill-in form data into the database if Cold Fusion tries to insert literal values from the first Form field into the Counter data type field. It is better to use the CF-QUERY tag to insert fill-in Form data into tables to avoid this problem.*

Building the CFQUERY Tag

When building the CFQUERY tag, use the Cold Fusion DATASOURCE name for your database. The DATASOURCE name is created by using the Cold Fusion Administrator panel, as shown in a previous section, "Creating the Cold Fusion Data Source." The CFQUERY Tag is made up several parts: the Data source and the INSERT INTO parameter. Here is the general form of the CFQUERY tag:

```
<CFQUERY DATASOURCE="the datasource name">
     INSERT INTO tablename (column names)
     VALUES (values)
</CFQUERY>
```

Programming Tip: The CFQUERY INSERT INTO tag does not use the "Name= "tablename" parameter. If you try to name the CFQUERY, it will not work. Also, by using this tag, Counter type fields are legal in your table. The CFQUERY tag inserts the fields that you specify into your table. A front-end HTML document containing a fill-in form to collect data is shown in Figure 8-9.

The following template listing shows how to use a CFQUERY tag. The remaining template code is used to send a message back to the end user. This template contains a CFQUERY tag, which inserts data into the Company table.

TEMPLATE USING A CFQUERY TAG

```
< — c8_3.cfm template uses the "Company" table — >
<CFQUERY DATASOURCE="Paradox DB">
     INSERT INTO Company (Company, Fname, Lname, Addr1,
          City, State, Zip, Email)
     VALUES ('#Form.Company#','#Form.Fname#',
          '#Form.Lname#', '#Form.Addr1#',
```

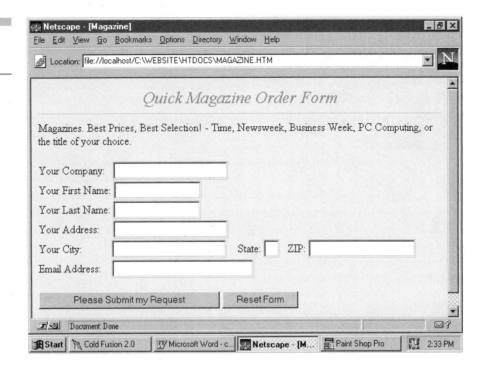

Figure 8-9
HTML Fill-in form
for CFQUERY

```
                    '#Form.City#', '#Form.State#',
                    '#Form.Zip#', '#Form.Email#')
</CFQUERY>
<HTML>
<HEAD>
<TITLE>Magazine Subscriptions Department</TITLE>
</HEAD>
<BODY>
<CENTER><H2>Thank you for your magazine order!</H2><CENTER>
<HR>
</BODY>
</HTML>
```

The Data source is named using the CF administrator. The phrase **INSERT INTO Customers** requires the use of the table name **Company**. Each Form field inserted must be named inside the parentheses; for example, **Company, Fname, Lname,** and so on. The VALUES parameter indicates that inserted fields are from an HTML fill-in form, and that literal values from the fill-in form will be entered into the respective table fields.

Also found in the VALUES statement are single quotes '…' used around each Form field name. Single quotes are necessary for all literal strings of alphanumeric characters. The hashmarks (found inside the single quotes) substitute the literal values collected from the Form fields into the Company table's fields. When building the CFQUERY tag, notice the position of the closing greater than character (>). Without proper placement of this tag, you do not have a working CFQUERY tag.

CONCLUSION

This introduction to the Paradox Database software shows how to create Paradox tables, how to build an HTML document to connect to a Paradox database mounted on a webserver, and how to use the CFQUERY Tag to retrieve data from Paradox tables. Later chapters on SQL show additional ways to use SQL to retrieve table data.

Introducing Microsoft's Visual FoxPro

- Building a Microsoft Visual FoxPro database
- Using the Tools Options Panel
- Creating FoxPro Programs
- Using the CF Administrator
- Verifying Cold Fusion database connections
- Using HTML Fill-in Forms with FoxPro Tables
- Building Cold Fusion Templates to query FoxPro tables

Overview

The Microsoft Visual FoxPro database uses the Rushmore technology to speed up data operations. It is a high-powered, object-oriented, hierarchical database, which is used, for example, by developers who are creating user-friendly, vertical market applications and by PC database *owners* to manage desktop databases.

OPENING VISUAL FOXPRO   To begin, double-click the Visual FoxPro icon. FoxPro opens and creates a Project (an organization area for files, data, documents, and objects) called *Proj1*. You will see the opening screen shown in Figure 9-1.

   Navigation Tip: Click any icon with a plus symbol to display its *hidden* icons.

NOTE: *When you open the Project Manager, FoxPro creates* **Proj1** *for you, but you must create a database with tables. Creating a database is not hard; a couple of mouseclicks is all that is needed to start building individual tables. Using the Table Wizard is also very easy to do. However, after you have created a*

Figure 9-1
Project Manager
opening screen

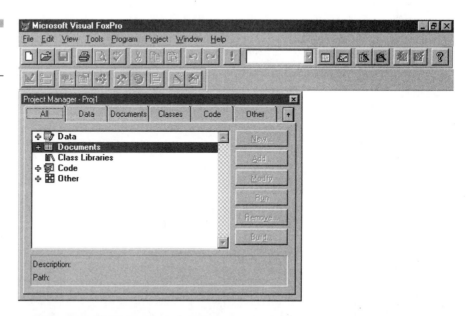

database, use the right mouse button to start up the Table Wizard. You can do each of these operations separately at different times. You can create and save a database, close FoxPro, reopen at another time, then create a Free *table, add the Free table to the database, and so on. This chapter will show you how to create the database and tables at the same time.*

CREATING A DATABASE WITH TABLES In the Project Manager, click the Data icon, click Databases, and then click New. Visual FoxPro displays the Create panel shown in Figure 9-2.

Click Save (unless you want to use the Enter text box to enter a different name, other than data1.dbc, for the database). The Database Designer—Data 1 panel appears. Click the right mouse button to start up the Table Expert. A pop-up menu is displayed. Select New Table, and then select the Table Wizard button. You are now creating a table, as an integral part of a database, inside a Project. Because you are creating the table as part of a database (rather than a *free table*), it is automatically part of the database. And because the table is part of a database, the task of relating one table to a second table is easier.

Figure 9-2
Database Create
panel: data1.dbc

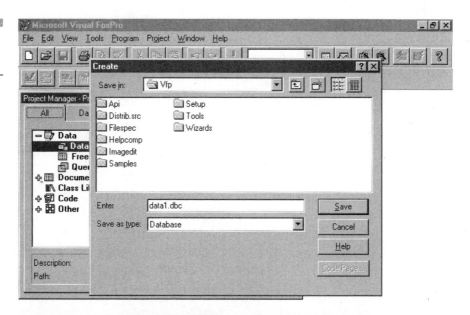

Using the Table Wizard

To create your first table, click the Data icon, click the Free Table icon, click New (no longer shaded), and then click the Table Wizard button. FoxPro displays the Table Wizard: Step 1—Field Selection shown in Figure 9-3.

In the first column titled *Sample Tables*, use the spin arrow to display the Customers table. Click Customers. Now the middle column displays a new group of fields. To move these fields into your table, click the double chevrons next to the Selected Fields column. The fields move to the Selected Fields column. Click Next, and the Table Wizard displays the Step 2—Field Settings panel.

DEFINING FIELDS In the Field Settings panel, the CustomerId field is highlighted and the default field type is Character. Character fields can contain alphanumerics, spaces, symbols, and punctuation. No computation can be done against a character field. Use the spin arrow to change the field width to 10. Leave the Null field Check Box blank. The CustomerId field will be a mandatory data-entry field, and so will never be

Figure 9-3
Table Wizard: Step 1
—Field Selection

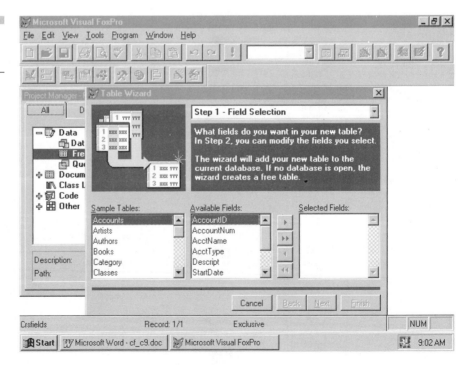

null (unknown contents). In the case of records from a table containing Null fields being copied into another table not having Null fields, the Null values (unknown) are interpreted as either blank, empty, or zero values in the second table, not as Null fields. This interpretation could give you unexpected results during SQL queries. Null fields are useful if you want to highlight the condition that a given field contains values that are unknown—that is, not equal to zero or blank, but is just unknown. Perhaps you expect in the future to enter real values into a null field and you don't want it evaluated to blank or zero (for example, a company name field or a quantity field).

If you need to do math against a field, choose the numeric field type; numeric fields can store numbers, decimals, and optionally a sign. Now click the Next button. Figure 9-4 shows a FoxPro table populated with several rows of data.

SELECTING A PRIMARY INDEX KEY   In the Table Wizard, the Step 3—Indexing panel allows you to select a Primary Index Key. Use the spin arrow to select the ContactID field. Click Next, and then save the file as the **data1.dbf table**. Index keys are used to speed up database searches —FoxPro creates a separate Index file, which can be much more quickly

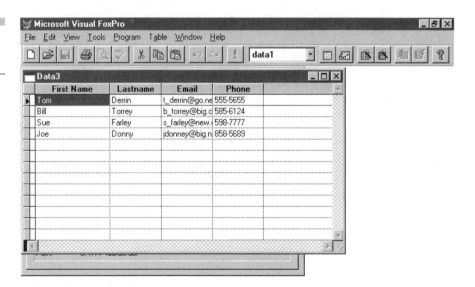

Figure 9-4
Entering data
into fields

sorted or searched than the corresponding data file with its multiple fields. Also, the Primary Index Key only displays the first instance of any duplicate record. Duplicate records can be marked for deletion and then deleted, but they will never be viewed or processed if the table contains a Primary Index Key. Thus, if a Customer transaction record table has duplicate entries, only one bill for any given transaction will ever be sent to a customer, even if the transaction has been accidentally entered twice and exists as a duplicate in the table.

Thus, for unique record identification, use a Primary Index Key for each record. If you only want to display unique records, click Tools, click Options, select the Data tab, and then put a check in the *Unique Records in Indexes* box. If the Index is unique, any records that are pointed to by the index will also be unique.

If a second table in the same database is created, which also contains a ContactID Index Key field as a Primary Index Key (now called a Foreign key from the perspective of the first table), the two tables can be related through the common ContactID field. Related tables can be given Referential Integrity Rules that govern both tables. A later section shows how to develop Referential Integrity.

USING THE TOOLS OPTIONS PANEL   The Options panel contains global database settings. This panel consists of 10 different tabs. In this chapter, although some of the more important tabs are described, you should tour through all 10 tabs in the Options panel to see what these tabs contain. For example, open the International tab and you have the option of setting Date and Time display formats, currency formats, and numbers of decimal places to be displayed. The Data tab allows you to select Ignore Deleted Records. (Deleted records are records marked for deletion but not yet erased from the database.) Also, you can click SET NEAR, which allows searches to find records that are close to the spelling of the desired field data but not spelled exactly like the search string. Thus, if *Smith* is accidentally data-entered in a last name field as *Smth*, it will still be retrieved by a search that has SET NEAR checked. The View tab controls the clock, status bar, and program opening defaults.

ADDING NEW FIELDS   If you highlight an existing table icon in the Program Manager and click Modify, FoxPro displays the table field structure, as shown in Figure 9-5. To insert a new field into the table structure, highlight the field and click the Insert button. FoxPro inserts a new field—a Character type with a default value of 10 characters immediately above the highlighted field. The Delete button removes fields.

Figure 9-5
Modifying the table
structure

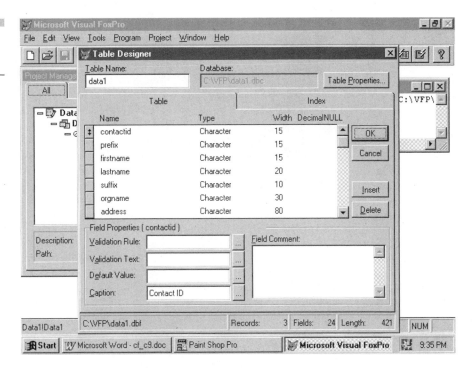

ADDING VALIDATION RULES Click the Validation Rule Button. FoxPro displays the Expression Builder. The Expression Builder has four categories of functions that can be used to specify which data values will be accepted into each field. These categories are: String, Math, Logical, and Date. Each category contains possible values, and after an expression is built, you can test its logical consistency and correctness by using Verify. Also, any field can have a comment attached by using the lower-right Field Comment text box. Figure 9-6 shows the Expression Builder Options panel.

STORING IMAGE FILES IN GENERAL FIELDS FoxPro allows you to store GIF or JPG images, sound files, and other binaries in General fields. By using Object Linking and Embedding (OLE), it is possible to store images in General fields. Cold Fusion does not support the object linking feature of OLE, but it does support embedding features, thus you can embed files in General Fields, which can later be retrieved and displayed. To place an object into a General field, use the Windows clipboard to help you paste a GIF into the General-Type field, as shown in Figure 9-7.

Adding a GIF image requires that you locate a GIF on your hard drive you can open and copy. You will use the Windows clipboard as an inter-

Figure 9-6
The Expression
Builder Options
panel

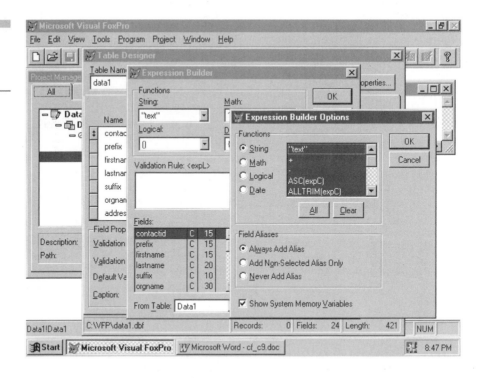

Figure 9-7
Adding GIF images
to a General-Type
field

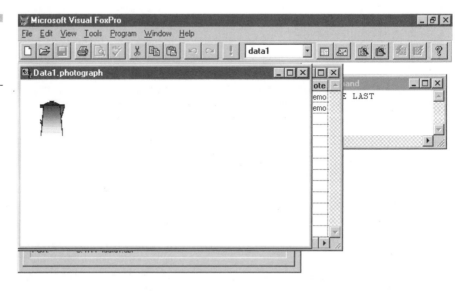

mediate holding area for the GIF image. First, open a GIF file using Paint Shop Pro, LVIEW PRO, or any Windows program that opens and displays GIF files. Then use the Edit and Cut command of that program to copy the GIF image to the clipboard. Next, open the FoxPro table that contains the General-Type field (in this case, `data1.dbf`—the General-Type field called *Photograph*), and then click the Browse button. The various fields of the table appear.

Now, in FoxPro, click View and then click Append mode. Highlight and open the General-Type field. Select Edit and then Paste Special to paste the GIF image into the field. The field appears as shown in Figure 9-7. Click x in the top-right corner to permanently save the GIF file in the General-Type field. You can use the Browse command to view the embedded GIF file in the General-Type field. You can use Crystal Reports Report Writer (see Chapter 15 and 16) to retrieve and display embedded files over the Internet.

RELATING TABLES BY USING PRIMARY INDEX KEYS   Use the Table Wizard to build a second table called Contact.dbf. When you open the Step 1—Field Selection panel, select the ContactId field and transfer it into the new table. Also, create an Orderid field and place it in the new table. In the next panel, which asks if you would like to index any fields, make the ContactID field a Primary Index Key field. Name this table Contact.dbf. Now both the Data1.dbf table and the `contact.dbf` field have a Primary Index Key called ContactID. The ContactID field will be used to relate these tables to each other.

Open the Database Designer by highlighting the Data1 (database) icon. Click the Modify button. FoxPro displays both tables, which make up the Data1 database shown in Figure 9-8. Notice that both ContactID fields are listed under an Indexes icon. In the next step, these two tables will be related using these ContactID fields (see Figure 9-8).

To relate the two tables, highlight the ContactID field in the Contact.dbf table and drag the field on top of the data.dbf ContactID field. FoxPro relates the two tables and draws a line between the two tables, as shown in Figure 9-9.

CREATING REFERENTIAL INTEGRITY BETWEEN TABLES   From the menu bar, click Database and then select Referential Integrity. FoxPro displays the Referential Integrity Builder panel and asks `Which rule do you want to apply when the key value in the Parent Table is modified?` The default is `ignore`, so choose `Cascade: Update all records in the Child Table with the new key value`. If the ContactID number

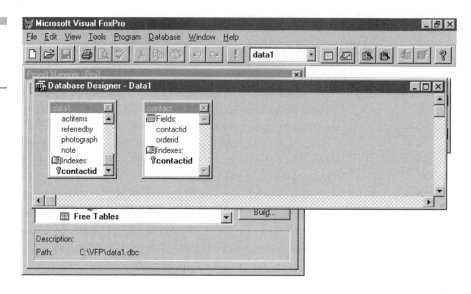

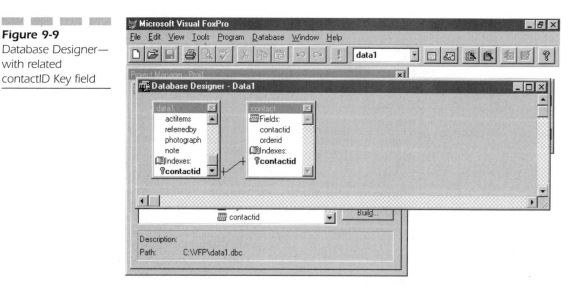

is changed in the parent table, it will be updated simultaneously in the child table. Notice that when you click the Cascade Radio button, the Update text box changed to Cascade. If you wanted to change the Delete text box to Cascade, click in that box and it turns into a list box that displays the word `Cascade`, which can then be selected. The same is true for the Delete list box.

When you are finished making Referential Rule changes, click OK. FoxPro asks, `Create the referential code now?` Reply `Yes` to generate the Referential Integrity. To delete a persistent relationship, open the Database Designer, display the two tables, click the line between the tables, and press the Delete key. Close the Database Designer by clicking the *x* in the top-right panel corner.

USING THE COMMAND WINDOW   If you want to test individual commands, write them in the Command window, which is displayed when FoxPro is opened. An example of an individual command would be *Use data1*. Type this command in the Command window exactly as shown, `Use data1`, and then press Enter. The status bar shows that the Data1 table is open by displaying the following at the bottom of the page: `Data1!Data1 Record 1/1 Exclusive`. If you now type in `browse fields First Name, Last Name, Work Phone, Email Name,` and press Enter, only those table fields are displayed in the Data1 panel. To close the table, type `Use`. All this and much more can be done from the command window.

CREATING FOXPRO PROGRAMS   But what if you get tired of having to type out commands such as `browse fields Firstname, Last Name, Work Phone, Email Name?` Or what if you forget one of the field names, or want to display even more field names? You will have to write longer and longer commands in the command window. An elegant solution to this problem is to write a small program that opens the Data1 table and displays the desired browse fields. Then whenever you want to run the program, click on the main menu, click Program, click Do from the popdown menu which appears, and then select the program you want to run.

Therefore, let's take a look at how to create a *browse fields* program. First, from the File menu, choose New. Select Program, and then click New File. FoxPro opens a new window called *Program1*. It is wise to put information on the first line of the file, stating the name of the program, the author, and the date of creation. If the program becomes complex, further comments can be added. Type in the comment line at the top (comments begin with at least one asterisk—I use several for style only). Then

Figure 9-10
Creating your first
FoxPro program

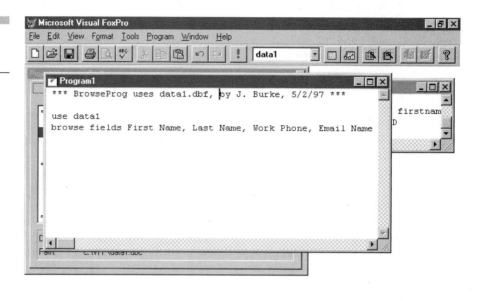

type in the other commands (use data1, browse fields First Name...) as shown in Figure 9-10.

The Program1 window responds to many of the same commands used in any word processor; for example, you can highlight and delete text, use the copy command, and so on. When you have finished entering the commands, click File, and then click Save. FoxPro names the file **prog1.prg**. You can type over the name **BrowsProg.prg**, and then click OK. To close the Program1 window, click *x* in the top-right corner.

DEBUGGING FOXPRO PROGRAMS   To run your new program, click Program, click Do, select Prog1.prg, and then click OK. Now, if you have gone this far, you will see FoxPro display an error. Inside the program, the *browse fields* command that worked so well in the command window must be slightly modified to work inside the program. Remove the space between the two parts of each of the field names (for example, make *first name* into *firstname*, and so on), and then click File, Save As (save as **prog1.prg** again). Again, click Program, click Do, select Prog1.prg, and then click OK. Now the program works. You have just debugged your first

FoxPro program. Programs run nicely, but when several commands are used in a given program, debugging is the rule rather than the exception. Fortunately, FoxPro ships with a number of Sample programs, which you can examine and *clone* commands that work correctly into your own programs. And most of the time, commands that work in the command window will work inside a program with little or no modification. (If that doesn't work, send an e-mail to request a solution to the FoxPro Web site on the Internet.)

ADDING FOXPRO PROGRAMS TO YOUR DATABASE Open the Project Manager, click the Code icon, click the Programs icon, click Add, and then click OK. FoxPro adds your program as a bulleted list item below the Programs icon in the Project Manager. Now you can double-click the Prog1 program to open it in the Program1 window. Remember to save your changes by clicking File, Save As, and then OK. Also, notice that you can now run Prog1 by clicking on Run in the Project Manager and selecting your program from the file list.

Obviously, programs can contain many commands, each of which does different functions such as opening data-entry forms, selecting fields for display in tables, or automatically printing out a report, just to name a few possibilities. And you can learn how to build these types of programs that can accomplish so much. When you do, you'll be on your way to creating a set of programs that can manage a complete database application.

The next sections show how to use HTML fill-in forms to retrieve data from server-based FoxPro tables by using Cold Fusion Professional 3. The first task is to install a FoxPro ODBC Driver.

Using FoxPro ODBC Drivers

To install the ODBC Driver, click the Cold Fusion icon (displayed by clicking Start) and select the Cold Fusion Administrator. Then select the Data Sources tab. Figure 9-11 shows the ODBC Data Sources Available to Cold Fusion Window used to verify a Data Source.

Cold Fusion displays the Data Sources panel. Click the Spin button, and then highlight the Microsoft FoxPro Driver that matches your version of FoxPro. In Cold Fusion 3.0, there is a new Visual FoxPro Driver that may not recognize older version FoxPro files. You may have to remake your database files using the latest version of FoxPro to be able to use this

Figure 9-11
The ODBC Data
Sources Available to
Cold Fusion window

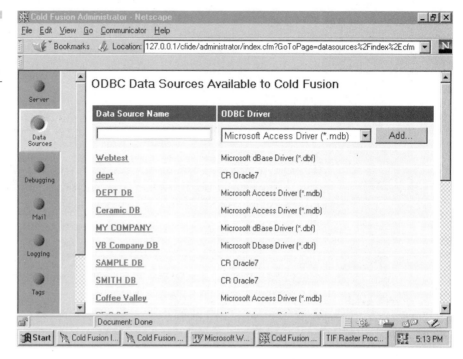

driver. (No Microsoft backward version compatibility.) Click the Add button. Cold Fusion displays the Create ODBC Data Source panel. Click the top Browse button. CF starts up a Java Applet and displays your top drive directory. In Windows 95, double-click the C root directory and the drive directory where you have installed FoxPro. Select a FoxPro subdirectory containing databases, and then select the one corresponding to the database you have created. Click OK. CF redisplays the Create ODBC Data Source page.

Type in the Data Source Name **FoxPro DB** (notice that Cold Fusion has filled in path information to your database table), and then click the Create button at the bottom of the screen. CF takes you back to the opening Data Source page, and lists your data source (FoxPro DB) with the other hypertext Data Source links. At the bottom of the page, the Verify ODBC Data Source text has a Spin button.

Click the Spin button, highlight *FoxPro DB,* and then click the Verify Button. If you have done everything correctly, Cold Fusion will verify the ODBC database connection by giving you the following message: **The connection to the data source was verified successfully**. Then click the Go Back button to return to the Add Data Source panel. You may now exit from this panel or close the System Administrator. You have now connected the database to the FoxPro ODBC Driver. When the HTML form sends a URL to the server, Cold Fusion will be able to *find* the table and retrieve data.

Using HTML Fill-in Forms to Connect to FoxPro Tables

HOW TO BUILD A FRONT-END HTML DOCUMENT An HTML document containing a form is used to start up the Cold Fusion Engine on the server. Cold Fusion uses tag-based instructions contained in a Cold Fusion template to retrieve the FoxPro Data1 table data. Cold Fusion opens a path to the table by using the Visual FoxPro ODBC Driver to connect to the FoxPro Customers table. Then, after Cold Fusion successfully queries the database table using SQL in the Cold Fusion template, a dynamic HTML page is generated back to the end user containing the results of the queried Sample table. The following code shows the HTML document used to start up the Cold Fusion template file on the server.

The bolded code shows the Form tag used to start up Cold Fusion on the server. The Form Action passes control to the Cold Fusion template named *c9_1.cfm*, which resides on the server, and Cold Fusion uses the FoxPro ODBC Driver to open and query the selected FoxPro table using

HTML Document which Start Up Cold Fusion on the Server

```
<HTML>
<! C9-1.html document uses C9_1.cfm ->
<HEAD>
<TITLE>FoxPro "Connect" Test</TITLE>
</HEAD>
<BODY BGCOLOR="#FFFF80">
<center><font size="+2" color="red"><i>FoxPro "Connect"
     Test Form</i></font></font></center>
<HR>
<B>Database "Connect" Test</B>
<FORM ACTION="c9_1.cfm" METHOD=POST>
<INPUT TYPE= "SUBMIT" VALUE="Please Submit my Request">
</FORM>
</BODY>
</HTML>
```

SQL instructions found in the CF template. The results from querying the FoxPro table are incorporated into a Cold Fusion dynamically generated HTML document sent back to the end user's screen. The following code listing shows the CF template used to query the FoxPro Data5 table.

This template uses the CFQUERY tag to select the entire contents of the Data5 table. Each CFQUERY must be given its own Data Source name using the Cold Fusion Administrator—in this case, FoxProSearch.

The SQL statement `Select * from Data5` retrieves data from the Data5 columns. The CFOUTPUT QUERY tag displays the contents of the Company column to the screen as part of a dynamically generated HTML document displayed to the users screen. This template file has been limited to a few table columns to help you get your first FoxPro Table Query up-and-running. A later chapter shows you how to use the CRYSTAL REPORTS Report Generator to generate highly formatted GAAP accounting-style reports. Figure 9-12 shows table data output from using the CFQUERY tag.

The CFOUTPUT tag allows you to insert various HTML tags, for example, an unordered list <UL> tag, inside of the CFOUTPUT tag to help format the output. The <BR> tag formats the output of the Company column into three separate lines of output instead of writing all three Company names to the same line. The next example shows how to use the CFOUTPUT tag to display data from several fields.

The code shows the <PRE> tag used to format individual columns. Using the <PRE> tag eliminates using Break tags, <BR>, at the end of each line. Also, an empty line is inserted after each record. The use

Cold Fusion Template used to query the "Company" Table

```
<! — c9_1.cfm TEMPLATE FILE, queries the "Data1.db" FoxPro
       Table. —>
<CFQUERY NAME="FoxProSearch" DATASOURCE="FoxPro DB">
  SELECT * FROM data5
</CFQUERY>
<BODY>
<UL>
<CFOUTPUT QUERY="FoxProSearch">
#firstname# #lastname# #workphone# #emailname# <BR>
</CFOUTPUT>
</UL>
<HR>
</BODY>
</HTML>
```

Figure 9-12
CFQUERY output
from Data5 table

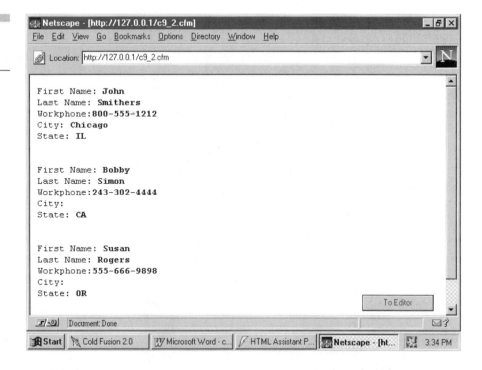

Cold Fusion Template
Listing with Special
Formatting

```
<! - c9_2.cfm TEMPLATE FILE, queries the "data1" Visual
     FoxPro Table. ->
<CFQUERY NAME="FoxSearch2" DATASOURCE="FoxPro DB">
  SELECT * FROM DATA5
</CFQUERY>
<BODY>
<CFOUTPUT QUERY="FoxSearch2">
<PRE>
First Name: <B>#firstname#</B>
Last Name: <B>#lastname#</B>
Workphone:<B>#workphone#</B>
City: <B>#city#</B>
State: <B>#state#</B>
  </PRE>
</CFOUTPUT>
<HR>
</BODY>
</HTML>
```

of tags, <B>...</B>, helps make the raw data stand out on the page.
Figure 9-13 shows the HTML document generated by running the CF
template.

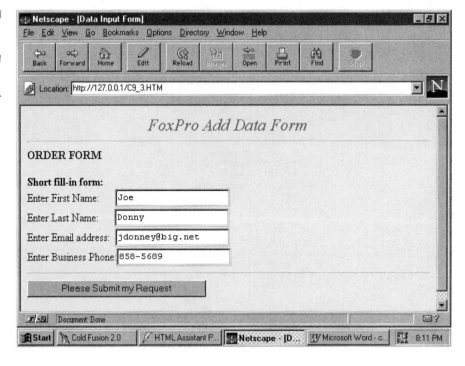

10

Using Cold Fusion with Microsoft SQL Server

- Creating an SQL database for Microsoft SQL Server
- Using Microsoft's SQL Server Database

This chapter will introduce you to Microsoft's SQL Server, show you how to use Cold Fusion to create an SQL Server database, and show you how to use Cold Fusion to access that database. But before we start, we need to be sure that you understand SQL—at least enough to understand what the SQL world is all about.

Becoming an SQL Pro in One Easy Lesson

Welcome to *An Introduction to SQL*. I hope that everyone is in the right class. I'll get started by taking a few questions. Okay, who wants to be first?

Q. What does SQL stand for?

A. SQL is shorthand for Structured Query Language.

Q. I've seen SQL in print, but I've never talked about it. Just how does one pronounce SQL?

A. Microsoft folks pronounce it *sequel*. Tradition-minded old-timers may just say the letters, *S–Q–L*. Some rebels pronounce it *squeal*.

Q. Just why do I need to know SQL?

A. SQL is by far the most popular language for database access. All major manufacturers of server-based databases support it. SQL has also become the language of choice for database access over the World Wide Web. If you use databases, you use SQL.

Q. Where can I get more in-depth information on SQL?

A. Chapters 12 and 13 of this book will cover SQL in much greater depth. If you want more than that, you can refer to the many books written about nothing but SQL.

Q. I'm a C++ programmer. Will my C++ knowledge help me with SQL?

A. Not much. But your knowledge of English will help a great deal. SQL is similar to the English language. SQL statements resemble COBOL more closely than any other programming language.

Q. Are you going to go into the theory of SQL in depth?

A. Please see me after class.

Well, maybe SQL isn't quite that simple, but you have to know very little to do some heavy duty work with SQL. If you didn't know anything about SQL when you started this book, by the time you finish, you should feel quite at home with SQL. But this chapter is about Microsoft SQL Server. So let's get started with that. First, let's look at just what makes up a database in Microsoft SQL Server.

Parts of an SQL Server Database

A SQL Server database contains more than just your data. It contains a definition of what each item of data should look like and how it should be presented (text, integer, and so on), and it contains who is allowed to access and change the database. Group/user management is done in SQL Server through the Enterprise Manager, the specifics of which will not be covered in this book. The part of a SQL Server database that is of interest to us is a collection of some or all six different types of objects: tables, views, stored procedures, rules, defaults, and user-defined datatypes.

- *Tables* contain the actual data in row/column format.
- *Views* are different ways of presenting the data from the database.
- *Stored procedures* are groups of SQL statements saved for later execution by database clients.
- *Rules* are objects bound to either a column or row or a user-defined datatype that is used to validate data when it is entered into the database.
- *Defaults* are used to provide a value when one is not entered for a specific column for which a data value is required.
- *User-defined datatypes* allow a user to specifically define the limitations and format of the data that is required for a specific column.

Create a Database Using Enterprise Manager

It is certainly possible, and in large installations desirable, to create databases using SQL statements. It is also possible to do this for Microsoft SQL Server using Microsoft SQL Enterprise Manager, and that is what we'll do in the following example, as shown in Figure 10-1. Here goes.

Enter the name of your new database in the Name box. Make sure that Master is selected and displayed in the Data Device box, because our example will be created in the existing Master device. Select a log device (if you desire) in the Log Device box. A log device is essential for running ac-

Figure 10-1
New Database
creation dialog box

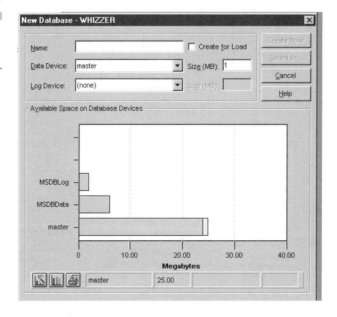

Figure 10-2
Enterprise Manager
tree with new
database

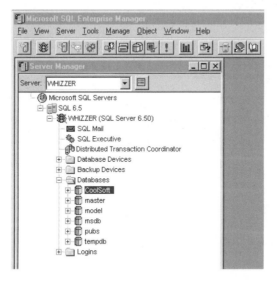

tual online databases, but not for our example. The default size of 1M is fine for our use. Click the Create Now button. When the dialog box disappears, your new database should be listed along with existing databases, as shown in Figure 10-2. Our example database is named *CoolSoft*, the name of our fictitious software company.

Creating Tables Using Enterprise Manager

Start Enterprise Manager as previously described. Click the + in front of your database to show the Groups/Users and Objects categories. Right click on Objects and select New Table from the context menu that appears. The Manage Tables dialog box appears, as shown in Figure 10-3. Enter **Products** in the Table box at the top of the form. Fill out the Column names, Datatypes, Sizes, Nulls, and Defaults as appropriate.

Adding a Primary Key

There is another concept that is very important in the world of databases —the concept of a key. A key consists of one column or a combination of columns in a table. There are several different types of keys. A primary key is used to uniquely identify a specific row in the table to which it belongs. For instance, we are going to make the ProductNumber column in our table the primary key. Because the user must be able to uniquely identify any single row in our table by using this key, SQL Server will never allow us to create two rows in our table that have the same value for ProductNumber. You will encounter other types of keys as you use SQL Server more and more. The term *primary key* is used in every database product with which the author is familiar, but some of the other types of keys may vary from product to product. When working with SQL Server, the following types of keys will be used.

■ Primary key—as previously defined

■ Common key—a key that relates two different tables in the database

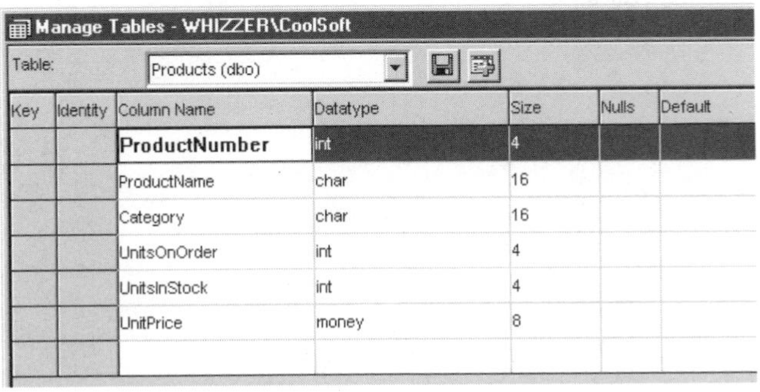

Figure 10-3
Column definitions
for Products table

Key	Identity	Column Name	Datatype	Size	Nulls	Default
		ProductNumber	int	4		
		ProductName	char	16		
		Category	char	16		
		UnitsOnOrder	int	4		
		UnitsInStock	int	4		
		UnitPrice	money	8		

Manage Tables - WHIZZER\CoolSoft

Table: Products (dbo)

- Composite key—any key that consists of more than a single column

- Foreign key—a column or columns whose values match the primary key in another table.

To create a primary key in the Products table, click on the Advanced Features button (the button with the + on it). Make sure that the *Primary Key / Identity* tab is selected. Click the down arrow on the right of the Column Name box to reveal the list of available columns. Click on ProductNumber. Click the Add button. A small key symbol will now appear in the Key column in the top part of the box, as shown in Figure 10-4.

When you have entered all the information needed to define the columns in the table and have added the primary key, click the Save Table icon (the one with the little floppy disk on it), enter the name of your table in the New Table Name box (in our example, the table name will be **Products**), and click OK. When the save has been completed, close the dialog box. The new table should now appear in the Enterprise Manager tree, as shown in Figure 10-5. Notice that we have created six columns.

- ProductNumber—an integer that defines the product internally

- ProductName—a text field that describes the product

- Category—another text field that defines the type of product

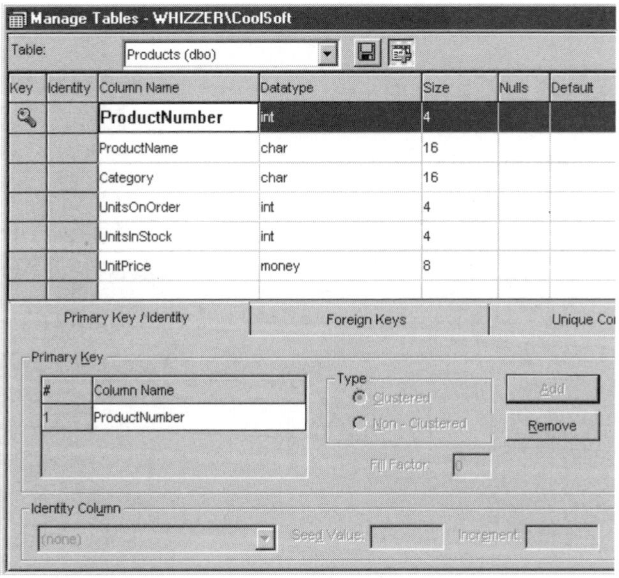

Figure 10-4
Table definition with primary key included

Figure 10-5
Enterprise Manager
tree containing
Products

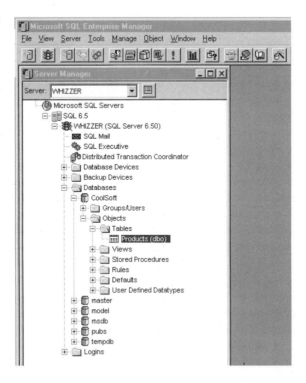

- UnitsOnOrder—an integer that indicates how many we have currently on order
- UnitsInStock—an integer that indicates how many we have currently in stock
- UnitPrice—a money field that contains the price per unit

Populating the New Database

We now have a database, but it contains nothing. We have a fancy box all ready to contain our data, but no data. So how do we get the data into our box? Microsoft provides tools to move in data from another database, but no specific tool with which to enter the data one row at a time. Why? Generally speaking, the IS folks who create databases are not the folks who enter the data into the database. The means of data entry is usually unique to the type of business for which the database is created. Small businesses or individuals generally do not need something as powerful as Microsoft SQL Server, so in those cases something such as Microsoft Access is a more appropriate database tool.

The purpose of this chapter, however, is to show you how to use Cold Fusion in conjunction with Microsoft SQL Server. Currently, you and I are the entire IS department as well as the data-entry personnel. Well, because we're featuring Cold Fusion, let's build a Cold Fusion application to use for entering the example data into our example database.

The HTML Side of Data Entry

We need to know a few HTML elements, a few Cold Fusion tags, and two SQL statements to build our data-entry example. First, the HTML. We will build a very simple Web page to act as the human interface to our under-the-covers data-entry program, as shown in Figure 10-6. Here it is.

This page consists primarily of one FORM element, which causes your browser to create a form that you can use to enter the data. The HTML element

```
<FORM ACTION=ch10_1.cfm METHOD=POST>
```

indicates that when you click the Submit Form button, the data that you have entered into the form will be sent (POST method) to the server. The .cfm extension in the ch10_1.cfm filename identifies the file as a Cold Fusion template, so the Cold Fusion Application Server will use that template to process the data sent from the form. The following steps show how the process works.

1. You tell your Web Browser to load the HTML page, ch10_1.htm.

Figure 10-6
Data-entry
HTML page

```
<HTML>
<HEAD>
<TITLE>
Simple Data Entry Page
</TITLE>
</HEAD>

<BODY>
<FORM ACTION=ch10_1.cfm METHOD=POST>
<FONT SIZE="+1">Enter Product Information</FONT>
<BR>

<B>Product Number</B>
<INPUT TYPE="TEXT" NAME="ProductNumber"><BR>
<B>Product Name</B>
<INPUT TYPE="TEXT" NAME="ProductName"><BR>
<B>Category</B>
<INPUT TYPE="TEXT" NAME="Category"><BR>
<B>Units On Order</B>
<INPUT TYPE="TEXT" NAME="UnitsOnOrder"><BR>
<B>Units In Stock</B>
<INPUT TYPE="TEXT" NAME="UnitsInStock"><BR>
<B>Unit Price</B>
<INPUT TYPE="TEXT" NAME="UnitPrice"><BR>
<INPUT TYPE="Submit" VALUE="Submit Form">
<INPUT TYPE="Reset" VALUE="Reset Form">
</FORM>
</BODY>
</HTML>
```

2. Your Web Browser sends a request to the server, asking for page ch10_1.htm.

3. The Internet Information Server processes the request and sends the page back to your browser.

4. Your browser displays the form described by the FORM HTML statement.

5. You enter your data into the displayed form and click the Submit Form button.

6. The data from the form is sent back to the server. Because of the ACTION=ch10_1.cfm part of the FORM statement, the data from your form is processed on the server by the Cold Fusion Application Server. The Cold Fusion statements contained in the ch10_1.cfm template file determine what Cold Fusion does with that data that is sent to it.

7. Cold Fusion builds an HTML page and sends it back to your browser for display.

The statements within the FORM block (starting from <FORM and ending with </FORM) that start with <INPUT TYPE="Text" create the boxes into which you enter the form data. The last two <INPUT TYPE elements define the Submit Form and Reset Form buttons.

The Cold Fusion Side of Data Entry

Figure 10-7 shows the code making up a Data Entry Cold Fusion Template. Figure 10-7 shows the contents of the ch10_1.cfm template. The first tag

```
<CFINSERT DATASOURCE=CoolSoft NAME=ProductData>
```

does all the actual work. That's all there is to it. This statement takes the data that you entered into the form and adds it as a new row to the Products table

Figure 10-7
Data entry Cold
Fusion template

```
<CFINSERT DATASOURCE=CoolSoft TABLENAME=Products>

<CFQUERY DATASOURCE=CoolSoft NAME=ProductData>
      SELECT * From Products
      WHERE ProductNumber=#Form.ProductNumber#
</CFQUERY>

<HTML>
<BODY>
<CFOUTPUT QUERY=ProductData>
<FONT SIZE="+1">
ProductNumber #ProductNumber#, ProductName #ProductName#, Category #Category#,
UnitsOnOrder #UnitsOnOrder#, UnitsInStock #UnitsInStock#, UnitPrice #UnitPrice
</FONT>
</CFOUTPUT>
</BODY>
</HTML>
```

in our CoolSoft database. The next CFQUERY block constructs a database query that returns the data that the CFINSERT tag just placed in the database. The CFQUERY tag identifies CoolSoft as the database to be queried, and names the query *ProductData*. The next two lines are pure SQL, which the CFQUERY tag sends to SQL Server. The SELECT statement says to return all rows (*) from the Products table (in the CoolSoft database) WHERE the ProductNumber field is equal to the ProductNumber value that was sent from your form—that is, the same record that was just placed in the database.

Because we created our table with the ProductNumber column as the primary key, if we try to enter the same Product Number twice, SQL Server will generate an error message and refuse to do our bidding, as shown in Figure 10-8. The CFOUTPUT block tells Cold Fusion to use the results of the ProductData query to fill in the parameters (delimited by pound signs) with the returned data, and to send the resulting HTML file back to your browser for display.

Now it's your turn. Use your favorite text editor to create the two files, ch10_1.htm and ch10_1.cfm. Place them both in the Cold Fusion default directory—the **\cfdocs** subdirectory of the root directory of your Web server. If you are using Microsoft Internet Information Server and installed the software using the defaults, place the files in **\IntePubs\wwwroot\cfdocs**. Make sure that you have created your database as we described earlier. But don't start trying to enter the data quite yet. There is one more step on this path.

Registering Your Data Source with Cold Fusion

There is one more thing to do before you can test and start entering data. You need to register your new database with Cold Fusion. Cold Fusion can

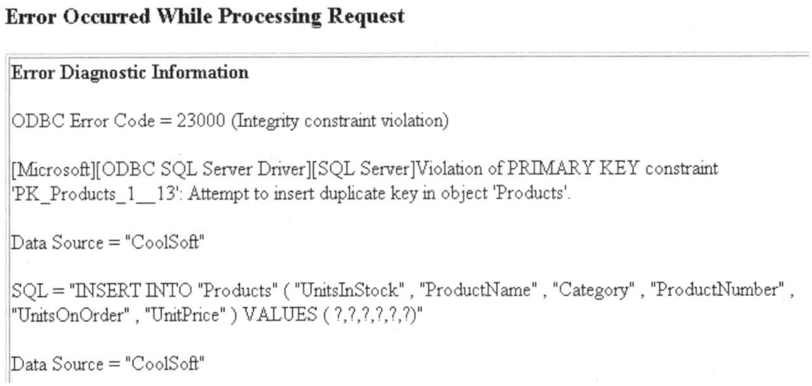

Figure 10-8

Error produced by duplicate Product-Number entry

Error Occurred While Processing Request

Error Diagnostic Information

ODBC Error Code = 23000 (Integrity constraint violation)

[Microsoft][ODBC SQL Server Driver][SQL Server]Violation of PRIMARY KEY constraint 'PK_Products_1__13': Attempt to insert duplicate key in object 'Products'.

Data Source = "CoolSoft"

SQL = "INSERT INTO "Products" ("UnitsInStock" , "ProductName" , "Category" , "ProductNumber" , "UnitsOnOrder" , "UnitPrice") VALUES (?,?,?,?,?,?)"

Data Source = "CoolSoft"

only connect to databases that have been properly registered. Here's how you do that.

Click Start, select Programs, select Cold Fusion Professional 3.0, and then click on Cold Fusion Administrator. Your Web browser will start and display the Cold Fusion Administrator Password Authentication page. Enter your Cold Fusion Administrator password and click Submit. When the Server Settings page loads, click on Data Sources on the left edge of the page. A list of data sources known to Cold Fusion will be shown (see Figure 10-9). Enter **CoolSoft** in the Data Source Name box. Select Microsoft SQL Server Driver in the OBDC Driver box, and then click Add.

The Create OBDC Data Source page appears, as shown in Figure 10-10. The Data Source name will be filled in with **CoolSoft**. Enter any description you like or leave it blank. Enter **(local)** in the Server box, because your database is on the local SQL server. Enter your database

Figure 10-9

Registering a new data source with Cold Fusion

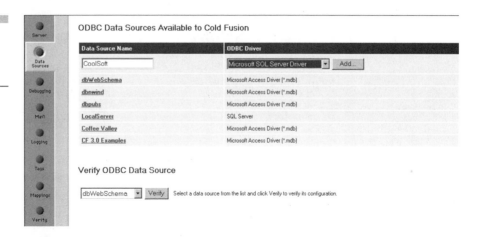

Figure 10-10

Creating the Data Source definition

name, `CoolSoft`, in the Database box. This box is the actual name of the database that you created. We have created a data source with the same name. Check the Use Trusted Connection box. Leave the other two boxes checked. Click on the Create button. Your database has been registered. To verify that the connection between Cold Fusion and your database can be made, select CoolSoft in the Verify OBDC Data Source box, then and click the Verify button. If all goes well, the message `The connection to the data source was verified successfully` will be displayed, as shown in Figure 10-11.

Testing The Form and Entering the Data

The function that will be used to populate our test database is now ready to use. Start up your browser and open the HTML page you just created (ch10_1.htm). If your Internet Information Server is Microsoft IIS, the URL will be http:\\127.0.0.1\Cfdocs\ch10_1.htm. The data-entry form should be shown (see Figure 10-12).

Populate the database by entering the records from Table 10-1 into the form. Click Submit to enter each record (see Figure 10-13).

Figure 10-11
Verifying the
data source

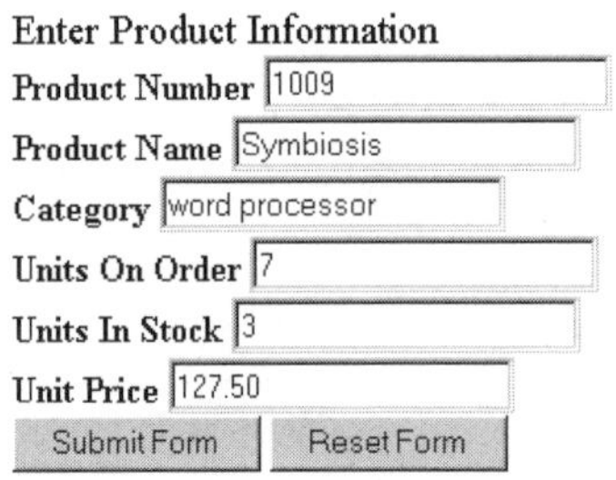

The connection to the data source was verified successfully.

Go Back

Figure 10-12
Data-entry form

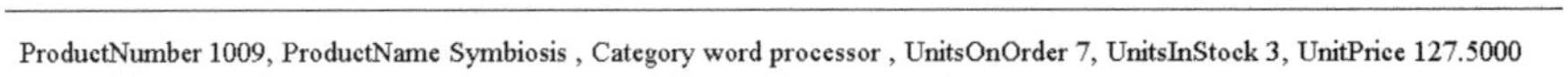

Enter Product Information
Product Number 1009
Product Name Symbiosis
Category word processor
Units On Order 7
Units In Stock 3
Unit Price 127.50
Submit Form   Reset Form

Figure 10-13
Data-entry
verification

ProductNumber 1009, ProductName Symbiosis , Category word processor , UnitsOnOrder 7, UnitsInStock 3, UnitPrice 127.5000

Table 10-1

Products
Table Data

Product Number	Product Name	Category	Units On Order	Units In Stock	Unit Price
1000	FastBase	database	10	5	$149.99
1001	FooBase	database	30	4	$275.00
1002	MyBase	database	45	19	$35.00
1003	MyBase2	database	5	6	$65.00
1004	MyBase3	database	5	27	$88.00
1005	Allegory	game	25	3	$27.50
1006	Trident	game	18	45	$36.95
1007	SpeedWrite+	word processor	36	19	$65.00
1008	HomeBase	database	12	7	$94.50
1009	Symbiosis	word processor	7	3	$127.00
1010	Quick Util II	utility	3	22	$46.50
1011	Frame Tool	utility	20	0	$65.00
1012	OS2000	os	5	16	$523.00
1013	OS3000	os	1	4	$721.00

Retrieving the Entire Database

You now have a working Microsoft SQL Server database table, populated with 14 records of data reflecting the software inventory of our imaginary software distribution company. Let's see some of what we can do with that data. The first and simplest function is to retrieve and print out the entire contents of the database. Create the file **ch10_2.cfm** in the **\cfdocs** subdirectory. Figure 10-14 shows how to create the template that retrieves the contents of the database table.

Notice that there is no HTML in this template. Cold Fusion will create all the HTML that is needed in the document that is sent back to your browser for display. Point your browser to Cfdocs/ch10_2.cfm. The contents of your database appears. As before, when your browser requests ch10_2.cfm from the server, the Cold Fusion Application Server recognizes the .cfm extension as that of a Cold Fusion template, and then processes it. The CFQUERY tag identifies the data source as CoolSoft, creates an

Figure 10-14

ch10_2.cfm template

```
<CFQUERY NAME="Getit" DATASOURCE="CoolSoft">
     SELECT * FROM Products
</CFQUERY>

<CFTABLE QUERY="Getit" MAXROWS=20>
     <CFCOL HEADER="<B>Number</B>" WIDTH=10 TEXT="<I>#ProductNumber#</I>">
     <CFCOL HEADER="<B>Product</B>" WIDTH=20 TEXT="<I>#ProductName#</I>">
     <CFCOL HEADER="<B>Category</B>" WIDTH=20 TEXT="<I>#Category#</I>">
     <CFCOL HEADER="<B>On Order</B>" WIDTH=10 TEXT="<I>#UnitsOnOrder#</I>">
     <CFCOL HEADER="<B>In Stock</B>" WIDTH=10 TEXT="<I>#UnitsInStock#</I>">
     <CFCOL HEADER="<B>Price</B>" WIDTH=12 TEXT="<I>$#UnitPrice#</I>">
</CFTABLE>
```

Figure 10-15

Output of SELECT *
Query

Number	Product	Category	On Order	In Stock	Price
1000	FastBase	database	10	5	$149.9500
1001	FooBase	database	30	4	$275.0000
1002	MyBase	database	45	19	$35.0000
1003	MyBase2	database	5	6	$65.0000
1004	MyBase3	database	5	27	$88.0000
1005	Allegory	game	25	3	$27.5000
1006	Trident	game	18	45	$18.4500
1007	SpeedWrite+	word processor	36	19	$65.0000
1008	HomeBase	database	12	7	$94.5000
1009	Symbiosis	word processor	7	3	$127.5000
1010	Quick Util II	utility	3	22	$46.4000
1011	Frame Tool	utility	20	0	$65.0000
1012	OS2000	os	5	16	$523.0000
1013	OS3000	os	1	4	$721.0000

SQL query named *Getit'* and sends the SQL statement SELECT * FROM Products to SQL Server. The SQL SELECT statement is the most frequently used of all SQL statements. It requests a database server to return data from a database based on specified qualifiers. SELECT * means select all records; FROM identifies the Products table within the database.

SQL Server returns the specified records to Cold Fusion. The Cold Fusion CFTABLE tag tells Cold Fusion to use the query named *Getit*, which was created by the CFQUERY tag, and to format the data into an HTML document using the CFCOL tags. The resulting HTML page is returned to your browser and displayed, as shown in Figure 10-15.

Selective Data Retrieval

The SELECT * SQL query retrieves all the data from the specified table. Adding one additional clause, using the WHERE clause, allows you to retrieve a subset of the data based on the qualifiers you use. For example, if you insert the clause *WHERE UnitPrice < 50.00*, you retrieve only those products in the database that have a unit cost of less than $50. Figure 10-16 illustrates the query and Figure 10-17 illustrates the output.

Figure 10-16
ch10_3.cfm template

```
<CFQUERY NAME="Q1" DATASOURCE="CoolSoft">
        SELECT * FROM Products
        WHERE UnitPrice < 50.00
        </CFQUERY>

<CFTABLE QUERY="Q1" MAXROWS=10>
        <CFCOL HEADER="<B>Number</B>" WIDTH=10 TEXT="<I>#ProductNumber#</I>">
        <CFCOL HEADER="<B>Product</B>" WIDTH=20 TEXT="<I>#ProductName#</I>">
        <CFCOL HEADER="<B>Category</B>" WIDTH=20 TEXT="<I>#Category#</I>">
        <CFCOL HEADER="<B>On Order</B>" WIDTH=10 TEXT="<I>#UnitsOnOrder#</I>">
        <CFCOL HEADER="<B>In Stock</B>" WIDTH=10 TEXT="<I>#UnitsInStock#</I>">
        <CFCOL HEADER="<B>Price</B>" WIDTH=12 TEXT="<I>$#UnitPrice#</I>">
</CFTABLE>
```

Figure 10-17
Output of SELECT *
Query with the
WHERE clause

Number	Product	Category	On Order	In Stock	Price
1002	MyBase	database	45	19	$35.0000
1005	Allegory	game	25	3	$27.5000
1006	Trident	game	18	45	$18.4500
1010	Quick Util II	utility	3	22	$46.4000

Figure 10-18
Cold Fusion diagnostic output

Error Occurred While Processing Request

Error Diagnostic Information

Cannot parse template file "F:\INETPUB\WWWROOT\CFDOCS\CH10_3.CFM"

The error occurred on (or near) line 6 of the template file F:\INETPUB\WWWROOT\CFDOCS\CH10_3.CFM.

```
1:
2:
3:
4:
5:
6: <CFQUERY NAM="Getit" DATASOURCE="CoolSoft">
7:        SELECT * FROM Products
```

Invalid token found on line 6 at position 10. Cold Fusion was looking at the following text "NAM="

Date/Time: 07/14/97 19:49:17
Browser: Mozilla/3.0Gold (WinNT; I)
Remote Address: 127.0.0.1
Template: F:\INETPUB\WWWROOT\cfdocs\ch10_3.cfm

Cold Fusion includes extensive validation for Cold Fusion templates. For example, if you misspelled NAME in the CFQUERY tag, Cold Fusion would detect the error and report it as shown in Figure 10-18.

You can begin to see just how powerful this combination of technologies can be. By changing the WHERE clause in the SELECT statement, you could display all the products that had zero units in stock. By using Category in the WHERE clause, you can select from only the products in one or more categories. But, of course, relational databases and SQL have been around for a while and are ubiquitous in business today. What Cold Fusion does is make it easy to access the power of the database through Internet and intranet technology.

Dynamic Selective Data Retrieval

The example we just described is limited in a very severe way. The templates we created were static. When we wanted to change what we selected, we had to edit or create a template. Clearly that would be of little use in a real business environment. So lets take it one step further and move the selection mechanism out of our text editor and back into our browser, where it will become much more useful. First, we will expand the HTML page that contains the data-entry form to look like the code you see in Figure 10-19.

When this page is displayed in our browser, it looks like the form in Figure 10-20.

Figure 10-19

Revised data-entry form—the code

```
<HTML>
<HEAD>
<TITLE>
Query Construction Page
</TITLE>
</HEAD>

<BODY>
<FORM ACTION="ch10_4.cfm" METHOD=POST>
<FONT SIZE="+1">Enter Your Product Selection Criteria, then
 Click <b>Submit Form</b></FONT>
<BR>
<BR>

<B>Product Number is </B>
<INPUT TYPE="TEXT" NAME="ProductNumber"><BR>
<B>Product Name is </B>
<INPUT TYPE="TEXT" NAME="ProductName"><BR>
<B>Category is </B>
<INPUT TYPE="TEXT" NAME="Category"><BR>
<B>Units On Order is less than or equal to </B>
<INPUT TYPE="TEXT" NAME="MinimumUnitsOnOrder"><BR>
<B>Units On Order is greater than or equal to </B>
<INPUT TYPE="TEXT" NAME="MaximumUnitsOnOrder"><BR>
<B>Units In Stock is less than or equal to </B>
<INPUT TYPE="TEXT" NAME="MinimumUnitsInStock"><BR>
<B>Units In Stock is greater than or equal to </B>
<INPUT TYPE="TEXT" NAME="MaximumUnitsInStock"><BR>
<B>Unit Price is less than or equal to </B>
<INPUT TYPE="TEXT" NAME="MinimumUnitPrice"><BR>
<B>Unit Price is greater than or equal to </B>
<INPUT TYPE="TEXT" NAME="MaximumUnitPrice"><BR>
<BR>
<BR>
<INPUT TYPE="Submit" VALUE="Submit Form">
<INPUT TYPE="Reset" VALUE="Reset Form">
</FORM>
</BODY>
</HTML>
```

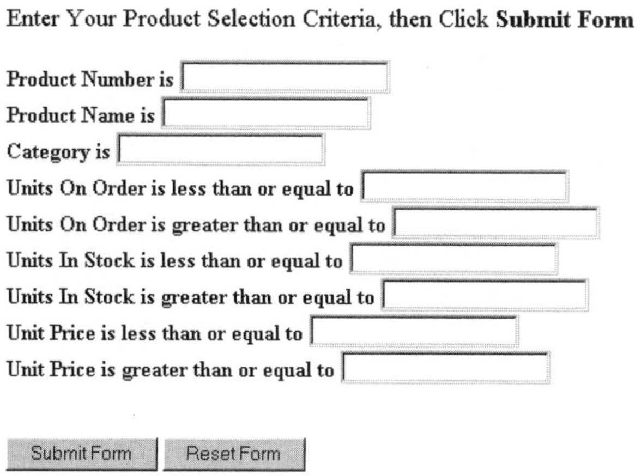

Figure 10-20

Revised data-entry
form—shown in
browser

Enter Your Product Selection Criteria, then Click **Submit Form**

Product Number is [ ]

Product Name is [ ]

Category is [ ]

Units On Order is less than or equal to [ ]

Units On Order is greater than or equal to [ ]

Units In Stock is less than or equal to [ ]

Units In Stock is greater than or equal to [ ]

Unit Price is less than or equal to [ ]

Unit Price is greater than or equal to [ ]

[Submit Form]   [Reset Form]

Figure 10-21

Revised data-entry
form—the result

Number	Product	Category	On Order	In Stock	Price
1001	FooBase	database	30	4	$275.0000
1012	OS2000	os	5	16	$523.0000
1013	OS3000	os	1	4	$721.0000

This simple form allows us to search our database based on the criteria that we supply to the form. The elements of the form are checked from top to bottom. If a Product Number is entered, all other elements are ignored and the database is searched for that Product Number. If no Product Number is entered, the same logic is applied to the Product Name. If neither Product Number nor Product Name is supplied, Category is checked. If Category is entered, all products in the database making up the specified Category are returned. A search can be made based on Units On Order, Units In Stock, or Unit Price, either all products greater than or less than an entered value.

We could, of course, carry this even further by allowing searches based on a combination of the elements. We could set up the template to allow a search for all products in a specific category that had a unit price of greater than $500 and which showed less than five units in stock. But we have gone far enough to illustrate the power that can be built into a Cold Fusion template. Using this page and template to search our sample database, the output, as shown in Figure 10-21, is produced when we specify all units that have a list price of $250 or greater.

The modified Cold Fusion template that processes the data we enter into the form is shown in Figure 10-22.

Figure 10-22
Revised Cold Fusion
template

```
<CFQUERY NAME="Query2" DATASOURCE="CoolSoft">
    SELECT * From Products
    <CFIF #Form.ProductNumber# is not "">
    WHERE ProductNumber = #Form.ProductNumber#
    <CFELSEIF #Form.ProductName# is not "">
    WHERE ProductName = '#Form.ProductName#'
    <CFELSEIF #Form.Category# is not "">
    WHERE Category = '#Form.Category#'
    <CFELSEIF #Form.MinimumUnitsOnOrder# is not "">
    WHERE UnitsOnOrder <= #Form.MinimumUnitsOnOrder#
    <CFELSEIF #Form.MaximumUnitsOnOrder# is not "">
    WHERE UnitsOnOrder >= #Form.MaximumUnitsOnOrder#
    <CFELSEIF #Form.MinimumUnitsInStock# is not "">
    WHERE UnitsInStock <= #Form.MinimumUnitsInStock#
    <CFELSEIF #Form.MaximumUnitsInStock# is not "">
    WHERE UnitsInStock >= #Form.MaximumUnitsInStock#
    <CFELSEIF #Form.MinimumUnitPrice# is not "">
    WHERE UnitPrice <= #Form.MinimumUnitPrice#
    <CFELSEIF #Form.MaximumUnitPrice# is not "">
    WHERE UnitPrice >= #Form.MaximumUnitPrice#
    </CFIF>
</CFQUERY>

<CFTABLE QUERY="Query2" MAXROWS=20>
    <CFCOL HEADER="<B>Number</B>" WIDTH=10 TEXT="<I>#ProductNumber#</I>">
    <CFCOL HEADER="<B>Product</B>" WIDTH=20 TEXT="<I>#ProductName#</I>">
    <CFCOL HEADER="<B>Category</B>" WIDTH=20 TEXT="<I>#Category#</I>">
    <CFCOL HEADER="<B>On Order</B>" WIDTH=10 TEXT="<I>#UnitsOnOrder#</I>">
    <CFCOL HEADER="<B>In Stock</B>" WIDTH=10 TEXT="<I>#UnitsInStock#</I>">
    <CFCOL HEADER="<B>Price</B>" WIDTH=12 TEXT="<I>$#UnitPrice#</I>">
</CFTABLE>
```

NOTE: *Either single or double quotation marks are used in Cold Fusion statement delimit strings. A pair of single or double quotation marks is used to indicate an empty string. A parameter from a form that is passed to Cold Fusion that contains a string consisting of one or more blanks is* not *an empty string. Therefore. the Cold Fusion tag*

<CFIF #Form.ProductNumber# is îî>

will evaluate to TRUE if the parameter is null, but will evaluate to FALSE if the parameter consists of one or more blanks.

CONCLUSION

This chapter described how to create a database in Microsoft SQL Server, how to create a table within that database, and how to populate that table with data using Cold Fusion. It has also shown how to retrieve data from that SQL Server database, retrieving both the entire contents of the table and retrieving data selectively using the Cold Fusion CFIF tag. More Cold Fusion tags and functions will be covered in the chapters 11 and 12 on using SQL and Advanced SQL.

11

New Features in Cold Fusion 3

- Fine-Tuning Server Settings from the CF Administrator
- Using the Create New Data Sources Tab
- Debugging and Error-Logging Options
- Creating Custom Tags and Mapping Options
- Using JAVA Controls, Tree Controls, and Talking to Other Servers

Many of the newest features of Cold Fusion 3 are targeted at experienced programmers and not at the audience of an introductory book.

Hard-core programmers tend to get miffed if they cannot use arrays; Cold Fusion 3 now includes arrays. Programmers feel hemmed in if they cannot connect to all their other favorite components and controls; Cold Fusion now includes connections to ActiveX components and COM-compliant objects. And, in the eternal chess game of programmers versus hackers and corporate spies, encryption technology has become a required property of any network product; Cold Fusion now contains a wide range of security measures, including encryption.

If you are just learning Cold Fusion, you might think these technologies are beyond your reach. In reality, Cold Fusion brings these complex methods to the beginner in a much simpler form than you might expect. You can now access all this power with the familiar and high-level syntax of CFML.

This chapter does not teach you to use all of these advanced methods. Instead, it gives you a broad overview of these new, specialized technologies, links to information sources, and, in a number of cases, a thumbnail sketch of how to use them. With the information in this chapter, you can create a simple custom tag or use the Verity search engine at its most basic level. For more in-depth information, however, consult the *Cold Fusion 3 Language Reference*.

On the other hand, this chapter provides a complete guide to using the Cold Fusion 3 Administrator pages. You may be especially interested in Tab 2: Creating New Data Sources, Tab 3: Debugging Options, Tab 6: Creating Custom Tags, and Tab 8: The Verity Search Engine.

New Features in the Cold Fusion 3 Administrator

An important new feature of the Cold Fusion 3 Administrator is that it is a web-based system. This enables administration access from one or more remote locations.

Although you could administer Cold Fusion 2 from a remote server, it required a more complex syntax to call it up, and you could not create or manage ODBC data sources from a remote location.

The fact that the Cold Fusion 3 Administrator is Web-based is in itself a real bonus for managing the site. Even if you manage your original site primarily from the server, this feature enables you to delegate parts of the job to individuals elsewhere in the company, or for several projects that are running on the server to be completely managed from different locations—as long as you are careful about security. Also, the new release uses JAVA to display file directories; however, your browser must fully support JAVA in order to bring up these directories.

Some of the differences are cosmetic. Instead of tabs, the Cold Fusion 3 Administrator has a navigation frame to move from template to template. (This does extract a small time cost on slower servers; moving from tab to tab was instantaneous in the Cold Fusion 2 Administrator.) Selecting the Administrator tab fills in the browser screen and provides additional options and more information. For instance, the help text is now displayed on screen.

The following is a description of what's in the new Cold Fusion 3 Administrator pages. The following tab sections are arranged in the order presented by Cold Fusion, although in setting up your first templates, you will probably first go to tab 2: Data Sources.

Tab 1: Increasing Efficiency with the Server Page

Most of the server settings enable you to fine-tune your performance or customize Cold Fusion to your environment (see Figure 11-1). The Oracle database driver, for instance, requires that simultaneous requests be limited to one, rather than the default of 15.

The defaults on the *Server page* are set at high values that should work for most situations. The timeout value, for instance, is rather long. It is very rare that you will have an application that requires more than the default of three minutes. If you do have complicated queries that push the time even close to three minutes, you might want to limit the number of simultaneous requests so that the computer can get each one done most quickly.

You might be interested in resetting the Template Cache Size—which has a default of 1024 kbytes—particularly if your templates contain a lot of memory hogs and load slowly. Before going on-line with a new cache size, however, test it on your server. On one configuration, increasing the cache size caused problems initially, though we were careful to increase the cache size by multiples of 1024 kbytes. This problem has apparently been addressed in Cold Fusion 3.

If you are using client management through the Web Application Framework, purging outdated client data from the data stored by Cold Fusion in your system is a good idea. It doesn't usually make sense to keep client data

Figure 11-1

The Server settings in the Cold Fusion 3 Administrator

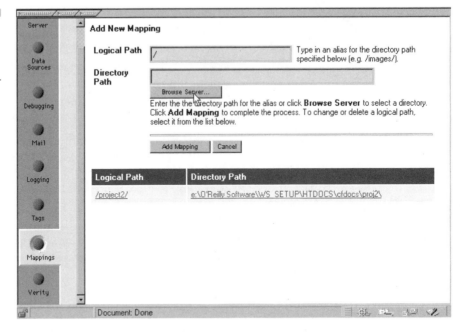

Figure 11-1
The Server settings in the Cold Fusion 3 Administrator

for extremely infrequent visitors in your server's memory. Purging old data automatically decreases the number of times you need to reset the Windows Registry size to accommodate new visitors to your site.

Finally, password access to the Administrator pages gives you strict control over who can use Cold Fusion on your system.

Tab 2: Creating New Data Sources

The Data Sources page is used to make a database available to Cold Fusion through the ODBC driver. On this page, you create a name by which you will refer to this data source whenever you run a <CFQUERY>. Then you associate it with an ODBC driver with a select box that lists the ODBC drivers on your system. The Submit button takes you to another page, which is customized to the ODBC driver you have chosen.

When you return to this page, another Submit button at the bottom of the page enables you to verify that the data source is properly configured to be accessed by Cold Fusion. If not, each of the data sources listed can be edited by clicking the name that you gave it when you created it. The following Figure 11-2 shows the ODBC Data Sources Available to Cold Fusion page.

Figure 11-2

The opening page of settings for creating a new data source

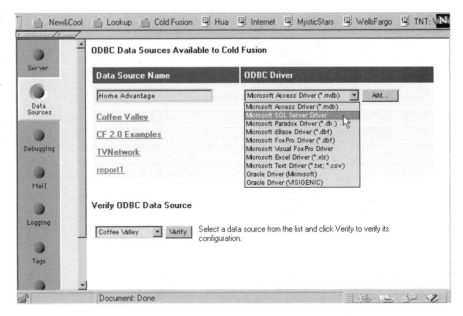

Clicking the data source you want to modify or delete takes you to the same template that is used to create the data source originally; only the title and the wording and number of Submit buttons are changed.

The only thing you have to do on most Create ODBC Data Source pages is click the Browse Server button beside the Database File input box (see Figure 11-3). Everything else is optional. It might be useful to write a description if you have lots of similar data sources. Most data source names, however, should be intuitive and easy to remember. After all, you need to use these names in all of your <CFQUERY> statements.

After you click Browse Server, Cold Fusion loads a Java applet that provides you with a directory tree, from which you can select the database file you are configuring. Once again, there's nothing new here about what to do: you select the file and click OK (or double-click the file).

What's most interesting about the displayed directory tree, however, is that it is an example of the new tag in Cold Fusion 3, the <CFTREE> tag. This Java device is presently available to display query results graphically in a tree format. The <CFTREE> tag does not yet enable users to display a directory, such as the one shown in Figure 11-4. For that, you'll need to wait for the next version.

ADVANCED DATA SOURCE PROCEDURES FOR PRECISE SECURITY CONTROL When you click the CF Settings button, Cold Fusion

Figure 11-3
The Create ODBC
Data Source page

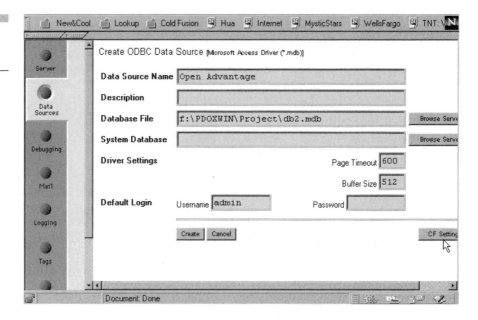

Figure 11-4
The Select File on the
Server page shows
the use of the
<CFTREE> tag

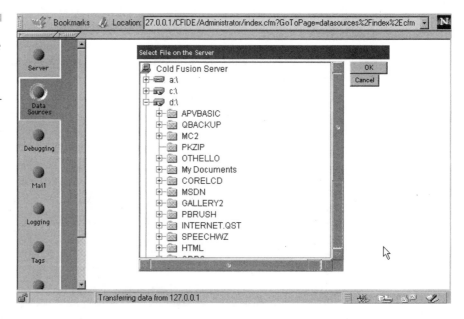

adds a number of additional choices to your screen. Most of these choices
enable you to specify levels of security so that many individuals can have
wider access to the program without compromising the most sensitive data.

Rather than accepting the global security options on the Server page, for instance, you can create a different login user name and password for an individual data source. Furthermore, you can specify that your developers can only do certain things with SQL.

Some relational databases, such as MS SQL Server, enable you to create mini-programs with SQL, which are then stored within the database. If you need to control the use of the data extremely tightly, you may want to restrict your developers from doing anything other than these stored procedures. Thus, Cold Fusion can prevent any insertions or deletions the would violate the referential integrity of the database.

In other words, you must handle linked tables in a way that preserves their system of links. Cold Fusion lets you do this easily.

In addition to providing increased security, the advanced data source procedures enable you to modify globally the settings from the Server page, (see Figure 11-5), which might not apply to the specific needs of an individual project.

Tab 3: Debugging Options

Cold Fusion provides four forms of debugging information, three of which are displayed at the bottom of the Web page generated by Cold Fusion.

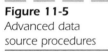

Figure 11-5
Advanced data
source procedures

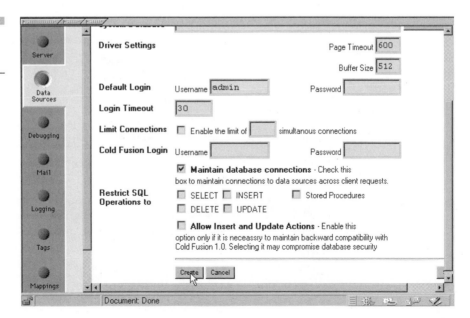

The fourth type of information is logged along with the error message itself in the error log files (see the section "Tab 5: Error Logging Options" later in this chapter). Each of these debugging options provides you with direct feedback about the output of the template as Cold Fusion turns it into HTML (see Figure 11-6).

The Show variables option lists the variables passed to the template by URLs, cookies or forms, and CGI variables. When the program is not working, this is one of the first places to look.

Even if you are meticulous about turning off this option when you are done with it, the existence of this option could be a security risk if it were not for the fifth item on the page. If someone wanted to hack your site, they could turn on debugging from anywhere in the world by appending the URL with the URL variable **?mode=DEBUG**. Appending **?mode=DEBUG** to the URL would enable them to see the actual location of your templates on your hard drive.

The fifth item enables you to restrict the display of debugging information to selected sites, preventing a hacker from accessing it. With this in place, you can leave debugging on all the time. After all, what Web site isn't constantly under construction?

The Show query information option is useful in tracking down variables that are used in creating dynamic queries. If a variable is processed

Figure 11-6
Turning on debugging options

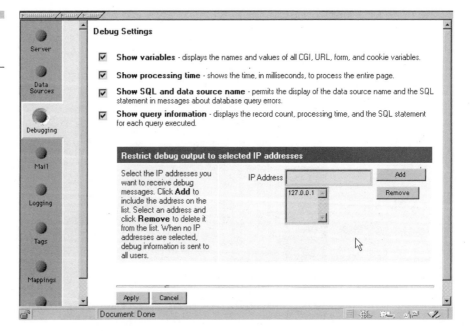

and then passed to the SQL query, it's useful to be able to check that the actual, raw query is exactly as you expect it to be. If it is, your error is in the SQL statement. If not, check the <CFSET> statements or other processing statements preceding the SQL.

Processing time (option 2), of course, is important in evaluating the performance of your templates, and logging information about the SQL and data source (option 3) makes maintenance and bug tracking easier.

Tab 4: Sending E-Mail

Cold Fusion makes it possible to generate e-mail messages automatically as users interact with your templates. New users can be welcomed after registering; purchases and other decisions can be confirmed by e-mail; files and documents can be sent as MIME attachments to e-mail messages.

The Mail page contains three input boxes (see Figure 11-7). In most cases, however, you need to fill in only the first one: the Mail Server. This is the same host name or IP address that you would use in any Internet software.

After you fill in the Mail Server field, Cold Fusion enables you to test it by sending a test message to an e-mail address.

Figure 11-7
Mail settings

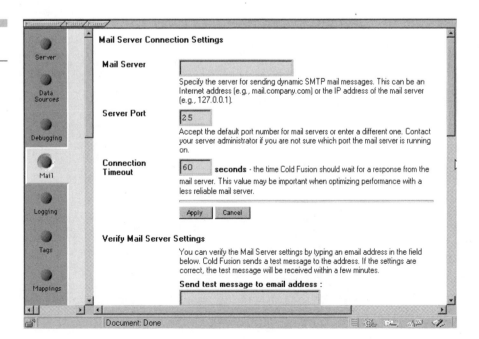

The Server Port and Connection Timeout input boxes are already populated with standard values that should rarely be changed. You can override all of the values on this page with the <CFMAIL> tag, using attributes of the same names.

Tab 5: Error Logging Options

Cold Fusion 3 automatically logs errors that occur during its operation into three files that are stored in a location specified on the Logging page (see Figure 11-8). Each logged error includes information about what the problem was, how severe the problem was, and when it occurred. These error messages are stored in a single line, with each element comma-delimited.

Thus, you can easily store the log file whereever you want on the server. If you then delete the file, Cold Fusion generates a new file by the same name, which you can import later for analysis.

The main log file of interest to you is cfserver.log, which reports every Cold Fusion error message displayed to a user. These are the errors that you can repair most easily. Included are application page errors, syntax

Figure 11-8
The Logging settings in Cold Fusion

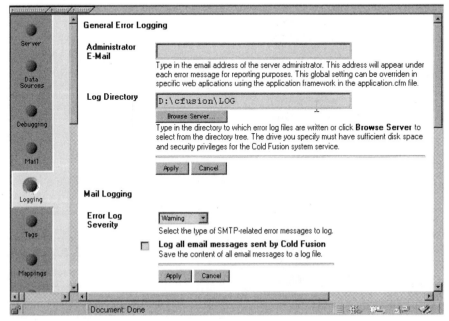

errors, ODBC errors, and SQL errors. The web page visitor's IP address and browser information is also included, if possible, which enable you to identify work-arounds for problems with unusual browsers that you may not have considered in writing the original code.

You will not personally use cfexec.log or server.log frequently. These files focus on problems with Cold Fusion service itself or communication between Cold Fusion and your web server. Both files include a Threaded ID field, which is meaningful only to Allaire technical support personnel.

Finally, Cold Fusion also logs all errors generated by an SMTP mail server; you can set the level of severity that you want to know about on this page.

Tab 6: Disabling Cold Fusion Tags or Creating Custom Tags — Possible Security Issues

The Tags page begins by enabling you to disable the <CFFILE> and <CFCONTENT> tags, which could be used maliciously to wreak havoc on your information system. Whether this applies to your site or not, it's a good thing to be reminded that Cold Fusion introduces security risks to your system of which you must be conscious and in control. You are most vulnerable to disgruntled employees and hackers if you do not plan to avoid them.

Custom tags are one of the more important innovations in Cold Fusion 3.

The rest of the page enables you to register custom tags created in C++. If you do not know C++, you might consider creating tags outside of your interest or ability, which is incorrect. Although this page does not address all of the issues involved in creating and using custom tags, the importance of custom tags should at least be mentioned in slightly greater depth.

Tags are simply a convenient way of reusing code that you have written. On the simplest level, using a custom tag is just like using the <CFINCLUDE> tag. The following two expressions are very similar, because both use the contents of a different template. If you can use the <CFINCLUDE> tag, there is no reason that you cannot create custom tags and use them all the time in your work.

```
<CFINCLUDE TEMPLATE="CustomTagName.cfm">
<CF_CustomTagName>
```

Although these two expressions do a similar job, two things are wrong with saying that they mean the same thing. First, in a custom tag, variables are protected. This means that even if your main template has a variable by the same name, it will not interfere with the operation of the custom tag.

Second, you cannot pass URL variables or attributes to a template when using a <CFINCLUDE> tag. With a custom tag, you simply name the variables as attributes and assign them some values. Thus, to pass three variables, you would write your tag expression as follows:

```
<CF_CustomTagName AttributeName1="Value"
        AttributeName2="Value" AttributeName3="Value">.
```

In both cases, you need to write another template, called "CustomTag-Name.cfm." You can also invoke this file with the tag <CFMODULE>, which gives you more options for advanced work, as described in *Cold Fusion 3 Language Reference*.

Creating a new tag with C++ gives you the ability to program at a much more powerful level than you can in Cold Fusion. When creating a new tag with C++, you store it inside of a Dynamic Link Library (DLL), and then you register it with this page. Figures 11-9 and 11-10 illustrate the two pages that you would use.

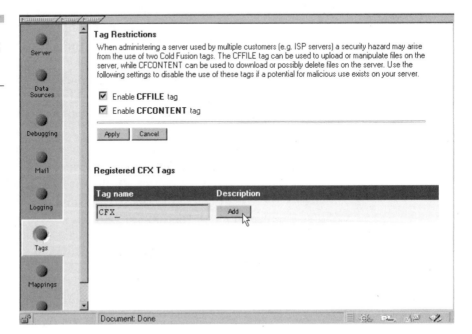

Figure 11-9
Registering new CFX tags that were created with C++

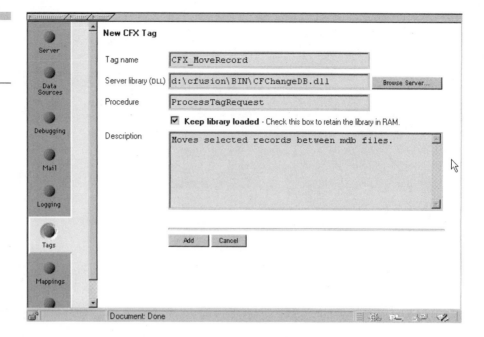

Figure 11-10
Specifying the DLL
that contains the
new tag

Tab 7: Mapping

Mapping is an important function, but chances are you will map your directories through your Web server rather than Cold Fusion.

Most Web servers recognize .cfm files as Cold Fusion application pages without mapping in Cold Fusion, because Cold Fusion supports the most common APIs (NSAPI, ISAPI, and WSAPI). Mapping directories is still necessary if you are running Cold Fusion as a CGI application.

Mapping is a useful for achieving several things. First, mapping enables you to hide the actual location of your templates on your server. By renaming the directory path where you store your templates, you can prevent unauthorized modifications to the templates. Protecting the location of your templates can be part of your security strategy.

Mapping also enables you to create a less complex URL for users to access. Finally, by creating more than one alias to the same directory, you can reuse templates and subdirectories in different applications. Although occupying the same space on your hard drive, they will have different virtual locations. Figure 11-11 shows how to map a documents/ templates directory to Cold Fusion.

Figure 11-11
The Mapping settings
in Cold Fusion 3

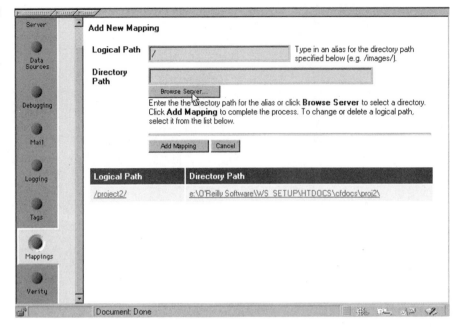

Figure 11-11
The Mapping settings
in Cold Fusion 3

Tab 8: The Verity Search Engine

Cold Fusion's incorporation of Verity Search 97 is a major innovation for creating a powerful data-driven Web site. Searching a large site for specific words is a difficult task in SQL; it's now become a simple matter with the Verity search engine.

The first step in using this technology is to use this page and create an index name for the information Cold Fusion will search. This index is called a *collection*. All you have to do is invent a name for it and click the Create button (see Figure 11-12).

Next, you have to populate your collection with data. The simplest way is to highlight the collection you want to index (in the Verity Collections box) and click the Index button. This will take you to the Index Collections page (see Figure 11-13). Here you choose the directory you want to index, the file extensions you want to include, and the URL to return with the list of files the search engine lists.

As soon as you've done this, you will be able to create an application that searches the collection using the <CFSEARCH> tag.

You can also create an index dynamically with the <CFINDEX> tag, described in the *Cold Fusion 3 Language Reference* book.

Figure 11-12
Use this page for creating a Verity search collection and indexing it

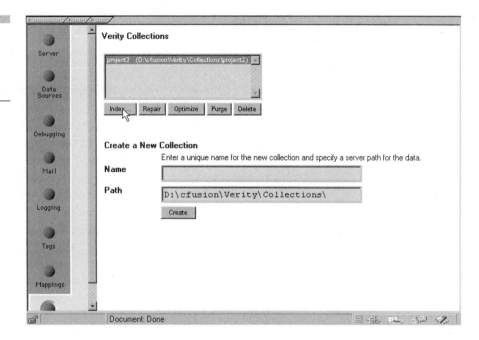

Figure 11-13
Indexing your collection

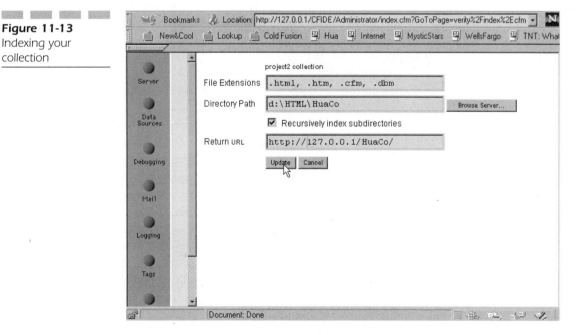

Using Other New features in Cold Fusion 3

Cold Fusion 3 has integrated many different technologies that were not available through Cold Fusion 2, making it a powerful vehicle for electronic commerce and enterprise-wide applications. The following tags and functions summarize some of the more important new features.

With the exception of the <CFFORM> tag, most of these new features will be of interest mostly to advanced users of Cold Fusion. They are included here, because it may be useful for you to know about them.

The <CFFORM> Tag and Java Controls

Previously, Cold Fusion simply used HTML forms as the method of allowing the user to enter information. HTML forms, however, are very limited in what they are able to do. Cold Fusion 3's <CFFORM> tag adds a number of Java controls, including a slider control, a tree control, and a text control. These are graphically pleasing, powerful, and allow for greater levels of data validation.

The downside is that only visitors to your site who have Java capability can use the forms you create.

The controls are invoked with Cold Fusion tags, and the parameters define how the html page looks and what information is presented to the user. The parameters generally provide you with the ability to specify the font, size, and even color in some cases. Some of the input forms allowed under <CFFORM> are very much like the HTML form fields; some forms are quite enhanced. For text input boxes, Cold Fusion now enables you to require that the input information is specifically formatted as a telephone number, a social security number, or a credit card number.

The Tree Control uses the <CFTREE> tag to create an information tree that looks like the Windows File Manager or Windows Explorer. It can be populated from a query, and a variety of images are built in as icons for information.

The <CFSLIDER> tag provides a control that looks like a volume control on a stereo and is used to adjust a numerical value up and down. The <CFGRID> tag enables you to put a table into the form, which, for instance, might list different parts for different cars in an auto repair shop. The Grid Control is not yet updateable in version 3.0, but it is supposed to be updateable in version 3.1. This means that in the next version of

Cold Fusion, customers will be able to order merchandise directly from the grid.

Talking to Other Servers Using the <CFHTTP> and <CFHTTPPARAM> Tags

The <CFHTTP> and <CFHTTPPARAM> tags allow Cold Fusion to contact other Web servers and interact with them. If a hotel is using Cold Fusion to let a customer make reservations and check in online, for example, the template might also ask if the customer wants to order supper, wine, flowers, and so forth.

Rather than forcing the customer to go to all these different sites for each transaction, however, the hotel's template would go to the other Web sites and fill in their order forms automatically with the <CFHTTP> tag. Using the POST method, the hotel would send the form fields required by the other web sites directly to them to complete the orders.

POST operations also enable you to send files, cookies, URLs, or CGI variables to other servers.

The <CFHTTP> tag also supports GET operations. An example of how you might use GET operations is to create a Cold Fusion robot agent for yourself. This agent would regularly visit important Web sites on the Net —for online magazines and newspapers, for example—and search for information that you need to find out about.

Your robot would then return and bring the information you needed. A sample application is included in Cold Fusion 3. To use this functionality, simply rewrite the example to suit your needs.

Finally, you can use GET operations to download binary and text files and to create a query object on your server from the contents of the text file. What is created is called a *query object* because it is exactly the same as the information stored in your computer's RAM when you run a <CFQUERY>.

Building an Enterprise-Wide Application with the <CFLDAP> Tag

Light Directory Access Protocol (LDAP) is a standard enterprise networking protocol that allows computers at different locations to share resources. One practical method you might use it for is to ask your customers or users to register when they first start using the system. This information is then stored in a central company database and is shared with web servers in your company at different locations around the country. Thus, after your customers have registered once, no matter which server they had contacted, they would be permitted to access every other server in the company at any location.

You can also use LDAP to create Internet White Pages for users to easily locate people and resources and to receive information about them. This directory can be managed and updated from various other sites, and customers can search the directory for a variety of information, using a form that you create.

LDAP has its own syntax and terminology, which you will need to learn to use the <CFLDAP>tag effectively. Two sites that can provide you with more information include:

▓ University of Michigan: http://www.umich.edu/~rsug/ldap/

▓ Netscape: http://developer.netscape.com/ (search for "LDAP")

Sending and Receiving E-Mail with the <CFMAIL> and <CFPOP> Tags

Cold Fusion's capability to generate and send e-mail is nothing new. The <CFMAIL> tag's use of SMTP is essentially the same as it was in Cold Fusion 2. The <CFMAIL> tag can be used to send messages to users—such as confirmation that a purchase was made or other automatic messages—generated while interacting with the user.

Cold Fusion 3, however, also supports the Post Office Protocol (POP), which means that it can also receive e-mail. This means that you can now design a mail box service, an e-mail discussion forum, a management tool to monitor a project's work flow, or a program to manage documents, which can be automatically sent by e-mail as attachments.

If you are familiar with e-mail, you will feel comfortable with the parameters to the mail tags, because they are mostly the headers you see on all e-mail. The addition of the <CFPOP> tag provides you with a great deal of new functionality.

Accessing and Interacting with External Components with the <CFOBJECT> Tag

Cold Fusion now gives you the ability to embed other applications and components into your templates, as long as they adhere to COM standards. In some instances, these will be third-party components that are supplied as DLLs or EXEs; others will be ActiveX server components, or perhaps external programs that you write in Visual Basic, Delphi, C/C++, or Java.

It is very useful, for instance, to use the <CFOBJECT> tag to interact with an accounting system such as Legacy, or to design custom interactive components with Java. This is a high-level programming feature that is very powerful, but beyond the scope of this book. You can find out more about what COM compliance means at http://www.microsoft.com.

Unless you are a hard-core programmer, you probably do not need to know much about arrays or query objects. This section is included so that you can understand a little about these concepts when you encounter them in the documentation provided by Allaire Corporation.

An *array* is essentially a single variable that contains a number of values. It is a little like having a database table stored in the computer memory, rather than on the hard drive.

A problem with this analogy is that database tables have only two dimensions. Cold Fusion has the capability to create arrays with many dimensions; three dimensions is the native or default number of dimensions in an array in Cold Fusion.

An example of using an array is having a list of automobiles and the parts needed for each on a two-dimensional array. A third dimension could be the car's year of manufacture so that you could access information about the car's muffler from one year to the next. In a database, you need a separate table for each year; in an array, every part for every car of any year would be part of the same array.

Cold Fusion 3 also has a variety of new functions that deal with query objects: QueryAdd, IsQuery, QueryAddRow, and QuerySetCell. These functions have nothing to do with the information you access from a database using SQL. Using SQL does create a query object that is stored in the computer's memory, but hard-core programmers need methods of creating query objects that did not originate in a database.

These new functions are methods of creating a query object that can be manipulated as if it had been drawn from a database. QueryNew creates column headers with no rows or data under them. QueryAddRow adds an empty row to the query object. QuerySetCell puts values into the cells of the query object you create.

After you have done all of this, you can access the query object of <CFOUTPUT>, just as if you had created the query object by using SQL to access a database.

CONCLUSION

Thus, Cold Fusion 3 is a step into a more complex, more integrated, and more powerful level of programming. You do not need to use its most advanced methods, however, to get what you need from it. It is still a very straightforward program that anyone can use.

12

Using SQL in Cold Fusion Templates

- Introducing Structured Query Language (SQL)
- Building Statements and Tables with SQL
  SQL Data Retrieval
  Columnar Formatting in Templates
- Using Conditional Logic in SQL Queries
  Passing Dynamic Parameters to CF Templates
  Searches with Pattern Matching—the "LIKE" Operator
- Updating Tables using SQL—The "Products" Table Example

Introducing SQL

The World Wide Web is now accessible from most hardware platforms; in a parallel fashion, SQL is now supported by most database software. And there are compelling reasons why SQL is so popular. SQL was first developed in the mid-70s to support the newly introduced relational model proposed by Dr. Codd of IBM. By the mid-80s the first ANSI (American National Standards Institute) version had been published. By 1996, SQL-89 and then SQL-92 had been proposed and accepted, and third-party vendors began adding powerful language extensions. Today, the latest version—SQL-92—is included as a programming tool in most existing database programs. In addition, SQL seems to have become an often chosen language to retrieve information from server-based databases over the World Wide Web. This chapter (and the next) show how Cold Fusion implements SQL-92 along with very handy language extensions.

SQL is a powerful, non-hierarchical, nonprocedural language to which conditional statements are added by vendors to make SQL into a more business-capable database language. SQL is used with web servers because it is high level, well-known, and can be easily implemented. After you create a database containing tables, you can easily access the database using Cold Fusion's implementation of SQL within CF templates.

Almost any database can have its SQL statements transported to another database application. Basic SQL code is highly portable among different database software. As soon as you create a table, you can create SQL statements to access the table easily without having to learn a lot of new commands, functions, and ways of manipulating data in the (probably much lower-level) proprietary database language. You can run most SQL statements unchanged against any of the PC-based databases covered in this book, including Personal Oracle 7. SQL makes it easier for you to try out different database software products; you can try out different products and find the one that is easiest for you to implement and then quickly hook it up to already existing SQL code and start working.

NOTE: *Most databases now include their own "flavor" of SQL as an add-in module. A few software companies have actually designed their database product around SQL; Personal Oracle 7 and SQL Server are two such examples described in this book. It is also possible to make the data definition for your tables (build the tables, fields, and their attributes) using SQL statements. In my opinion, it is generally easier to use native database table wizards to build*

tables than to use SQL to build the initial tables and data definitions. Regardless of how you build a table, however, you can connect an ODBC driver to the table and then use the SQL statements along with Cold Fusion to retrieve information from the table.

WHAT IS SQL? SQL is based on set theory, rooted in relations, and derived mathematically from rules that govern data associations. SQL's principal benefit is ease of use; it is truly a high-level English-like language. Its principal deficiency is a lack of procedural tools—which are usually added by database vendors. To remedy native SQL's deficiencies, the Cold Fusion implementation of SQL adds quite a bit of procedural functionality to generic SQL.

SQL is a high-level language. Not completely pure English, but compared to Visual Basic, C, Pascal, COBOL, or other computer languages, SQL is very English-like. This is a good reason to use the language. Do not be fooled, however. Even though SQL is a high-level language, it does contain subtleties, which is the reason for this chapter.

BUILDING SQL STATEMENTS The most basic SQL statement retrieves what is called "the entire data set" of a database table (all the records making up the table). SQL uses the verb "SELECT" at the beginning of retrieval statements, as in the following statement:

```
SELECT * From MYTABLE
```

This short statement reads as follows: "Select all the rows from MYTABLE." It accesses all of the columns (the asterisk stands for "everything," thus no specific column(s) needs to be listed in a SELECT statement) and all the data rows of "MYTABLE." This is straightforward. And in some situations, this statement is the only statement you actually need. In other cases, however, you only want to retrieve a part of the database. This chapter shows you how SQL can work on specific rows or specific columns of a database table.

Anyone who has worked with procedural databases knows that database users generally work with specific subsets of a database; that is, with specific columns, specific rows, or combinations thereof. To develop a model, assume there is a software distribution company called "CoolSoft, Inc." that sells a wide variety of software products. CoolSoft needs to know how to use SQL to retrieve its data. Table 12-1 shows the CoolSoft,Inc. company's first table, a products table.

Table 12-1

Products1 Table

Product No	Product Name	Category	Units on Order	Units in Stock	Unit Price
1000	FastBase	Database	10	5	$149.99
1001	RelateBase	Database	3	10	$149.95
1002	SpreadData	Database	14	8	$99.95
1003	Quick Spread	Spreadsheet	19	1	$69.95
1004	Quick Spread Pro	Spreadsheet	5	7	$169.95
1005	QuikUtility II	Utility	12	5	$39.95
1006	FrameTool	Utility	22	4	$121.99
1007	OS2000	OS	4	10	$300.00
1008	OS3000	OS	10	22	$600.00

NOTE: *The Products1 Table could contain more fields, but this is sufficient to show the features of SQL quite nicely. Adding more columns means adding additional field names to SQL statements.*

ABOUT DESIGNING SQL TABLES   There are several ideas to keep in mind when designing a database, ideas that reach beyond just thinking about what data to include or leave out. Assume, for example, that you want to transform a paper-driven system into an SQL-driven, Internet-based system. What else should you be thinking about? You should be thinking about meta-data categories; that is, information about information. The exercise of building a database can be very frustrating if it is allowed to develop into a sort of giant electronic hall closet, an undisciplined repository for all the information floating through a company. In contrast, using meta-data categories helps you organize your information very effectively.

What is meta-data? To appreciate what it is, spend a couple of moments thinking about using categories. Almost all information can be thought of as fitting into larger categories. It is a curious thing that the human mind has its own sense of dimension, its own ups and downs, its own peculiar ways of arranging information. A friend once observed, "You can carry $300,000 dollars worth of business in your head, but after that, forget it."

It's true, databases as well as SQL statements can create some numerical categories on the fly. Selecting product categories by dollar amounts, for example, is easy. Using SQL, you can get a list of all products that cost more than $20.00 but less than $100.00, all products starting with the letters A through F, or a list of all products with Units in Stock less than two. You can even make hard copy reports quickly. When you want to know whether some spreadsheets are selling better than similar-priced databases that are for sale, however, you might not be able to quickly quantify the answer.

Unless, of course, you have already thought about this question and included a column in your database, breaking down each software product by category in a category field. You can then answer that question using SQL fairly easily. Spend some extra time creating the categories, and it will be easy to use SQL to select that particular subset of the table. That is what SQL is designed to do.

If you are the primary proprietor of a business and you spend every day with your products, you can probably carry quite a few products in your head pretty well; you do not need an SQL query to tell you whether certain spreadsheets are selling better than others during the previous quarter or month. If you are always multitasking, always having half a dozen projects going at the same time, however, it is difficult to remember all the bits and pieces of software version—usage across multiple platforms, prices, and so forth. Multiply this situation times ten in your business and factor in a business trip or two or a side job plus constant customer contact, and you can see that trying to keep it all in your head may not be the best idea.

Therefore, to make life more hassle-free, make the database keep track of important categories, rather than having to someday create artificial columns, and then have to go through and mark every member of a group (out of a group of ten thousand or more records in a database table) before you are able to use an SQL SELECT statement to manipulate the group.

Most programmers, of course, think ahead and always include additional table columns to track categories long before any need for specialized data retrieval comes up, and so have never had to mark every related record in a database table. This highly theoretical course of action that might occur at the end of a given month on a Friday night is only discussed from the position of a good-humored but essentially disinterested third-party observer. And besides, it's probably as much fun as you can possibly imagine to have the task of searching a whole database by hand to see whether or not you've missed a member or two, a real-life experience no-one should miss, especially if you can schedule it to fall on a Friday evening or even better yet, an otherwise open weekend.

BUILDING CATEGORIES INTO TABLES Coolsoft Inc., is Products table that has some useful features. Each product has a unique ProductNo; if there are several versions of a product, the ProductNo identifies the correct version. Each software product is also under a category; a general Category field contains key words that help you look at smaller related datasets of the main table. Thus, you can use a key word to help you select all the "OS" products, all the "Database" products, or all the "Utility" products category.

Next, you will use SQL to select individual columns of information (and then subgroups of information inside of those columns). The example in the following section shows the SQL statement. (Adding the word **DISTINCT** in the adjective position before the column name prohibits duplicate entries from being displayed.)

Retrieving and Displaying Table Information

An HTML Fill-in form and a CF template are used to retrieve and then display server-based table information. The following HTML Front-End Form shows how to select one or more columns from a table and then start up a CF Template. The template then dynamically generates an HTML document (an HTML document created on the fly by a Cold Fusion template) that displays the SQL data retrieval results to the end user.

Listing: HTML
Front-End Form

```
<HTML>
<HEAD>
<TITLE> Form used to start up CF Template</TITLE>
</HEAD>
<BODY BACKGROUND="redbackg.jpg" BGCOLOR="#FFFF80" >
<center><font size="+2" color="red"><i>ACCESS "QUERY1"
     </i></font></font></center>
<HR>
<FORM ACTION="c12_1.cfm" METHOD=POST>
<B>To run Query, press the Submit button:</B><BR>
<HR>
<INPUT TYPE= "SUBMIT" VALUE="Please Submit My Request">
<HR>
</FORM>
</BODY>
</HTML>
```

The bolded code shows the Form tag that starts the Cold Fusion template c12_1.cfm on the server. This form has only one active element: the

Submit button input field. The following code segment shows the c12_1.cfm template it activates:

Listing: CF Template used to Query the Products1 Table

```
<!- c12_1.cfm template uses "products1" table - >
<CFQUERY NAME="ACCESSQ1" DATASOURCE="CERAMIC DB">
     SELECT DISTINCT Category FROM PRODUCTS1
</CFQUERY>
<HTML>
<b>Products Table Data:</b><br>
<CFOUTPUT QUERY="ACCESSQ1">
#Category#<BR>
</CFOUTPUT>
</HTML>
```

This code shows the Cold Fusion SQL query tag. Use the name of the query in the CFOUTPUT tag portion of the template so that Cold Fusion will find the right query to use when outputting retrieved query information. (This example displays only the Category data column, but you can easily add more display fields.) You can put the results of several queries on one HTML page—another reason why Cold Fusion requires the use of a specific query name in the CFOUTPUT tag. When you run this query against the Products table (created using Access with the above data), you get the following SQL output:

Listing: Output From CFQUERY "ACCESSQ1"

```
Products Table Data:
Database
OS
Spreadsheet
Utility
```

If you run the same SELECT statement without the DISTINCT adjective, you get a list of every row of the table, as follows:

Listing: Output From CFQUERY "ACCESSQ1" -without the query adjective "DISTINCT"

```
Products Table Data:
Database
Database
Spreadsheet
Spreadsheet
Utility
utility
OS
OS
```

To increase the usefulness of this query, you can select multiple columns to print, as shown in the following code segment. (Only the code necessary to print multiple fields from the table is shown. The results, which are very much like the output shown previously, is not shown.)

```
<!- c12_2.cfm template uses "products1" table - >
<CFQUERY NAME="ACCESSQ2" DATASOURCE="CERAMIC DB">
     SELECT ProductName, Category, UnitPrice   FROM
          PRODUCTS1
</CFQUERY>

<HTML>
<b>Products Table Data:</b><br>
<CFOUTPUT QUERY="ACCESSQ2">
#ProductName#  #Category#  #UnitPrice#<BR>
</CFOUTPUT>
</HTML>
```

Notice that the name of the Datasource is still QUERY1 but that the name of the query has been changed in to ACCESSQ2 in two places in the template. That's because *each query must have its own unique name*. Also, make sure you spell column names exactly. If you get an error message, such as **No such field name**, check the spellings in the template against the database table spellings. They must match exactly. If you need to save time, you can use SELECT * to select all of the columns from the table. In the CFOUTPUT tag, only list the columns that you need to display.

RETRIEVING AND DISPLAYING INDIVIDUAL TABLE RECORDS
The preceding section described how to design a CATEGORY. After you have included a category in your table, you will use it to select and display rows that match a particular type of category. This section shows how to use SQL to select and display records matching a single member of a category.

BUILDING TEMPLATES THAT SELECT INDIVIDUAL TABLE ROWS The following template example shows how to select rows which match a specific software category subgroup, in this case, "database".

```
<!- c12_3.cfm template uses "products1" table - >
<CFQUERY NAME="ACCESSQ3" DATASOURCE="CERAMIC DB">
```

```
      SELECT * From PRODUCTS1
      WHERE Category = 'database'
</CFQUERY>
<HTML>
<b>Products Table Data:</b><br>
<CFOUTPUT QUERY="ACCESSQ3">
#Category#  #UnitPrice#<BR>
</CFOUTPUT>
</HTML>
```

The text shows how to select a single member of a category. Also it is proper to read the Select statement from the inner-most condition to the outer-most condition as follows: **Where Category = 'database,' SELECT all instances from the Products1 table.**

This SQL statement is very precisely written; if the single quotes around the word **database** are omitted, the statement will not execute. If the asterisk is omitted, the statement will not run. The output is not highly formatted, but some formatting is not difficult if you use a **<CFCOL>** tag as shown in the following template code example, **cf12_3.cfm)**. See XXX for more information on using these commands.)

```
Template Output:
Products Table Data:
Database 149.9900
Database 149.9500
Database  99.9500
```

DISPLAYING QUERY RESULTS IN A TABULAR FORMAT This preceding example displays results that can be more carefully formatted using preformatted tables. The CFTABLE and CFCOL tags are used together to structure query results. The following CFTABLE tag example formats the output from the c12_3.cfm template:

```
Template using the CFTABLE tag with <CFCOL Header>
<!— c12_3a.cfm template uses "products1" table — >
<CFQUERY NAME="ACCESSQ3" DATASOURCE="CERAMIC DB">
     SELECT * From PRODUCTS1
</CFQUERY>
<HTML>
<CFTABLE QUERY="ACCESSQ3" MAXROWS=8>
     <CFCOL HEADER="<b>Products</b>"  WIDTH=20
          TEXT="<I>#ProductName#</I>">
     <CFCOL HEADER="<b>Category</b>"  WIDTH=15
          TEXT="#Category#">
     <CFCOL HEADER="<b>Units</b>"  WIDTH=15
```

```
            TEXT="#UnitsInStock#">
</CFTABLE>
</HTML>a
```

The CFTABLE/CFCOL tag replaces the CFOUTPUT tag. You can also add HTML bold and italics tags inside of the CFCOL HEADER tag for additional formatting. CFCOL HEADER tags do not need closing tags. Because the MAXROWS limits the number of data rows to be displayed, you might want to show only a single screen's worth of table information if most of your users only have 14-inch monitors. In this case, use MAXROWS=22. You can also specify the WIDTH of each of the data columns. The following shows the output from the CFTABLE/CFCOL tags:

Products	Category	Units
FastBASE	Database	5
FrameTool	Utility	4
OS2000	OS	10
OS3000	OS	10
Quick Spread	Spreadsheet	1
Quick Spread Pro	Spreadsheet	7
QuikUtility II	Utility	5
RelateBase	Database	10
SpreadData	Database	8

BUILDING SQL QUERIES CONTAINING CONDITIONAL LOGIC

The preceding query can be modified to include additional conditions. If you want to select two categories, for example, you can use the following SQL statement. Notice that the column name *must* be repeated with the second data search condition and that the CFQUERY NAME must also be changed (in two places, the second place is in the CFOUTPUT tag). Also, remember to use OR. If you use AND, both of the conditions must be met before a row can be selected.

```
<CFQUERY NAME="ACCESSQ4" DATASOURCE="CERAMIC DB">
    SELECT * From PRODUCTS1
    WHERE Category = 'database'  OR  Category= 'OS'
</CFQUERY>
```

If the table contains a great number of different database column entries, you might want to limit the search to only those database products that have fewer than 9 units in stock. The following example shows how to use AND.

```
<!- c12_5.cfm uses products1 table ->
<CFQUERY NAME="ACCESSQ5" DATASOURCE="CERAMIC DB">
    SELECT * From PRODUCTS1
    WHERE Category = 'database'  AND  UnitsInStock < 9
</CFQUERY>
<HTML>
<b>Units in Stock:</b><br>
<CFOUTPUT QUERY="ACCESSQ5">
#ProductName#  #UnitsInStock#<BR>
</CFOUTPUT>
</HTML>
```

This query produces the following output:

```
Units in Stock:
FastBase 5
SpreadData 8
```

The preceding example shows how to use `Category= 'database' AND UnitsInStock <9` as two conditions to retrieve table records that match both conditions. Notice that the actual information displayed is from two entirely different columns in the table, not the columns searched on. This process shows how SQL is designed to work. When query conditions are satisfied, SQL retrieves the entire row. When the entire row is retrieved, any field(s) in the row can be displayed.

Using Dynamic Parameters in SQL Statements

One of the most useful features of Cold Fusion's implementation of SQL is the capability to enable the end user to enter form data, which is then passed to a Cold Fusion template residing on a server, and is then used to search a database table. Cold Fusion recognizes this special parameter information, because it is enclosed in hash marks (#). Upon receiving a parameter value, Cold Fusion searches the SQL variables until it finds the variable that matches the parameter, and then "substitutes in" the value. This enables the end user to customize database searches by entering varying information into HTML fill-in forms. The following example shows how to create an HTML fill-in form by allowing entered values to be used as parameters:

```
<HTML>
<HEAD>
<TITLE>Query Containing Form with Parameters</TITLE>
</HEAD>
<BODY BACKGROUND="redbackg.jpg" BGCOLOR="#FFFF80" >
<center><font size="+2" color="red"><i>ACCESS "QUERY"
      </i></font></font></center>
<HR>
<FORM ACTION="c12_6.cfm" METHOD=POST>
Please enter a quantity number to search for Units In Stock
      below that quantity.
<INPUT TYPE "Text" NAME="UnitsInStock"><BR>
<HR>
<INPUT TYPE= "SUBMIT" VALUE="Please Submit my Request">
<HR>
</FORM>
</BODY>
</HTML>
```

The number entered in the form is passed as a parameter to a CF template. The following template is an example of parameter passing:

```
CF Template Using Form-passed Values (Parameters)
<!— c12_6.cfm uses products1 table —>
<CFQUERY NAME="ACCESSQ6" DATASOURCE="CERAMIC DB">
      SELECT * From PRODUCTS1
      WHERE UnitsInStock < #Form.UnitsInStock#
</CFQUERY>
<HTML>
<b>Units in Stock:</b><br>
<CFOUTPUT QUERY="ACCESSQ6">
#ProductName#   #UnitsInStock#<BR>
</CFOUTPUT>
</HTML>]
```

```
Units in Stock:
FastBase   5
SpreadData 8
Quick Spread 1
Quick Spread Pro 7
QuikUtility II 5
FrameTool 4
```

The CFQUERY tag uses hash marks (#) around the **#UnitsInStock#** to indicate to Cold Fusion that the parameter value passed from the form to be substituted into that member of the SQL expression. Also, text needs single quotes ' ' around it, numbers (1,2,3,4) do not.

RETRIEVING DATA USING PATTERN MATCHING A useful technique is to retrieve records containing information that is close to the search key but not exactly the same as the search key. This is done by using the SQL LIKE operator along with at least one wildcard character (the % character, for example), as shown in the following SELECT statement:

```
SQL = SELECT * FROM PRODUCTS1 WHERE  UnitsInStock  LIKE
      #UnitsInStock%#
```

Use an HTML fill-in form to pass parameters to a CF template containing the above **SQL=Select…** statement. Then type the first few letters into the fill-in form text input field, and submit it. The LIKE operator in the SQL statement works wonders. Entering **os**, for example, finds the table ProductName entries **OS2000** and **OS3000**.

USING CFIF WITH CFQUERY The preceding example passed inputted values (parameters) to the template. For even more flexibility, you can insert a CFIF tag inside of the CFQUERY tag to allow conditions to be added to the main SQL statement. The CFIF tag can execute or not execute a secondary condition, based on values entered (or left blank) by the end user. When writing the CFIF tag, you must use the AND operator carefully. The following example shows how to build a CFIF tag inside of a CFQUERY tag:

```
<!- c12_7.cfm uses products1 table ->
<CFQUERY NAME="ACCESSQ7" DATASOURCE="CERAMIC DB">
    SELECT * From PRODUCTS1
    WHERE Category = '#Form.Category#'

    <CFIF #Form.UnitsInStock# is not " ">
       AND UnitsInStock < #Form.UnitsInStock#
    </CFIF>

</CFQUERY>
<HTML>
<b>Units in Stock:</b><br>
<CFOUTPUT QUERY="ACCESSQ7">
#ProductName#  #UnitsInStock#<BR>
</CFOUTPUT>
</HTML>
```

The preceding code creates the following form shown in Figure 12-1.

The code shows the <CFIF> tag. The word **AND** adds the second condition to the main **SELECT * From PRODUCTS1 WHERE** … statement. If a zero is entered in the **UnitsInStock** input box, no category entries are displayed. If a large number is entered, all the entries are displayed. If the user enters a Product Name and types in a number for **Units In Stock**,

Figure 12-1

Fill-in Form used to enter table search parameters

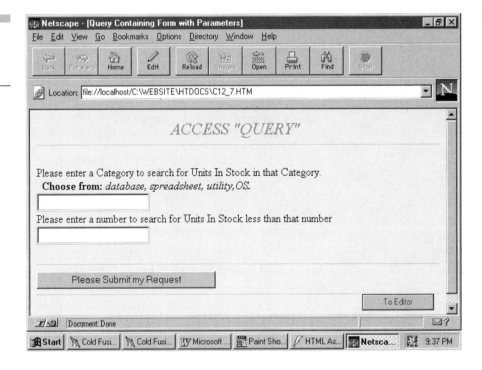

all Units in Stock record entries less than that number are retrieved and displayed.

If you have a large database, being able to create exception reports using SQL conditional statements showing low stock levels is a valuable tool. You can also modify the preceding template to add an OR condition to the main template. Because of the power of CFIF conditional statements, you should survey user needs, and then build special search features into both HTML forms and CF templates.

NOTE: *When you build special capabilities into a template, add specific instructions about how to use these special capabilities. Otherwise, the custom-built features may remain invisible and unused.*

Updating a Table

Updating a table involves the following steps:

1. A form is built that uniquely identifies the record to be updated.

2. The table to be updated must include a key field, and the key field must be included in the HTML form. (A hidden Input field can be used, see following example.) The CFUPDATE tag uses the key field to uniquely identify the specific record in the table to be updated.

3. The template generates a dynamic HTML form that the end user uses to make changes to the fields to be updated by new information.

4. The form is then submitted, which causes Cold Fusion to open the database table and update the record.

NOTE: *Make sure your table does not have a counter-type field as the primary key field. The CFUPDATE tag can not process a counter-type field used as a primary key field.*

After you enter the ProductNo and press the Submit button, the specific record identifying the information is sent to the server, which then starts the c12_9x.cfm update template. The template retrieves the columns to be updated, asks you to make changes to the values to be updated, starts a second template c12_9a.cfm to do the actual update, and then sends the user a confirming HTML document showing the updates made to the UnitsOnOrder and UnitsInStock fields. The first Update template, c12_9x.cfm, is shown in the following example:

```
Dynamic Data Input Template
<! —c12_9x.cfm   uses Customers, Orders tables   — >

<CFQUERY DATASOURCE="CERAMIC DB" NAME=PRODUPDATE>
     SELECT * From Products1
     WHERE ProductNo = '#Form.ProductNo#'
</CFQUERY>
<HTML>
<HEAD><TITLE> Product Name Update </TITLE></HEAD><br>
<BODY>
<CFOUTPUT QUERY=PRODUPDATE>
<FORM ACTION=c12_9a.cfm   METHOD=POST>
<FONT SIZE="+1">Please Update Inventory Units for: </font>
     "#Form.ProductNo#"<br>
<HR>
<b>Change ProductName:</b>
<INPUT TYPE="HIDDEN" NAME="ProductNo"
     VALUE="#ProductNo#"><p>
```

```
<INPUT TYPE="TEXT" NAME="ProductName" VALUE=
     "#ProductName#"><p>

<INPUT TYPE="Submit" VALUE="Submit Form">
<INPUT TYPE="Reset" VALUE="Reset Form">
</FORM>
</BODY>
</HTML>
</CFOUTPUT>
```

Figure 12-2 shows the preceding template on-screen.

The Dynamic Data Update template enables the user to make data changes and then submit those changes to the second CFUPDATE template. The CFUPDATE template uses the following line of code to write the changes to the database table:

```
<CFUPDATE   DATASOURCE="CERAMIC DB"   TABLENAME=Products1 >
```

After the changes are written to the database, the updated product name information is displayed to the user. To keep this example short and easy to read, only a single field was updated; obviously many items can be up-

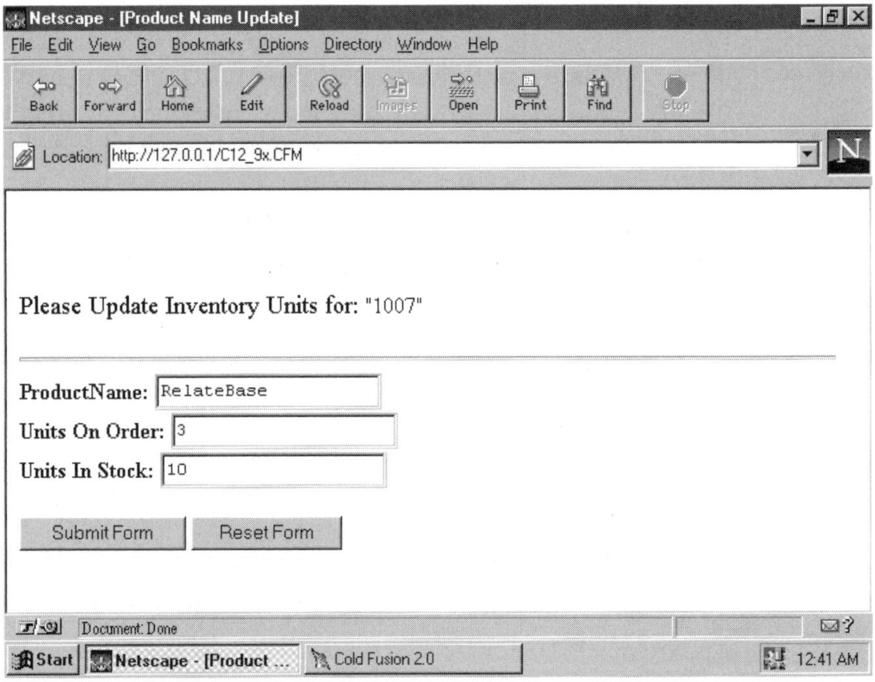

Figure 12-2
The Data Change
template

dated at once. Also, Access requires that the ProductNo field be a key field, otherwise it will not permit a search and update operation. If an incorrect name is entered, it is easy to use the Back button on the browser to resend the correct update values. You can also easily add a button, which would use a FORM tag to start the UPDATE fill-in form a second time.

The following CF template uses the CFOUTPUT tag to display the results of the UPDATE operation, as shown in Figure 12-3.

```
CFUPDATE Template
<! — c12_9a.cfm called from c12_9x.cfm— >
<CFUPDATE   DATASOURCE="CERAMIC DB" TABLENAME=Products1 >
<CFOUTPUT >
<HTML>
<TITLE>Products1 Table Update </TITLE>
<BODY>
<font size="+1">Updated Inventory Product Name</font><BR>
<HR>
ProductName: #ProductName#

</BODY
</HTML>
</CFOUTPUT>
```

Figure 12-3
The CFUPDATE
template results

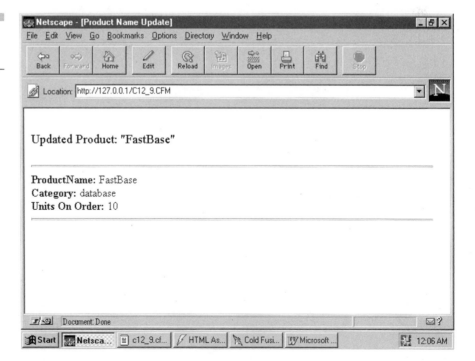

CONCLUSION

This chapter discussed how to design tables that SQL can use to effectively search databases. The Cold Fusion implementation of SQL with the use of conditional logic, such as CFIF, OR, and AND operators, was also discussed. The next chapter, which covers advanced SQL, shows how to use subqueries to further refine data retrievals, and how to use multiple SQL queries to produce an even more powerful HTML page. Chapters 17 and 18, which contain a detailed Cold Fusion programming example, discusses SQL operators even further.

Advanced Database and Cold Fusion 3.0 Programming

13

Using Advanced SQL with Cold Fusion

- Using the Microsoft Access SQL Wizard
- Creating Nested/Grouped SQL Statements
- Building SQL Subqueries
- Using SQL Joins & Order-By Parameters with Access Tables

Microsoft Access—Using the SQL Wizard

You can use Microsoft Access SQL wizard to create SQL statements, and understand and analyze how they are constructed. You can also use the Access SQL wizard to relate two tables to one another, (Access displays the relationship visually). To start the SQL wizard, open Access, click Query, New, and then click the New Query button (not the Query Wizard button). Then click Add to display, sample tables such as the `Customers` table in the window. Next, highlight `Orders` and click Add to display the `Orders` table in the window. Click `Close`. Access draws a line from the `Customers` table and field `CustomersID` to the `CustomerID` field in the `Orders` table. These two tables are now related by means of the common CustomerID field. Click the Field tab to display all of the fields in both tables. (To view hidden Access fields, you can display all the Orders fields by clicking the spin arrow repeatedly).

Using the spin arrow, highlight the `FirstName` field in the drop-down menu box. As soon as you release the mouse button, `FirstName` automatically becomes your first field selection. Click the adjacent empty square on the top row across from the word Field. Once again, a drop-down menu of field choices appears. Select `LastName`. Click the empty box on the top row to bring up the spin arrow and display a list of field choices. Find the `Billed` field. If you cannot see the fields that belong to the Orders table, scroll down with the spin button until you get to the Orders Table fields. Select the Billed field. When the Billed field appears, go vertically down to the fourth empty box (across the row from the word Criteria) and right-click on that box. Click on the word Build.

Access displays a window in which you can choose any condition you want as a field criteria. Click the greater than (>) symbol; (used to show that one number is greater than another) Access displays the greater than symbol in the window. Type `$50.00` right after the greater than symbol. Click OK. You have now created a field condition in which only records having billed amounts greater than $50.00 appear.

SAVING (AND DEBUGGING) THE QUERY To save the query, click the "*x*" in the top-right corner of the query window, name the query `prodquery`, and then click Save. Access saves the "prodquery" under the Query tab. Double-click the query to run it. The `Type Mismatch` error message appears, meaning that the Billed column expects a simpler query expression. Open the Query Design tool and change the criteria from `>$50.00` to `>50`. Close the query. Double-click the query again and watch it give you a list of products more expensive than $50.00. (You can also add `<100` after the `>50` to show products more than $50.00 but less than $100.00.

VIEWING MICROSOFT ACCESS SQL CODE   After writing your SQL query, click the word **Design.** When the Query Design window opens, right-click anywhere in the window. Access displays a list of choices. Click **View SQL.** Access displays the underlying SQL code making up the query, as follows:

You can use this code as a model to develop SQL code in Cold Fusion templates. Notice that each field is identified with a prefixed table name, which helps SQL keep track of how to select the correct field. You will

Listing: Microsoft Access Auto-generated SQL Code

```
SELECT DISTINCTROW Customers.FirstName, Customers.LastName,
     Orders.Billed
FROM Customers INNER JOIN Orders ON Customers.CustomerID =
Orders.CustomerID
WHERE ((Orders.Billed>50));
```

probably have some identical field names in tables—for example, key field names. Looking at the code that was created, you can leave off the word INNER; it is only useful in helping document the code. INNER JOINS "join" a first table with a second table using a common column found in both tables. This SQL statement also has a WHERE condition used to select all orders over $50. On the last line, a semicolon is the marker of the end of an SQL statement in Access. Cold Fusion uses a less than (>) sign for the same purpose.

USING NESTED CFOUTPUT TAGS WITH GROUPINGS   When implementing SQL, some commercial applications are able to generate several thousand lines of SQL code per query. This kind of complex coding is very daunting to read through; an alternate approach is to break down each complex query into groups of individual queries. Taken this way, you can write individual queries quickly and easily. There is an individual benefit of being able to check your work at several stages of the operation; sometimes program logic seems very correct until you look hard at the results. After you retrieve table information using several individual SQL queries, you can also use grouped CFOUTPUT statements to display the information onscreen. Nested output statements can quickly draw a data picture for users who need summary data reporting.

If you want to group all Software Products by Category and individual software type, use an SQL statement with the ORDER BY parameter. You must choose the Category field to group on in order to produce the desired subgroups. Figure 13-1 shows the results from the preceding query of ordering by Category on the PRODUCTS1 table.

The following code line shows how to produce groups. Notice how a condition is placed on the field UnitsInStock:

```
" WHERE UnitsInStock < #UnitsInStock# ".
```

Figure 12-1 in the preceding chapter shows the front-end HTML form which can start up the templatecode. To run this template using that HTML form, you only need to change the template reference to `c13_1.htm`. Notice how WHERE conditions are inserted into the following CFQUERY tag, giving you a great deal of freedom in retrieving and displaying very specific parts of a table:

```
<!- c13_1.cfm uses products1 table ->
<CFQUERY NAME="Access13Q1" DATASOURCE="CERAMIC DB"
SQL =       "SELECT * From PRODUCTS1
     ORDER BY CATEGORY" >
</CFQUERY>
<HTML>
<font size="+1">PRODUCTS:</font>
<CFOUTPUT QUERY="Access13Q1" GROUP = "CATEGORY" >

<H4>#Access13Q1.CATEGORY# </H4>
<UL>
<CFOUTPUT>
```

Figure 13-1
The grouped output
from tables

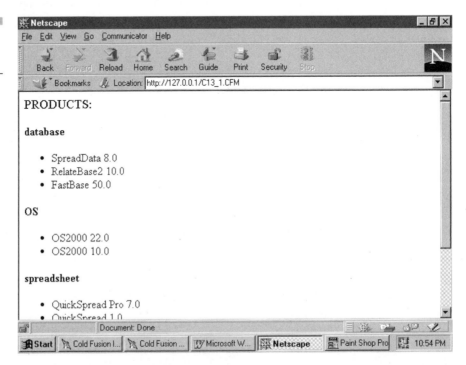

```
<LI> #ProductName#   #UnitsInStock# <BR>
</CFOUTPUT>
</UL>
</CFOUTPUT>
</HTML>
```

In the preceding code, the line

```
<H4>#Access13Q1.CATEGORY# </H4>
```

is used to print the ORDER BY product categories. This line creates the titles for each subgroup grouping. Another useful feature is that this code automatically cycles until it displays all of the record data meeting the conditions of the WHERE clause. You do not need to add a LOOP command. Each time a new category appears, all of the product names meeting the WHERE condition requirements in that category are displayed, and then control is passed back to the outer CFOUTPUT tag. If you need to have multiple levels of grouping, you also must have multiple levels of sorting in the SQL query. (For example, ORDER BY Category, Product Type.)

Building SQL Subqueries

You can use SQL to search two or more tables by using a subquery. Subqueries use a careful approach when handling several tables at a time. Subqueries contain two parts: the outer Select statement and the inner Select statement (which can also be an Update, Insert, or Delete statement). The outer Select statement has the same form as a stand alone Select statement. The inner Select statement searches the second table during its intermediate processing. To search two tables, each must have a common field that relates the two tables to each other. In the following example, the two sample tables are Customers and Orders.

```
Customers Table      Orders Table
CustomerID           CustomerID
First Name           Product Name
Last Name            Ship City
Address              Ship State
City                 Ship Postal Code
State                Billed
Zip
```

The two tables share a common key field, CustomerID, which is used to relate the tables to each other. The Orders table can have multiple instances of records containing the same CustomerID. This occurs when a customer places a second or third order. The following template (see

Figure 13-2) shows how to select only those customers who have actual orders in the Orders table. (This query skips new customers who have not yet ordered merchandise.) The inner query, represented in the following example, searches the Orders table for a record containing a given CustomerID and compares it against the Customers table. If a CustomerID exists in both tables, a match has occurred. In the final section of the template, CFOUTPUT tags are used to display the results onscreen.

SUBQUERY EXAMPLE TEMPLATE

```
<! —c13_2.cfm  uses Customers, Orders tables  — >

<CFQUERY DATASOURCE="CERAMIC DB"   NAME=ORDERSUBQ>
     SELECT FirstName, LastName From Customers
     WHERE EXISTS
           (SELECT *
           FROM Orders
           WHERE Customers.CustomerID = CustomerId)
</CFQUERY>
<HTML>
<HEAD><TITLE> Select Orders </TITLE></HEAD><br>
<BODY>
<b>Customer Name:<br>
<CFOUTPUT QUERY=ORDERSUBQ>
```

Figure 13-2

A graphical relationship between Customers, and Orders tables

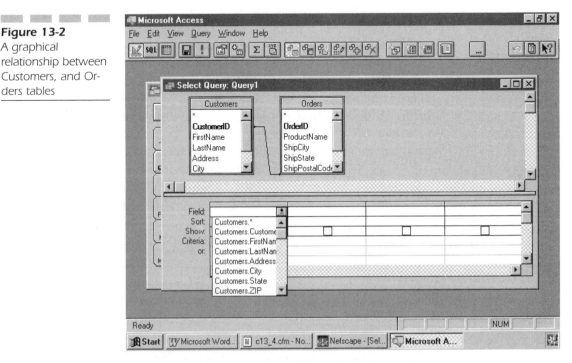

```
</b>#FirstName# #LastName# <BR>

</FORM>
</BODY>
</HTML>
</CFOUTPUT>
```

This query produces a list of first and last names of customers who have existing orders in the orders database. After running this query, if you examine the Customers Database, you will find that several CustomerId's exist that were not reported because they had no corresponding Orders Table record.

When writing this query, the inner query must be completely bounded by parentheses. When referring to the CustomerID field in the Customers table, include the table prefix as: `Customers.CustomerID`. The SQL statement `Where Exists` finds the instances of customers who have already made orders. The use of the DATASOURCE name allows access to all tables making up the database.

USING JOINS Sometimes it is useful to display column information retrieved from two or more tables. *Joins* enable you to select and display columns that are controlled by a condition that reaches across both tables —in this example a WHERE clause. Notice that the second table must have its columns prefixed with its own table name, or the Select statement cannot find them. Also, the listing order of column names must correspond to the listing order of the table names; otherwise, SQL looks for the field names in the wrong table and returns an error code.

GENERAL JOINS A *general join*, selects all columns from both tables and has the following form:

```
<CFQUERY DATASOURCE="CERAMIC DB"   NAME=ORDERSUBQ>
    SELECT *
    FROM  Customers, Orders
        WHERE Customers.CustomerID = Orders.CustomerID
</CFQUERY>
```

Notice the `Select *` statement preceding the WHERE clause, it selects all of the rows of the table. A general join can produce a huge report with many outputted columns. If you want fewer columns, a different technique is used. The following example shows how to select only a limited number of columns. The bolded code shows how to refer to the columns of the second table. Interestingly, in order to be "seen" by SQL, both table names must prefix the respective column names inside the WHERE statement.

```
<! —c13_3.cfm  uses Customers, Orders tables  — >

<CFQUERY DATASOURCE="CERAMIC DB"  NAME=ORDERSUBQ>
     SELECT FirstName, LastName, Orders.ProductName
     FROM  Customers, Orders
          WHERE Customers.CustomerID = Orders.CustomerID
</CFQUERY>

<HTML>
<HEAD><TITLE> Select Orders </TITLE></HEAD><br>
<BODY>
<b>Customer:   </b> Purchase<br>
<CFOUTPUT QUERY=ORDERSUBQ>
<b> #FirstName# #LastName# - </b>#ProductName#<BR>

</FORM>
</BODY>
</HTML>
</CFOUTPUT>
```

Figure 13-3 shows the output from the preceding template.

ORDERING RESULTS IN AN ASCENDING PATTERN   SQL also enables you to order column results in an ascending order. The following code shows how to use the Billed column to create a Products report with increasing billed dollar amounts.

```
<! —c13_3.cfm  uses Customers, Orders tables  — >

<CFQUERY DATASOURCE="CERAMIC DB"  NAME=ORDERSUBQ>
     SELECT ProductName, Orders.Billed
     FROM  Customers, Orders
          WHERE Customers.CustomerID = Orders.CustomerID
          ORDER BY Orders.Billed
</CFQUERY>
<HTML>
<HEAD><TITLE> Select Orders </TITLE></HEAD><br>
<BODY>
<b>Item:      Price</b><br>
<CFOUTPUT QUERY=ORDERSUBQ>
<b> </b>#ProductName# - #Billed#<BR>
</FORM>
</BODY>
</HTML>
</CFOUTPUT>
```

Figure 13-4 shows the results of running the preceding template.

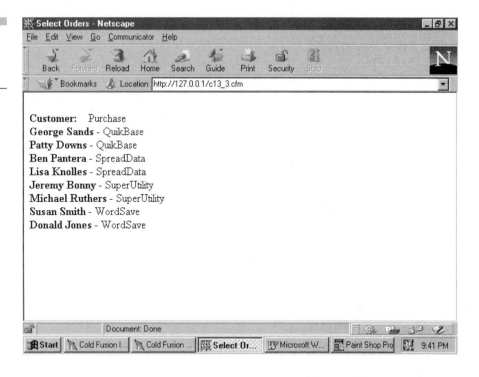

Figure 13-3
Displaying columns
from two tables
using a join

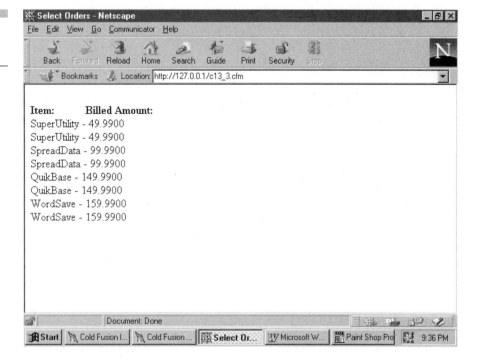

Figure 13-4
Ordered billed
amounts

CONCLUSION

This chapter discussed some of the multi-table manipulation features of SQL. Programming Examples have shown how to select subgroups from within columns by adding conditional statements to basic SQL code. Chapters 16 through 19 introduce additional SQL features that enable you to further exploit the capabilities of this language. The complete language specification is hundreds of pages long and includes many details of the SQL language that could not be covered in this chapter. Nevertheless, most installations are now using some form of SQL that has been enhanced with proprietary language extensions, (for example, Cold Fusion).

14

Advanced Cold Fusion Templates Design

- Designing Cold Fusion templates
- Dynamically generated HTML documents
- Building master templates with reusable templates— using the **CFINCLUDE** tag
- Insider's view: how to really build a corporate intranet

Understanding how to build Cold Fusion templates will change the way you work on the Web. By themselves, HTML documents can only do certain kinds of work, such as display text, images, and sound, do data validation, play Java applets, or run animated GIFs. Getting beyond strictly client-side activities, however, requires a different order of information management using server-based Cold Fusion templates.

Web databases can contain terabytes of information, an amount equal to all the editions of a newspaper for 300 years. Being restricted to working with Web sites containing only static HTML documents sitting on a server does not allow you to meet all information needs in a timely manner. You can use Cold Fusion templates (containing HTML, SQL, and CFML tags) to process client information requests against server-based databases., Retrieved database information can be incorporated into dynamically generated HTML documents sent back to the requestor. The best part is that you can save time and give yourself a real flexibility by using Cold Fusion templates.

Creating Cold Fusion Templates

To understand fully how templates work means to understand that the three major building blocks making up templates—HTML tags, CFML tags, and SQL statements—can be arranged in almost any order and can be made to do almost any activity that you can think of. It may be very useful, for example, to use an SQL query in the opening lines of the template. In this case, the SQL statement makes up the opening program lines, and allows database information to be immediately retrieved by a pre-written query and then used to generate a dynamic HTML document back to the end user showing the query results. Or perhaps you need to get clarifying information from the end user before querying the database. In this case, an HTML document containing a fill-in form can be used; then the form information is used to search the database. The results of the database query are then combined with the HTML fill-in form information and sent back to the end user. Additionally, you can feed the SQL query results directly into the Crystal Reports Report Writer (see chapter 15 and 16)to make GAAP accounting-style reports. The possibilities are unlimited. You can make templates into reusable modules simplifying the task of maintaining a group of HTML. Let's take a look at some Cold Fusion templates.

Using Templates to retrieve database information

You can build templates to process data queries from end users such as the following: What is the *current* price of our company's standard widgets? Which technical support personnel *at this time* support the Superware software product? How many stock items are *currently* at our XYZ site? The important concept in each of these requests is represented by the italicized time reference word.

You can answer each of these questions by creating static, hard-coded HTML pages that contains the necessary data. If you process the same information request each time, you can create a number of HTML hyperlinked Web pages to do the job. Look at the bigger picture, however, and consider how much Web page maintenance overhead will be required. If you have ever spent time building a large number of HTML pages containing legacy text-based information, you soon realized that there must be an easier way to do the job than having to build a new HTML page each time an end user needs to retrieve data. Building HTML pages involves careful, painstaking work, and revising HTML pages is an even more exacting job.

Therefore, if an easier way to retrieve some of the data you need is available, you should seriously considered it. A smart decision is to put the information into a database, use a Cold Fusion template containing SQL to retrieve the information, and then generate a dynamic HTML document back to the requester. This solution often is avoided because it necessitates writing fairly complex PERL or C/C++ scripts. With Cold Fusion, however, the whole process is much more doable because Cold Fusion uses easily written tags that can easily create a dynamic HTML page that looks just like a hyperlinked HTML document.

Static HTML Web Pages versus Dynamically Generated CF Web Pages

The following example shows the strengths and weaknesses inherent in using static HTML pages for data retrieval. The sample shown in Table 14-1 contains software products offered for sale in a hypothetical products table.

Table 14-1

Products Table

Product Name	Units on Order	Units in Stock	Unit Price
FastBase	10	5	$149.99
RelateBase	3	10	$149.95
SpreadData	14	8	$99.95
Quick Spread	19	1	$69.95
Quick Spread Pro	5	7	$169.95

You can permanently hard-code the preceding data into an HTML page using <PRE> tags as follows. (Many legacy text-based intranets are putting reams of data on modified text-based pages like the following)

```
<HTML>
<! Products.html document >
<TITLE> <CENTER><I>Products Database</I></CENTER></TITLE>
<HEAD>
<FONT SIZE="+2">Products Data</FONT>
<HR>
<PRE>
Product Name       Units on Order Units in Stock    Unit Price
FastBase              10                5             $149.99
RelateBase             3               10             $149.95
SpreadData            14                8              $99.95
Quick Spread          19                1              $69.95
Quick Spread Pro       5                7             $169.95
</PRE>
<HR>
</HTML>
```

If you try to display the HTML page created by this code some further formatting is required to produce a reasonably legible HTML page. (Using <PRE> tags for formatting does not always produce vertical columns of data). Instead of using <PRE> tags, to make the data look a little nicer, you could format the data into HTML tables, which takes even more time and effort. Figure 14-1 shows the resulting "static" HTML output page.

This table contains numeric as well as text information, and 5 different model numbers are used to identify the product information. What if there were 2000 model numbers and 20 fields of information; how would you create the vast number of HTML pages needed to display 2000 model numbers? And perhaps you would be ready to go on permanent vacation when you are informed that 50 of the model numbers and products (scattered throughout the range of serial numbers, of course) are scheduled to

Figure 14-1
The Products.htm
static HTML
document

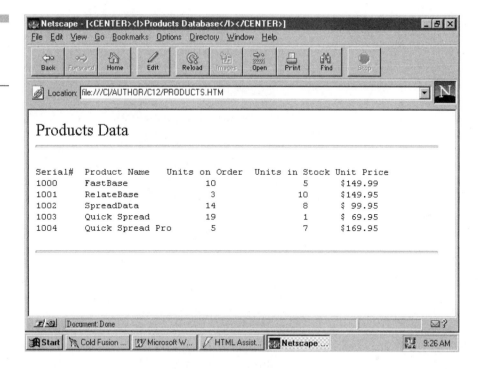

be retired each month and replaced by new products and, of course, new model numbers. Storing this information in a database table, and using SQL and Cold Fusion to retrieve the data and create dynamic HTML pages is much more manageable than creating a huge group of hyperlinked HTML pages.

Chapters 5 to 9 review five popular desktop databases, and demonstrate how to build tables using any one of these software products. This chapter uses Microsoft's Access database. (See Chapter 5 if you have any unanswered questions about using Access to build the database and table.)

To get started, open a project in Microsoft Access, and use the Access Table wizard to select fields for the table (adding any additional fields you need). Save the table, and then begin populating the table with data. No HTML tags to think about just yet! As soon as you have added a half dozen or so rows of data, save your work and close the table.

Next, open the Cold Fusion Administrator, and change the table to a Data source by linking it to an ODBC driver (also covered in Chapter 5). Now you are ready to build an HTML page to use as a front-end to start

Front-end HTML form

```
<HTML>
<HEAD>
<TITLE>Query Front-End Form</TITLE>
</HEAD>
<BODY BACKGROUND="redbackg.jpg" BGCOLOR="#FFFF80"
     TEXT="#00000" >
<center><font size="+2" color="red"><i>ACCESS "QUERY"
     </i></font></font></center>
<HR>
<FORM ACTION="c14_1.cfm" METHOD=POST>
<B>To run Query, press the Submit button:</B><BR>
<HR>
<INPUT TYPE= "SUBMIT" VALUE="Please Submit my Request">
<HR>
</FORM>
</BODY>
</HTML>
```

a Cold Fusion template can retrieve database information. That HTML page could resemble the following HTML document:

The CF template, which retrieves the information from the database, uses a combination of SQL, HTML, and CFML tags. The following is a working template:

```
<! —c14_1.cfm  uses Products1 table — >

<CFQUERY DATASOURCE="CERAMIC DB"  NAME=ch14a>
     SELECT *
     FROM  Products1
</CFQUERY>
<HTML>
<HEAD><TITLE> Select Products </TITLE></HEAD><br>
<BODY>
<PRE>
<b>Product:    Order  Stock#   Price</b>
</PRE>
<CFOUTPUT QUERY=ch14a>
<PRE>
<b>#ProductName#</b> #UnitsOnOrder#   UnitsInStock#
     #UnitPrice#
</PRE>
</FORM>
</BODY>
</HTML>
</CFOUTPUT>
```

The following Figure 14-2 shows the dynamically generated HTML page sent back to the user resulting from running the **c14_2.cfm** template.

Up to this point, the results of the template are the same as the results of a dynamically generated Cold Fusion HTML page. This shows the power of Cold Fusion templates. (You can do further **CFCOL** tag formatting with the Cold Fusion results, but that is not the purpose here.) Consider, rather, a database that contains many hundreds of records. The benefits of using Cold Fusion templates to generate HTML-ormatted pages using retrieved records from the database become readily apparent, because you can selectively retrieve the records you want from the database and do not have to code page after page of HTML. That ability is based on using conditional language inside of SQL statements, as discussed in the chapters 12 and 13 covering SQL.

A second task is the job of tying together Web pages from different departments. You can use Cold Fusion to simply this task and its subsequent

Figure 14-2

The database output from the CF template

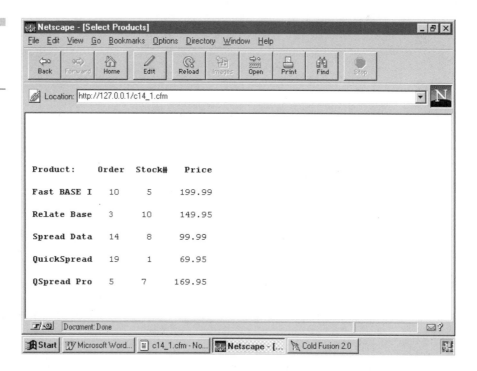

maintenance. (Departmental staff will always want to update their Web page content.) The next section discusses using Master templates and re-usable templates to speed up repetitive Web page development.

Using Master Templates

One of the most useful and powerful Cold Fusion tags is the **CFINCLUDE** tag. The **CFINCLUDE** tag enables you to create a master page that incor-porates many re-usable templates. Each of the sub-templates is included in the main Web page and in the sub-Web pages; you can use a single tem-plate to generate a dozen or more sub-pages. The capability to reuse tem-plates becomes extremely useful in helping develop a uniform look and feel for expanding intranets. Reusable templates also save you a great deal of time and effort.

Suppose, for example, that you have the task of creating an intranet that containing home pages for twelve separate departments, and that each department has requested corporate recognition and visibility to showcase the department to Web page visitors. You may not yet realize it, but you really need reusable templates to keep your development work-load down. As each department gets used to using its part of the intranet, the requests for additional services and Web pages will increase, and you will find that having reusable templates is far superior to maintaining several hundred individual HTML documents. This is not to say that you may not still have some legacy documents on the bottom of the Web page heirarchy.

Using the CFINCLUDE Tag

How can you save yourself from having to replicate HMTL pages? Cold Fusion uses the **CFINCLUDE** tag to help create reusable web pages. All sub-templates use the **CFINCLUDE** tag to produce dynamic Web pages on the fly. You can place templates and sub-templates in the same directory as the master template. Each template is activated by a single **CFINCLUDE** tag in the master template. And each departmental sub-template can use the same modularized and reusable template. (Reusing templates has a secondary benefit of achieving design uniformity in terms of look and feel). The master template dynamically creates each departmental Web page upon demand. Once a user logs in to the departmental Web page, that Web page can contain documents—PDF files, GIFs, JPEGs, sound files, and so on.

The following example shows how to build a master template containing reusable sub-templates (which work in an analogous manner to HTML "server-side includes").

The following Figure 14-3 shows the top Web page for SuperCorp, Inc. using a master template with **CFINCLUDE** tags.

The first **CFINCLUDE** template is the **environ.cfm** template, which is used to control background and link colors, and determine other Web page characteristics. The second template is the **header.cfm** template, which displays a Web page header. The third template is the **mastmenu.cfm** template, which creates a stack of navigational "hot" buttons on the left side of the Web page.

Master Template Incorporating reusable subtemplates

```
< ! — Uses c14_2.cfm template with reusable sub-templates
     —>
< ! — by J. Burke, 5/31/97 — >
<HTML>
<HEAD>
<TITLE> Supercorp Home page </TITLE>
<! — incorporates web page environment template — >
<cfinclude TEMPLATE="environ.cfm">
<cfinclude TEMPLATE="header1.cfm">
<center>
<TABLE align=center width=100%>
<TD width="150" valign="top" align=left>
< !— Menu template contains lefthand column of "stacked"
     template menu buttons — >
<cfinclude TEMPLATE="mastmenu.cfm">
</td>
<!— spacer follows — >
<TD width=2> </td>
<TD width=400>
<BR><BR><BR><FONT COLOR=red>News Item:</FONT> SuperCorp
     achieves record profits in third quarter on database,
     spreadsheet and webserver sales. Common stock split
     receives favorable market reaction. New marketing
     V.P. created to head world-wide software sales.
<P>
New office will be opened in U.K. in response to increased
     demand for webserver products.
</TD>
</TABLE>
</BODY>
</HTML>
```

Figure 14-3
SuperCorp's top Web
page using a master
template

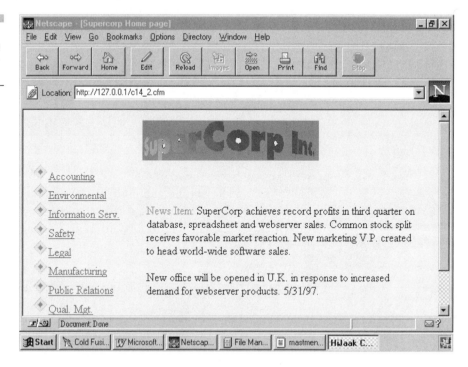

The following is the **Environ.cfm** template:

```
Environ.cfm Template
<BODY BACKGROUND="redbackg.jpg" BGCOLOR="#FFFF80"
      TEXT="#00000"
 LINK="#0000FF" VLINK="#FF00FF" ALINK="#0000FF" >
```

The following is the **Mastmenu.cfm** template:

```
Mastmenu.cfm Template
<! — mastmenu.cfm calls sub-templates  —>
<HTML>
<BODY>
<IMG SRC="rect.gif"><A HREF="mastmenu.cfm">Homepage</a><br>
< IMG SRC ="rect.gif">< A HREF
      ="accountg.cfm">Accounting</a><br>
< IMG SRC ="rect.gif">< A HREF
      ="environ.cfm">Environmental</a><br>
< IMG SRC ="rect.gif">< A HREF
      ="infomgt.cfm">Information Serv.</a><br>
< IMG SRC ="rect.gif">< A HREF
      ="hlthsaf.cfm">Safety</a><br>
< IMG SRC ="rect.gif">< A HREF ="legal.cfm">Legal</a><br>
```

```
< IMG SRC ="rect.gif">< A HREF
     ="manufact.cfm">Manufacturing</a><br>
< IMG SRC ="rect.gif">< A HREF
     ="pubrel.cfm">Public Relations</a><br>
< IMG SRC ="rect.gif">< A HREF ="qualmgt.cfm">Qual.
     Mgt.</a><br>
< IMG SRC ="rect.gif"><a
     href="shiprcv.cfm">Shipping/Receiv.</a><br>
</BODY>
</HTML>
```

The `c14_2.cfm` master template is designed to dynamically generate the top Web page. It contains the three **CFINCLUDE** templates, which build all the sections of the top Web page. The `header1.cfm` template, for example, contains the company logo and any other title messages. The `mastmenu.cfm` template contains stacked buttons as navigation aids to departmental Web pages and template links representing each department in the corporation. The second level of Web pages, the departmental Web pages, is also created by using **CFINCLUDE** tag templates. Each Web page appears to the end user as a standard HTML Web page.

When someone clicks a department button, such as Accounting, Cold Fusion activates the Accounting template on the server and dynamically creates the Accounting HTML Web page. Because reusable templates are in use, the Accounting sub-page is able to reuse the `mastmenu.cfm` template to dynamically generate the navigation button list, which it displays on the left side of the Accounting Web page. This causes the Accounting page to have the uniform look and feel of the top Web page. It also gives the end user a highly recognizable navigation system that can be used to get back to the top page.

Using templates in this manner allows you to use reusable code togreatly reduce the amount of code needed to create individual Web pages and departmental sub-pages. If the Accounting department needs to create a page with a third-level template, you can build that page by once again recycling existing template information. At the lowest level, the Accounting Web page itself can contain document links and news items that serve the visitorís needs. The following is the code for the Accounting Web page:

```
Accounting Web Page - Employs Reusable Templates
< ! — Uses mastmenu.cfm template to re-display department
     navig. buttons  —>
< ! — by J. Burke, 5/31/97 — >
<HTML>
<HEAD>
```

```
<TITLE> The Accounting Page </title>
<! - incorporates webpage environment template - >
<cfinclude TEMPLATE="environ.cfm">
<CENTER>
<TABLE align=center width=100%>
<TD WIDTH="140" valign="top" align=left>
< !- Menu template contains lefthand column of "stacked"
      template menu buttons - >
<cfinclude TEMPLATE="mastmenu.cfm">
</TD>
<!- spacer follows - >
<TD width=2> </td>
<TD width=400>
<BR>
<CENTER><b><FONT SIZE="+3"><i>Corporate
      Accounting</FONT></I></B></CENTER>
<BR>
<UL>
<LI><a href="director.htm">Third Quarter Financial
      Report</a><p>
<LI><a href="stockqt.htm">The Week's Stock Prices </a><p>
<I>News Item:</I> The New Expense Report Format goes into
      effect at the first
of next week. Please use on-line form found at
      "server1\corporate.Forms.cfm"
for all normal expensed items. Any Individual expense items
      greater than $250 must
be approved by your department head and submitted with
      receipt. Thank you in advance for your cooperation.
</UL>
</TD>
</TABLE>
</BODY>
</html>
```

The following Accounting Web page shows how subpages can contain links to other subpages by using re-usable templates.

The Accounting department Web page employs reusable templates shown by bolded CFINCLUDE statements. Using this system of dynamic HTML Web page creation, as well as using SQL to retrieve database information, enables you to manage and control a large number of Web pages simply by changing the CFINCLUDE templates. Having centralized templates also means less HTML writing errors and debugging.

A second topic that needs to be covered is the actual creation of intranet content. At this point, it is worthwhile to spend a little time discussing intranet use, data storage requirements, and retrieval options. The next section describes how to construct intranets and the kind of information to include on individual Web pages.

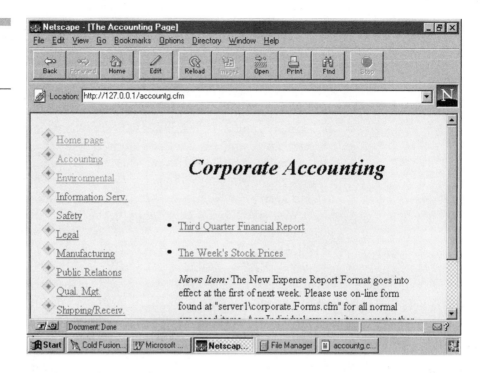

Figure 14-4
The Accounting
department
Web page

How to Really Build an Intranet!

Marshall McCluhan's book, "The Media is the Message," probably needs an appendix to cover the growing impact of the Internet. What would McCluhan say today about the impact of the intranet on the end user? In his most famous work, "The Media is the Message," McCluhan opined that text-based information was a "hot" medium, whereas television represented a "cool" medium. According to his view, reading print engages critical thinking in a more active way than watching television. It would be interesting to hear his opinion on the impact of information presentation via the Internet.

Most intranet Web pages—at least at the second level and below—contain significant amounts of text, and demand interactivity. Does this qualify the intranet as a "hot" or "cool" medium? The answer is unclear. Because both print messages and visual images are present on the Internet, does its media impact fall somewhere between hot and cool? Don't Web pages contain both text and images, and so function simultaneously as both a hot and a cool medium?

What significance does this have? Brain researchers say that text is processed mostly on the left, logical side of the brain, whereas images are processed on the right, intuitive, parallel processing side of the brain. If a Web page has significant amounts of text and significant numbers of images, viewers may find themselves jumping from text blocks to images and back to text blocks in a new sort of computer-like "deadly embrace" between the right side and the left side of the brain. The main problem of the "deadly embrace" in computers (and people) is that it effectively keeps any work from being done because all the resources are tied up trying to initiate the next operation while already being tied up processing the previous operation. To keep your Web site visitors from such interesting dilemmas, DESIGN WEB PAGES TO COMMUNICATE EITHER BY USING IMAGES with subordinate text, OR BY USING TEXT with subordinate images. DO NOT USE BOTH IMAGES AND TEXT HEAD TO HEAD; THEY WILL VIE WITH EACH OTHER FOR VIEWER ATTENTION!

Notice how the use of uppercase text in the preceding paragraph creates an image-like effect, which immediately dominates the page. If a visual effect can be achieved just by changing the typeface from lowercase to uppercase, imagine how distracting a whole group of images would be to a Web page visitor (unless that is what you want to happen). Web page stylists (a new profession) are beginning to lay down rules about the interaction of text and images. One proposed rule states that if a Web page is to convey vital *textual* information, you should limit the number of font sizes. A Web page does not need a half dozen different fonts or font sizes; bolded captions one font size greater than the normal text are quite sufficient to set off individual paragraphs. If the Web page is primarily a graphic—such as a map, building layout, schematic, or picture—use brief text captions that visitors can scan at a glance. In this case, the text is the subordinate element.

Graphics on a Web page can overwhelm the accompanying text and render it a poor second in terms of visual interest. There are times, however, that you may want to do exactly that. Your top Web page should be very graphically interesting to the visitor; Web surfers have come to expect carefully rendered graphics on the top page. You want people to stop and stare a little to get interested, but then go to the next level. The next level should be quite different in terms of the balance between graphics and text. It should include some small orienting images tha preserve the look and feel of the top page.

If the top page is 60–75 percent graphics, the first sub-page may use graphics as navigation guides or for other specific uses. Web pages must be visually interesting, but beware of making excessively visually distracting Web pages. If you do, no other meanings will be remembered. On the positive side, because visual memory works so well (for example, almost anyone can quickly recall a mental picture of any number of famous faces or places), you can use the same header images or button "stacks" on the same place on a Web page to help orient your visitors.

Therefore, you will probably want to reuse headers on "related" second-level Web pages because of their instant visual recognition and orientation value for visitors. The header should be fairly small and may include text, directions, or other information. That the header is consistently color-coded for a particular function or department of a business contributes to its recognition and orientation power.

Soliciting Intranet and Internet Material

What content should you chose for an Inter/intranet? To answer that question, you must find out what is important to the intranet end users before you start designing intranet Web pages. There is something you should always remember before you start the process: When you build an intranet, news is always news no matter what the media!

The Inter/intranet has been called the new media of the 90s. And just like people turn on the television at 6 p.m. to watch the news, news on the intranet can attract attention and help generate hits. News can take the form of company stock quote information, employee recognition and awards, physical improvements to the facility, cafeteria menus (a hot item!), new business developments, and so forth. You can put all these items on the front (top) page of your intranet. Once lured to the top page, people will go to individual sub-pages for additional information. Why not have people visit your site on a regular basis to keep up with ongoing company- and industry-wide developments? Also, if you have stunning graphics on subpages, consider creating "thumbnails"(images less than 2-3K) of the originals to lead to these graphics.

What Makes Up an Intranet?

What else can go into an intranet? To properly accommodate your visitor's needs while maintaining control over the look and feel of the intranet, you should solicit raw Web page material from active company departments, rather than waiting for departments to send in blasé contributions. After the call goes out, you will probably receive a blank stare or two, some questions, and perhaps a few paper documents. What's the problem? There is no problem, but rather a need to interpret the mission; that is, to explain what the Internet is about. Businesses are hotbeds of potential intranet material, but you must get the eyes of the people you serve on their own work and reporting what's going on back to you. You need to develop an Web page example or two to help your coworkers understand what you need from them. The intranet is like a "two-way" television set that enables workers to communicate with each other as well as download data. Help them to think visually and dynamically in terms of live news and demonstrations, instead of in the "memo mode" of using black ink on white paper.

And there's more. Because corporate departments have honest-to-goodness functionality in companies, they continue to exist over the long term. Although a great deal is murmured regarding the inefficiencies, workarounds, and general bureaucracy of corporations (think of the Dilbert comic strip for a moment), look past that and into the actual working heart of a given area. There people are busy producing and creating who may not easily recognize what they do or why it is newsworthy; yet each day they make their contribution, and the company stays alive because of what they do. Your task is to become the investigative reporter using the five W's to get the story: who, when, where, why, and what. Go out and find the stories, find the people who are creating the new products, the people who interact with customers, the people on the cutting edge. Take pictures, get the story, and create the Web page around it."

Here are the kind of results you can expect at the first data gathering stage.

You will collect paper documents that represent daily work operations. People will tell you about "secret" operations. You will get electronic documents, charts, PDF documents, and printed out spreadsheets and databases. You will interview the big people and the little people of departments. Go where the action is. Regularly used legacy documents can be good candidates to put on the intranet. Product manuals, installation guides, processes, schematics, maps, product pictures, and a host of other working documents can be hyperlinked into departmental Web pages. Keep your eyes open for the practical. After you have gleaned the best, do quick layout on paper, revisit the departmental head for content approval and get to work.

CONCLUSION

This chapter discussed how to build an intranet using re-usable master templates and sub-templates. Web page content and the impact of Web pages on visitors was examined with some ideas about how to gather raw material to include on intranets. The following two chapters discuss how to use Crystal Reports Report Generator to dynamically create beautiful reports in HTML document form.

Introducing Crystal Report's Report Writer

- Using the Crystal Reports Expert
- Inserting Crystal Reports into CF templates
- Using custom formatting controls
- Adding images, calculated subtotals, and totals
- Using the Crystal Query Designer

Crystal Report Writer from Seagate Software delivers a great deal of functionality in a very user-friendly format. Database programmers look for report writers that can deliver stunning reports without requiring excessive or complex coding. Easily meeting this challenge, the Crystal Reports Report Writer (CRW) brings as much flexibility and power to intranet and Internet report creation as most database programmers could want. CRW automates the task of making classy report formats, uses WYSIWIG Experts to manipulate images and data inside a Windows-based environment, and brings dynamic report-generation capabilities to your web site. CRW generates dynamic HTML webpages back to the end user and is called by a single line of code from inside a Cold Fusion template.—Crystal Report Writer software is bundled with Cold Fusion at no additional cost.

When Cold Fusion databases are linked to an ODBC driver, they are immediately available to be used by CRW reports. As discussed in Chapter 5, the Cold Fusion Administrator is used to connect a given database to an ODBC driver. An Access ODBC driver, for example, is connected to an Access database, and so on. CRW uses these ODBC-linked databases as the data sources for its reports. When testing your database connection, you can use CRW to retrieve and display underlying live data from ODBC-linked databases without having to create a live web connection using an HTML Form. This feature greatly speeds up the process of creating reports, because the server is not needed to test report data retrieval.

Using the Crystal Reports Expert

To open Crystal Reports, click its icon. A welcome screen appears, as shown in Figure 15-1. Start by clicking the New Report button. (You can turn off the welcome screen by disabling the `Show welcome dialog at startup` check box.) After you click the New Report button, Crystal Reports displays the Report Gallery, a group of eight different report icons, as well as a custom report icon. For your first report, a Standard Format report will be constructed. (The section, "Designing a GAAP-Style Crystal Report with Totals" describes how to create a more complex, GAAP-style report.) To make the standard report from scratch, click the Standard Report icon in the upper-left corner of the Report Gallery.

The Create Report Expert panel appears. Clicking the Report Expert button enables you to choose the database table(s) to be included in your report. To display the list of available databases, click the SQL/ODBC but-

15-1
Opening Crystal
Reports Writer

ton. Crystal Reports displays a directory list of ODBC-connected databases, as shown in Figure 15-2.

Furthermore, any database to which you can hook an ODBC driver—including the databases described in this book—can be used as a data source to make a Crystal Reports report).

Inserting a Crystal Report in a Template

You can easily include a finished report in a template by using the CFREPORT tag, as follows:

```
<CFREPORT REPORT="C:\crwdir\Report1.rpt">
      ...
   </CFREPORT>.
```

NOTE: *You must use a full pathname for the report, including the name of the root directory and subdirectory. Without a full pathname, Cold Fusion generates a* **Report not found** *message.*

Figure 15-2

A directory of
ODBC-connected
databases

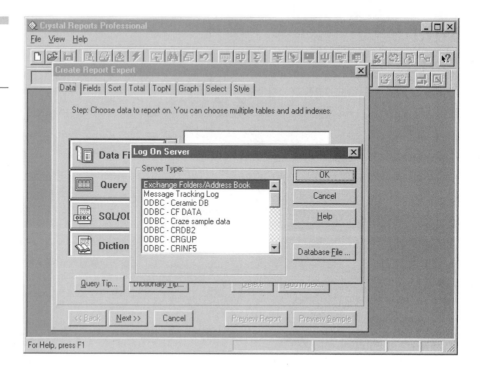

Selecting an ODBC Database

When the directory list of available ODBC-connected databases appears highlight the ODBC - Ceramic DB and click OK. Crystal Reports displays the Choose SQL Table screen shown in Figure 15-3. Highlight the Personel table. Click the Add button to make the Personel table available to Crystal Reports. Notice that CRW adds the Personel table to the underlying Create Report Expert Screen.

Before closing the panel, click the Done button. CRW removes The Choose SQL Table screen. Click the Next>> button at the bottom of the screen. The Create Report Expert panel appears as shown in Figure 15-4.

Selecting Report Columns

To select columns for your report from the Personnel table (part of the Staff database), click the Fields tab on the Create Report Format panel (second tab from the left). Before you choose any fields, the report exists as an empty shell. As you select individual fields for the report, Crystal Reports places those fields into the shell meaning that you do not have to

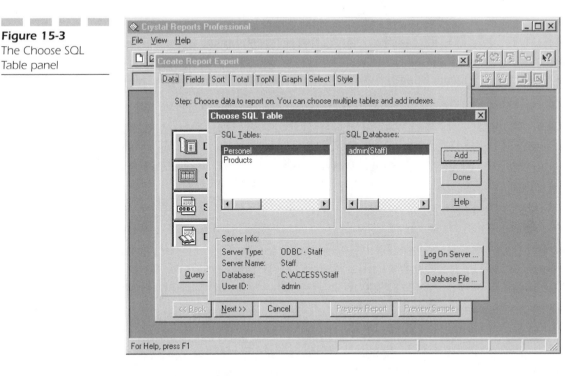

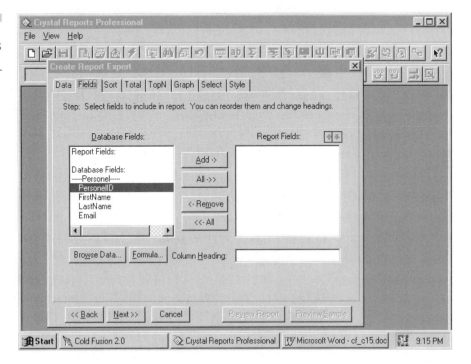

do anything with fields using a Cold Fusion template. When you click the Fields tab, Crystal Reports displays a complete list of all the Personel table fields (see Figure 15-4).

There are many useful features available on the Create Report Expert panel. If you want to check the contents of a field in the table, for example, instead of closing the report and opening the table, or paging back and forth between the table and the report, simply highlight any field (such as Email) and click the Browse Data button. Crystal Reports displays the contents of the selected Email field. This feature saves time from having to open the Personnel table (or any other table) as a separate window in Windows 95 or Windows NT. This feature also verifies that a live ODBC data connection exists from Crystal Reports to your database and table(s).

To place fields into the report, highlight the desired field in the Database Fields window, and click the Add button. Crystal Reports displays the field in the Report Fields pane. Each report field name is made up of the table name, a period (.), and the field name. For example, a typical report field name is `Personel.email`, which is a longer name than you might first expect. Table names are prefixed to field names to make sure the report can distinguish two identical fields from two different tables. This problem can arise with key fields of the same name that relate two tables together. Even after you move a field into the report, you can still use the Browse Data button to view the underlying table data.

You can click the All button to move all the fields into the report. You can click the Remove button to remove a single highlighted field, or the All button with the chevrons pointing left to remove every field from the report. Find the Column Heading box. To change the name of the field, replace the old column name Email with Web Address or whatever you want.

If you need to add sales tax to a dollar amount field, you can write a quick formula adding 8.25 percent to the selling price and use the Formula button to add the formula to the report. The section "Creating a Calculated Field in a Report" explains the process of building this kind of calculated field.

Using the Preview Tab to Customize Formatting

The Preview Report button enables you to see how the included fields will be displayed as a report by Crystal Reports. Figure 15-5 shows your preliminary report.

Figure 15-5
The preliminary
Personel Table report

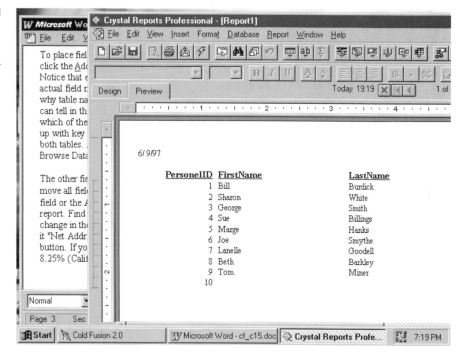

A quick glance shows that the new report lacks appropriate spacing between the columns. Use the small upside-down triangle tabs on the ruler line to move the position of fields to where they look better (and will not "crowd off" the right side of a 14 inch monitor). This operation, which is very much like true WYSIWIG, takes less than a minute. Make sure you take advantage of this feature! Figure 15-6 shows what one minute of formatting can do. The gray area beneath the LastName field shows how many characters you allotted to this field, even though there is no data longer than seven letters in the field. To shorten the LastName field, highlight and drag a left or right edge toward the center. Figure 15-6 shows the results of some preliminary report editing.

When you display the report on your browser over a network, you may want to drag the fields around further, and shorten the lengths of the titles and the display areas of the fields. If either the title or the detail part of a field is in the wrong position or is too long or short, the report may not look presentable even though it contains correct information. Make sure the **FirstName**, **LastName**, and **EMAIL** fields are toward the middle of the page by using the Design tab with its drag-and-drop functionality.

Figure 15-6
Crystal Reports
Professional [Report1]
Design Tab

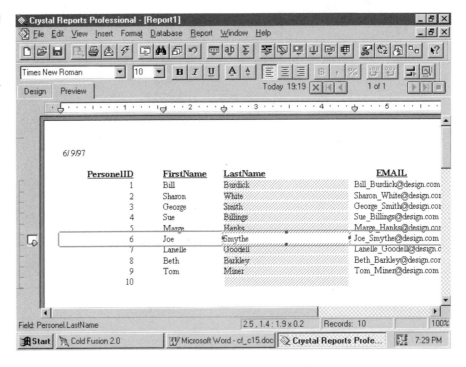

Using the Design Tab to Customize the Report

To display the underlying report structure, click the Design tab. All the elements of the report appear as "bands" stretching across the report. The top band, the page header, could be compared in use to the header section of an HTML page, it will display as a non-repeating top part of a web page. You can do some awesome things in this space; logos, images, text boxes, underlines, text font changes, nearly any formatting change you can think of can be incorporated in this area. Do not be surprised, however, if you have to fuss with these customizing elements to make sure the overall design comes out looking the way you want.

REMOVING UNNEEDED REPORT FIELDS   You may be wondering what happened to the `PersonelID` field. It was removed by a two-step process. To remove a field, click it, and then press Delete. Additionally, to move fields, click any field once, and then drag the field to its new position. You can even move or delete date fields. (Fields are only deleted from appearing on the CRW report, not the underlying table).

After highlighting a field, you can change the font type and size. You can also apply italics or bold. To relocate the field title to a different position above the field, use the left, center, and right formatting buttons. These are just the beginning of formatting changes.

ADDING IMAGES TO THE REPORT HEADER   To add an image to the report header, click the Insert Picture icon. (To see the name of an icon, position the mouse cursor over an icon on the toolbar. The name of the icon appears on the lower-left of the screen.) Crystal Reports displays the CRW directory with a list of image files. Click on a name, for example Crazeb.bmp, and click Open. The image is opened in a box on the report header. (You can also change directories and insert a custom image.) You can size the box by clicking a corner and reducing the box size or by dragging and dropping the box anywhere desired, and then clicking outside the box to imbed the picture in the report. To alter the size further, click on the image. The image again appears in an edit sizing box, from which you can then resize, move, or delete the image.

ADDING TEXT TO THE REPORT HEADER OR FOOTER   To add text to the report header or footer, click the Insert Text Object icon (the "ab" icon). Type `Personnel Report` in the text box that appears. To change the font size, highlight the text, click the font change box, and change to font size to 14 or larger for the title. Change the font type to Comic Sans Serif (or another font). Drag and drop the text box to where desired, and then resize the text box to fit your design scheme.

Using the Details Section

The Details section of the report is used to show report records. In this example, the Details section shows the following columns: `FirstName`, `LastName`, and `EMAIL`. If the report contains columns with numbers, the Details section can include subtotals and totals. Finally, the Footer section can include page numbers and other items that need to appear on the last page of the report. You will probably not want to put page numbers in Internet reports that will only be viewed on-line.

To view the report, click the Report Preview button. If you have not gotten carried away customizing the report, you should see the Personnel Report, as shown in Figure 15-7.

To demonstrate how to create a GAAP-style accounting report, the next report example uses a table containing numerical data.

Figure 15-7
Displaying a CRW
report over a
network

Designing a GAAP-Style Report with Totals

To begin designing an Accounting style report, open the Report Expert and choose the New report button. Select the DB4 database and the Products Table. Click the Fields tab. CRW displays all of the tables and fields in the DB4 database. Highlight the following fields and use the "greater than" (>) button to move them into the Report Fields box:

"Order Report by
Product" Report

Table fields:

Orders.ProductName

Customers.FirstName

Customers.LastName

Customers.Address

Customers.City

Customers.ZIP

Products.UnitPrice

Products.UnitsOnOrder

■ Calculated fields:

ExtPrice (Unit Price * Units on Order)

GrandTot (Summed ExtPrice)

■ Group-By field:

Products1.Category

The following Figure 15-8 shows the accounting-style Orders by Product report. Report data is taken from several different related tables.

Creating Reports using Calculated Fields

Generally, accounting-style reports include dollar amount totals at the lower-right side of the report. To create this type of report, you must create a calculated "total amount" field, and position it where desired in the report. In addition, if you want subtotals in the body of the report, at least one Group By field must be used in the report. This example uses the **Products1.Category** Group By field.

If your table lacks a Group By field, you will have to add an appropriate Group By field to the table, and then populate it with data. In this example, the Group By field is **Category**. Each category represents several different kinds of software products (see the following list showing product names and categories.) The members of each category are subtotaled and printed each time a new category is encountered. The following list shows how software products can be thought of as being a part of a category. The first category, Database, is made up of three different software products: FastBase, RelateBase, and SpreadData. The next category, Utility, is made up of FrameTool, QuickUtility, and so on. You can group almost every database into categories. Notice the following table data, it is in natural input order, the way data is entered into a databases in real life. When Group By fields are added to the report, CRW will use the Group By fields to sort raw data into categories. Then, for example, all the products in the Database Category will be displayed together on the report. To learn how to do this see the following section called "Adding a Group By Field To a Report."

Figure 15-8
A Detail report with
calculated fields

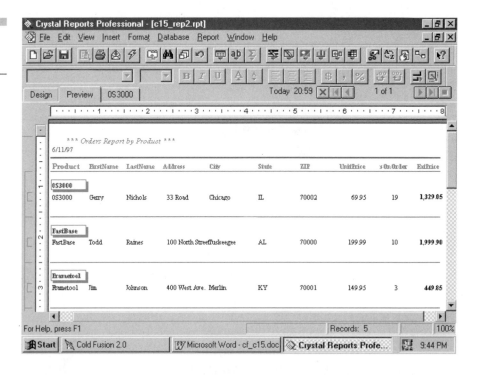

Figure 15-9
A Detail report with
calculated fields

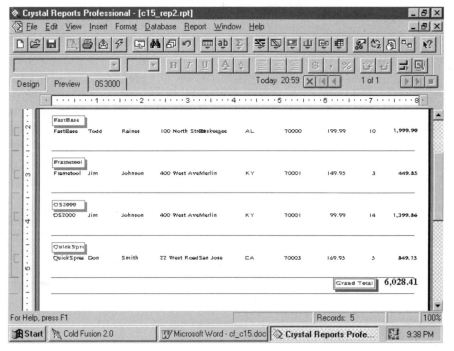

Product Name	Category
FastBase	Database
OS2000	OS
OS3000	OS
QuickSpread	Spreadsheet
QuickSpread Pro	Spreadsheet
QuickUtility II	Utility
RelateBase	Database
SpreadData	Database

Formatting the Report

Reports should reflect user needs. Although 17 inch monitors are becoming more common in offices and homes, most reports going out over networks should probably be able to be displayed on a 14 inch monitor. This means you will have to do some customization to get all the fields on the screen. When using the Report Expert, you might find that even though you can select a number of report fields rather easily, the Report Expert may position fields off-screen. To fit all the fields on a standard size monitor, you have to drag them closer together and shorten the display length of the fields.

When you are building the Products report, for example, you should drag the **Product** field very close to the other fields to save space for additional fields. When creating the report, do not hesitate to delete irrelevant report columns to produce a clean, easily read report. Even if you delete a column, you can always put it back later. (Use Edit, Undo to recover from hasty decisions.) The best report is created by experimenting until you have produced a work of art.

Adding a Group By Field to a Report

To use a Group By field, open the Create Report Expert, select the ODBC-CERAMIC database, and then add the **Orders**, **Customers**, and **Products** tables to the report. Click Done when you are finished. CRW displays the three tables that will make up the report. Click the Fields tab, and then select each of the fields listed in the "Designing a GAAP-Style Crystal

Report with Totals" section previously in this chapter. Click the Sort tab to move to the next screen, and then use the spinner button to display potential Group By fields. Look for the **Products1.Category** to transform into a Group By field. Highlight the **Products1.Category** field and use the Add button to move it from the Report fields box to the Group Fields box. The report creates a subtotal on **Products1.Category** each time the Category field value changes in the database.

Creating a Calculated Field in a Report

To create a calculated field, you must use the Field Expert. To start this process, click the Preview Report button. To create the **ExtPrice** field, choose Insert, then click Formula Field. You will create the calculated field **ExtPrice (UnitPrice * UnitsOnOrder)** to subtotal on.

To create a formula field, click the New button, enter **ExtPrice** as the name of the field, and then click OK. Crystal Reports displays an options window. A number of basic algebra functions, such as **x+y, x-y, x*y**, and so on, appear in the far-right Operator window box. To create the extended price, use the asterisk multiplier symbol (*) to show one field being multiplied against a second field. The exact formula to be written in the expression box is shown as follows. (Click the Check button to check the formula.)

        {Products.UnitsOnOrder} * {Products.UnitPrice}

NOTE: *To avoid excessive typing, highlight the field entry you want to use, such as* **Products.UnitsOnOrder**, *and then click the Select button. CRW enters the* **Products.UnitsOnOrder** *field into the Formula text box. To finish writing the formula, select the multiplier symbol (*), and then select the* **Products.UnitPrice** *field. The complete formula should now appear in the Formula Box. To check your formula, click the Check button. To close the formula box, click Accept.*

INSERTING A FORMULA INTO THE REPORT   To position the formula in the report, click Insert. Drag and drop the formula to the "body" band of the report where desired. (see Figure 15-10 to see where calculated fields are placed).

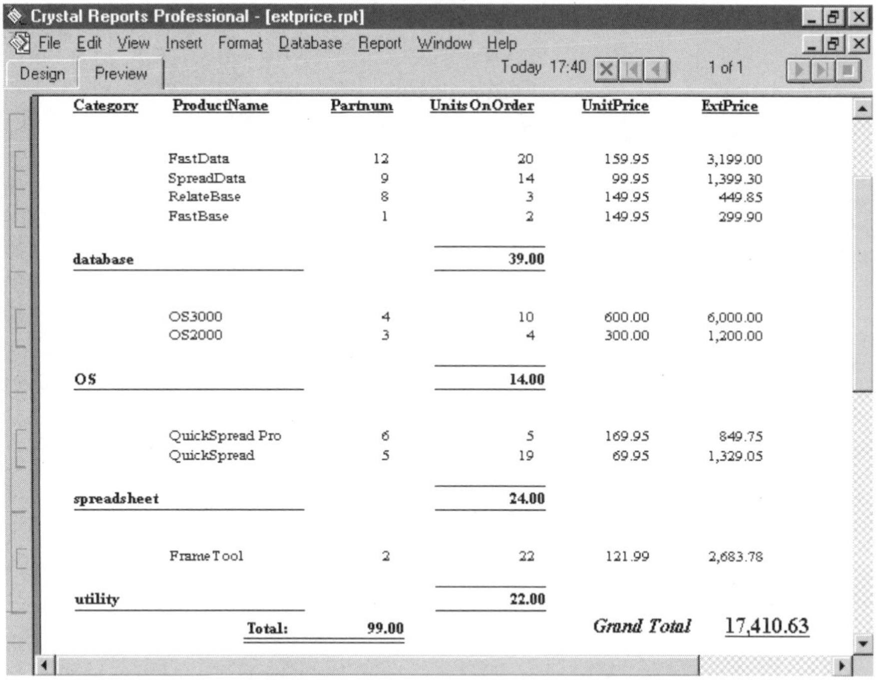

Figure 15-10
ExtPrice report with
calculated fields

```
Crystal Reports Professional - [extprice.rpt]

 File  Edit  View  Insert  Format  Database  Report  Window  Help

 Design    Preview                               Today 17:40             1 of 1
```

Category	ProductName	Partnum	Units On Order	UnitPrice	ExtPrice
	FastData	12	20	159.95	3,199.00
	SpreadData	9	14	99.95	1,399.30
	RelateBase	8	3	149.95	449.85
	FastBase	1	2	149.95	299.90
database			39.00		
	OS3000	4	10	600.00	6,000.00
	OS2000	3	4	300.00	1,200.00
OS			14.00		
	QuickSpread Pro	6	5	169.95	849.75
	QuickSpread	5	19	69.95	1,329.05
spreadsheet			24.00		
	FrameTool	2	22	121.99	2,683.78
utility			22.00		
	Total:	99.00		Grand Total	17,410.63

CREATING A GRAND TOTAL CALCULATED FIELD

The basic report is almost finished except for the creation of the Grand Total field. To create the **ExtPrice Grand Total** field, choose Insert, then click , Formula Field. Give the formula field the name **ExtPriceTot**. Click the New Button, enter **ExtPriceTot** as the name of the field, and then click OK. Crystal Reports displays the Options window. To create the extended price total, use the summation symbol to add the contents of the **ExtPrice** field. The exact formula is as follows. (After you finish creating the formula, click the Check button to ensure you have correctly written the formula.)

```
Sum ({@ExtPrice})
```

The Sum formula is used to calculate the **ExtPriceTot** field. Be careful to use the two different types of separators (parentheses and braces) in the function part of the formula. This formula gives the grand total of the extended price amounts. Figure 15-10 shows the extended price **Grand Total** field in the report.

This report organizes data into subgroups and gives report details for each report record. Individual unit prices, extended unit prices and an extended price grand total are displayed. If you have trouble getting the report to correctly subgroup your data, you may find it useful to quickly presort the data before running the report.

NOTE: *If you do not know how to correctly write a formula, but a CRW sample report has a calculated field presentation which suggest that the formula you want must exist in that field, highlight the field containing the underlying unknown formula and click the right mouse button. CRW displays the needed underlying formula in the formula edit box. Copy the formula to your report. Also, if you have made changes to the data, to refresh the report data, choose Report, Refresh Data.*

Using the Section Expert

The Section Expert simplifies the process of customizing reports. To open the Section Expert, click the Section Expert button on the right side of the toolbar. When the Section Expert opens, notice that each section of the report is listed on the left. When you highlight a section on the left, the Section Expert brings up numerous change options for that section. If you highlight the Group Header or Details sections, for example, you can checkmark **Suppress Blank Section** to skip empty records. Checkmarking the Color tab allows you to shade the header, footer, or any other section of the report to the color of your choosing.

Using the Crystal Query Designer

The Crystal Query Designer contains Experts that you can use to write SQL queries against database tables. Existing SQL queries can be pasted in and modified, or the New Query Expert can be used to start from scratch and select columns and add conditional statements without requiring any SQL coding on your part.

After opening the Crystal Query Designer, click the New button. CRW displays the New Query panel (see Figure 15-11). Click the Use Crystal

Figure 15-11
The Crystal Query
Designer's New
Query panel

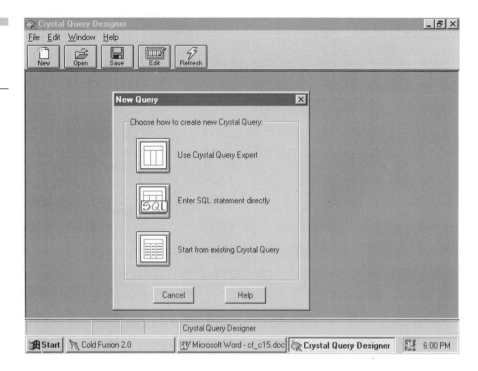

Query Expert button. CRW displays the Create Query Expert panel. Click the SQL/ODBC button to select a SQL/ODBC-linked database. SQL queries can only be run against ODBC-linked databases. CRW displays a Log On Server panel with a directory list of ODBC-databases.

Highlight the ODBC-CERAMIC DB database and click OK. CRW displays the message text, `Logon to ODBC-Staff Server Succeeded`. This means that a correctly written SQL query will successfully retrieve data from the ODBC-Staff database and its tables. Click OK. CRW displays a Choose SQL Table panel (see Figure 15-12). Highlight the Products table, click Add, and then click Done. At the bottom of the Create Query Expert panel, change `Untitled Query` to `Products`.

To choose fields, click the Next button. The Fields Tab is selected. Add the following fields to the Query Fields window: `Products.Category`, `Products.ProductName`, `Products.UnitsOnOrder`, and `Products.UnitPrice`. Highlight `Products.UnitsOnOrder` in the Query Fields window and use the Total "spinner" button to display the out-of-view Sum command. Click the Expression Button, CRW displays the SQL Expression text box. Type in any name for the SQL expression, click OK. CRW displays a SQL Expression Text Input Box. Write the SQL query that fits your data needs.

Figure 15-12

Choosing a SQL
query table

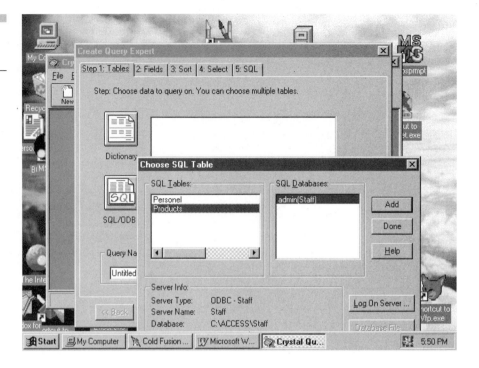

Click OK. CRW displays your new SQL query name in the Database
Fields box under the heading called SQL Expressions. (If you're not sure
about SQL syntax, open Help, choose SQL Topics, and then select the SQL
verb that looks interesting.)

Click Next. CRW displays the **Sort** tab. Sort on category (highlight the
Products.Category and Click Add to move the Products1.Category into the
Group Fields Box. (Notice that the default Order is Ascending.) Click
Next. CRW displays the Select tab.

When you move a field to the Select Fields Box, for example, UnitsOnOrder (a calculated numeric field), CRW displays in the Select Field
box **Sum(Units on Order)** and also displays two additional conditions
boxes which contain further conditions such as: **any value** (default)
equal to, less than, greater than, and so on. (To preview field data in
order to make a decision about applying a filter condition, click the
Browse Data Button. CRW displays the actual field data in a separate
popup message box.) When you apply a condition, you are putting a filter
on the UnitsOnOrder field before performing any other calculations. Click
Next. CRW displays the SQL tab containing the following Products query:

Products query
created by
crystal query

```
SELECT
   Products.'Category',
   Products.'ProductName',
   SUM (Products.'UnitsOnOrder'),
   Products.'UnitPrice'
FROM
   'Products' Products
WHERE
   Products.'Category' = 'database'
GROUP BY
   Products.'Category',
   Products.'ProductName',
   Products.'UnitPrice'
ORDER BY
   Products.'Category' ASC
```

Each field is enclosed by a single quotation mark. The conditional value is introduced by the following WHERE clause:

```
WHERE Products.'Category'='database'
```

You may want to edit the query and delete the second and third GROUP BY expressions. Highlight unwanted code lines and use the Scissors button to remove unwanted SQL code. Click the Preview button to run the query. Click the Edit button to return to the Crystal Query Designer and make any further changes to the query. Save the query as **product.qry** in the directory of your choice. Figure 15-13 shows the query results.

Inserting the Query into a Report

When you are completely satisfied with the query results, you can incorporate the query into a report. You can use the query to retrieve information in the report. The query can display information on-screen or print a paper report.

To select a Crystal query for a report, open Crystal Reports and click the New button. Select Report Expert from the Report Gallery. The Report Expert appears. Click the Query button. The File Open panel appears. Find the directory containing Product.qry, highlight Product.qry, and click OK. CRW displays the word Query on the Data tab of the Create Report Expert.

Figure 15-13
The Products SQL
Crystal query

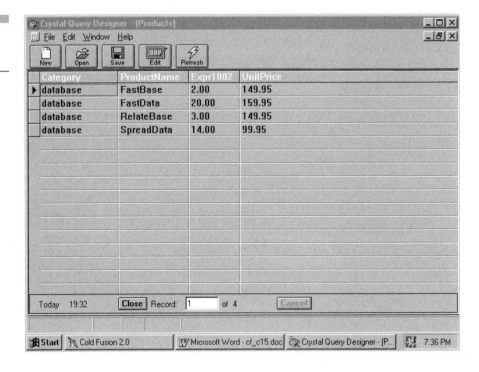

Click Next. Notice that the Fields tab now displays the fields you previously selected when creating the Products query (see Figure 15-14).

You can click the All->> button to include all the query fields in the report. Click Next to go to the Sort tab. Highlight the **Products.Category**
field and click the Add button to add the fields to the report. The Report
Generator inserts the fields on the report. Now you must do some customization.

Drag each field to where it looks best, and rename the field titles to
more compact names if you lack space on the report. Select Format, Border and Colors to customize your final presentation. Figure 15-15 shows
the GAAP-style report.

Incorporating Your CRW Report into a Cold Fusion Template

Incorporate your report into a Cold Fusion template is an easy process because this database is already an ODBC-database. Here is the working
code:

Figure 15-14

Inserting query fields into a report

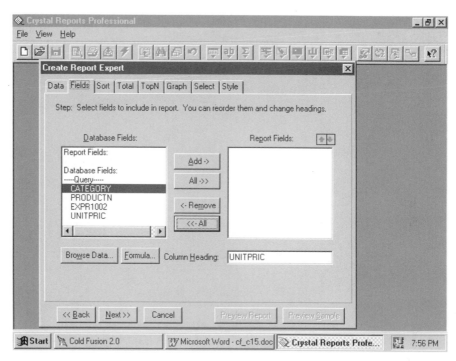

```
<! —c15_1.cfm  uses Products.qry and Products1 table — >
<HTML>
<BODY>
<CFREPORT REPORT="c:\website\htdocs\C15_rep1.rpt">
</CFREPORT>
</BODY>
</HTML>
```

You must use an absolute report pathname. If you use an incomplete pathname, the Cold Fusion service issues the **Not able to find report or the message: Report does not exist** error.

CONCLUSION

Crystal Reports Writer contains powerful report creation tools that make report writing easier. You can drag and drop report fields, which are displayed in a WYSIWIG format. The Crystal Query Expert guides novice SQL writers through the development of queries. The Crystal Report Expert guides new report writers through the stages of field selection, field

Figure 15-15
An SQL query with
conditional statement
report

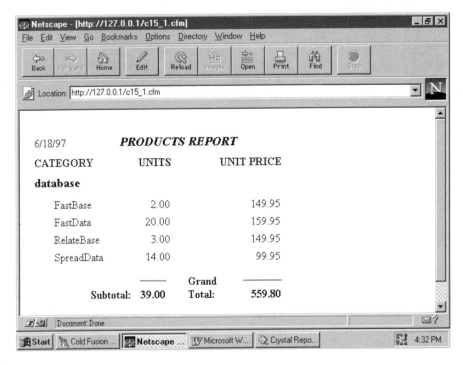

sorting, report customization using fonts and background colors, and calculated field creation. Fields can be moved around and displayed during
each step of creating the report. The next chapter shows how to build over
80 different graphs using the fully automated graph experts found in the
Crystal Reports Generator.

16

Advanced Crystal Reports with Graphics

- Building graphs with Crystal Report Writer
- Using the Graph/Chart Expert
- Using the PG Editor to build 80 different custom graphs
- Specialized PG Editor features

Crystal Report Writer (CRW) can graph live, drill-down table data, as well as present that data in tabular form. To build embedded graphs easily, CRW includes a highly sophisticated and automated Graph/Chart Expert, additionally, CRW contains the powerful PG Editor, containing more than 80 different chart and graph formats, as well as 3D and Special Effects Palettes. You can use the 3D and Special Effects Palettes to change the orientation and shape of the finished graph or chart in three-dimensional space using the live Redraw option. Very little is missing in this software.

Building Graphs With Crystal Report Writer

A Contacts table containing data grouped by state will be used to build a CRW graph. CRW only graphs table data that has been previously summarized or totaled by Crystal Reports. This section discusses ways to ensure that data is included in your graph, and uses an MS Access 'Ceramic DB' database containing a table called Contacts for this purpose (see Table 16-1).

Building Reports Containing Graphs

To create reports containing graphs, you must first create a standard report that contains grouped or summarized data by using CRW's Report Expert. Then, having created a report with grouped data, you can begin building a graph or chart as shown in Figure 16-1.

1. To build a basic report, open Crystal Reports, click the New Report button, and then select the Standard Report button. CRW displays the Choose New Location pane.

2. Click Cancel. Crystal Reports brings up the Create Report Expert panel, and displays the Choose Database File pane and a file directory structure.

Table 16-1

The Contacts.mdb
table data

Contact ID	Orders	Company	First Name	Last Name	City	State	Work Phone
1	2	FarEast, Inc.	Joe	Blount	Chicago	IL	(454) 555-6666
10	4	Petrovsky	Author	Petrovsky	St. Louis	MI	(252) 456-5222
11	1	Donnell Co.	Harry	Bennett	St. Louis	MI	(252) 456-8365
12	3	Janners, Inc.	Mona	Perry	New York	NY	(478) 989-9999
13	2	Duncan Works	Maxwell	Penner	New York	NY	(477) 988-9999
14	9	Painter Co.	Lisa	Montage	New York	NY	(479) 999-8212
2	1	Western States	Donna	Smith	Chicago	IL	(454) 556-9999
3	2	Engels Ltd.	Peter	Donne	Chicago	IL	(454) 858-9797
4	5	Antoine Co.	James	Antoine	Chicago	IL	(454) 858-9494
5	4	Jones Ltd.	Payne	Jones	Kansas City	KA	(121) 555-6666
6	2	Burnes	Roland	Burnes	Kansas City	KA	(121) 845-9797
7	1	Maxwells	Larry	Maxwells	Kansas City	KA	(121) 548-9944
8	2	Fournier Co.	Alicia	Fournier	Kansas City	KA	(121) 466-8213
9	1	Zebrunner	Tomas	Zebrunner	Saint Louis	MI	(252) 456-9874

3. Highlight the `ceramic.mdb` database file. CRW moves `ceramic.mdb` into the File Name box. When it displays, click the Done button. The Create Report Expert displays the two tables that make up the `ceramic.mdb` database.

4. Highlight the Contacts table, and then click the Fields tab to begin selecting report fields.

Use the Add -> button to put the Company, City, Orders, and State fields into the report. Use the Browse Data button to display raw field

Figure 16-1
Create Report
Expert Panel

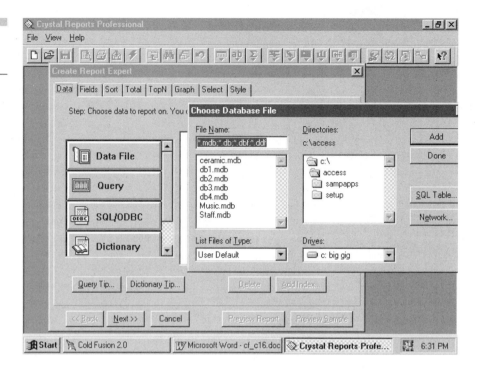

data and test for yourself the link between the **Products.mdb** table and the CRW report you are creating.

After you have selected a database and tables, the next step is to prepare table records for graphing. Usually, data files are "grown" by inputting records day by day. Tables become full of raw data and unordered records. The commands found under the Sort tab can be used to organize and summarize raw data records into ordered groups.

Using the Sort Tab to Create Summarized Data

Select the Sort tab and add the **Contacts.State** field to the Group Fields box by highlighting **Contacts.State** and then clicking the Add Button.

Click the Total button, and then add the **Contacts.State** field by using the Add button. Click the Next Button to display a preview graph.

To create the Contacts report shown in Figure 16-1, highlight each field and drag to the left until the report is readable and fits on a single page.

Leave almost a third of a page of space on the right side for the graph. Because a graph or chart is visually dominant, only those parts of the database that directly refer to the graph will be displayed on the same page as the graph.

Using the Graph/Chart Expert

After you have created and modified a preliminary report, leaving sufficient space for the chart or graph, open the Graph/Chart Expert inside the basic CRW report by clicking the Insert Chart button on the top toolbar. To create the graph, perform the following steps when the Graph/Chart Expert opens:

For your first chart, choose the Pie chart by clicking the Pie button on the Step 1: Type tab (see Figure 16-2). The Step 1: Type tab enables you to choose from twelve pre-made charts and graphs, or to create custom graphs and charts of your own.

Next, click the Step 2: Data tab (see Figure 16-3). This tab gives you the option of placing a graph on each page of the report or just once per report. The On Change of box displays your earlier Group-By field choice

Figure 16-2
The Graph/Chart Expert's Step 1: Type tab

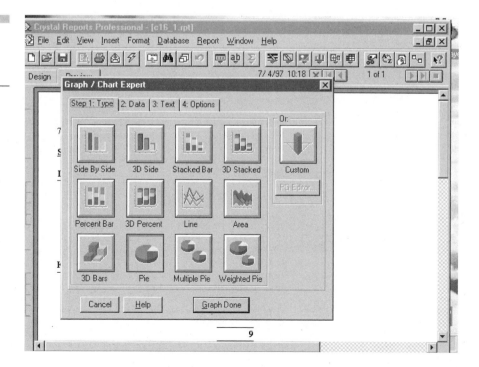

Figure 16-3
The Graph/Chart
Expertís Step 2:
Data tab

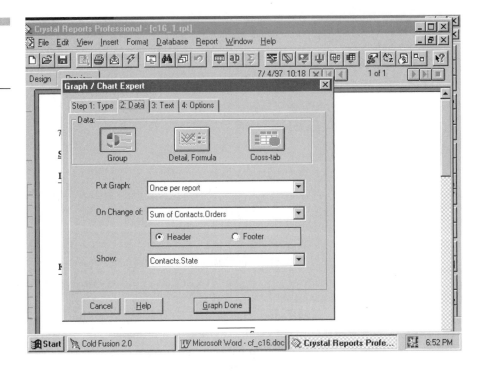

(in this case the **state** field) and also shows what information is going to be summed up (in this case, the **Contacts.State** field). A radio button enables you to display the graph in either the header or the footer. (Because you will likely want to display your graph as the first element on the Internet page, select the header rather than the footer).

Next, click the Step 3: Text tab (see Figure 16-4). This tab enables you to fully customize the Title, Subtitle, Groups and Series Titles, and X, Y, and Z axes titles, as well as give the graph a footnote directly underneath. When building a pie graph, you only need to use three of the chart heading selections, as follows:

1. In the Title entry box, type **Orders By State**.

2. In the Sub Title entry box, type **Percent of Total**.

3. In the Footnote entry box, type **US Region**.

For the final step, click the Step 4: Options tab (see Figure 16-5). The **Show legend** box is already checked. You can select a different font by clicking the Font spin arrow. At the bottom of the pane, enter **0** as a Minimum value and **100** as a Maximum value. Entering minimum and maximum graph data values filters out any incorrect data that inadvertently

Figure 16-4
The Graph/Chart
Expert's Step 3:
Text tab

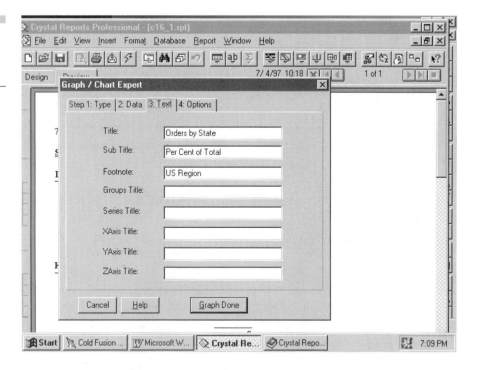

Figure 16-5
The Graph/Chart
Expert's Step 4:
Options tab

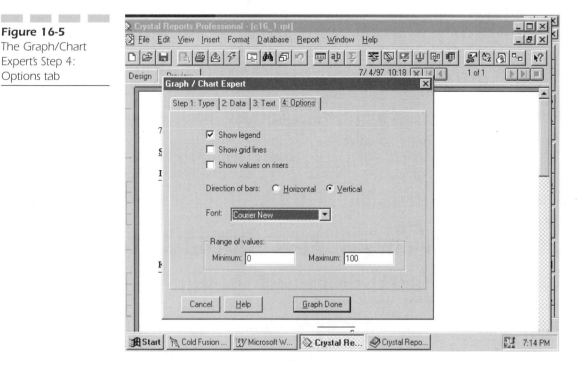

entered the database, and that would make your graph very skewed in appearance and therefore lose usefulness.

To view the completed graph, click the Graph Done button; the graph appears across the top of your CRW report. You can resize the graph by clicking one of the boundary lines, and then dragging the handle toward or away from the center of the graph—to shrink or expand the graph, respectively. If your graph is going over any kind of a public network, remember to keep it to a reasonable byte size to facilitate rapid transmission.

Removing Unwanted Graph White Space

You may find that you have some unwanted white space between the graph and the data in the report. This could be because the header section is empty in the report, causing this part of the report to contain unwanted white space. To suppress the blank header section and display much more information on the opening page of the report, choose Edit, Show/Hide Sections. CRW displays the Section Expert (see Figure 16-6). Highlight the Page Header to bring up the Header control pane. When the Header pane appears, check the Suppress Blank Section and the Underlay Following Sections options. CRW suppresses the blank header and displays the data directly next to the chart or graph. (Normally, the graph would take a horizontal band all the way across the page so that you could not display any live data immediately next to the graph.)

You can also drag the titles of the report (State, City, Company, and Orders) until they are immediately adjacent to the corresponding data sections. If the report title does not show up clearly, highlight the title, click Format, Font, and choose a larger font size. On this report, the title has been dragged from its position above the graph to the left side of the graph in order to display database information on the opening page. Figure 16-7 shows the final report with the imbedded graphics.

Using the PG Editor to Build a 3-D Side Chart

To activate the PG Editor, open the Graph/Chart Expert, and then click the Custom button. Use The Custom button to activate PG Editor. Next, click the PG button. A default graph appears (see Figure 16-8).

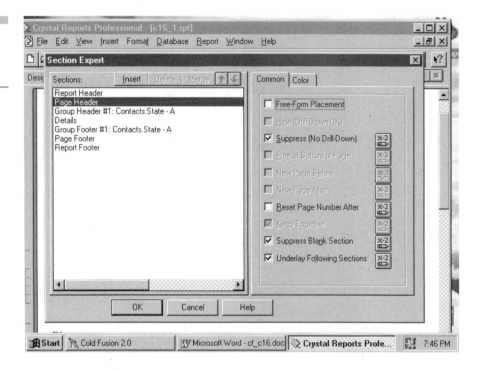

Figure 16-6
Section Expert -
Suppressing page
headers

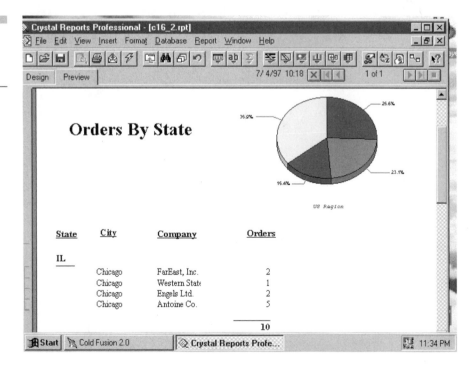

Figure 16-7
The Orders By State
report with an
imbedded chart

Figure 16-8
Sample Embedded
Crystal Chart

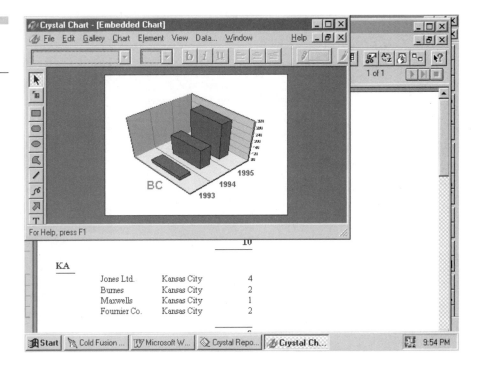

Selecting a Chart Type Menu

To quickly select one of the 80 chart formats, choose Gallery. The available formats include the following: Bar, Line, Area, Pie, Scatter, and Histogram.

To modify the appearance of any given chart, click Chart, Preset Viewing Angle. A drop-down list shows the available chart display angles and proportions (see the Figure 16-9).

CUSTOMIZING CHART RISER APPEARANCE Whenever you begin thinking about customizing charts, invariably, someone will want you to make the risers taller, thicker, or flipped this way or that. CRW is more than equal to this task. This section shows you how to make the small visual changes to the graph which make a big difference in the finished product. Start by clicking Choose Chart, Vertical Z Axis. A drop-down list opens. Click Scale Range, and then select the Manual Scale radio button. Enter the upper and lower numerical limits you want the vertical chart axis to display. To show only typical data values, exclude values outside of the normal range of data.

Figure 16-9

The preset chart viewing angles

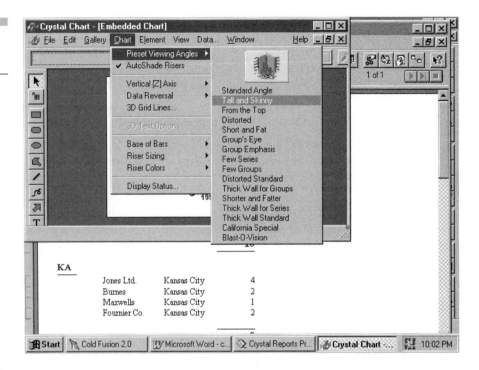

Next, choose Chart, Riser Sizing. As your cursor travels over each displayed percentage width for the risers (and there are many), a riser preview appears. Select, for example, **25% x 75%** to display a thin, easily distinguishable riser that causes your data to stand out from its surrounding. You should try using every major option in the PG Editor, you will not be disappointed.

To see all the titles and text labels currently in use, choose Chart, Display Status.

Choose View, 3D View Palette. CRW displays a 3-D view palette. Clicking any of the arrow tips shown in the 3-D View Palette will begin resizing the graph in three dimensional WYSIWYG manner. Use the Redraw option on the 3D Palette to permanently reposition the graph after moving the graph using the arrow tips. Each of the 3D buttons sizes, repositions, or rotates the graph in a precise direction.

Use the Special Effects Palette to give individual risers a mottled, textured, or gradient color. Each of the selections in the Special Effects Palette has its own range of special effects, textures, and variations. The power to change graph's appearance puts this program almost into the category of desktop publishing. The PGE Editor is the strongest graph development tool that the author has seen that is available for use on the Internet at a low cost.

Another feature of the Crystal Chart panel is the ability to paint the background using gradient colors. Notice the paintbrush icon in the upper-right corner. To use the Paintbrush icon, click a part of the graph, such as a panel of the background, and then click the paintbrush icon. CRW displays a color gradient. Highlight the desired color; the background changes to the selected color. Click a series number in the graph; the Bold, Font, Italic, Underline, and Justification buttons are activated and may be used on any given element. What is quite nice about this process is that only the highlighted number is affected, the other numbers inside a series stay the same.

On the left side of the Crystal Charts panel are several premade resizable shapes that you can drop onto the graph. You can add text inside a given shape by using the Text tool. Crystal Reports enables you to choose an almost infinite variety of graph types, colors, and orientations. No serious database designer should ever be concerned about not being able to produce a visually arresting graph.

When you are finished designing the graph, save it under its own name to use later as a template.

CONCLUSION

This chapter focused on building standard graphs such as pie charts and 3D graphs, as well as creating custom graphs by using the PG Editor. The PG Editor, special palettes, and individual element customization features were explored. For the a wide range of users, the PG Editor makes possible highly developed charts and graphs reflecting the individual, corporate, and business needs of sophisticated users.

A Multi-Chapter Cold Fusion 3 Programming Example

17

Introduction to CF Programming with Functions and Conditional Logic

- Introduction to variables and functions
- Debugging as you go
- Programming in tiny chunks
- Introduction to cookies
- Other ways to pass variables from template to template
- Introduction to conditional logic
- Using conditional logic for navigation

Overview: Learning to Program With Cold Fusion

Cold Fusion is an application development tool, rather than a pure programming language, because it requires the Cold Fusion run-time program and because it lacks some of the flexibility of a true programming language. (This description is admittedly oversimplified.) Nonetheless, it provides non-programmers with simple access to some of the power available to professional programmers. By using Cold Fusion, you can create applications that would take much longer using the true programming languages.

Programming languages are often ranked by how many special codes one must memorize to write a program. High-level, intuitive languages use a lot of English key words and eliminate background details. Lower-level languages have fewer user-friendly features built in and operate closer to the computer's bare bones.

Although it is not a programming language per se, Cold Fusion uses concepts and methods that are common to all programming languages, whether obscure or intuitive. Therefore, this chapter will focus on the programming aspects of Cold Fusion as if it was a high-level, intuitive programming language. (Cold Fusion is actually most similar to a scripting language.)

With Cold Fusion, for instance, applications can be programmed to make choices, depending on what information the program receives. Cold Fusion can also be programmed to repeat a series of pre-planned actions on cue. Finally, Cold Fusion uses *expressions* to tell the computer what to do—just like true programming languages—expressions that use functions and operators to manipulate variable data and constant data.

These dynamic elements—conditional logic, expressions, functions and variables—are what separates programming from using a mark-up language such as HTML. Cold Fusion brings dynamic programming into web page design through the use of programming expressions and their components.

Planning a Cold Fusion Project in Advance

Traditionally, most programming books began with discussion about the use of flow charts to plan the program flow from information, through various processes to obtain the outcome. With the advent of object-oriented programming tools, this technique has become less important today, and some experts do not recommend it at all.

With Cold Fusion, flow charting is still very useful for keeping track of loose ends. The more complicated the application you are writing, the more likely that you'll forget to finish one little detail, which will, in turn, affect the entire operation of the web site you are developing.

In addition, flow charts are useful to explain to other people how the system works. Sometimes, a well-designed flow chart can be a crucial element of documenting the system for others—particularly if you have different groups of people that get different types of information out of the same system. A single picture can demystify a complex process so that everyone involved knows how it fits into the whole system.

In making a flow chart for a Cold Fusion project, however, doodling with circles and arrows of your own design will help you organize your thoughts, but you probably don't need to learn any formal system of flow charting (see Figure 17-1).

You might make a circle in the middle of a piece of paper and label it **Home Page**. Perhaps you are planning to put five links onto your home page, so you make and label five more circles and connect them with arrows to the first circle. When you start labeling the global and temporary variables you need to add to the system to indicate program loops and delineating areas of multiple levels of limited access, a flow chart may become increasingly useful in keeping track of details.

For instance, flow charts would be useful in describing the complex flow of information in a large corporation: Who's got the information at the beginning, where it goes next, what happens to it, where it gets stored, who keeps track of all the loose ends, and corrective measures built into the system.

In most applications, however, planning requires very little flow charting. Suppose you are designing a Cold Fusion system for a television network so that users can query the database through a web site to locate

Figure 17-1

Doodling with circles and arrows may be all the flow charting you'll need

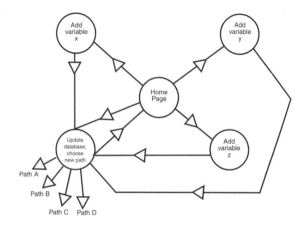

movies, rerun series, and other TV shows. Furthermore, you want to know a little bit about the people querying the site in order to assist the programming department, which will create demographic reports from web traffic.

For such an example, each of the templates will interact directly with the database, and complex charting of information flow will not be necessary—except perhaps to explain it later in the docs. Most of the access permissions and other details can be handled through existing procedures in the database, rather than through the application.

Whatever planning system you use, focus first on clarifying the goals of the application. Make certain that you obtain a complete list of "feature requests" from everyone involved. In other words, the focus of programming in Cold Fusion is not what the technology can do, but what people want.

Cold Fusion is about information exchange. Therefore, define very clearly what information you want the user to enter into the system, how much of it you need to store, and which information you want them to receive.

Recycling Existing Sources

In this chapter and the next, we will design a dynamic TV program guide for a network that broadcasts "oldies" to the entire nation via cable, without adjusting the broadcast time to local time zones.

If you were assigned to this project, you would start your planning by compiling everything the network already had, which would probably include an online viewer information form and a static TV program guide. You would also explore the existing database to discover what kinds of information are missing that you would need to use.

The next step is to search the Cold Fusion documentation for examples that are similar to what you want to do. It's also useful to use the Web Application Wizards that are bundled with the program to provide you with basic applications that you can change as you go.

Even master programmers often find it easier to modify something that works rather than to create new programs from scratch. Especially at the beginning, it's most efficient to recycle.

Almost any book on Cold Fusion will provide examples of many of the things that you would need to provide television scheduling information to viewers. It's easy to find sample programs for accessing information in forms, passing that information to a databa!se, retrieving information from a database, and populating a table with that information. As you start to collect the pieces of your project, you will discover that you already have a large number of details in place, which will simplify the final development process considerably. You may notice, for instance, that most of the template names used in this chapter and the next are the exact names generated by the Web Application Wizards or similar to programming codenames from other sources.

At the same time, you'll notice that the examples in these chapters bear little resemblance to the originals. I left the template names the same as the originals to illustrate the usefulness of recycling code.

Because Cold Fusion has such a short learning curve, you may want to start planning your first real-world project before you start learning it. In this way, you will be able to collect code to recycle as you learn.

Introduction to Variables and Functions

In all computer programming, information that varies from one operation of the program to the next is assigned to a *variable*. The name of this variable is used in expressions to store and process the information that is assigned to it. By using variables, one expression can fit every situation.

For instance, in the network TV guide example, variables would be assigned to information that each TV viewer enters into the search form, the time and date that the television show(s) will air, information stored in the browser that the viewer is using (so that the person doesn't need to register repeatedly), and information about the time zone where the TV viewer lives.

Using the CFSET Tag

You can define variables directly with the CFSET tag. The following expressions store the specific name "The News" and the hour of broadcast in the variables **ProgramName** and **ProgramHour**.

```
<CFSET #ProgramName# = "The News">
<CFSET #ProgramHour# = "23:00:00">
<CFSET #ZoneHour# = #ProgramHour#+#FORM.TVTimeZone#>
```

You'll notice that the **ProgramHour** variable includes hours, minutes, and seconds, even though no television programming would require scheduling in seconds. In Cold Fusion, time and date variables are formatted according to the ODBC standard, which is used in many Windows programs. When you present it to the user, the extra information is simply stripped off with the **TimeFormat** function.

Second, notice that in the third statement, CFSET is creating a new variable, **ZoneHour**, which is defined by adding two other variables. The variable **FORM.TVTimeZone** was created via a form that had an HTML <INPUT> tag.

Our sample application will not use the third statement, which is incorrect, and is included only to illustrate the concept simply. If this expression were used as is, it would produce the value 3.958333333333, instead of "2:00 a.m." for a viewer on the east coast. The mathematics to correctly adjust the broadcast time by the time zone of the viewer will be illustrated in the section on functions later in the chapter.

NOTE: *In Cold Fusion documentation, variables are also referred to as* parameters *or* dynamic parameters. *All of these terms mean the same thing.*

Variables can also be defined through the use of a SQL SELECT statement, through an HTML form or through a URL reference (e.g., http://filename.cfm?URLparameter=value). The only difference between variables created by any of these methods is that form variables and URL variables cannot be inspected by the <CFPARAM> tag.

Using Functions

Functions are operations that are already set up, and all you need to do is fill in the blanks for the operation to work. The blanks that you have to fill in are called *arguments*. When the function provides an answer to your question, it's called *returning a value*.

The following sentence displays the variables in online TV Guide example, using functions to process the data. Note that the actual output for someone on the East Coast would read "'The News' will air at 11:00 PM broadcast time (PST), 2: 00 AM local time."

In the first half of this example, the Evaluate function inspects the variable **ProgramHour** and returns the number 23:00:00. This is done so that the **TimeFormat** function will recognize that it stands for the time. The **TimeFormat** function then gets rid of the inaccurate default date and formats the time as desired (11:00 PM).

In the second half of this example (which is in italics), the CreateTimeSpan function is used to interpret the variable **TVTimeZone** as hours so that it can be added to **ProgramHour** before it is formatted.

```
<CFOUTPUT>
"#ProgramName#" will air at #TimeFormat(Evaluate
    ("ProgramHour"), "h:mm tt")# broadcast time (PST),
    #TimeFormat(Evaluate("ProgramHour")+CreateTimeSpan(0,
    Evaluate("FORM.TVTimeZone"),0,0), 'h:mm tt')# local
    time.
</CFOUTPUT>
```

In this example, notice that:

▒ The output containing the functions is enclosed by <CFOUTPUT> tags.

▒ Both expressions and variables are delimited between two pound signs.

▒ Arguments (the fill-in-the-blanks part) are written in parentheses behind the function.

▒ If there's more than one argument, they are separated by commas.

▒ Unless they are enclosed in square brackets (i.e., [ ]) all arguments are required.

▒ Functions can be nested as arguments to other functions.

▒ One of the important issues you will face when using functions is getting the syntax exactly correct, including using quotes, pound signs, and brackets in the precisely required way

Details on Using These Specific Functions

TimeFormat(time, mask)

▒ In most cases, both the "time" and "mask" arguments should be enclosed by quotes.

▒ "Time" can use a string, a number, or another function that can be converted to a time value.

▒ A mask is the code that tells Cold Fusion how you want the time formatted.

- In the mask, use *h*, *m*, and *s* for hours, minutes, and seconds, and *tt* for AM or PM. Double letters add a leading zero to single digit numbers.

- Punctuation and spaces between the letters will be part of the format.

- Use a capital **H** to convert the time to a 24-hour clock.

```
CreateTimeSpan(day, hour, minute, second)
```

- This function is necessary to add a numeric value to a Time/Date variable.

- Use numbers (without quotes) for days, hours, minutes, and seconds.

- The variable *FORM.TVTimeZone* needed to be evaluated to be recognized as a number before it could be added to Program Hour.

- An alternative function, **DateAdd**, would have worked equally well in the example, to accomplish the same ends. See the Cold Fusion Language Reference for syntax.

```
Evaluate(string_expression1, [string_expression2, [....]])
```

- This function evaluates (e.g., calculates) each string expression from left to right. It returns the results of evaluating the last argument.

- Only one argument is required—all others are optional.

- All arguments should be enclosed by quotes.

How Will You Use This Information in the Future?

TimeFormat and **CreateTimeSpan** are very similar to many formatting and time manipulation functions, such as **NumberFormat**, **DollarFormat** and **DecimalFormat**. The arguments and masks are different, but it's easy to use the above procedures with most of the functions described in the *Cold Fusion Language Reference* book. Take a few minutes to read about the functions **DateDiff** and **Now**, which are especially versatile and useful.

The masks in **NumberFormat** are only a little more complicated than the date formatting functions. However, you may need to refer to the Language Reference each time you use the function. The arguments used in **NumberFormat** are not as obvious as the arguments used in the time formatting functions (the first letter of time words). **NumberFormat** not only uses either the character **9** or _ for the mask, but the placement of other characters (to obtain other specific results) is too complicated to memorize instantly.

On the other hand, certain functions, such as **DollarFormat** and **DecimalFormat**, are extremely simple. In both cases, the function has only one argument—the number you are formatting, and in both cases, the function returns a number with two decimal places. The only difference is that **DollarFormat** also inserts a dollar sign.

The **Evaluate** function will also be regularly useful to you . You will often need to get specific information out of a variable for use in a function, and that's one of the things **Evaluate** does. Whenever you have written an expression that doesn't work, one of the first things to try may be to stick in the **Evaluate** function to see if it will help.

TO TRY OUT THE TV GUIDE EXAMPLE   You will need two files to run this simple example. Call the first one **time.cfm** and the second, **time2.cfm**. We will use the methods in these templates for the rest of the chapter.

Finally, although not necessary, it's useful to create a simple html file to act as your example home page as you test your work. After you run it, bookmark it. Link different pieces of your projects to this one page and use this file to document the differences between many similar templates that you create along the way. This index will help you access the best approach when you start putting the puzzle pieces together.

Here's how these two simple templates look when you run them. You will notice that both of them have the Cold Fusion Administrator Debugging options turned on. These options will be described in the following section.

Note that debugging options are enabled, including Execution Time which is disabled for Figure 17-3.

Note that debugging options are enabled. In the CGI section, you can see the values for the cookies described later in this chapter.

Time.cfm

```
<HTML>
<HEAD><TITLE>TV Show Scheduling Example</!TITLE></HEAD>
<BODY BGCOLOR="#FFFFFF">
<FORM ACTION="time2.cfm" METHOD="POST">
<INPUT TYPE="radio" NAME="TVTimeZone" VALUE=4> Atlantic
     Time<BR>
<INPUT TYPE="radio" NAME="TVTimeZone" VALUE=3> EST<BR>
<INPUT TYPE="radio" NAME="TVTimeZone" VALUE=2> CST<BR>
<INPUT TYPE="radio" NAME="TVTimeZone" VALUE=1> MST<BR>
<INPUT TYPE="radio" NAME="TVTimeZone" VALUE=0 CHECKED>
     PST<BR>
<INPUT TYPE="radio" NAME="TVTimeZone" VALUE=-1> Alaska
     Time<BR>
<INPUT TYPE="radio" NAME="TVTimeZone" VALUE=-2> Hawaii
     Time<BR>
<INPUT TYPE="submit" VALUE=Process> <BR>
<HR>
</FORM>
</BODY>
</HTML>
```

Time2.cfm

```
<HTML>
<HEAD><TITLE>TV Show Scheduling Example #2</TITLE></HEAD>
<BODY BGCOLOR="#FFFFFF">
<CFSET #ProgramName# = "The News">
<CFSET #ProgramHour# = "23:00:00">
<CFOUTPUT>
"#ProgramName#" will air at #TimeFormat(Evaluate
     ("ProgramHour"), "h:mm tt")# broadcast time (PST),
     #TimeFormat(Evaluate("ProgramHour")+CreateTimeSpan(0,
     Evaluate("FORM.TVTimeZone"),0,0), 'h:mm tt')# local
     time.
<HR>
</CFOUTPUT>
</BODY>
</HTML>
```

Myindex.html

```
<HTML>
<HEAD>
<META HTTP-EQUIV="Content-Type" CONTENT="text/html;
     charset=windows-1252">
<TITLE>My index</TITLE>
<X-SAS-WINDOW  TOP=26 BOTTOM=33!4 LEFT=28 RIGHT=558></HEAD>
<BODY LINK="#0000ff" VLINK="#800080">
<P><A HREF="time.cfm">Register</A> This registration screen
     sets time zone, then changes the scheduled time for
     the news. </P>
</HTML>
```

Figure 17-2

Setting up a time zone adjustment variable with radio buttons

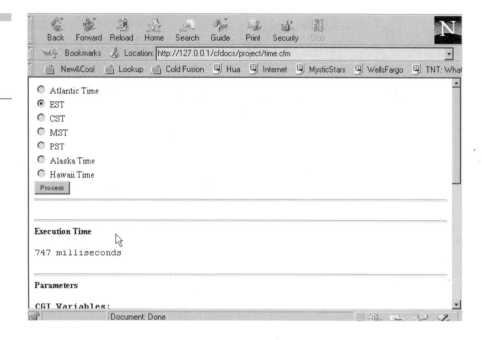

Figure 17-3

Output screen after a time zone adjustment has been made

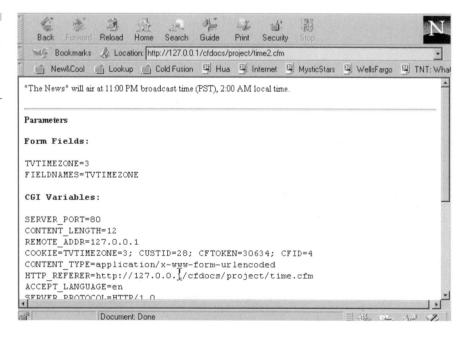

Debugging as You Go—and an Introduction to the <CFSET> and <CFABORT> Tags

When you're programming in Cold Fusion, there are two debugging measures you should use continuously: 1) built-in debugging, and 2) debugging code in your template. When your templates are not working, you need to get immediate feedback about why not.

First, you should open the Cold Fusion Administrator, go to the Debugging screen and enable all of the debugging options. This causes Cold Fusion to display all of the variables that your templates are passing (and other information) underneath the Cold Fusion output page.

NOTE: *If you are developing an application that is already available on the net, you should restrict the display of debugging information to your machine by using the Cold Fusion Administrator, Debugging screen.*

Second, as you move through the template, making improvements, insert the following lines immediately after the section you're working on. Run the template regularly to test it. <CFOUTPUT> prints the variable on the web page, and <CFABORT> stops the program immediately after the section you've been working on.

The <CFSET> line at the beginning enables you to test any expression directly by assigning a temporary variable name to it. If the following expression does not work, you could take it apart, piece by piece, to discover whether you are getting the expected results at every location within the expression.

```
<CFSET> TempVariable = #TimeFormat(Evaluate
    ("CreateODBCTime(""1:00 AM"") +CreateTimeSpan(0,
    #TVTimeZone#,0,0)"), `h:mm tt')#
<CFOUTPUT> #TempVariable#
</CFOUTPUT>
<CFABORT>
```

These measures will help you to ensure that every function, expression, and variable is behaving as planned.

Finally, Microsoft Access and Microsoft Query provide you with tools for testing and debugging SQL queries as you work through your Cold Fusion project templates.

(If you need more information about what went wrong, you might find it in one of the error logs that Cold Fusion generates. Error logs can be found in the "logs" directory that is probably in your main Cold Fusion program directory. If not, you can find the location in the Cold Fusion Administrator, Logging screen.)

PROGRAMMING IN TINY CHUNKS   If this is your first excursion into programming, you'll notice that the general strategy is to start with something simple that works and then to improve it step-by-step until it reaches your goal. The previous examples are included as an illustration of this. They are an extremely simple test of one function that will be included in a larger application. The remaining examples in this chapter and the next are all drawn from the complex application that was built by using simple tests, such as `time.cfm` and `time2.cfm`. Building your application in tiny pieces will save you a lot of time waiting to see how the whole application runs.

In the TV guide example, several major tasks are immediately obvious for further development. First, most people do not want to choose their time zone every time they visit the site. Second, people want more program information than just "The News," and "11:00 p.m." Third, this example doesn't yet query a data source to provide dynamic data. And fourth, many people like to study a grid of shows from which to choose. Let's assume that the network already has a static TV guide grid on its web site. Here are the first improvements we might want to work on:

1. To generate the results from a query of the datasource.
2. To automatically modify the entire TV guide grid according to the user's time zone.
3. To store the time zone information on the user's computer and to automatically access that information when the user logs on to your site.
4. To link the TV guide grid to a detailed description of the scheduled shows and movies.

Introduction to Cookies

The simplest of these challenges is storing the time zone information on the user's computer. One simple way to do this is to send a cookie to the user. *Cookies* are variables that are stored on the user's machine and submitted with every web page request. This means that the variable is available for immediate use, no matter which template the user is viewing. After registering once, the viewer will never need to do it again.

Insert the following line of code at the top of **time2.cfm**. You'll note that it creates a cookie with the same name as the variable created in time.cfm. The **EXPIRES** attribute is set to **NEVER** so that the user never will need to register again. You could also set the attribute to expire after a certain number of days, on a certain date, or immediately as follows: (**EXPIRES=10**, **EXPIRES=10/10/1998**, or **EXPIRES=NOW**)!

```
<CFCOOKIE NAME="TVTimeZone" VALUE="#Form.TVTimeZone#"
    EXPIRES=NEVER>
```

If you have turned on the debugging options in the Cold Fusion Administrator, you will be able to verify the existence of this cookie in the section called "CGI variables." (See Figure 17-3.)

For the remainder of this example application, you will notice another cookie as well, **CustID**. You might be curious about why both cookies are needed. With a customer identification number (**CustID**), after all, it would be possible to query the database and obtain accurate time zone information from it.

The main reason for using two cookies is that running an extra query could add five seconds more processing time to your application. This is probably not a big problem most of the time, but because the web is already inconsistent in transmission speeds, the more efficiently your templates operate, the better.

As easy as they are to use, cookies do have limitations. In particular, some older browsers not support cookies in their browsers, though this is becoming less and less of a limitation. You can program around the problem or suggest that your page requires newer software. You are also limited to 20 cookies per domain. In the next chapter, alternative means of accomplishing the same ends are presented in the section on the Web Application Framework.

OTHER WAYS TO PASS VARIABLES FROM TEMPLATE TO TEMPLATE   In previous chapters, you learned how filling out a form passes form variables to the next template. If you wanted your user to register their time zone at the beginning of each session, you could use the following line to pass **TVTimeZone** from template to template, throughout the session. In this way, there would always be the variable **FORM.TVTimeZone** passed from any template or file with a form, even though it would always be invisible to the user.

```
<INPUT TYPE="hidden" NAME="TVTimeZone" VALUE=#TVTimeZone#>
```

If a template does not contain a form, you can pass a URL variable from template to template by embedding the variable in a link. This is done by identifying the variable and its value behind a "?" in the linking URL.

NOTE: *Include only letters, numbers, equals signs, and pound signs when setting URL variables.*

For example, if you were to create the variable **TVTimeZone** in the **Myindex.htm** file, you could pass the variable to **time.cfm** by changing the link as follows:

```
<A HREF="time.cfm?TVTimeZone=#TVTimeZone#">Register</A>
```

Each of these techniques is most useful for passing variables to a limited number of templates. If your application is large, using cookies or the Web Application Framework is most efficient and flexible, and less prone to mistakes.

In the TV Network example, a great many decisions are made using parameters that are cookies or that are passed from template to template. The following example, included on the CD, looks very basic and, indeed, the only difference between this page and many web pages is the inclusion of URL variables.

The status bar in Figure 17-4 shows the URL under the cursor and the URL variable—**Welcome.cfm?goal=search**—that is passed to the next template. Beneath Figure 17-4 is the template listing. You'll notice that every user link points to one template: **welcome.cfm**. The only difference between the links is that the variable **goal** has different values.

The reasons for navigating in this unusual way are described in the next section. The only link that does not go to welcome.cfm is called "Remote administrator access to customer database through Cold Fusion." But this link doesn't really count as an exception, of course, because it will be removed or hidden before the application is posted on the web.

Introduction to Conditional Logic

Cookies, of course, are only useful if your program can make decisions because of them. In this case, we want the cookie to eliminate the registration screen for people who have already registered. So how do we create a template that will make this decision?

Computer programming generally makes decisions through *conditional logic*. Conditional logic in Cold Fusion uses the tags <CFIF>,

Figure 17-4
Setting Up URL Variables on the Index Page

<CFELSE>, and <CFELSEIF>, and ends with </CFIF>. It is frequently useful to create complex conditional logic using the Boolean operators AND, OR, NOT, XOR, EQV, and IMP or to nest conditional logic statements within other conditional logic statements.

Conditional logic and Boolean operators are not as mysterious as they sound. We all learned extremely complex conditional logic and Boolean operators from our parents, who offered us options such as the following. Note that after the first <CFELSE> below, we are presented with an entirely new set of conditions: a nested <CFIF> statement. The nested statement tells you your options if you do not clean your room and if you do not do your homework.

```
<CFIF you clean your room AND you do your homework>
     You get your allowance.
<CFELSE>
     <CFIF you help your sister with dishes OR you butter
          up mom>
          You get a late supper and a possibility of still
               earning your allowance tomorrow.
     <CFELSEIF you display a bad attitude>
          You go to bed without supper and no hope of an
               allowance.
     <CFELSE>
```

```
                    Dad talks to you and gives you a new set of
                              options.
                </CFIF>
            </CFIF>
```

TONindex.cfm

```
<-- Page setup information -->
<HTML>
<HEAD>
<META HTTP-EQUIV="Content-Type" CONTENT="text/html;
    charset=windows-1252">
<TITLE>TONindex</TITLE>
</HEAD>
<BODY TEXT="#000000" LINK="#0000ff" VLINK="#800080"
    BGCOLOR="#ffffff">
<B><FONT FACE="Arial" SIZE=7><P ALIGN="CENTER">Welcome to
    T.O.N.<BR>
The Oldies Network!!!</P>
<IMG SRC="NIXON.gif" ALIGN="LEFT" HSPACE=12 WIDTH=255
    HEIGHT=297>
<--Links to the rest of the application. Note that each
    option passes a URL variable to the next template.-->
</B></FONT><FONT SIZE=5><P ALIGN="CENTER">After your free
    registration**, you will be able to:</P>
</FONT><P ALIGN="CENTER"><A
    HREF="Welcome.cfm?goal=search">Search the upcoming
    season lineup for a movie or TV series of your
    choice.</A></P>
<P ALIGN="CENTER"><A HREF="Welcome.cfm?goal=static">
    Instantly see next week's static program
    grid.</A></P>
<P AL!IGN="CENTER"><A HREF="Welcome.cfm?goal=grid">View a
    programming grid for any week of your choice. (Search
    takes around 60 seconds.)</A></P>
<P ALIGN="CENTER"><A HREF="Welcome.cfm?goal=change">Change
    registration information.</A></P>
<P ALIGN="CENTER"> </P>
<P ALIGN="CENTER">(Note: All grids in with example are
    limited to four days. All include detailed episode
    summaries.) </P>
<P ALIGN="CENTER"> </P>
<P><HR></P>
<P ALIGN="CENTER">**Purpose of registration: to translate
    your request into your time zone, and to allow our
    programming department to serve your interest
    better.</P>
<P ALIGN="CENTER"><A HREF="empadmin.cfm">Remote
    administrator access to customer database through
    Cold Fusion.</A></P></BODY>
</HTML>
```

Using Conditional Logic for Navigation

All of the links on the index page of the TV guide application (**TONindex.htm**) point to the following template. You'll also notice that this cfm file does not generate an html page and only serves to redirect the program through the tag <CFLOCATION>.

To accomplish this, the variable #goal# is evaluated against a series of <CFIF>, <CFELSE>, and <CFELSEIF> conditions. For each of these conditions, a link is indicated within the <CFLOCATION> tag.

You might wonder why anyone would bother creating an extra file, simply to redirect the program flow. Why not link the index page directly to the destination template?

The only reason is to provide an opportunity to evaluate whether the cookie "TVTimeZone" exists or not. Without this cookie, none of the other pages would work accurately. If TVTimeZone exists, the user is directed to one of three files. If TVTimeZone does not exist, the user is directed to the registration template, **empau3.cfm**. The user is then returned to the index page to choose again.

After users are registered and their cookies are returned to the server, the index template acts completely differently because of the conditional logic in **Welcome.cfm**. Clicking the very same link that led to the registration page now leads to the different options available to the user.

There is another alternative that would accomplish the same thing even better. Instead of creating a separate navigation template, the following template could be created and inserted into every file on the web

Welcome.cfm

```
<CFIF ParameterExists(TVTimeZone)>
    <CFIF #goal# EQ "Search">
        <CFLOCATION URL="Search.cfm?goal=search">
    <CFELSEIF #goal# EQ "grid">
        <CFLOCATION URL="Search.cfm?goal=grid">
    <CFELSEIF #goal# EQ "static">
        <CFLOCATION URL="static.cfm?goal=static">
    <CFELSEIF #goal# EQ "change">
        <CFLOCATION URL="empau3.cfm?goal=
            change&NewRecord=No">
    </CFIF>
<CFELSE>
    <CFLOCATION URL="empau3.cfm?NewRecord=
        Yes&goal=#goal#">
</CFIF>
```

site. If something happened on the user's computer to erase the cookies, the user would be required to reregister, no matter which file was bookmarked.

Checkcookie.cfm would only need three lines:

```
<CFIF #ParameterExists(TVTimeZone)# is "No">
      <CFLOCATION URL="empau3.cfm?NewRecord=Yes">
</CFIF>
```

Whenever **Checkcookie.cfm** was run, the <CFLOCATION> tag would check for the existance of the cookie, and if the cookie did not exist, it would run the registration template instead. To run **Checkcookie.cfm** with every template, you would need to insert only the following line in any other template:

```
<CFINCLUDE TEMPLATE="Checkcookie.cfm">
```

The <CFINCLUDE> tag runs the checkcookie template and returns to the original template if the cookie exists.

DETAILS ON USING THESE SPECIFIC FUNCTIONS AND TAGS

CONDITIONAL LOGIC, <CFIF>, <CFELSE>, <CFELSEIF> AND </CFIF>

- Whenever you use <CFIF>, you must also use </CFIF> to avoid generating an error.
- The syntax of conditional logic can be very confusing because different conditions require different punctuation. Especially while you're learning, find a working sample to use as a guide.
- Decision operators return the values TRUE or FALSE (without quotes) or "Yes" or "No" (with quotes). The decision operators in each category below are interchangeabl!e.
- IS, EQUAL, or EQ compares two values to see whether they are identical. This comparison is case sensitive. Their opposites are IS NOT, NOT EQUAL, and NEQ.
- CONTAINS and DOES NOT CONTAIN checks to see whether the value on the left is contained in the value on the right.
- The following operators can be used to compare the rank or size of dates, numbers, and strings (according to alphabetical order). The value on the left is compared to the value on the right, just as if it were part of a normal English sentence.
- GREATER THAN (alternately GT)

- LESS THAN (alternately LT)
- GREATER THAN OR EQUAL TO (alternately GTE or GE)
- LESS THAN OR EQUAL TO (alternately LTE or LE).

Complex conditional logic evaluates more than one condition in deciding the outcome (e.g., You must clean your room XOR do your homework { but NOT both.} OUTCOME: to get your allowance.)

- The following Boolean operators connect two conditions and return a true value in the following circumstances:
- AND requires both conditions to be true.
- OR requires one or both to be true.
- XOR requires one to be true, but not both
- EQV requires both to be true or both to be false.
- IMP requires the second value to be true whenever the first value is. (Condition A implies B.)
- NOT reverses the value of the argument.

```
<CFLOCATION URL="TargetTemplate.cfm" ADDTOKEN="Yes">
```
- This is a very common tag to use in response to conditional logic statements. It can pass the user to any standard cfm or html file.
- ADDTOKEN is optional and only used if CLIENTMANAGEMENT is enabled.

```
<CFINCLUDE TEMPLATE="TargetTemplate.cfm">
```
- It is often very useful to place all header or footer information into a single file, and to include it at the top or bottom of the page. This practice means that system-wide programming changes and cosmetic enhancements can be handled simply by changing only one file.

```
ParameterExists(Variable)
```
- Conditional logic usually depends on the existence of the variables that it uses. If those variables don't exist, you need to catch the problem and correct it before running the rest of the program.
- In other words, if it's possible for someone to operate the program wrong, they will. This function helps you stay one step ahead of them.

How will You Use This Information in the Future?

After you have understood the basics of conditional logic, you can accomplish vast numbers of tasks with your programming. Almost any task can be broken down into, "If this specific thing occurs, then I want the computer to do something specific. Otherwise, something else should happen instead."

The next chapter takes conditional logic several steps further and provide some looping techniques-for repeating the same steps over and over as needed. In addition, it provides more sophisticated methods of keeping track of client variables (such as cookies.) Additionally, we will continue exploring the different types of functions that you will find useful in your programming.

18

More Programming with Functions, Loops, and the Web Application Framework— Part 1

- Reusable Templates
- Conditional Logic Lets You Use the Same Template for Different Purposes
- Using Cold Fusion Parameters and Variables
- Using the Same Template in Different Ways, Pt 2
- Using Conditional Logic to Run Different Queries in the Same Template

This chapter, even more than Chapter 17, contains additional information that does not fit directly into the subheadings. The description part of each section describes how the application works and is not limited to the immediate section topic.

For instance, the first three lines of the template **search.cfm** have nothing to do with the first section, "Conditional Logic Lets You Use the Same Template in Different Ways," although they easily fit the topic of the second section.

When you are developing an integrated application such as the TV Network Program Guide, you need to consider many factors at the same time. Please read this chapter for the main topics, for certain, but also read it for the information that is included around the edges of the main topics. Much of the information around the edges will help you become a better Cold Fusion programmer quickly.

Conditional Logic Lets You Use the Same Template for Different Purposes

Conditional logic (using <CFIF>, <CFELSE>, and <CFELSEIF>) was introduced in the last chapter as a means of navigation. You may have noticed, however, that in **Welcome.cfm**, two links went to the exact same template: **search.cfm**.

Below are these two links. The only difference between them is the variable #goal#, which is passed to the new location as a URL variable. In one case, the definition of **#goal#** is **search**. In the other case, it's **grid**.

```
<CFIF #goal# EQ "Search">
    <CFLOCATION URL="Search.cfm?goal=search">
<CFELSEIF #goal# EQ "grid">
    <CFLOCATION URL="Search.cfm?goal=grid">
```

If you trace these two links back to the TONIndex.cfm file, you'll see that the purpose of the links is quite different for each one:

1. Search the upcoming season lineup for a movie or TV series of your choice.

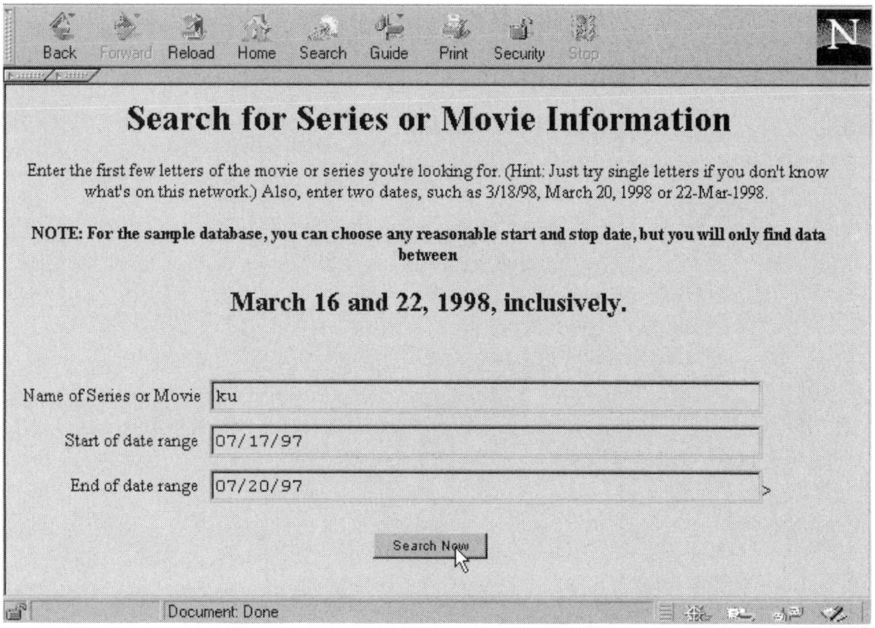

Figure 18-1
Output screen
produced by
search.cfm?goal=
search

Search for Series or Movie Information

Enter the first few letters of the movie or series you're looking for. (Hint: Just try single letters if you don't know what's on this network.) Also, enter two dates, such as 3/18/98, March 20, 1998 or 22-Mar-1998.

NOTE: For the sample database, you can choose any reasonable start and stop date, but you will only find data between

March 16 and 22, 1998, inclusively.

Name of Series or Movie   ku

Start of date range   07/17/97

End of date range   07/20/97

Search Now

2. View a programming grid for any week of your choice.

Furthermore, the output screens are quite different, depending on how the **#goal#** variable was set, as demonstrated in Figures 18-1 and 18-2.

The trick, of course, is that **search.cfm** uses conditional logic to act differently when passed a different value for **#goal#**. Depending on the value of **#goal#**, the output screen will do either of the following:

1. Produce three input fields for the name of the program sought and which dates to consider. The Submit button then links to **results.cfm**.

2. Produce input fields to choose the first date for a four-day grid. The Submit button links to **grid.cfm**.

In general, producing one template that handles several purposes in this way is a time saver, for initial programming, testing, and system maintenance, among other things. If you have to make a change that looks the same in both conditions, what better way than to make it on one template only?

Figure 18-2
Output screen
produced by
`search.cfm?`
`goal=grid`

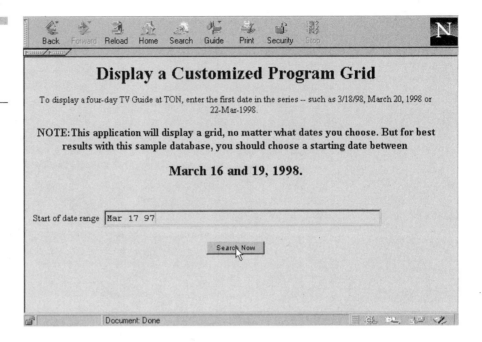

Figure 18-2
Output screen
produced by
`search.cfm?`
`goal=grid`

NOTE: *The following section contains the complete listing of search.cfm. It is broken up by text rather than trying to include all of the text as comments within the code itself. Notes on new functions and syntax are at the bottom of this template listing. This is the case with all the templates for the rest of the chapter.*

Description of Search.cfm

Search.cfm starts by ensuring that the program has something to do, even if expected variables aren't there. Perhaps, for instance, the page was bookmarked, and the user doesn't start with **TONIndex.cfm**. Would the variable exist under every possible situation?

This is probably an unnecessary precaution because all (or almost all) browsers include passed URL variables in their bookmarks. But what if, for instance, the person didn't make a bookmark, but manually copied the link address and not the variable assignment? This may seem so unlikely that you wouldn't want to worry about it, but even so, the possibility is dealt with in the first three lines.

Whenever a template depends on the existence of a variable to work, it's a good idea to include bits of code to create the variable if it's not there. (See notes on the CFPARAM tag in the discussion section following this code.) It simply can't hurt, and it might help—in some situations, more than you expect.

```
<CFIF #ParameterExists(goal)# is "NO">
    <CFSET #goal# = "search">
</CFIF>
    <HEAD><TITLE>Search for Customized
    Information</TITLE></HEAD>
    <BODY>
```

The next section of code is where the form begins to act differently, depending on the value of **#goal#**. If the user requests a customized grid of TV shows for the week, this is the HTML that becomes active.

The code contains two things, based on the value of **#goal#** in the CFIF expression. First, it produces the screen in Figure 18-2 by activating the HTML for the heading and on-screen instructions that are displayed. Second, it sets up an HTML <FORM> that is used only to produce a grid.

```
<CFIF #goal# is "grid">
    <FORM ACTION="grid.CFM?RequestTimeout=500"
        METHOD="POST">
    <CENTER><H1>Display a Customized Program Grid</H1>
    To display a four-day TV Guide at TON, enter the first
        date in the series-such as 3/18/98, March 20,
        1998, or 22-Mar-1998. <P>
<H3>NOTE:This application will display at least an empty
        grid, no matter what dates you choose. But for best
        results with this sample database, you should choose
        a starting date between </H3><H2>March 16 and 19,
        1998.</H2><P><BR></CENTER>
```

If, on the other hand, the user chose to search for a specific TV show, none of the previous HTML would apply. In this case, the following code is invoked to produce Figure 18-1. The second alternative HTML is invoked whenever **#goal#** is not defined as **grid** because it uses only the <CFELSE> tag.

It might seem like a sticky point, but #goal# does have other definitions in this application. They're not supposed to lead to this template, but if through programmer error they somehow do, there's no special code written for them. With <CFELSE>, anything that's not **grid** leads to **search**.

You will notice further down the template that other conditions are also defined as **NEQ** **"grid"** (not equal to grid), rather than is **"Search"**. This was to keep the conditional logic consistent. —

You'll also notice that the HTML <FORM> tag in this section invokes **results.cfm**, rather than **grid.cfm**, even though you're using the same submit button. Thus, the same button takes you to different places, depending on how **#goal#** is defined.

```
<CFELSE>
    <FORM ACTION="Results.CFM" METHOD="POST">
    <CENTER><H1>Search for Series or Movie Information</H1>
Enter the first few letters of the movie or series you're
    looking for. (Hint: For the sample database, just try
    single letters if you don't know what's on this
    network.) Also, enter two dates, such as 3/18/98,
    March 20, 1998 or 22-Mar-1998. <P>
<H4>NOTE: For the sample database, you can choose any
    reasonable start and stop date, but you will only
    find data between </H4>
    <H2>March 16 and 22, 1998, inclusively.</H2><BR>
</CENTER>
</CFIF>
```

Each of the previous two sections of code uses a different <FORM> tag, and each of the two forms thus invokes a different template. However, both use the same HTML table for alignment, and both the search and grid forms also share one input field: StartDate.

The next two lines start the table and invoke Cold Fusion.

```
<TABLE>
<CFOUTPUT>
```

In the next section, you'll notice that conditional logic adds two more input fields to the custom grid form than it does to the program search form. The TV program grid form needs only a starting date. The program search form also needs an end date and the name of the movie, series, or other TV program that the user wants to find.

The following form field, in which the user asks for a specific show, only goes on the search form:

```
<CFIF #goal# NEQ "grid">
    <TR><TD ALIGN="right">Name of Series or Movie</TD>
    <TD><INPUT TYPE="text" NAME="Schedule__ProgName"
```

```
         SIZE="50" MAXLENGTH="40"></TD></TR>
</CFIF>
```

Both the grid and the search form get the following form field. Therefore, it does not need to be part of any <CFIF> statement. It's just there.

You'll notice that the default form field value is set to display the current date as the starting date because most TV viewers are only concerned with what they're going to watch tonight or in the next few days.

```
<TR><TD ALIGN="right">Start of date range</TD>
<TD><INPUT TYPE="text" NAME="StartDate" SIZE="50"
    MAXLENGTH="40" VALUE=#DateFormat(Now(),"mm/d/yy")#>
    </TD></TR>
```

The end date form field listed next is only invoked for creating a search form. The default value here displays three days after the current date because most TV viewers are concerned only with what they'll be watching in the next few days.

```
<CFIF #goal# NEQ "grid">
<TR><TD ALIGN="right">End of date range</TD>
<TD><INPUT TYPE="text" NAME="EndDate" SIZE="50"
    MAXLENGTH="40" VALUE=#DateFormat(Now()+
    CreateTimeSpan(3,0,0,0),"mm/d/yy")#></TD></TR>
```

In the next half dozen lines, Cold Fusion checks to make sure that the user entered dates and not garbage. The template **results.cfm** cannot search the database for dates that do not exist.

The dates are validated by using the built-in mechanisms provided by Cold Fusion. Unfortunately, these built-in mechanisms cannot guarantee that the user didn't mix up the start date and the end date. (Don't forget Murphy's law!) Therefore, which date comes first must be validated in the next template, **results.cfm**, using conditional logic.

One more thing to notice is the location of </CFIF>. This tag, which closes the conditional logic, occurs after validating the end date and program name because they are required only for the Program Search page.

Validations that are required for both the search form and the grid come after </CFIF>.

```
<INPUT TYPE="hidden" NAME="Schedule__ProgName_required"
    VALUE="You must enter at least one letter for the
    program name.">
<INPUT TYPE="hidden" NAME="EndDate_Date" VALUE="You must
```

```
      enter valid dates.">
<INPUT TYPE="hidden" NAME="EndDate_required" VALUE="You
      must enter valid dates.">
</CFIF>
</TABLE>
<INPUT TYPE="hidden" NAME="StartDate_Date" VALUE="You must
      enter valid dates.">
<INPUT TYPE="hidden" NAME="StartDate_required" VALUE="You
      must enter valid dates.">
<P>
<CENTER><INPUT TYPE="submit" VALUE="Search Now"></CENTER>
</CFOUTPUT>
</FORM>
</BODY>
</HTML>
```

Details on Using These Specific Functions and Tags

The first function was not used in the code. It is discussed here because it's an extremely useful function to know about, and because it's closely related to the function used in the code.

<CFPARAM NAME="VARIABLENAME" DEFAULT="VALUE IF IT DOESN'T ALREADY EXIST">

- The first three lines of **search.cfm** use the function
  #ParameterExists(goal)#. In a different situation,
  the same results might have come from
  <CFPARAM NAME="goal" DEFAULT="search">

- <CFPARAM> checks to make sure a variable exists. If not, it provides one and puts the default value into it. However, if the variable already does exist, the value of the variable doesn't change. The variable is set to the default value only if it doesn't exist in the first place.

- The reason <CFPARAM> could not be used in this situation is that it cannot evaluate form variables and URL variables.

- If you could use this tag here, the first three lines of the program would be condensed to **<CFPARAM NAME="goal" DEFAULT= "search">**

DATEFORMAT (DATE [, MASK]).

- In most cases, both the **"date"** and **"mask"** arguments should be enclosed by quotation marks.

- The **"date"** argument can use a string, a number, or another function that can be converted to a date value.

- A mask is the optional code that tells Cold Fusion how you want the date formatted. Without a mask, the date returned uses the format 02-Aug-93.

- In the mask, use **"m,"** **"d,"** and **"y,"** for day of the month, month, and year. Double letters add a leading zero to single digit numbers.

- **"mmm"** and **"ddd"** produce three-letter abbreviations for the month or the day of the week

- **"yyyy,"** **"mmmm,"** and **"dddd"** produce a four-digit year or the complete name of the month or the day of the week

- Punctuation and spaces between the letters are part of the format.

- For this function (and the next two) to work, make sure it is placed somewhere between a <CFOUTPUT> and a </CFOUTPUT> tag.

CREATETIMESPAN (DAY, HOUR, MINUTE, SECOND)

- The CreateTimeSpan function is necessary to add a numeric value to a Time/Date variable.

- Use numbers (without quotes) for days, hours, minutes, and seconds.

- This example of CreateTimeSpan is less complex than the example in the previous chapter, which needed to evaluate the variable **#TVTimeZone# first**.

NOW ( )

- This function takes no arguments.

- Unless formatted otherwise, Now( ) returns the current ODBC time stamp.

VALIDATING FORM FIELD VARIABLES WITH COLD FUSION

- Cold Fusion enables you to require that the user enter the right type of data, using the following syntax.

```
<INPUT TYPE="hidden" NAME="VariableName_required" VALUE=
    "You must enter something to go to the next
    template.">
```

- The variable name is given a suffix that starts with an underline, and an error message of your choice is assigned to it.

▨ All attribute values are surrounded by quotes.

▨ In the previous example, the suffix **"_required"** returns the error message if the user leaves the form field blank.

▨ Numerical validations require the user to enter a number.

"_integer" rounds the number to an integer.

"_float" allows the number to have decimal places.

"_range" lets you specify the minimum and/or maximum values in the Value Attribute (rather than an error message). Example: VALUE="MIN=15 MAX=99"

▨ Time validations require the user to enter a time or date. Cold Fusion turns them into ODBC time stamps before passing them to the next template.

"_date" accepts a wide number of formats, from 3/21/99 to Mar 3 1997 to September-5-98.

"_time" requires a valid time format.

"_eurodate" requires that the person use a European date format.

REQUESTTIMEOUT=500

▨ This variable prevents Cold Fusion from automatically timing out when the search reaches the default of 180 seconds (which can be reset to any length from the Cold Fusion Administrator, Server Settings page).

▨ This variable was necessary on the 486-100 machine that this application was developed on, and only during certain experimental parts of the development process. It is only left in the program as a teaching illustration.

▨ Most servers will be significantly faster than the development machine so that the grid will be produced in a fraction of a minute. However, for any search that takes more than a few seconds, the user should be warned about the delay in response. In this application, the user was warned on **TONIndex.cfml**.

How Will You Use This Information in the Future?

In general, you will want to use conditional logic for recycling code as often as possible. Not only will you save time in development, but system-wide changes will be easier to manage as you update the look and functionality of the system.

Whenever writing any template, you should always assume that there will be times that the variables you are using didn't get passed to the template or weren't created correctly. Expressions using <CFPARAM> and **ParameterExists(variable)** take little time to build but enable you to avoid being trapped by the many things that could go wrong—whether generated by the user or by your own errors in planning. Make a habit of putting these error-trapping expressions into the templates you write—even if you're certain that the errors could never occur.

You will use **DateFormat ()** and **Now ()** in most of the applications that you write because most organizations do not require a greater level of precision than the date when they record a time stamp. People like to receive the level of precision that they're used to. Many people with digital watches, for instance, round off to the nearest five minutes to avoid irritating other people who ask what time it is, even though it takes a little more thought. In many situations, the date is all you need.

Use of the built-in Cold Fusion validation techniques (and the conditional logic method in the next section) will serve your purposes most of the time and will save you the trouble of writing Javascript validation routines.

Finally, you will probably never need to use the RequestTimeout variable—but it's probably good to know that it's there if needed.

Using the Same Template in Different Ways, Pt 2.

If you have been following the program flow, or plot, this section will take a little detour from what we've been doing. Up until now, we've been following the user of the application as the start to search for the TV show or TV Program Grid that they want. This plot will be continued later in Chapter 19's section titled, "Using Conditional Logic to Verify the Existence and Validity of Form Fields."

For now, this section will develop the theme of the last section: "Conditional Logic Lets You Use the Same Template for Different Purposes," using the viewer registration templates. In other words, the **empau3.cfm** template is used to register new viewers or to update the records of old viewers. In fact, **empau3.cfm** looks different for each condition.

By now, you should have a general idea of how a simple form can be used in two different ways with conditional logic. Yet the reasons for doing so may not be very compelling for you.

Using the Empau3.cfm Template

`Empau3.cfm` is a much more complex-looking template. Combining two purposes in one template definitely saved considerable time in development and testing because of conditional logic. Please do not be intimidated by the size of the template, though. As we go through it, you'll see that it's really fairly simple, after you understand the internal structure.

You may recall that there were two other options in the `Welcome.cfm` template which linked to the same file. First of all, if the TV viewer had never registered, forced registration occurs, no matter what was clicked on. Notice that the new variable `#NewRecord#` is created and set to `Yes` in this line of code, taken from `Welcome.cfm`. Figure 18-3 shows the final screen.

```
<CFLOCATION URL="empau3.cfm?NewRecord=Yes&goal=#goal#">
```

On the other hand, the user may have been simply updating an address or changing a maiden name to her married one. In this case, the new variable `#NewRecord#` is set to `No`. Figure 18-4 shows the output screen.

```
<CFLOCATION URL="empau3.cfm?goal=change&NewRecord=No">
```

DESCRIPTION OF EMPAU3.CFM   The template begins by checking for crucial variables and setting defaults. Notice that for a new record, `#TVTimeZone#` is set at 44. This value turns on the radio buttons in the screen shown in Figure 18-3 so that users can adjust their time zone properly.

If `#TVTimeZone#` is a cookie that is already set to one of the existing time zones, only two radio buttons will show up, as illustrated in Figure 18-4. Users can still change their time zone, but they must first resubmit the form.

```
<CFIF ParameterExists(URL.NewRecord) IS "NO" OR
ParameterExists(TVTimeZone) IS "NO">
    <CFSET #NewRecord# = "Yes">
    <CFSET #TVTimeZone# = 44>
</CFIF>
```

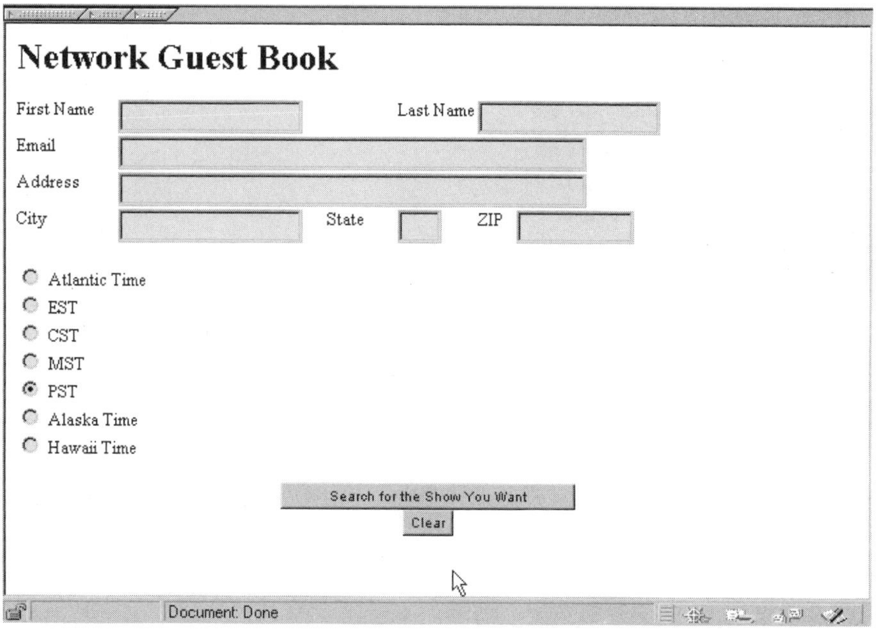

Figure 18-3
The output screen
produced by
cmpau3.cfm?
NewRecord=Yes

For users who are just changing their registration, we want to populate the form with existing information from the database. This way, the user only needs to type in new information.

Notice in this query the DEBUG attribute **""**. This attribute displays the actual SQL query that is submitted to the database, including the actual number inside the variable **#CustID#**. Notice in Figure 18-4 that this number was 28 for the user Phil Barrett.

```
<CFIF #NewRecord# EQ "No">
    <CFQUERY DATASOURCE="TVNetwork"
    NAME="CustomerChange" DEBUG>
    SELECT LastName, FirstName, Email, Address, City,
        State, ZipCode, TVTimeZone
FROM Customer
    WHERE CustID=#CustID#
    </CFQUERY>
</CFIF>
```

The following code changes the title in the browser window, as well as the unprocessed HTML output, depending on the conditional logic that leads up to it. This would also be a good location to provide focused promotional material for newcomers versus old-timers. Because a query has

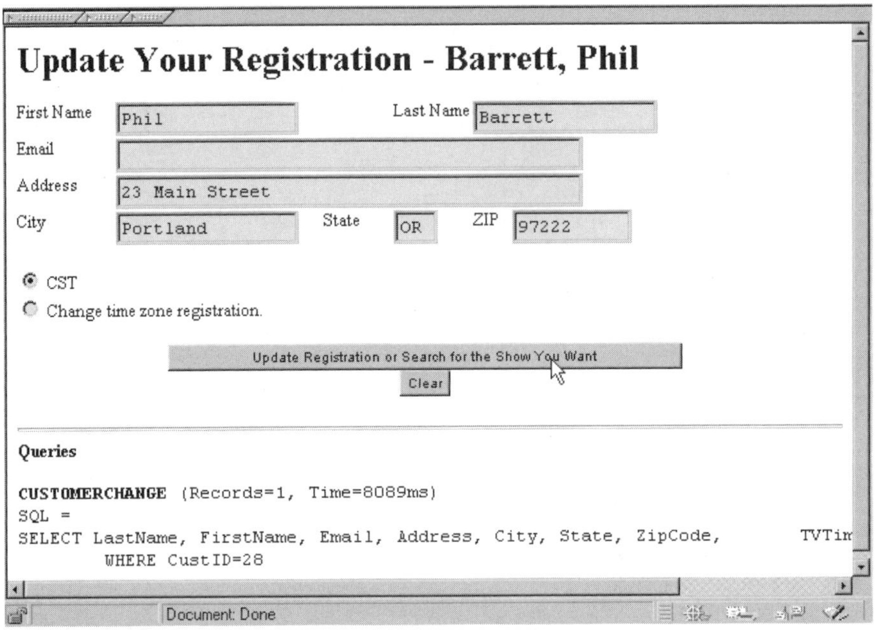

Figure 18-4
Output screen
produced by
empau3.cfm?
NewRecord=No,
showing the existing
data that person has
registered with. No-
tice that the <CF-
QUERY DEBUG> at-
tribute is turned on,
thereby displaying
the query on the
screen with all
variables evaluated

already accessed the customer database, highly focused promotions could be inserted here, with several layers of conditional logic.

Selective promotion is an excellent use of conditional logic to control the look and content of the page. This all depends on what kinds of demographics you are obtaining from your users. In this application, name, address, and phone number are about all you obtain. You could, however, schedule a short questionnaire every 10 times they log on or focus promotions based on the types of shows they ask about in their searches.

Because network advertising departments have already linked advertisers to programming, inserting web page links to their advertisers could be automated through existing database tables. But that's another story and another application.

```
<HTML>
<HEAD>
<CFIF #NewRecord# IS "Yes">
    <TITLE>Network Guest Book</TITLE>
<CFELSE>
    <CFOUTPUT QUERY="CustomerChange">
    <TITLE>Update Your Registration - #LastName#,
        #FirstName#</TITLE>
    </CFOUTPUT>
</CFIF> </HEAD>
```

```
<BODY BGCOLOR="#FFFFFF">
<CFIF #NewRecord# IS "Yes">
    <H1>Network Guest Book</H1>
<CFELSE>
    <CFOUTPUT QUERY="CustomerChange">
    <H1>Update Your Registration - #LastName#,
        #FirstName#</H1>
    </CFOUTPUT>
</CFIF>
```

The form fields in this template are processed with conditional logic in the `tvtzchng.cfm` template. Notice that no URL variables are passed through the <FORM ACTION> attribute. When you are processing a form, you can pass variables only as cookies or as hidden form fields (or as client variables, but we haven't dealt with them yet.)

You'll also notice that **#TimeOfVisit#** and **#CustID#** are being passed as hidden form fields. Why would **#CustID#** be passed as a form field when it is already a cookie? Because in the `tvtzchng.cfm` template, all of the form fields are used to update the record specified by the primary key, which is #CustID#.

```
<FORM ACTION="tvtzchng.cfm" METHOD="POST">
<CFIF #NewRecord# IS "No">
    <CFOUTPUT QUERY="CustomerChange">
    <INPUT TYPE="hidden" NAME="CustID" VALUE="#CustID#">
    </CFOUTPUT>
</CFIF>
<CFIF #NewRecord# IS "Yes">
    <INPUT TYPE="hidden" NAME="TimeOfVisit"
        VALUE="CurrentDateTime()">
</CFIF>
```

USING FORM FIELDS   In the next section of the template, each form field is addressed in two ways, depending on whether the person is registering for the first time. First, the form field is made into a required field through a hidden input tag. Then the blank is created for the user to type a name. Finally, if this is not a new record, the blank form field is filled with the existing information in the database.

```
<TABLE CELLSPACING=0 BORDER=0 CELLPADDING=0 WIDTH=574>
<TR><TD WIDTH="18%" VALIGN="TOP">
First Name </TD>
<TD WIDTH="22%" VALIGN="TOP" COLSPAN=2>
<INPUT TYPE="hidden" NAME="FirstName_required" VALUE="You
    must enter a first name to proceed. Note: If you
```

```
            enter invalid data, your registration will be
            invalidated within a week.">
<INPUT TYPE="text" NAME="FirstName" SIZE="16"
        MAXLENGTH="16"
<CFIF #NewRecord# IS "No">
        <CFOUTPUT QUERY="CustomerChange">VALUE=
                "#Trim(FirstName)#"
        </CFOUTPUT>
</CFIF>
        >
```

If you're new to programming, the amount of code that follows may seem intimidating. Notice, however, that the remaining <INPUT TEXT> fields are exactly the same as the FORM.FirstName field shown previously. The only difference is that the `#FORM.email#` is not a required field because some users may have chosen not to have email.

This is an example of recycling code that works. To complete the entire form, it was only necessary to work out code for the FORM.FirstName field above. The code was then copied over and over, and tiny changes were made each time. No big deal.

```
    </TD>
    <TD WIDTH="16%" VALIGN="TOP" COLSPAN=2>
    Last Name </TD>
    <TD WIDTH="48%" VALIGN="TOP" COLSPAN=3>
    <INPUT TYPE="hidden" NAME="LastName_required" VALUE="You
            must enter a last name to proceed. Note: If you enter
            invalid data, your registration will be invalidated
            within a week.">
    <INPUT TYPE="text" NAME="LastName" SIZE="16" MAXLENGTH="16"
    <CFIF #NewRecord# IS "No">
        <CFOUTPUT QUERY="CustomerChange">
                VALUE="#Trim(LastName)#" </CFOUTPUT>
    </CFIF>
    >
    </TD>
    </TR>
    <TR><TD WIDTH="16%" VALIGN="TOP">
    Email </TD>
    <TD WIDTH="84%" VALIGN="TOP" COLSPAN=7>
    <INPUT TYPE="text" NAME="EMail" SIZE="42" MAXLENGTH="42"
    <CFIF #NewRecord# IS "No">
    <CFOUTPUT QUERY="CustomerChange">VALUE="#Trim(EMail)#"
            </CFOUTPUT>
    </CFIF>
    >
    </TD>
    </TR>
    <TR><TD WIDTH="16%" VALIGN="TOP">
    Address </TD>
    <TD WIDTH="84%" VALIGN="TOP" COLSPAN=7>
```

```
<INPUT TYPE="hidden" NAME="Address_required" VALUE="You
     must enter an address to proceed. Note: If you enter
     invalid data, your registration will be invalidated
     within a week.">
<INPUT TYPE="text" NAME="Address" SIZE="42" MAXLENGTH="42"
<CFIF #NewRecord# IS "No">
<CFOUTPUT QUERY="CustomerChange">VALUE="#Trim(Address)#"
     </CFOUTPUT>
</CFIF>
>
</TD>
</TR>
<TR><TD WIDTH="16%" VALIGN="TOP">
City </TD>
<TD WIDTH="27%" VALIGN="TOP">
  <INPUT TYPE="hidden" NAME="City_required" VALUE="You must
     enter your city to proceed. Note: If you enter
     invalid data, your registration will be invalidated
     within a week.">
<INPUT TYPE="text" NAME="City" SIZE="16" MAXLENGTH="16"
<CFIF #NewRecord# IS "No">
<CFOUTPUT QUERY="CustomerChange">VALUE="#Trim(City)#"
     </CFOUTPUT>
</CFIF>
>
</TD>
<TD WIDTH="15%" VALIGN="TOP">
State </TD>
<TD WIDTH="10%" VALIGN="TOP" COLSPAN=2>
  <INPUT TYPE="hidden" NAME="State_required" VALUE="You
     must enter your state to proceed. Note: If you enter
     invalid data, your registration will be invalidated
     within a week.">
<INPUT TYPE="text" NAME="State" SIZE="3" MAXLENGTH="3"
<CFIF #NewRecord# IS "No">
<CFOUTPUT QUERY="CustomerChange">VALUE="#Trim(State)#"
     </CFOUTPUT>
</CFIF>
>
</TD>
<TD WIDTH="8%" VALIGN="TOP" COLSPAN=2>
ZIP </TD>
<TD WIDTH="20%" VALIGN="TOP">
<INPUT TYPE="hidden" NAME="ZipCode_required" VALUE="You
     must enter a ZipCode to proceed. Note: If you enter
     invalid data, your registration will be invalidated
     within a week.">
  <INPUT TYPE="text" NAME="ZipCode" SIZE="10"
     MAXLENGTH="10"
<CFIF #NewRecord# IS "No">
  <CFOUTPUT QUERY="CustomerChange">VALUE="#Trim(Zip-
     Code)#" </CFOUTPUT>
</CFIF>
>
```

Using Recycled Code

Here's another place where a lot of work is done by a little bit of code, copied over and over. First, for each time zone, a <CFIF> or <CFELSEIF> tag identifies the time zone where the viewer lives. Two radio buttons then identify that default location and offer the person a chance to change the time zone (for instance, if they move a long distance.) This is illustrated by Figure 18-4.

If this is a new record or if the user wants to change the time zone, the variable **#TVTimeZone#** is set at 44. This invokes radio button choices for every time zone on the continent, as illustrated by Figure 18-3.

```
</TD>
</TR>
</TABLE><P>
<CFIF #TVTimeZone# EQ 4> <BR>
    <INPUT TYPE="radio" NAME="TVTimeZone" VALUE=4 CHECKED>
        Atlantic.<BR>
    <INPUT TYPE="radio" NAME="TVTimeZone" VALUE=44> Change
        time zone registration.<BR>
<CFELSEIF #TVTimeZone# EQ 3>
    <INPUT TYPE="radio" NAME="TVTimeZone" VALUE=3 CHECKED>
        EST. <BR>
    <INPUT TYPE="radio" NAME="TVTimeZone" VALUE=44> Change
        time zone registration.<BR>
<CFELSEIF #TVTimeZone# EQ 2>
    <INPUT TYPE="radio" NAME="TVTimeZone" VALUE=2 CHECKED>
        CST<BR>
    <INPUT TYPE="radio" NAME="TVTimeZone" VALUE=44> Change
        time zone registration.<BR>
<CFELSEIF #TVTimeZone# EQ 1>
    <INPUT TYPE="radio" NAME="TVTimeZone" VALUE=1 CHECKED>
        MST<BR>
    <INPUT TYPE="radio" NAME="TVTimeZone" VALUE=44> Change
        time zone registration.<BR>
<CFELSEIF #TVTimeZone# EQ 0>
    <INPUT TYPE="radio" NAME="TVTimeZone" VALUE=0 CHECKED>
        PST<BR>
    <INPUT TYPE="radio" NAME="TVTimeZone" VALUE=44> Change
        time zone registration.<BR>
<CFELSEIF #TVTimeZone# EQ -1>
    <INPUT TYPE="radio" NAME="TVTimeZone" VALUE=-1 CHECKED>
        Alaska Time<BR>
    <INPUT TYPE="radio" NAME="TVTimeZone" VALUE=44> Change
        time zone registration.<BR>
<CFELSEIF #TVTimeZone# EQ -2>
    <INPUT TYPE="radio" NAME="TVTimeZone" VALUE=-2 CHECKED>
        Hawaii Time<BR>
```

```
        <INPUT TYPE="radio" NAME="TVTimeZone" VALUE=44> Change
            time zone registration.<BR>
<CFELSEIF #TVTimeZone# EQ 44>
        <INPUT TYPE="radio" NAME="TVTimeZone" VALUE=4> Atlantic
            Time<BR>
        <INPUT TYPE="radio" NAME="TVTimeZone" VALUE=3> EST<BR>
        <INPUT TYPE="radio" NAME="TVTimeZone" VALUE=2> CST<BR>
        <INPUT TYPE="radio" NAME="TVTimeZone" VALUE=1> MST<BR>
        <INPUT TYPE="radio" NAME="TVTimeZone" VALUE=0 CHECKED>
            PST<BR>
        <INPUT TYPE="radio" NAME="TVTimeZone" VALUE=-1> Alaska
            Time<BR>
        <INPUT TYPE="radio" NAME="TVTimeZone" VALUE=-2> Hawaii
        Time<BR>
</CFIF>
<P> <CENTER>
```

Finally, conditional logic provides different wording on the Submit buttons, depending on whether it is a new record.

```
<CFIF #NewRecord# IS "Yes">
        <INPUT TYPE="submit" VALUE="Search for the Show You
            Want"> <BR>
        <INPUT TYPE="reset" VALUE="Clear">
<CFELSE>
        <INPUT TYPE="submit" VALUE="Update Registration or
            Search for the Show You Want"> <BR>
        <INPUT TYPE="reset" VALUE="Clear">
</CFIF>
</CENTER>
</FORM></BODY></HTML>
```

Details on Using These Specific Functions

If you've been reading Chapters 17 and 18 sequentially, you will have already been exposed to most of the functions in the template empau3.cfm. These two chapters are structured to provide you small bites of syntax in an actual application, but nothing more than you can chew at a time. Thus, for this section, there are only two new vocabulary items, and you may already know them.

```
<INPUT TYPE="hidden" NAME="VariableName"
        VALUE="#VariableValue#">
```

- Using hidden form fields is one method of passing variables to the next template which is supported by all browsers. For all practical purposes, hidden form fields are not limited in size or number, but they require a form before you can use them.

- They are clumsy for global variables because they must be passed to every template that uses them.

TRIM(STRINGVARIABLE)

- Trim removes spaces from the beginning and end of any string variable.

- Enclose the string in quotation marks.

- Some databases, such as Microsoft SQL Server, create variables that are padded with spaces to fill the field size completely. These must be trimmed after queries—especially if the user will be modifying the variables in a form.

- Spaces entered into form fields by a query are not ignored by Cold Fusion.

How Will You Use This Information in the Future

Every time a web page is created, it is a system unto itself. There are no automatic methods of moving a variable from one page to the next. Indeed, one of the most challenging aspects of creating a foolproof application is passing variables from one template to another. No system works perfectly for all purposes.

Passing variables with hidden form fields is certainly one method that you will need to employ at various times in your programming. However, you'll need to be careful when doing this so that you do not accidentally update or insert variables into your database that you do not intend to. To prevent this, you may need to list your form fields with the <CFINSERT FORMFIELDS> attribute. Of course, with the SQL INSERT statement, you are required to do this anyway.

Trim(string) is one of those nit-picky things that may cost you hours of pain if you don't know how to do it. If your database doesn't pad variables with leading or trailing spaces, you may not run into a problem until you try recycling your code in another environment. If you become proficient with Cold Fusion, this could happen to you.

It's a good practice to use Trim() when populating a form from a database—at least some of the time—so that you know how to use it. After that, be lazy if you want, but don't forget the issue.

Using <CFTRANSACTION> to Obtain the Results of a Current Operation

After the user fills the registration form, Cold Fusion has to either update an existing record or insert a new one into the database. This is also the right time for creating cookies and deciding where the program should go next.

These details cannot be taken care of in the same template as the form because the variables do not exist as variables until they are submitted. At the same time, taking care of these details doesn't require generating an HTML page.

The following template simply takes care of all the little details and sends the user back to the **TONindex** page—or, in one case, back to **empau3.cfm**. Other than that, it's invisible to the user.

DESCRIPTION OF TVTZCHNG.CFM The first conditional statement pertains to a new record entered by a new viewer of the network. This record is inserted into the datasource, and a query is immediately run to find out what the customer ID (CustID) is. That's because **#CustID#** just doesn't exist until after the information is inserted.

#CustID# is the primary key of the database table that holds customer information. This means that each **#CustID#** is completely unique, and, furthermore, it is generated automatically by Microsoft Access whenever a new record is inserted into the table.

Cold Fusion has no way of determining what **#CustID#** is before inserting the new record. So after inserting the record, it immediately queries the database to get the ID number. There's a problem with this, however. The database normally handles commands and queries in more or less the order that they are received. If two users are simultaneously registering, the commands sent by the server to the database might become mixed up — especially in a large database which is being used heavily. The Customer ID generated automatically by a new user in New York might be sent as a cookie to a new user in Hawaii, along with the wrong time zone information.

So the following conditional statement begins with the tag <CFTRANSACTION>, which locks up the computer until the complete transaction is finished, and the computer receives </CFTRANSACTION>. This way, there is no way for the **#CustID#** fields to get mixed up. As long as Hawaii is doing its transaction, New York must wait. (The wait is a few milliseconds, so don't sweat it.)

Notice the syntax for the SELECT clause in the **GetID** query. SQL asks for the largest **#CustID#** and gives it a temporary name. Before anything can go wrong, it CFSETS another temporary variable and creates a cookie in the user's machine. Only then can the transaction close, and the computer is freed up to handle another request.

```
<CFIF #ParameterExists(CustID)# IS "No">
    <CFTRANSACTION>
<CFINSERT
        DATASOURCE="TVNetwork"
        TABLENAME="Customer">
    <CFQUERY DATASOURCE="TVNetwork"
      NAME="GetID">
      SELECT max(CustID) as newcustid FROM Customer
    </CFQUERY>
        <CFOUTPUT QUERY="GetID">
    <CFSET #NewCustID# = #GetID.NewCustID#>
        </CFOUTPUT>
        <CFCOOKIE NAME="CustID" VALUE="#NewCustID#"
            EXPIRES=NEVER>
        <CFCOOKIE NAME="TVTimeZone" VALUE="#Form.TVTimeZone#"
EXPIRES=NEVER>
        </CFTRANSACTION>
```

Here's what happens if the TV watcher is already registered with the network. First, the customer database is updated. The <CFUPDATE> command needed the optional FORMFIELDS attribute because one of the form fields was the hidden variable of **#NewRecord#**, which is not part of the database. It therefore needed to be excluded from the database update.

Finally, new cookies are created, and the user is sent to one of two places: empau3.cfm—if the user wanted to change the time zone information—or TONindex.cfm otherwise.

<CFTRANSACTION> was not needed for this step, because **#CustID#** doesn't change. No confusion is possible. You might wonder, however, why <CFINCLUDE> was used to redirect the user rather than <CFLOCATION>.

If a cookie"" is created just before <CFLOCATION>, the cookie won't take. To be sure that the customers gets their cookies, the step needs to be separated from <CFLOCATION>. However, in trying various combinations of commands, I could not get the cookies to register, even before the database update.

Beyond that, if the TV viewer wants to change the time zone, the cookie `#TVTimeZone#` set at 44. This directs the person back to `empau3.cfm` and turns on the radio buttons for the entire range of possible time zones.

```
<CFELSE>
    <CFUPDATE
    DATASOURCE="TVNetwork"
    TABLENAME="Customer"
FORMFIELDS="custid,firstname,lastname,email,address,city,
    state, zipcode,tvtimezone">
    <CFCOOKIE NAME="TVTimeZone" VALUE="#TVTimeZone#"
    EXPIRES=NEVER>
    <CFCOOKIE NAME="NewRecord" VALUE="#NewRecord#"
        EXPIRES=2>
    <CFCOOKIE NAME="CustID" VALUE="#CustID#" EXPIRES=NEVER>
    <CFIF #TVTimeZone# EQ 44>
        <CFINCLUDE TEMPLATE="empau3.cfm">
    <CFELSE>
        <CFINCLUDE TEMPLATE="tonindex.CFm">
    </CFIF>
</CFIF>
```

You might wonder why the final section is even here, considering that it duplicates the navigation commands in the conditional statements just above it. This navigation section should only apply to new records, rather than updated ones. Why even have a section for `#TVTimeZone#` being set at 44?

It certainly seems unnecessary at this point, and, logically, there should be no reason to leave it this way. However, at one point in development, it was necessary. There may be some reason for suspecting that `#FORM.TVTimeZone#` = 44 could get passed along to this conditional statement, and it may just be that I can no longer remember how it would get there.

When you're cleaning up code, it often doesn't hurt to leave extra precautions in the code, even if you no longer remember why they were put there in the first place. When you remove something that you think is no longer needed, you sometimes do damage that can cost you hours of troubleshooting when you finally realize it's not working anymore. The troubleshooting starts after you realize something's not working. But finding what's wrong can take hours. Conditional logic does not slow down the program visibly, so if it ain't broke, why fix it?

```
<CFIF #TVTimeZone# EQ 44>
    <CFINCLUDE TEMPLATE="empau3.cfm">
<CFELSE>
    <CFINCLUDE TEMPLATE="Tonindex.cfm">
</CFIF>
```

DETAILS ON USING THIS SPECIFIC TAG: <CFTRANSACTION>

- <CFTRANSACTION> protects your program from doing something that's wrong if it doesn't finish. If a glitch happens, if the system crashes, if the program times out before it's done, or if the computer operator spills coffee onto the keyboard, the entire transaction is wiped out, from the beginning.

- Use <CFTRANSACTION> in situations where more than one user is entering information into the same database field from different locations—such as two partners accessing the same bank account through two different ATMs.

- For specialized multiuser environments, read about the optional ISOLATION attributes in the Cold Fusion docs. These are very specialized levels of protection; don't bother learning them until you need them.

- The ODBC drivers for MS FoxPro 2.x, MS Excel, and Borland Paradox do not support the <CFTRANSACTION> tag.

How Will You Use This Information in the Future?

<CFTRANSACTION> is another one of those precautions against a mistake that you will never see during your development time. While you're creating your application, the multiuser errors that <CFTRANSACTION> addresses are completely hypothetical. Using it is a matter of preventative problem solving, of working with foresight, and running through scenarios mentally before they happen.

Knowing about <CFTRANSACTION> is important to understanding the state of mind you must possess to be a programmer. This what a programmer does. If you want to be a programmer, learn how to think in this nit-picky, scenario-running manner. For programmers, worrying about details is a positive trait.

On the other hand, the SQL clause `"SELECT max(CustID) as newcustid FROM Customer"` contains a lot of new syntax that you don't need to learn about at all for Cold Fusion. Just remember how to find this clause when you need it. Then copy it exactly. Don't try to understand it —just do it.

That's the other side of thinking like a programmer.

CONCLUSION

Chapter 19 continues this program's development and shows how to use conditional logic to verify the existence and validity of Form Fields.

19

More Programming with Functions, Loops, and the Web Application Framework— Part 2

- Using Conditional Logic to Verify the Existence and Validity of Form Fields
- Conclusion of the User's Search and Drill-Down: `Time2.cfm` Revisited
- Using Program Loops to Repeat Instructions
- Wrapping Up—the Instant Weekly Static Grid
- Using the Web Application Framework for Persistant Client Variables

Using Conditional Logic to Verify the Existence and Validity of Form Fields

Now we return to the program flow, or *plot*, in which the TV viewing audience searches for the TV show or TV Program Grid that they want. We took a detour from this plot after the first section of Chapter 18 so that we could stay with one programming theme.

In this chapter, conditional logic is used to verify data in a number of ways, including the following:

1. In the previous chapter, conditional logic is used at the beginning of **search.cfm** to ensure that the variable **#goal#** actually exists and to create this variable with a default value if not.

2. Similarly, at the end of **results.cfm**, which follows, a <CFIF> statement uses conditional logic to produce an appropriate message if a query produces no results. In order to do this, however, you must structure your SQL query so that it doesn't generate an error message that you didn't control.

3. Finally, at the beginning of **results.cfm**, conditional logic is used to determine whether the beginning and end dates for the search are in the correct order.

If you've run the sample templates and database from the TV Network Program Guide on your system, using an internal server, such as O'Reilly's WebSite, the entire application will be working just fine, and you'll have no indication that anything could go wrong. It's tempting to assume that the job is done because it works on your machine, but this is not the case and is true of the TV Network Program Guide application, as well.

By the end of this chapter, I hope to show you some of the potential problems in this application that might not be obvious to you. Hopefully, this will assist you in evaluating your own work with a more critical eye.

As a programmer, you should always include code to handle those instances when you don't (or the user doesn't) get the expected results. This section of the chapter illustrates this point by taking the **search.cfm** template to its conclusions, using the **results.cfm** and **detail.cfm** templates (see Figure 19-1).

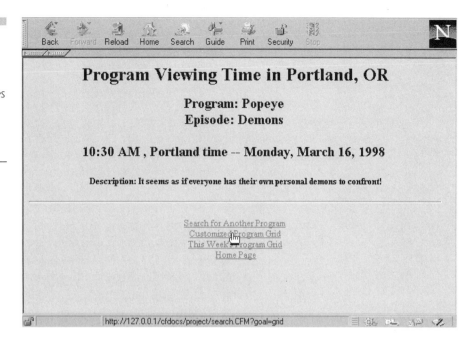

Figure 19-1
Output screen produced by **results.cfm**. Note: Episode names are fictional, as are the episode descriptions they link with.

Description of results.cfm

The first lines of any template are probably the best places to test whether the necessary variables exist. **Results.cfm**, for instance, validates whether the end date is the same as the starting date or comes after it by using conditional logic to test the form fields against each other. Notice the use of <CFABORT> to stop the program flow after delivering an error message.

Could this have been done with the Cold Fusion **_range** validation technique described in the previous chapter? Not easily, because the starting date variable does not exist until after the form is submitted. Thus, you could not set a minimum value for the end date variable from the form. And, even if you could overcome such a problem, your ability to create a custom error message would still be limited.

```
<CFIF #Form.StartDate# GT #Form.EndDate#>
    <H2>Invalid Date Range</H2>
    <UL>
        <LI>The beginning date must come before the end
            date, if they are not the same.<BR>
```

```
    </UL>
        Use your browser's Back button to go back and enter
                a valid date range.
  <CFABORT>
  </CFIF>
```

Now that the data is fully verified, we need to get to the business of this template, which is to perform a search of the database by using the user's search criteria. This would be very easy if the user was in the same time zone as the viewers of their programs. So the first job of the template is to adjust the variables that will be used in the query by the time zone.

In other words, the new variables (**#NewStart#** and **#NewEnd#**) need to be set up before they can be used in the SQL query that follows.

The following code is very similar to the code in **time2.cfm** of Chapter 17's section, "Introduction to Variables and Functions." The purpose of the code in **time2.cfm** is to adjust 11:00 PM to the user's time zone and to display it on the screen. In this template, the purpose is to create a variable, adjusted according to the time zone, to use in a query.

For this reason, the main difference between the code in **time2.cfm** and the code in **results.cfm** is the function that is used. Because the previous example needed to display the results, it used the function **TimeFormat**. Because the present example needs to create an accurate variable for a SQL query, it uses the function **CreateODBCDateTime**.

Notice one more thing before going to the next section. The End Date is not simply adjusted by the time zone. The first argument in **CreateTimeSpan** is the numeral one, which adds one day to the End Date. This is because **#NewEnd#** must be at midnight after the day has passed —technically the next day. When most people request two days of programming, they mean from midnight at the beginning of the first until midnight at the end of the last.

Using the CFABORT Tag

```
<CFSET #NewStart# =
CreateODBCDateTime(Evaluate("FORM.StartDate")
    +CreateTimeSpan(0,
Evaluate("TVTimeZone"),0,0))>
<CFSET #NewEnd# =
CreateODBCDateTime(Evaluate("FORM.EndDate")
    +CreateTimeSpan(1,
Evaluate("TVTimeZone"),0,0))>
```

The variable definitions in the preceding code are extremely complex, and it is often difficult to avoid syntax errors when creating them. This is therefore an excellent time to use the <CFABORT> debugging method described in Chapter 17. After each CFSET expression, sandwich **#NewStart#** or **#NewEnd#** between a pair of <CFOUTPUT> tags and follow up with <CFABORT>. This method will give you instantaneous feedback without having to wait for Cold Fusion to run a query.

Using the SQL LIKE Condition

Following is the SQL query that uses **#NewStart#** and **#NewEnd#**. In the WHERE clause, notice the program's use of the LIKE condition. This enables the user to run the query after entering only a few letters.

This was the situation in Figure 18-1, where the user only entered the letter *P* into the **#FORM.Schedule_ProgName#** variable. In the sample database, this query produces a list of 35 episodes of Popeye (see Figure 18-3).

```
<CFQUERY NAME="GetResults" DATASOURCE="TVNetwork"
    SQL="SELECT DISTINCTROW Schedule.ProgName,
        Schedule.Episode,
    ScheduleID,Time
      FROM Schedule
      WHERE   0=0
    AND Schedule.ProgName LIKE '#Schedule_ProgName#%'
    AND ((Schedule.Time BETWEEN #NewStart# And #NewEnd#))
    ORDER BY Schedule.Time">
<HTML>
<HEAD><TITLE>Episodes Available</TITLE></HEAD>
<BODY>
```

The query cannot function unless it produces a list of one or more TV shows. If it doesn't, SQL returns an error message that you did not write, which is why the first condition in the SQL WHERE clause is 0=0. This condition always is true, even if there are no records in the database that match the other criteria. This way, you can test for whether there were any records returned through the use of a <CFIF> expression, and, if not, display your own customized message. You are not stuck with the automatic error messages generated by a SQL. In this example, the custom message is listed in the last six lines of **results.cfm**.

The following <CFIF> statement checks to ensure that there are one or more shows using **RecordCount**. **RecordCount** is one of the two output attributes of <CFQUERY>. A **RecordCount** showing more records than zero is the first of two possible conditions recognized by Cold Fusion, using this conditional logic.

```
<CFIF #GetResults.RecordCount# IS NOT 0>
        <CENTER><H1>Titles Matching Your Request</H1>
```

Using the CFCOL Tag with URLs

The Cold Fusion table created by the following code displays the data from the database query. Notice that each cell is linked to the **detail.cfm** template. What is different about each row in the table is that each one passes a different value for the variable **#ScheduleID#** to the **detail.cfm** template. Each of the different values for **#ScheduleID#** stands for a different episode of Popeye. (**#ScheduleID#** is the primary key for the database table.)

#ScheduleID# is the most important result of the query. Passing it to the next template as a URL variable ensures that the **detail.cfm** template can find the requested episode easily.

Pay particular attention to the syntax for the CFCOL TEXT attribute. Each instance of this attribute is a standard HTML link, starting with **A HREF=**. The purpose is to let the TV viewer click on the desired episode to see a plot summary. What's strange about this link to the next page is that instead of one double quote around the link information, there are two double quotes.

The reason that the double double quotes are used is because an **A HREF=** link is nested within the string that the TEXT attribute requires. The TEXT string therefore is enclosed in quotes. If the string that comes after **A HREF=** was also enclosed with quotes, it would confuse the program. Cold Fusion would think that the TEXT string ended with **TEXT="A HREF="**. The rest of the link information would cause an error.

For a nested string to retain its identity as a string, use two double quotes together. This syntax tells Cold Fusion that it is dealing with nested strings as shown in the following template code fragment:

```
<CFTABLE HTMLTABLE QUERY="GetResults">
<CFCOL HEADER="<B>Program</B>" WIDTH="30" TEXT=
"<A HREF=""Detail.CFM?ScheduleID=#ScheduleID#"">
    #ProgName#</A>">
<CFCOL HEADER="<B>Episode</B>" WIDTH="30" TEXT=
"<A HREF=""Detail.CFM?ScheduleID=#ScheduleID#"">
    #Episode#</A>">
```

Using DateFormat

The next code produces the Time column. You'll notice that this one column uses the variable **#Time#** in three ways, simply by formatting it differently each time, as follows. (Of course, it's always adjusted to the time zone.)

- First, it's formatted as the day of the week.
- Second, it's formatted as a date.
- Last, it's formatted as the programming hour and minute.

No matter how it's formatted, it's the same variable.

```
<CFCOL HEADER="<B>Time</B>" WIDTH="40" TEXT=
"<A HREF=""Detail.CFM?ScheduleID=#ScheduleID#"">
#DateFormat(Evaluate(""Time"")+CreateTimeSpan(0,
Evaluate(""TVTimeZone""),0,0), 'ddd.')#,
#DateFormat(Evaluate(""Time"")+CreateTimeSpan(0,
Evaluate(""TVTimeZone""),0,0), 'mmm. d, yyyy')#,
#TimeFormat(Evaluate(""Time"")+CreateTimeSpan(0,
Evaluate(""TVTimeZone""),0,0), 'h:mm tt')#</A>">
</CFTABLE>
</CENTER>
```

Finally, the following code is invoked when no records are found and tells the user what to do when no results are retrieved. This is the final alternative provided by the conditional logic that was invoked immediately after the query at the top of this template.

```
<CFELSEIF #GetResults.RecordCount# IS 0>
<H2>No records were found matching your criterion</H2>
<P>Please press the BACK button and try again.
</CFIF>
</BODY></HTML>
```

Thus, although this template performs many functions, most of the template is enclosed in a <CFIF> statement that provides either records or a customized error message if there are no records found.

Details on Using These Specific Functions

CREATE ODBC DATETIME (DATE AND/OR TIME)

- When you enter a date and convert it to an ODBC DateTime variable, the time defaults to midnight at the beginning of the date, which enables you to add or subtract other time values (such as the Time Zone) from it accurately.
- The ODBC time stamp is formatted in this manner: `"{ts '1995-03-24 02:4!5:17'}"`
- Always pass date/time strings enclosed in quotes.

SQL WHERE CONDITIONS, SUBQUERY USAGE

▨ `Results.cfm` uses the following conditions to the WHERE clause: LIKE and BETWEEN.

▨ LIKE enables the user to search for partial words using the percentage symbol (%) as a wild card for any number of letters.

`'#Schedule__ProgName#%'` returns records that start with letters the user enters.

`%#Schedule__ProgName#%` returns records that contain the pattern of letters that the user enters.

`%#Schedule__ProgName#` returns records that end with letters the user enters.

▨ The SQL clause `"WHERE Schedule.Time BETWEEN #NewStart# And #NewEnd#"` is self explanatory.

▨ Mathematical operators mean exactly what they meant in high school. They are =, <> (not equal to), < (less than), <= (less than or equal to), > (greater than) and >= (greater than or equal to).

▨ IS (NOT) NULL returns records or rows in the database where the column or field is empty (or not empty, when using NOT). `"WHERE email IS NOT NULL"` produces a list of people with e-mail addresses.

▨ EXISTS and IN are operators that are mostly used in subqueries. For a full treatment of subqueries, see Chapter 13.

▨ A *subquery* is a nested SQL, in which a different data source is used as the criterion for sorting the main data source. The subquery (or inner query) is part of a WHERE or HAVING clause of the main query (or outer query). Nested subqueries are indented a few spaces and are enclosed in parentheses.

▨ An outer query with WHERE EXISTS, followed immediately by an inner query, which will return results only if the inner query returns a result. For instance, a television genre table could be linked to TV viewer table to notify only those viewers who have e-mail accounts. You could generate automatic announcements to only these viewers and ignore everyone else.

▨ An outer query with WHERE CustID IN, followed immediately by an inner query, returns results in which the inner query returns CustID. For instance, a television genre table could be linked to TV viewer table to determine what kinds of programming are preferred by viewers in different time zones.

CFQUERY OUTPUT ATTRIBUTES: RECORDCOUNT

▨ Every <CFQUERY> you run has two attributes to describe the results: `RecordCount` and `CurrentRow`.

▨ `#QueryName.RecordCount#` reports the total number of records returned by the query.

▨ `#CurrentRow#` reports the row number of each record as it is processed. Include it with your <CFOUTPUT> expression as if it were a field name from the data source.

How Will You Use This Information in the Future?

You will usually need to use a formatting function with your time functions. Most often, you will not want to display the time and date in the ODBC time stamp format.

The ODBC time stamp format is the standard format to transfer dates between applications in Windows. In fact, the default output of the functions `CreateTime`, `CreateDate`, and `CreateDateTime` is always an ODBC time stamp, containing both the date and the time. `CreateDate` defaults to 12:00 midnight (00:00:00), and `CreateTime` defaults to December 30, 1899. The exceptions are `CreateODBCDate` and `CreateODBCTime`, which return only the named part of the time stamp.

All of these different functions to create an ODBC time stamp exist because their arguments are different. Having so many options is useful because they provide the user with many ways to input information.

Suppose you want the users to enter a date or time in any format with which they are comfortable. What you would want to use is a function that accepts user formats. You would therefore choose a function in which the name starts with `CreateODBC___`. In these functions, the argument is a formatted time or date string, enclosed by quotation marks.

On the other hand, you might have a situation in which you have a separate variable for each of the parts of the date—such as for the hour, minute, and second. In such a case, you would need a function which takes arguments that are separate numerals. In this case, you would choose a function does not contain "ODBC" as a part of the function name. Although this general rule doesn't apply to every function that deals with time, it can help you keep the create functions straight in your mind.

The SQL WHERE clause conditions are crucial to having an efficient template. In a large database, if you retrieve all the data and then sort out the bits that you need, your query will take too long; your system will get overloaded too quickly; and your application will time out too often. It's much better to retrieve only the data you need by sorting with SQL before retrieving the data.

Though not within the scope of this chapter, nested SQL queries are sometimes the only way you can sort your data with the precision you need. It is unlikely that you will ever have all of your information in one table in your data source; nested queries are one of the tools that will let you evaluate one table with information from another.

The <CFQUERY> record number attributes are obviously useful if you want to number the records as you display them or if you want to tell the user how many records there are. However, these uses border on the cosmetic, which isn't the main reason for having these attributes available. **Results.cfm**, for instance, uses **#RecordCount#** to test whether there are any records returned at all and then displays a message if not.

Your application could also loop through some instructions, repeating them over and over, until **#RowNumber#** is the same as **#RecordCount#**. When these two numbers are the same, you would use conditional logic to move on to the next step in the application.

Conclusion of the User's Search and Drill-Down: **Time2.cfm** Revisited

When you look over the last template in the user's search for a specific movie or series, you'll notice that it's quite similar to **time2.cfm**, which was the trial application used to introduce variables and functions in Chapter 17. This template displayed the time that the news would be broadcast, adjusted to time zone.

This template searches for the desired episode of the requested TV show and adjusts the time in the same way. It's the same functionality, made fancier. There are therefore no new functions or programming tips included with this section.

You'll notice in this template that there are two <CFQUERY> tags—one for the broadcast information and one to retrieve the viewer's location. Using two tags in this manner enables us to access two different tables within the data source. In other words, it lets us tell the viewer in Fairbanks, Alaska, that this programming time schedule (from the schedule table in MSAccess) has been adjusted specifically for the city of Fairbanks (from the customer table in MSAccess). This provides a personalized output page like the one in Figure 19-2.

Using the user's information subtly like this is more appropriate and slicker than gratuitous personalization, such as "Hello, Mr. Jones. Welcome back to The Oldies Network! We love to have you visit, Mr. Jones, and hope that the weather in Thunder Bay is gr-r-reat!" Gratuitous personalization, becoming more and more evident in promotional material, is really nothing more than technological bragging, and most people realize how phony it is.

However, personalization that serves the customer better is appreciated.

Description of `detail.cfm`

Two queries are run to retrieve first, the broadcast information and second, viewer location for creating a personalized grid.

```
<CFQUERY NAME="GetDetailData" DATASOURCE="TVNetwork">
    SELECT Schedule.ProgName,Schedule.Episode,
        Schedule.Time,
```

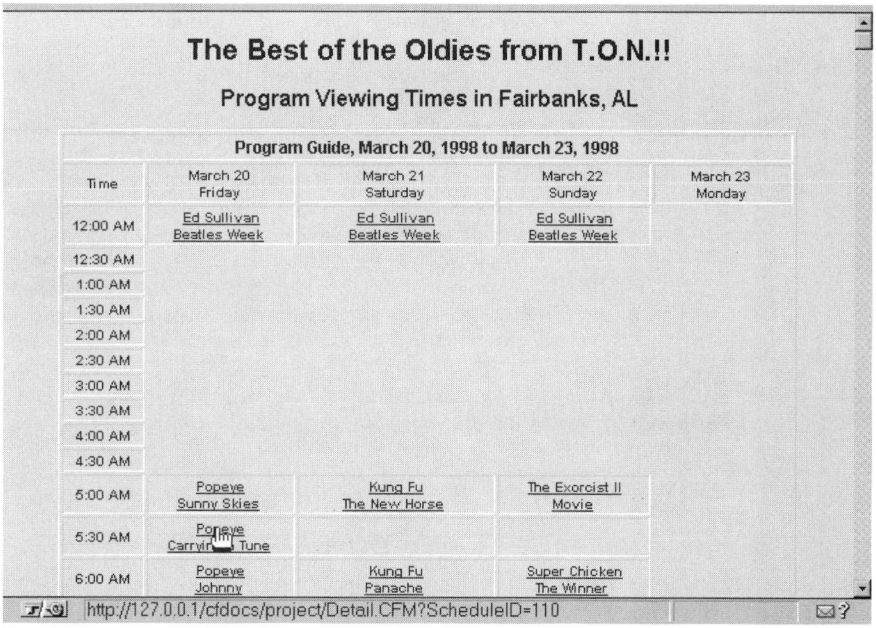

Figure 19-2
Output screen produced by **detail.cfm**. Note: Episode names and descriptions are fictional.

```
Schedule.Description
      FROM Schedule
         WHERE ScheduleID= #ScheduleID#
</CFQUERY>
<CFQUERY NAME="GetCustomerData" DATASOURCE="TVNetwork">
SELECT Customer.City,Customer.State
FROM Customer
         WHERE CustID= #CustID#

    </CFQUERY>
```

Necessary HTML to display the page, along with the personalized header.

```
<HTML>
<HEAD><TITLE>Program Viewing Time</TITLE></HEAD>
<BODY>

<CFOUTPUT QUERY="GetCustomerData">
<CENTER><H1>Program Viewing Time in #City#,
      #State#</H1></CENTER> <P>
</CFOUTPUT>
```

The following code produces the results of the query. As in the previous template, the single variable **#time#** is an ODBC time stamp that is formatted in three different ways: as the day of the week, the date, and the time. The episode description is only available on this page.

```
<CFOUTPUT QUERY="GetDetailData">
<CENTER><H2>
    Program: #ProgName# <BR>
    Episode: #Episode# <P>
#TimeFormat(Evaluate("Time")+CreateTimeSpan(0,
    Evaluate("TVTimeZone"),0,0), 'h:mm tt')# </CFOUTPUT>
<CFOUTPUT QUERY="GetCustomerData">, #City# time -
    </CFOUTPUT> <CFOUTPUT QUERY="GetDetailData">
    #DateFormat(Evaluate("Time")+CreateTimeSpan(0,
    Evaluate("TVTimeZone"),0,0), 'dddd')#,
    #DateFormat(Evaluate("Time")+CreateTimeSpan(0,
    Evaluate("TVTimeZone"),0,0), 'mmmm d, yyyy')# <P>
</H2>
<H4>
Description: #Description#</H4>
</CFOUTPUT>

    <hr>
```

So far, none of the other templates include any navigation other than what is necessary for the program flow. A navigation file such as the following could be included in many of the templates with the <CFINCLUDE> TAG.

```
<P><A HREF="search.CFM?goal=search">Search for Another
    Program</A>
<BR><A HREF="search.CFM?goal=grid">Customized Program
    Grid</A>
<BR><A HREF="static.CFM">This Week's Program Grid</A>
<BR><A HREF="TONIndex.cfm">Home Page</A></P>
</CENTER>
    </BODY></HTML>
```

Using Program Loops to Repeat Instructions

Most people like to have a TV programming grid for picking the shows that they want to watch. This is especially valuable for a network with a specialty genre, like the fictional TON network, which is devoted to Oldies.

Producing such a grid is challenging because no matter how you sort a query with SQL, the results do not fit into a grid of date columns and time rows. If you sort your results by an ODBC date/time stamp, each 24-hour period is returned consecutively, which means that a program that airs at 7 p.m. Tuesday cannot be placed on the same row as a program that airs at 7 p.m. Monday.

In programming, there are always a hundred solutions to any given problem. For instance, you might consider the following strategy, not the one employed in **grid.cfm**.

It would be possible to include a field in the data source that is not an ODBC time stamp, but that only contains the program hour and minute. One query could be run to extract all of the 7:00 p.m. programs between two dates to populate the first row; a second query could then extract all the 7:30 p.m. programs to populate the next row, and so on.

This solution contains several problems that would be challenging to solve. First of all, the date of the program schedule information would be inaccurate after being adjusted by the cookie **#TVTimeZone#**. If an ODBC time stamp is adjusted for the time zone, Cold Fusion automatically adjusts the date for programs near midnight.

Someone in Newfoundland, for instance, would have four hours of Sunday programming listed in the Monday column. This might not be so terrible a fate for viewers in North America, but viewers in Australia, South Africa, and England might find it quite confusing.

A second problem is dealing with blank spots in the programming grid. If the query returned two 7:00 p.m. programs from a four-day range, it would be challenging to get those two programs into the correct columns.

None of these problems are necessarily insurmountable. They simply represent a set of challenges that I did not choose to pursue.

In particular, I felt that the second of the challenges would have been most difficult. The strategy I was considering was to evaluate each record that was returned by the query and renaming it according to the column at which it would be targeted—such as calling it `#Column2Record#`. Then, in generating the grid, I would have accessed the records according to their new names.

Thus, in generating the grid, `#Column2Record#` would always go into the second column as the program moved from time slot to time slot.

In the end, I do not know if this would have been a better strategy than the one I chose, which is used in the template `grid.cfm` and described in the following sections. As a programmer, you will continuously make choices like this without knowing how to weigh all the factors that will influence the performance of the application in the end.

The point of this discussion is to emphasize that you should always be aware of the myriad options that are available to you. If one strategy doesn't work, there's always another strategy to try. There's never just one way to skin the cat.

Figure 19-3 illustrates the output screen produced by the method I chose to use in `grid.cfm`. As you can see, the program continues to work,

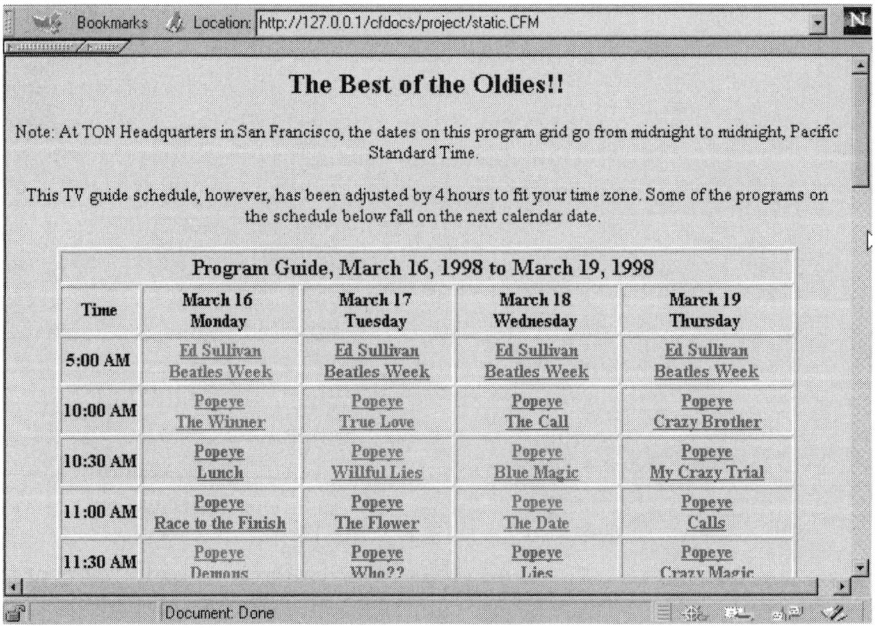

Figure 19-3
Output screen produced by `grid.cfm`.

| Bookmarks | Location: http://127.0.0.1/cfdocs/project/static.CFM |

The Best of the Oldies!!

Note: At TON Headquarters in San Francisco, the dates on this program grid go from midnight to midnight, Pacific Standard Time.

This TV guide schedule, however, has been adjusted by 4 hours to fit your time zone. Some of the programs on the schedule below fall on the next calendar date.

Program Guide, March 16, 1998 to March 19, 1998

Time	March 16 Monday	March 17 Tuesday	March 18 Wednesday	March 19 Thursday
5:00 AM	Ed Sullivan Beatles Week	Ed Sullivan Beatles Week	Ed Sullivan Beatles Week	Ed Sullivan Beatles Week
10:00 AM	Popeye The Winner	Popeye True Love	Popeye The Call	Popeye Crazy Brother
10:30 AM	Popeye Lunch	Popeye Willful Lies	Popeye Blue Magic	Popeye My Crazy Trial
11:00 AM	Popeye Race to the Finish	Popeye The Flower	Popeye The Date	Popeye Calls
11:30 AM	Popeye Demons	Popeye Who??	Popeye Lies	Popeye Crazy Magic

Document: Done

even in a situation in which an entire day is missing from the database. Empty cells do not interfere with the correct placement of program information in other cells, as you can see. The query start date was March 20, one day after the recommended start date. This left the Monday column completely blank, but did not cause program errors. In addition, the grid extends from midnight to midnight, no matter which time zone the user is in.

In Figure 19-3, note the appearance of times that do not have any scheduled programming. For example, the query start date was March 20, one day after the recommended start date. This left the Monday column completely blank, but did not cause program errors.

The solution chosen for **grid.cfm** runs 192 different queries to produce programming information for four consecutive dates. Each query is essentially the same; however, the time and the date is changed for each one. A query for Monday at 12:00 a.m. is followed by a query for Tuesday at 12:00 a.m. After the query for Thursday, the date is reset to Monday, and the time is reset to 12:30 a.m. Between queries, the time and date are changed with the CreateTimeSpan function. The same query is then run again, but with the new ODBC time stamp, which is already adjusted for the time zone.

Repeating a query again and again is done with an *index loop*, which means that whenever the query runs and the results are processed, the program "loops" up and does the same thing again until all 192 cells are filled. Part of the loop, of course, is changing the variables so that the results are different each time.

What's wrong with this approach? For one thing, on a very slow server, each query could take half a second or so—up to two minutes in total. On a faster server, it might take half a minute, but that is still too long. This application solves these problems in two ways: it provides an instant programming grid for the current week, and it warns viewers that they might have to wait for the customized grid.

Description of grid.cfm

Grid.cfm starts by initializing a group of variables. *Initializing* means creating the variables and giving them an initial value. In a complex loop, there are many variables that have to change regularly to keep the loop on track.

These variables are all set to values that are required for the loop to start at the correct place. **#Flag#** must not be true until a full row is set up. The cell count has to be correct for the queries to populate the correct columns. `#RowTime#` has to have 30 minutes subtracted from it because the loop automatically adds 30 minutes before running the first query.

This segment of code is commented to tell you what each variable does, and why it is necessary.

```
<!---#Flag# is used to indicate when one row is finished
      and when it's time to start a new one. At the end of
      every row on the grid, #Flag# is set to true. After 3
      days are subtracted from #RowTime#, #Flag# is set to
      false again.-->
<CFSET Flag = False>

<!---#CellNbr# is the cell number. Every time the program
      loops through a query, the number 1 is added to
      #CellNbr# until it reaches 193. The first thing that
      the loop does is divide #CellNbr# by four and look at
      the remainder. If the remainder is 1, the query
      populates the first cell in a row. If there is no
      remainder, #Flag# is set to true, and a new row is
      started.-->
<CFSET #CellNbr# = 1>

<!---#NewEnd# is the same as it has been in every other
      template: It's the user's EndDate for the query,
      adjusted by time zone. In this template, #NewEnd# is
      only used once-to tell the loop when to stop looping
      by comparing it to #RowTime#. -->
<CFSET #NewEnd# = CreateODBCDateTime(Evaluate
      ("FORM.StartDate")+CreateTimeSpan(4, Evaluate
      ("TVTimeZone"),0,0))>

<!---You'll notice that #NewStart# isn't part of this
      template. #RowTime# essentially takes it's place.
      Why? #RowTime# is much more descriptive. #RowTime# is
      used in the WHERE clause of every query; it's used to
      label the time in every row; it tells the application
      when to stop. -->
<CFSET #RowTime# = CreateODBCDateTime(FORM.StartDate -
      CreateTimeSpan(0,Evaluate("TVTimeZone"),30,0))>
```

The following code creates basic aesthetics and sets up the HTML. It runs a simple query to personalize the header to the viewer's city. Nothing here is new information.

```
<CFQUERY NAME="GetCustomerData" DATASOURCE="TVNetwork">
      SELECT Customer.City,Customer.State
      FROM Customer
      WHERE CustID= #CustID#
</CFQUERY>
```

```
<HTML>
<HEAD>
        <TITLE>Program Grid</TITLE>
</HEAD>
<BODY>
<CENTER>
<H1>The Best of the Oldies from T.O.N.!!</H1>
<CFOUTPUT QUERY="GetCustomerData">
<H2>Program Viewing Times in #City#, #State#</H2> <P>
</CFOUTPUT>
```

The following code sets up the table headers. You might be wondering why the variables #Day1# through #Day4b# are set up separately as variables. Why not simply put the code for the dates into the column headers?

I felt that in the complete application, it might be effective to have arrow buttons to move to the previous and next grids without going back to the search form. In such a case, I felt that the code for changing the column headers would be simpler to read with summary variables like these —as well as being easier to diagnose errors.

```
<TABLE BORDER=1 WIDTH=90%>
<COLS=5>
<TR ALIGN="center">

<---Table header--->

<CFOUTPUT>
        <TD COLSPAN="5"><STRONG><FONT SIZE="4">Program
            Guide, #DateFormat(FORM.StartDate, "mmmm d,
            yyyy")# to #DateFormat(FORM.StartDate +
            CreateTimeSpan(3,0,0,0), "mmmm d, yyyy")#
</FONT></STRONG></TD>
</TR>

<---Set summary variables.--->

<CFSET Day1 = #DateFormat(FORM.StartDate, "mmmm d")#>
        <CFSET Day1b = #DayOfWeekAsString(DayOfWeek
            (FORM.StartDate))#>
        <CFSET Day2 = #DateFormat(FORM.StartDate +
            CreateTimeSpan(1,0,0,0), "mmmm d")#>
        <CFSET Day2b = #DayOfWeekAsString(DayOfWeek
            (FORM.StartDate +
            CreateTimeSpan(1,0,0,0)))#>
        <CFSET Day3 = #DateFormat(FORM.StartDate +
            CreateTimeSpan(2,0,0,0), "mmmm d")#>
        <CFSET Day3b = #DayOfWeekAsString(DayOfWeek
            (FORM.StartDate +
            CreateTimeSpan(2,0,0,0)))#>
        <CFSET Day4 = #DateFormat(FORM.StartDate +
            CreateTimeSpan(3,0,0,0), "mmmm d")#>
```

```
<CFSET Day4b = #DayOfWeekAsString(DayOfWeek
       (FORM.StartDate +
       CreateTimeSpan(3,0,0,0)))#>

<TR>

<---Row headers--->

    <TH WIDTH="12%">Time</TH>
    <TH WIDTH="22%">#Day1# <BR> #Day1b#
       </TH>
    <TH WIDTH="22%">#Day2# <BR> #Day2b#
       </TH>
    <TH WIDTH="22%">#Day3# <BR> #Day3b#
       </TH>
  <TH WIDTH="22%">#Day4# <BR> #Day4b#
       </TH>
</TR>
</CFOUTPUT>
```

Using CFLOOP

The following code segment is the beginning of the program that will loop 192 times. Each time it loops, **#loopcount#** is increased by one. The loop includes almost all of the rest of the template, down to the </CFLOOP> tag.

```
<CFLOOP INDEX="loopcount" FROM="1" TO="192">
```

#Flag# is set to true at the end of every row in the table. The conditional logic in the following code subtracts three days from the ODBC time stamp to start the next row and resets the flag to false. Until the next row is populated, one day is then added to the time stamp for each new column.

```
<CFIF #Flag# EQ "True">
       <CFSET #RowTime# = CreateODBCDateTime(#RowTime#+
       CreateTimeSpan(-3,0,0,0))>
       <CFSET Flag = False>
</CFIF>
```

The next segment of code uses the MOD operator to target each record into the appropriate column. The MOD operator in the <CFIF> expression returns the remainder of division when no decimals are used. At the beginning of the template, **#CellNbr#** was initialized to be 1. Since 1 divided by 4 = 0, remainder 1, the first subsection of the following code is invoked when the program first runs. Note that **#CellNbr#** is immediately set to **#CellNbr#** plus one, so that the next time the program loops around, it will invoke the second condition instead of this one.

Notice that the query is named **BuildGrid#CellNbr#**. This was done because a query could not be run more than once per template in Cold Fusion 2. To reuse a query, it was necessary to include a changing variable in the query name—such as **#CellNbr#** or **#loopcount#**.

Cold Fusion 3 now permits you to run the same query several times without changing the name. However, having a dynamically changing query name was useful for debugging this application during the initial writing stages. With debugging turned on in the Cold Fusion Administrator, it was possible to locate any specific query by number on the output screen.

The **#CellNbr# MOD 4 IS 1** condition is the condition that starts a new row; therefore, the following is where the show time schedule is advanced by thirty minutes (**#RowTime#**) and where the displayed show time is adjusted by the viewer's time zone (**#ProgTime#**). The show and episode names are linked to **detail.cfm**, discussed in the previous section, and the **#ScheduleID#** is passed to **detail.cfm** as a URL variable.

```
<CFIF #CellNbr# MOD 4 IS 1>
        <CFSET #CellNbr# = #CellNbr# + 1 >
        <CFSET #RowTime# = CreateODBCDateTime(#RowTime#+
        CreateTimeSpan(0,0,30,0))>
          <CFSET ProgTime = #TimeFormat(Evaluate
                ("##RowTime## +CreateTimeSpan(0,
                TVTimeZone,0,0)"), "h:mm tt")#>
        <CFOUTPUT>
        <TR><TH>#Progtime#</TH><TH>
        </CFOUTPUT>
        <CFQUERY NAME="BuildGrid#CellNbr#"
        DATASOURCE="TVNetwork"
        SQL="SELECT ScheduleID, Schedule.Time,
                Schedule.ProgName, Schedule.Episode
        FROM Schedule
        WHERE Schedule.time = #RowTime#">!
<CFOUTPUT QUERY="BuildGrid#CellNbr#">
<A HREF="Detail.CFM?ScheduleID=#ScheduleID#">
    #ProgName#</A><BR><A HREF="Detail.CFM?ScheduleID=
    #ScheduleID#">#Episode#</A>
    </CFOUTPUT>
    </TH>
```

The next two sections are essentially the same as the first, except that a day is added to each **#RowTime#**, rather than half an hour. The repetitious nature of these sections indicates that the viewer could be allowed to decide how large a grid he or she wants—from three days to a week or more.

This would add some additional complexity to the controlling logic, but it could be done. Doing this would also probably require using logic, rather than a counting variable, to control when the main loop stops looping.

That's your homework for tomorrow, class.

```
<CFELSEIF #CellNbr# MOD 4 IS 2>
    <CFSET #CellNbr# = #CellNbr# + 1 >
    <CFSET #RowTime# = CreateODBCDateTime(#RowTime#+
    CreateTimeSpan(1,0,0,0))>
    <CFQUERY NAME="BuildGrid#CellNbr#"
    DATASOURCE="TVNetwork"
     SQL="SELECT ScheduleID, Schedule.Time,
           Schedule.ProgName, Schedule.Episode
FROM Schedule
    WHERE Schedule.time = #RowTime#"   >
    <TH>
    <CFOUTPUT QUERY="BuildGrid#CellNbr#">
    <A HREF="Detail.CFM?ScheduleID=#ScheduleID#">
          #ProgName#</A><BR><A HREF="Detail.
          CFM?ScheduleID=#ScheduleID#">#Episode#</A>
    </CFOUTPUT>
    </TH>

<CFELSEIF #CellNbr# MOD 4 IS 3>
    <CFSET #CellNbr# = #CellNbr# + 1 >
    <CFSET #RowTime# = CreateODBCDateTime(#RowTime#+
    CreateTimeSpan(1,0,0,0))>
    <CFQUERY NAME="BuildGrid#CellNbr#"
    DATASOURCE="TVNetwork"
    SQL="SELECT ScheduleID, Schedule.Time,
           Schedule.ProgName, Schedule.Episode
    FROM Schedule
    WHERE Schedule.time = #RowTime#"   >
    <TH>
    <CFOUTPUT QUERY="BuildGrid#CellNbr#">
    <A HREF="Detail.CFM?ScheduleID=#ScheduleID#">
          #ProgName#</A><BR><A HREF="Detail.
          CFM?ScheduleID=#ScheduleID#">#Episode#</A>
    </CFOUTPUT>
    </TH>
```

The last section is another repetition, except that **#Flag#** is set to True and the tag </TR> is included to end one row in the table and prepare to start the next. The process of starting a new row is really simple and could have been accomplished in other ways. However, the logic might have become too convoluted if every viewer convenience had been created.

```
<CFELSE>
    <CFSET Flag = True>
    <CFSET #CellNbr# = #CellNbr# + 1 >
    <CFSET #RowTime# = CreateODBCDateTime(#RowTime#+
```

```
                    CreateTimeSpan(1,0,0,0))>
                    <CFQUERY NAME="BuildGrid#CellNbr#"
                    DATASOURCE="TVNetwork"
                    SQL="SELECT ScheduleID, Schedule.Time,
                         Schedule.ProgName, Schedule.Episode
                    FROM Schedule
                    WHERE Schedule.time = #RowTime#"   >
                    <TH>
                    <CFOUTPUT QUERY="BuildGrid#CellNbr#">
                    <A HREF="Detail.CFM?ScheduleID=#ScheduleID#">
                         #ProgName#</A><BR><A HREF="Detail.
                         CFM?ScheduleID=#ScheduleID#">#Episode#</A></TH>
                    </CFOUTPUT>
                    </TR>
            </CFIF>
            </CFLOOP>
            </TABLE>
            </CENTER>
            </BODY></HTML>
```

Details on Using Loops

<CFLOOP INDEX="variable" FROM="1" TO="100" STEP="10">

■ Index loops (or FOR loops) are simplest because they repeat the number of times you tell them to.

■ The optional STEP attribute enables you to count by something other than one. The above example counts by ten. You can also count backwards with a negative number.

■ One reason you might want to use the step attribute is if you are using the index for some other purpose, such as evaluating it to control condition logic inside of the loop.

■ All loops, of whatever type, end with </CFLOOP>.

```
<CFLOOP CONDITION="Time LESS THAN OR EQUAL TO NewEnd">
```

■ Conditional loops (or WHILE loops) run the loop until the condition is no longer true.

■ The previous example would let the user control the number of dates (and even the viewing hours) in the TV Network Program Grid example.

```
<CFLOOP QUERY="ChooseTemplate" STARTROW="#UserChoice#"
     ENDROW="#FiveMore#">
<CFINCLUDE TEMPLATE="#TemplateName#">
```

- Query loops loop over query results and return the same output as <CFOUTPUT>. However, <CFLOOP> does not have the same restrictions as <CFOUTPUT>, which does not allow <CFINCLUDE> and other tags.
- The STARTROW and ENDROW attributes enables you to set a dynamic range for the results, which is not allowed by <CFOUTPUT>.

```
<CFLOOP LIST="FieldNames" INDEX="item" DELIMITERS="," >
```

- List loops allow you to go through the contents of a list (contained in a string variable) and deal with each one of the items, one at a time. You can print the list, but this is not as useful as analyzing the output with conditional logic.
- List loops are especially useful in working with forms. In the above example, the word *FieldNames* is a reserved CFML variable name that is created by using a submit button in a form. This variable, `FieldNames`, passes a list of all the form fields within a form and to all of their contents to the next template.
- In `grid.cfm`, each of the 192 queries was given a dynamic name by including a counting variable. The same technique can be used to create a form with dynamic form field names. The list loop can be used to analyze all of the results and to insert them into a database table.

<CFBREAK> is used inside any loop to terminate it. The program immediately starts to process the line immediately after </CFLOOP>.

How Will You Use This Information in the Future?

Loops are an engine that enables you to repeat steps over and over, so long as the information is in a definable pattern—which is what computers create. Learning to use loops effectively increases your power to manipulate data many times over.

When you're stymied in your programming, explore whether you could solve the problem with some form of a loop. To be sure, it will also help to revisit the manuals, investigate functions you're not yet comfortable with, or look into more advanced SQL queries, for instance.

However, the four types of looping structures supported by Cold Fusion are both powerful and versatile in processing information in several ways.

In `grid.cfm` there were actually two ways that loops could have been used. As indicated previously, the simplest option was to create a grid of one size only—24 hours, four days, generated by exactly 192 queries, counted with an index loop.

Another option, though more complicated, would have been to allow the user to set both the range of hours and a range of dates. These more complicated criteria would be controlled through a conditional loop and a nested index loop with a dynamic index. The conditional loop would control the hours chosen for the beginning and end of the search, and the nested index loop would control the number of days displayed by the application.

Among the complications this would cause would be the following:

- Nesting the query within two loops would introduce more difficulties in debugging and would make the code harder to read or explain.

- Stopping the program at the correct time would require setting a temporary variable for each cell. This variable would be printed to the screen only after being tested by the conditional loop to see if the last cell in the row exceeded the ODBC target. This approach is less direct than displaying the content of the cells directly, and would make the code harder to read, at the very least.

- This process would increase the complexity of the search.cfm template and the conditional logic required to set up the additional variables that would be needed to control the template.

- It is also far more complex to modify the SQL queries to match both the time and date ranges set by the user, adjusted according to `#TVTimeZone#`, before running the query.

As you can imagine, such a grid would be superior.

Wrapping Up — the Instant Weekly Static Grid

Since many people may simply want to access this week's TV shows instantly, that option has also been created. It was done by running a query with `grid.cfm`, using Netscape's View/Page Source command and copying parts of the source code into a different template.

The new template was then modified to automatically adjust to **#TVTimeZone#**, and it was ready.

Sounds like a lot of programming to do on a weekly basis, right? In fact, the entire grid can be created by any computer-literate clerical person in about ten minutes. This is much faster than manually typing it the grid (which a network might be doing already) and not much slower than running a query of a database and formatting it. The advantage of doing it through the existing Cold Fusion **grid.cfm** template is that every show is linked to the **detail.cfm** grid, where the viewer can read the episode description for the evening.

The technique that would enable a secretary to set up the template so quickly is a macro written in Microsoft Word '97, (part of Office 97). It's a very simple macro that can easily be re-created in earlier versions of Word, even though earlier macros were not written in Visual Basic. (For the secretary to do this, YOU will need to create the macro and teach them to use it. But that will not be hard to do, once you've created the macro. And that won't be hard for you since the macro code is included later in this chapter. All you have to do is copy it.)

All the secretary would need to do is run a seven-day version of the grid.cfm template, copy the source code generated by Cold Fusion from Netscape, paste the correct lines in the new template **static.cfm**, change the date in the new template, and activate the macro 24 times by pushing a button on the tool bar. It's a little complicated, but if the procedure is documented, it would cause problems for few secretaries.

Note how the introductory text announces that because of the four-hour time zone adjustment, some of the shows will fall on the next calendar date. If the viewer had been in Hawaii, rather than Newfoundland, the text would have read "-2" and "previous."

Description of static.cfm

The code in this template's description section is chopped off in the middle to save space. The entire template is on the CD, and it would also be easy for you to recreate it with **grid.cfm** and the MS Word macro listed after this template.

The first section of this template sets up the introductory paragraphs. Notice that if **#TVTimeZone#** is equal to zero, the introduction is not displayed. West Coast viewers do not need an introduction about how the program times are adjusted to their time zone.

```
<HTML>
<HEAD>
<TITLE>Program Grid</TITLE>
</HEAD>
<BODY>
<CENTER>
<H2>The Best of the Oldies!!</H2>
<CFOUTPUT>
<CFIF #TVTimeZone# LT 0>
    <CFSET #shift# = "previous">
<CFELSE>
    <CFSET #shift# = "next">
</CFIF>
<CFIF #TVTimeZone# NEQ 0>
```

NOTE: *At TON Headquarters in San Francisco, the dates on this program grid go from midnight to midnight, Pacific Standard Time.*

```
<P>
```

This TV guide schedule, however, has been adjusted by **#TVTimeZone#** hours to fit your time zone. Some of the programs on the schedule below fall on the **#shift#** calendar date.

```
</CFIF>
<P>
```

The secretary will need to enter the correct date in the following. **#Currentdate#** is essentially the same variable as **#StartDate#** in other applications. This, however, is not a form field entered by the user. It is hard coded by the secretary.

```
<CFSET #Currentdate# = "March 16, 1998">
```

The next section sets up the table. It is almost the same as the table set-up section in **grid.cfm**. In this section, however, **#Currentdate#** is used instead of **#StartDate#**.

This section could have been a little more different—especially if TON has viewers overseas. Since the grid itself is created according to Pacific Standard Time, adjusting the grid to a different time zone no longer lists programs from midnight to midnight. For overseas viewers, this might be such a large problem that the network might create two static grids. Which one is displayed would be controlled through conditional logic and cookies.

In any case, the column headers might have been labeled: "From #Day1#
 #Day1b#
to #Day2#
 #Day2b#." This would only apply, of course, to instances where **#TVTimeZone#** is a positive number. In instances where **#TVTimeZone#** is a negative number, the date corrections would be different, controlled by a <CFIF> tag. Finally, conditional logic would be used to label the columns with just one date for West Coast viewrs.

```
<TABLE BORDER=1 WIDTH=90%>
<COLS=5>
    <TR ALIGN="center">
            <TD COLSPAN="5"><STRONG><FONT SIZE="4">Program
    Guide, #Currentdate# to #DateFormat(Currentdate +
    CreateTimeSpan(3,0,0,0), "mmmm d, yyyy")#
</FONT></STRONG></TD>
</TR>
    <CFSET Day1 = #DateFormat(Currentdate, "mmmm d")#>
    <CFSET Day1b = #DayOfWeekAsString(DayOfWeek
        (Currentdate))#>
    <CFSET Day2 = #DateFormat(Currentdate +
        CreateTimeSpan(1,0,0,0), "mmmm d")#>
    <CFSET Day2b = #DayOfWeekAsString(DayOfWeek(Currentdate
     + CreateTimeSpan(1,0,0,0)))#>
    <CFSET Day3 = #DateFormat(Currentdate +
        CreateTimeSpan(2,0,0,0), "mmmm d")#>
     <CFSET Day3b = #DayOfWeekAsString(DayOfWeek
        (Currentdate + CreateTimeSpan(2,0,0,0)))#>
    <CFSET Day4 = #DateFormat(Currentdate +
        CreateTimeSpan(3,0,0,0), "mmmm d")#>
    <CFSET Day4b = #DayOfWeekAsString(DayOfWeek(Currentdate
        + CreateTimeSpan(3,0,0,0)))#>
<TR>
    <TH WIDTH="12%">Time</TH>
    <TH WIDTH="22%">#Day1# <BR> #Day1b#
    </TH>
    <TH WIDTH="22%">#Day2# <BR> #Day2b#

        </TH>
    <TH WIDTH="22%">#Day3# <BR> #Day3b#
    </TH>
    <TH WIDTH="22%">#Day4# <BR> #Day4b#
    </TH>
</TR>
```

Finally, the following is the section of the template into which the clerical person simply pastes code which was taken from View/Page Source in Netscape. Only the first column of every row is different than the code generated by Cold Fusion and **grid.cfm**. (For this example, I also removed all the blank rows.)

In the original page source code, the first column simply said **1:00 AM.** The purpose of the MS Word macro is to insert all the functions and syntax needed to adjust this time by **#TVTimeZone#**. How the macro works is explained next. Since the following code is very repetitious, only three rows will be left in this example.

```
<TR>
<TH> #TimeFormat(DateAdd("h", Evaluate("TVTimeZone"), "1:00
    AM"), 'h:mm tt')# </TH>
<TH><A HREF="Detail.CFM?ScheduleID=203">Ed
    Sullivan</A><BR><A HREF="Detail.CFM?ScheduleID=203">
    Beatles Week</A></TH>
<TH><A HREF="Detail.CFM?ScheduleID=191">Ed Sullivan</A>
    <BR><A HREF="Detail.CFM?ScheduleID=191">Beatles
    Week</A></TH>
<TH><A HREF="Detail.CFM?ScheduleID=193">Ed Sullivan</A><BR>
    <A HREF="Detail.CFM?ScheduleID=193">Beatles
    Week</A></TH>
<TH><A HREF="Detail.CFM?ScheduleID=197">Ed Sullivan</A><BR>
    <A HREF="Detail.CFM?ScheduleID=197">Beatles
    Week</A></TH>
</TR><TR>
<TH> #TimeFormat(DateAdd("h", Evaluate("TVTimeZone"),
    "6:00 AM"), 'h:mm tt')# </TH><TH><A
    HREF="Detail.CFM?ScheduleID=1">Popeye</A><BR><A
    HREF="Detail.CFM?ScheduleID=1">The Winne!r</A></TH>
<TH><A HREF="Detail.CFM?ScheduleID=28">Popeye</A><BR><A
    HREF="Detail.CFM?ScheduleID=28">True Love</A></TH>
<TH><A HREF="Detail.CFM?ScheduleID=55">Popeye</A><BR><A
    HREF="Detail.CFM?ScheduleID=55">The Call</A></TH>
<TH><A HREF="Detail.CFM?ScheduleID=82">Popeye</A><BR><A
    HREF="Detail.CFM?ScheduleID=82">Crazy Brother</A></TH>
</TR>
<TR>
<TH>#TimeFormat(DateAdd("h", Evaluate("TVTimeZone"),
    "11:00 PM"), 'h:mm tt')# </TH><TH><A
    HREF="Detail.CFM?ScheduleID=202">News</A><BR>
    <A HREF="Detail.CFM?ScheduleID=202">News</A></TH>

        <TH><A HREF="Detail.CFM?ScheduleID=200">
    News</A><BR><A HREF="Detail.CFM?ScheduleID=200">
    News</A></TH>
<TH><A HREF="Detail.CFM?ScheduleID=198">
    News</A><BR><A HREF="Detail.CFM?ScheduleID=198">
    News</A></TH>
<TH><A HREF="Detail.CFM?ScheduleID=190">News</A><BR><A
    HREF="Detail.CFM?ScheduleID=190">News</A></TH>
</TR>
```

Finally, here's the end of the template that is not generated by Cold Fusion and **grid.cfm**.

```
</CFOUTPUT>
</TABLE>
</CENTER>
</BODY></HTML>
```

Description of the MS Word Macro Used in Creating This Template

A macro is a tool that records the actions you take when using a program. After you've recorded a macro, anyone can use it to perform all of the intricate and complex operations that you recorded—simply by pushing a button on a toolbar or using the keyboard. That's how this particular macro makes it possible for an untrained secretary to produce the web page that contains a complex programming grid.

In Word, this recording is automatically turned into a Visual Basic program. You can either record macros or edit them from within Word by using the commands found in the Tools/Macro menu.

In the Visual Basic macro that is automatically generated when you simply turn on the recorder, there is a lot of information you don't need. Most of these are attributes and methods that are part of the syntax, but which mean nothing to the current case. Nonetheless, if you simply copy the Visual Basic code, as is, into any machine running Word 97, the macro will repeat the steps that were recorded when it was generated.

The Visual Basic macro starts by finding "<TR>," which starts each new row. This command is executed after 14 lines of code. You really don't need to understand the lines in between if you don't want to. (If you do want to learn more about Visual Basic macros in Word, order the book *Microsoft Office 97/ Visual Basic Programmer's Guide* from Microsoft at (800) MS-PRESS in the U.S. or (800) 667-1115 in Canada, or order through the CompuServe Electronic Mall (GO MSP).)

Then the macro moves the cursor six characters to the right, which puts it right after the <TH> tag. It then inserts the first three quarters of the functions that are needed to adjust to the time zone.

At this point, it moves forward four words. The reason not to count the number of characters to move is that a two-digit hour would produce different results than would a one-digit hour.

Finally, the rest of the syntax for the required functions is inserted. As soon as the secretary observes that the macro has run correctly, he or she pushes the customized button in the button bar again so that the process can repeat itself for the next row.

The MS WORD Macro

```
Sub ChangeStaticGrid()
    Selection.Find.ClearFormatting
```

```
            With Selection.Find
            .Text = "<TR>"
            .Replacement.Text = "Currentdate"
            .Forward = True
            .Wrap = wdFindContinue
            .Format = False
            .MatchCase = False
            .MatchWholeWord = False
            .MatchWildcards = False
            .MatchSoundsLike = False
            .MatchAllWordForms = False
        End With
        Selection.Find.Execute
        Selection.MoveRight Unit:=wdCharacter, Count:=6
        WordBasic.Insert "#TimeFormat(DateAdd(""h"",
          Evaluate(""TVTimeZone""), """
        Selection.MoveRight Unit:=wdWord, Count:=4
        WordBasic.Insert """), 'h:mm tt')#"
    End Sub
```

So how does this macro get attached to a custom button? (Word 97 method.)

1. Use menu command Tools/Macro/Macros to open the Macros dialog box.

2. Type the macro name and click the Create button.

3. Paste the macro into the space provided in the Visual Basic window. Do not duplicate the "Sub" or "EndSub" lines.

4. Return to MS Word's main application window.

5. Click the right button over the tool bars and choose Customize.

6. In the Customize dialog box, click the Commands tab, locate the Macros category, and find the new macro you just wrote in the Commands list box.

7. Click on your new macro with the left mouse button and drag it to anywhere on the toolbar that you want to put it. Use the Modify button in the Customize dialog box to make it look the way you want.

8. Return to the Visual Basic window and save.

How Will You Use This Information in the Future?

There might have been a way to automate this process even further, so that the secretary wouldn't need to do anything with it. However, no template is going to operate forever, untouched by human hands. The automation needed to generate this entire grid is beyond what is practical, necessary, or even useful.

The secretary should know what the HTML and CFML code looks like so that late-breaking changes to the program line-up can be handled manually. Furthermore, it is in your best interest to train staff to create and use macros and manipulate the button bar.

Using the Web Application Framework for Persistent Client Variables

So far, we have explored three ways to pass variables from one template to the next: cookies, URL variables, and form fields. Cookies were the only technique we used for global variables, and, as noted before, cookies do have important limitations you must remember. One limitation is that certain older browsers do not support cookies. In addition, each domain may have only a limited number of cookies, which in some cases could limit your options significantly.

The complete set of tools in the Cold Fusion Web Application Framework is beyond the scope of this chapter. This chapter only describes it as a means of overcoming the problems with using global variables.

The basis for using this framework is a special template called APPLICATION.CFM, which is processed by Cold Fusion every time any other Cold Fusion template is processed in your application. For this reason, APPLICATION.CFM must be in the root directory of your application so that Cold Fusion can find it.

What follows is the first line you might put in **application.cf**, which is all you need in the template to make it start to work for you.

```
<CFAPPLICATION NAME="TVNetworkVariables"
    CLIENTMANAGEMENT="YES">
```

Giving your application a name keeps client variables from this application from being confused with client variables in another application. Naming is optional and is recommended if you are running several applications.

CLIENTMANAGEMENT is also an optional attribute, but it has to be turned on for persistent client variables. And even though the Web Application Framework can be used as an alternative to using cookies, it uses cookies when possible.

Using ClientManagement for Global Variables

If the user's browser accepts cookies, two cookies are sent to the person's computer and stored in **cookies.txt** in the browser directory. The only cookies that you have to pass to the users are a client ID called **#CFID#** and a security token called **#CFToken#**.

All other client variables, from that point on, are stored on your server. Thus when TV viewers log on, they only send you **#CFID#** and **#CFToken#**.

From these two cookies, Cold Fusion locates all of the other client variables that you need in the computer's system registry. Once you have **#CFID#** and **#CFToken#**, Cold Fusion locates **#TVTimeZone#** and **#CustID#** on your own server.

This gives you one maintenance job that is not automatic when using the Web Application Framework. If a lot of people visit your site, the registry will fill up quickly. You will need to regularly reset the registry's size in the Windows NT Control Panel.

So why bother? First of all, no matter how many client variables you need, you only have to worry about making sure that **#CFID#** and **#CFToken#** get to the template. If so, all the other client variables are automatically available in that template.

Secondly, It's easy to make sure that **#CFID#** and **#CFToken#** get to all of your templates. If you redirect the program flow by using <CFLOCATION>, **#CFID#** and **#CFToken#** get passed automatically. If you are using a URL link, you need to append only one variable to the URL-a special variable called **#URLToken#**. When you use it, it automatically contains both **#CFID#** and **#CFToken#**.

When you're using a form to pass variables, you have to include both **#CFID#** and **#CFToken#** as hidden form fields, which is certainly less complex than keeping track of all the client variables you might want passed around your system.

Creating and Using Client Variables

Client variables are both created and used in the same way as any other variable type.

```
<CFSET #CLIENT.TVTimeZone# = #FORM.TVTimeZone#>
<CFOUTPUT>
```

The programming schedule has been adjusted by **#CLIENT.TVTimeZone#** hours.

```
</CFOUTPUT>
```

In addition, Cold Fusion automatically creates three useful variables.

- **#HitCount#**, which tells how often the viewer uses the site.
- **#LastVisit#**, which tells the date and time of the person's last visit.
- **#TimeCreated#**, which tells the date and time the person first visited.

What to Do If There Are No Cookies

First of all, <CFAPPLICATION> is the logical place to test whether cookies exist. If they do not, <CFAPPLICATION> can pass new visitors to the registration template. But first, you might want to ask if they have, indeed, registered before. If they did, you might enable them to identify themselves with a password.

Thus, users whose browsers do not support cookies would not need to fill out the whole form each time they sign on. And users whose browsers do support cookies would never be asked for their password.

The conditional logic to do this is very simple. On the form that is located in **empau3.cfm**, an additional space could be inserted for a password. For security reasons, this could be combined with the phone number before being inserted into the database.

Later, when the user entered the password, the SQL query would use a WHERE clause with a LIKE condition to locate anyone with that password. If there were more than one, the person could be required to enter their phone number as well.

Other Uses of the Web Application Framework

The Web Application Framework is also very powerful at providing you with global customized error messages, global defaults for various required variables, and security measures to kick in before any other template is invoked.

Thus, the Web Application Framework provides you with numerous possibilities that might be very hard to accomplish otherwise. It is worthwhile studying this technique further in the Cold Fusion docs.

CONCLUSION

This chapter has developed a full programming example, illustrating how to use a Cold Fusion functions and variables. A MS WORD 97 macro was introduced to reduce repetitive maintenance tasks.

HTML
Language
Extensions

20

Introducing JavaScript Script Writing

- Creating JavaScript Functions
- Building JavaScript Windows with Included Help Messages
- Using JavaScript Event Handlers
- Validating Data Input
- A Cool Internet Explorer-Type JavaScript Interface

JavaScript is a versatile, powerful language that extends the functionality of HTML documents. Seamlessly imbedded within HTML documents, JavaScript can be used for client-side data validation and to display warning messages, open new instances of Netscape, create popup help screens, and do a host of other things. JavaScript is a line-by-line interpreted language, in contrast to the Java language, which must be compiled and uses passed parameters and applets to control its actions.

If you have had the experience of filling in and submitting a form only to have a message sent back to you asking you to start all over again and resubmit because you skipped a field, then you'll understand why it is good to learn how to use JavaScript to do client-side data validation. Going through data resubmission is the sort of thing that causes people to become irritated and to leave a Web site. JavaScript can be used to avoid this outcome. It may be easier initially to validate alphanumeric data using Cold Fusion controls but read this chapter carefully to learn about alternative ways to validate client-inputted form data.

This chapter focuses on building compact, easily written JavaScripts; it will not be as formidable as learning C or Java. (I rate it at just about the same level of complexity as writing a Cold Fusion template—as long as you don't try to write large, complex JavaScript modules that would force it to begin to show its C language roots.) JavaScript is not a tag-based language like HTML or Cold Fusion; you must therefore learn some new things. The JavaScript presented in this chapter will be made as accessible as is possible. If you don't want to hack the code, automatic JavaScript writers are in development right now (Intrabuilder from Borland has a built-in automatic JavaScript writer for use with validating fill-in form information), or you can adapt already written JavaScripts. Most of the JavaScripts currently on the Web are freeware and so can be modified to fit your needs as long as you give author credits.

Getting Started with JavaScript

JavaScript is an interpreted language. This means that it doesn't run as fast as C++ because each line must be interpreted before being run, but it also means that you don't have to use a compiler (or debugger) to build working blocks of code, nor do you use externally passed parameters as in JAVA applets. It also means that you can build up lines of code and test new lines very easily—very easy debugging compared with compiled languages.

JavaScript functions are usually placed in the header of an HTML page (or at the top of a Cold Fusion Template) because JavaScript functions must be first be defined before they can be used in a Web page. Also, it is wise to place your JavaScript after a HTML commented-out line, for example, (`!- javascript code goes here…`). The reason is this: if a browser cannot process the JavaScript, it will ignore the code if the code is placed immediately after a commented-out line. (See how to do this later in the chapter). However, with the widespread standardization on Netscape Navigator (versions 2.0, 3.0, and 4.0) browser and Microsoft's Internet Explorer Browser, version 4.0 (one million copies were downloaded the first week) it is fair to say that a majority of WWW users are now able to access JavaScript functions without major problems.

Creating a Javascript Function

To embed a JavaScript function in your Web page, use the following new opening and closing HTML-like tags:

```
<script> … </script>
```

Also, you usually identify the type of script language to be used, for example, `<script language=JavaScript>`. JavaScript is case sensitive so you must be careful when using mixed caps and lowercase when writing functions. A single statement can cover several lines and a *function*, a working group of statement(s), is set off by curly braces {} at the beginning and the end, as shown in the following example:

```
j1.htm (contains JavaScript)
<html>
<script language="JavaScript">
<!-This is a commented-out line which continues for several
    lines
document.write("Hello World!")
<!- the end of the comment ->
</script>
</html>

< - JavaScript Output - >

Hello World!
```

The code shows how to create a JavaScript function: the words to be displayed on-screen are set off by double quotes inside of parentheses. The actual statement uses a "noun.verb" command structure with the noun being called an *object* and the verb called a *method*. If you have studied any C or Visual Basic, you'll recognize that JavaScript is part of the same language family.

NOTE: *If you place just the <script> ... </script> tag inside commented-out lines in the Internet Explorer Explorer browser 3.0, it will not be executed. Therefore, put it before the start of the commented-out section, which contains the rest of the script function, or better yet, download Version 4.0 from the Internet).*

JavaScript Windows with Embedded Program Help

When building Web pages, having sufficient screen display area can be a development challenge. HTML-powered HyperText buttons can be used to bring up an URL that contains a help screen, but the user is moved off the current page when they press the hypertext link. This is not a good outcome because the user may have had trouble getting to your current Web page in the first place, and now the page must be reloaded. If you put a lot of graphics on the page and they have a slow connection—ouch! A better solution is to use JavaScript to pop-up a window displaying a scrollable HTML Help document. This works better because the browser creates a new instance of itself (you can create as many new instances as you want), while holding the original Web page in memory. When the user wants to return to the original Web page, they can then close the new instance(s) and be immediately back, without having to reload. By using a JavaScript message window, you can also display a sized Help window that it does not completely block the originally opened HTML Web page.

Figure 20-1 shows a standard-sized full screen HTML help document, in contrast to Figure 20-2, which shows a sized JavaScript popup Help window. Notice that by using a sized popup window, most of the underlying Web page is still visible on a 14-inch monitor.

The following HTML code contains the JavaScript that opens a pop-up window containing a help information screen. (I am going to leave off the commented-out lines at the beginning and the end in these JavaScript examples because they run quite nicely without it).

```
Java2.htm

<html>
<title>Help Screen</title>
```

Figure 20-1
Standard HTML Help
document.

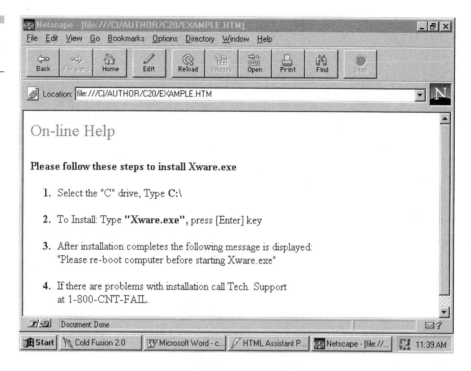

Figure 20-2
JavaScript-powered
popup Help
window.

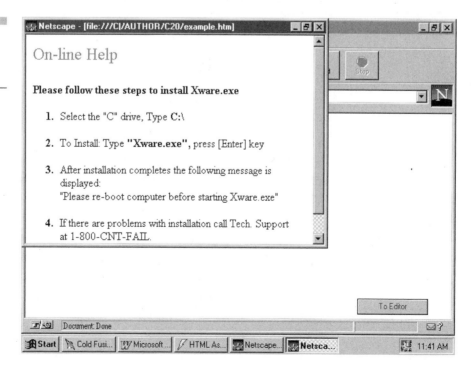

```
<body bgcolor="ffffff">

<SCRIPT LANGUAGE="JavaScript">

function statusExam()
    {
    msg=window.open("example.htm","StatusWindow",
        "toolbar=no,width=440,height=300,
    directories=no,status=no,scrollbars=yes,
        resize=no,menubar=no");
    }

</SCRIPT>
<form>
<INPUT TYPE="button" VALUE="Help button" NAME="button1"
 →       onClick="statusExam()">
</form>
</html>
```

HOW IT WORKS   The JavaScript function is called `statusExam()`. The arrow shows the JavaScript function which activates the Help button. (The Help button displays on the screen like a Submit or Reset button anywhere you want on the HTML page following the function). The various parts of the function are as follows:

1. { . . . } Curly Braces enclose the entire function and are required.

2. `msg=window.open()` This opens a browser window. The window is an object, and open( ) is a *method* (an action that can be applied to an object).

3. `example.htm` HTML document to be displayed in the popup window. You could use a full pathname such as `HTTP://` `www.mysite.com/example.htm.`

4. `,` Each parameter is separated by a comma.

5. `StatusWindow,toolbar=no,width=440,height=300,directories=no, status=no, scrollbars=yes, resize=no,menubar=no`

   The width,height can be changed to any desired value.

   If the window is too large, it blocks the original underlying Web page. If the help screen information is less than one screen, set scrollbar=no. *Notice the semicolon at the end of this statement.*

6. `onClick=statusExam()` `onClick` is an object *property* that executes when the button is clicked. Notice that this property activates the `statusExam` function. The onClick button can be placed

anywhere on the HTML page after the **statusExam()** function has been defined. Surround the function with double quotation marks.

7. The button must be inside an HTML **<form>** ... **</form>** tag.

Using a Message Window — To Display Text Only

Text can also be displayed in a window without using an HTML document. In order to do this, each text line must be preceded by a **msgWindow.document.write** statement. This is a little less graceful than using a HTML document, but requires no HTML document. Place a **<center>** ... **<center>** tag around the actual message text to make sure the text is centered in the message window; it gets lost otherwise. Figure 20-3 shows text displayed in a window without using an HTML document.

The following code shows how to open a message window, which can be defined with very specific width and height and displays selected text without using an HTML document.

Figure 20-3
Text-only message window.

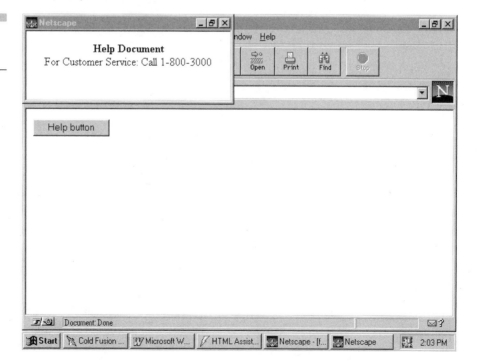

```
<html>
<SCRIPT LANGUAGE="JavaScript">
function windowOpen()
  {
→   msgWindow=window.Open ("",  "displayWindow",
      "width=300,height=100" )
    msgWindow.document.write
      ("<center><b>Help Document</b></center>")
    msgWindow.document.write
      ("<center>For Customer Service: Call
          1-800-3000</center>")
  }

</SCRIPT>
<form>
<INPUT TYPE="button" VALUE="Help button" NAME="button2"
      onClick="windowOpen()">
</form>
</html>
```

The arrow shows the working part of the windowOpen function. Notice in the code that where the HTML document name was previously inserted is replaced by double quotes. Also, the term displayWindow is used, and the double quotes are placed on the outside of the width and height parameters. The **msgWindow.document.write** line must be used each time a new line is added to the message window; it writes only one line at a time in the window. You could write a very long line in your browser, which would simply be wrapped if you needed to write a multiline paragraph.

Adding a Close Button

The following code shows how to close the opened window. The function **closeWin1()** reuses the argument definition from the **openWin1()** function. The close method is activated by an onClick event button. The open and close button-activated msgwindows are shown in Figure 20-4.

The bolded function shows the function **closeWin1()**. Notice that the definition of the open window (underlined in the example) is used to exactly define the object to be closed. The **onClick="closeWin1()"** button invokes the **closeWin1()** JavaScript function.

An interesting variation in an open window is to use a GIF or JPG (substitute in place of the **window.htm** parameter) in the HTML document example. A GIF can be downloaded along with the main page as an invisible

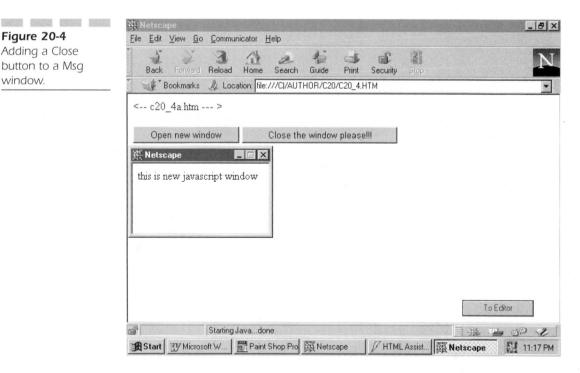

Figure 20-4
Adding a Close
button to a Msg
window.

c20_4a.htm
document

```
<html>
<- c20_4a.htm - >
<head>
<script language="JavaScript">
<!- Comment starts here...

function openWin1() {
  msgwindow = open("window.htm", "displayWindow",
      "width=200,height=10");
}

function closeWin1() {
 msgwindow = open("window.htm","displayWindow").close()
  win = null
}

// ->
</script>
</head>
<body>

<form>
```

Continues

```
<input type="button" value="Open new window"
     onclick="openWin1()">
<input type="button" value="Close the window please!!!"
     onclick="closeWin1()">
</form>

</body>
</html>
```

```
<html>
<script language="JavaScript">
<!- Comment starts here...

function openWin1() {
   newWindow = open("test.htm", "newWindow",
      "scrollbars=yes,
      resizeable=yes,width=150,height=250");
}

function closeWin1() {
newWindow.close();
   win = null
}
// ->
</script>
</header>
<b><font size="+2">A second Window Example </font></b><p>
This is a good place to put some interesting text.

<center>
<form>
<input type="button" value="Open a Cool Window"
     onclick="openWin1()">
<input type="button" value="Close" onclick="closeWin1()">
</form><p>
</center>
```

GIF, and it can be made to be almost invisible if it is given a height parameter =1 (pixel) and a width parameter =1 (pixel).

The GIF is then available to be "popped up" as a full-sized help screen (resize the object when you pop it up) from a JavaScript, and no further downloading from the server is required, which enables the user to access a Help screen without ever leaving the current page. (You could also accomplish the same effect by using a number of **document.write** statements—tedious).

This window also has Open and Close buttons, each managed by a separate function from the original Web page.

Using JavaScript for Data Validation

JavaScript is often used to validate Form input data. JavaScript functions are usually defined in the header HTML document section and called by using one of the following event handlers, for example, from a text input button by using an onChange event handler. Many different actions (methods) are available, as is shown in Table 20-1.

The majority of events are activated by user mouse pointer movements (except for the onLoad event) and occur as a response to mouse cursor

Table 20-1

JavaScript Event Handlers

Event Handler	Action	Result
onBlur	Select,Text,Textarea field left by user	JavaScript Function is called.
onChange	Select,Text,Text area	Field value checked modified by user and exited.
onClick	Form Object clicked	JavaScript Event occurs
onFocus	Cursor into field causes Value checked in	Cursor moves into Textarea input focus event.
onLoad	Netscape Navigator finishes loading frames or windows within a frameset.	Onload event occurs after windows or frames load
onMouseOver	Each time mouse pointer moves over object	Mouse pointer causes JavaScript event to occur
onSelect	Some of the text (in text or textarea field is selected by the user.	Event occurs when text is highlighted.
onSubmit	User submits a form, event occurs	"Return" statement can prevent a form from being "Submitted."
onUnload	Document is exited, event occurs	Javascript executed when user leaves document.

moves. Most of the Event handlers are placed inside of form tags and are used to do data validation, as is shown in the next section.

Using JavaScript to Check Data Input Values

The following JavaScript OnChange event handler is imbedded in the c20_4.htm HTML document. The validate function in the header, is completely separated from the form tag enclosed onChange event handler, which is put in later in the HTML document following the function definition.

```
<html>
<blockquote>
<script language="JavaScript">
function validate(param1, lowval, hival) {
if  ((param1.value < lowval) || (param1.value > hival))
    alert("Re-enter a Value between 5 and 25!")
}
</script>

<form>
<B> Enter a dollar amount between $5 and $25</b><br>
<INPUT TYPE = "text" NAME = "amount" SIZE = 3
  onChange="validate(this, 5, 25)"><p>
  </form>
<font size="+2">To run  click anywhere outside input
      box.</font>
</blockquote>
</html>
```

The resulting screen is shown in Figure 20-5.

Code Lines 4–7 show the location of the validate function. The following explains the elements of the validate function:

```
function validate(param1...
```

The **this** parameter is passed to the **param1** parameter in the function. The calling function and the function definition each have three values.

```
if  ((param1.value < lowval) || (param1.value > hival))
```

The double vertical lines || equal *or*. Notice that the value can be tested for being less than 5 or greater than 25. This causes a warning to be displayed for numbers outside of the acceptable range, whether too small or too large.

Figure 20-5
The onChange data
input event handler.

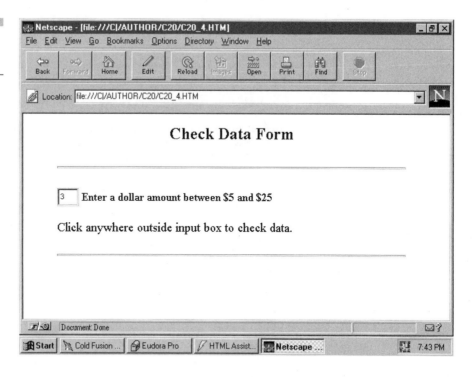

```
alert("Re-enter a Value between 5 and 25!")
```

The alert is displayed every time values greater or lesser than the stated limits are entered. After clicking the OK msg button and turning off the alert, users get a second chance to reenter a number correctly.

```
onChange="validate(this, 5, 25)"
```

NOTE: *Remember to place the entire function inside curly braces.*

The onChange Event Handler is defined by using the name of the function, in this case `validate(this,5,25)` parameters, such as `this`, do not have to be declared before being used, they can be created and used on the spot.

```
SIZE = 3
```

Shows the width (in characters) of the input box.

Using the onmouseover Event Handler

This rather cool event handler enables you to simply point the cursor at an object (such as a GIF or JPG file) or a hypertext link and a Java-Script Alert message will be displayed. The code is given here:

```
<a href = onmouseover="alert(here's a place for a cool help
    message');">
<img src="yourgifhere.gif">optional text </a>
```

You can also use text to activate the function (just put the text in place of the img src tag.)

USING JAVASCRIPT VARIABLES   Use the following code to initialize a variable and store a string to the variable.

```
var mystring="Please enter a value"
document.write(mystring.fixed())
< - OUTPUT - >
Please enter a value
```

In a similar manner, to override a preset font color by using a variable, use the following code snippet:

```
var mystring="Please enter a value"
document.write(mystring.fontcolor("red") +
    " is displayed as red text")
```

This example is equivalent to the following HTML code:

```
<font color="red">Please enter a value</font> is displayed
    as red text
```

Validating JavaScript String Expressions

JavaScript can be used to check text inputs to see whether an exact number of characters has been entered. The following code checks a field, called "State," to see whether a two-letter state code has been entered correctly. The text field input is automatically changed to uppercase if the user enters lowercase or mixed lower- and uppercase. (This can be important for database inputs). Figure 20-6 shows the error message of a two-character (for State abbreviation) input screen.

Figure 20-6
Data Validation—
State Field example

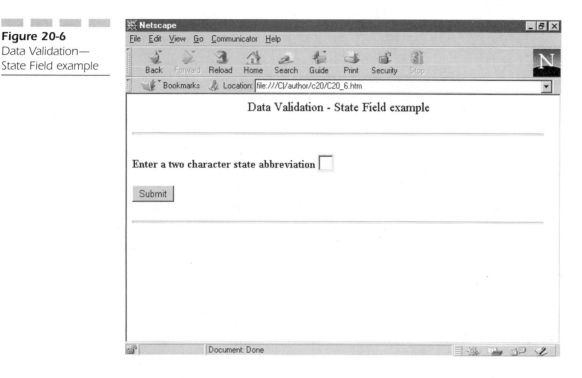

```html
<html>
<head>
<center><font size="+1">Data Validation - State Field
     example</font></center>
</head><P>
<hr>
<script>
var dataOK=false
function ValidData (){
if (document.form1.twoChar.value.length == 2) {
   return true}
   else {
       alert("Enter exactly two characters. " +
             document.form1.twoChar.value + " is not
             valid.")
       return false}
}
</script>
<body>
<form name="form1" onsubmit="return ValidData()">
<b>Enter a two character state abbreviation</b>
<input type="text" name="twoChar" size=2>
<p><input type="submit" value="Submit" name="submit1"
   onclick="document.form1.twoChar.value=document.
         form1.twoChar.value.toUpperCase()">
</form>
```

```
<hr>
</body>
</html>
```

The text shown next refers to the document form and its twoChar field.

```
(document.form1.twoChar.value.length == 2)
```

The variable twoChar is a variable that expects exactly two characters. JavaScript uses a double equal sign (= =) to show exact equivalency. Notice also that the object **document** has **form1** (the JavaScript name for the form) as part of its definition. The field name **twoChar**, is used in the form tag and passes its values to the function. The onClick function uses an equals sign to cause the input to be changed to uppercase letters.

The ValidData function can be easily modified to check whether a field has been skipped (left empty). The following listing shows how to modify the ValidData() function to check for empty fields.

```
<html>
<head>
<title>Data Validation - First Name Field example</title>
```

Figure 20-7

A fill-in form with exact field input validation.

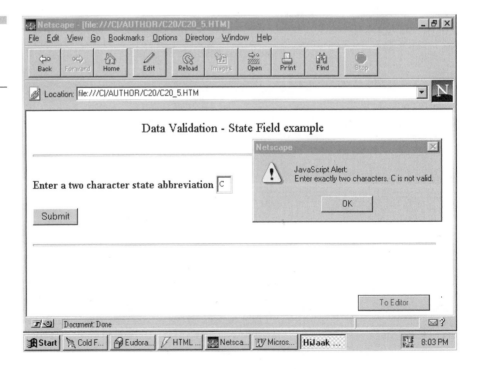

```
</head>
<script>
var dataOK=false
function ValidData (){
if (document.form1.oneChar.value.length > 0) {
   return true}
   else {
       alert("Enter a value in this field please " +
             document.form1.oneChar.value + " is not
             valid.")
       return false}
}
</script>
<body>
<form name="form1" onsubmit="return ValidData()">
<b>Please enter your first name</b>
<input type="text" name="oneChar" size=10>
<p><input type="submit" value="Submit" name="submit1"
   onclick="document.form1.oneChar.value">
</form>
</body>
</html>
```

The bolded text shows how to substitute a greater than symbol (>) in the place of the double equal signs to test for empty text fields. The input text tag is given a larger size (10) to hold inputted first names up to 10 characters.

JavaScript has many ways to open windows and display text or images. Frames may also be created and controlled by using JavaScript. (Check the **http://www.netscape** site for help in using frames with JavaScript.) JavaScript also controls many different data input validation techniques, some of these techniques have been shown in this chapter. As a further resource, the World Wide Web search engines Lycos, Alta Vista, and Yahoo point to many JavaScript sites when you enter the search word **JavaScript**. The great majority of JavaScript examples listed on the WWW are freeware.

An Internet Explorer-Style Navigation Menu

The following JavaScript Navigation Menu is more difficult, but it creates and displays a cool HTML frames-driven menu tree using very familiar folder icons (see Figure 20-8). This JavaScript works equally well with Netscape Navigator 3.0 or 4.0, or Internet Explorer 3.0 or 4.0. If you want to modify this program a little, notice the variable **foldersTree= foldernode("Start folder")**, which creates the top folder label. Any

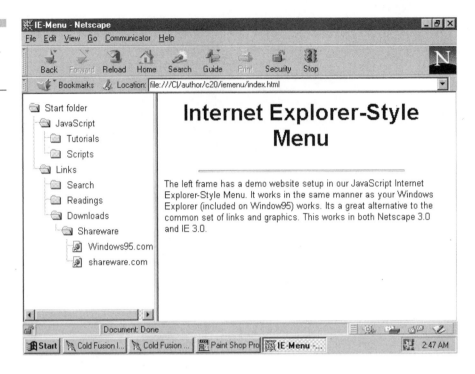

name could be used here because this is only a folder label. Continue reading down the tree until you get to the following line:

```
appendChild(aux2, generateDocEntry(0, "JS World
    Tutorials","www.mydesktop.com/javascript/help/", ""))
```

This line contains the label "JS World Tutorials," as well as an URL leading to an HTML doc. If you are modifying this JavaScript to fit your own needs, this is where you put the first HTML document or CFM template to be displayed as content in the right frame. In a similar manner you can go down one more level to the aux3 variable and substitute in further links. You can remove blocks of code that you don't need, but I recommend that you first make a backup of the original file before altering any of the code. Also, be careful with curly braces and, for that matter, parenthesis and all forms of punctuation. It all has a place in the code. This code is meant to be added to; it is a skeleton to which you can insert your links and use it on your Web site.

At the end of this script are a few lines of HTML; notice that the two frames are named **basetree.htm** and **basefolder.htm** and that the main HTML doc is called **index.html** (a correct name choice if you want this document to be your initial loading document on your Web site). Finally, index.htm will not work properly unless you place the many icon GIFs in the working directory. If you want to substitute your own very small GIFs to individualize the menu structure, carefully replace GIFs in the code without disturbing the surrounding lines of code, each of the curly braces must be left untouched.

(The following JavaScript is used with the permission of Marcelino A. Martins (martins@hks.com), the script has been annotated.)

```
<HTML>
<HEAD>
<title>Menu</title>
<script LANGUAGE="JavaScript">
<!- to hide script contents from old browsers

//each node in the tree is an Array with 4+n positions
//    node[0] is 0/1 when the node is closed/open
//    node[1] is 0/1 when the folder is closed/open
//    node[2] is 1 if the children of the node are documents
//    node[3] is the name of the folder
//    node[4]...node[4+n] are the n children nodes

// ***************
// Building the data in the tree
function generateTree()
{
var aux1, aux2, aux3, aux4
        foldersTree = folderNode("Start folder")
                aux1 = appendChild(foldersTree,
                        folderNode("JavaScript"))
                        aux2 = appendChild(aux1,
                                leafNode("Tutorials"))
appendChild(aux2, generateDocEntry(0, "JS World Tutorials",
     "www.mydesktop.com/javascript/help/", ""))
                                appendChild(aux2,
                                        generateDocEntry(0,
                                        "FAQ",
                                        "www.mydesktop.com/
                                        javascript/help/
                                        qa/", ""))

                        aux2 = appendChild(aux1,
                                leafNode("Scripts"))
                                appendChild(aux2,
                                        generateDocEntry(0,
                                        "Enhancements",
                                        "www.mydesktop.com/
                                        javascript/scripts/
                                        enhance/", ""))
                                appendChild(aux2,
                                        generateDocEntry(0,
                                        "Accessories",
```

```
                                    "www.mydesktop.com/
                                    javascript/scripts/
                                    accessories/",
                                    ""))
                        appendChild(aux2,
                            generateDocEntry(0,
                            "Games",
                            "www.mydesktop.com/
                            javascript/scripts/
                            games/", ""))

            aux1 = appendChild(foldersTree,
                folderNode("Links"))
                    aux2 = appendChild(aux1,
                        leafNode("Search"))
                        appendChild(aux2,
                            generateDocEntry(1,
                            "Search Com",
                            "www.search.com",
                            ""))
                        appendChild(aux2,
                            generateDocEntry(1,
                            "Yahoo",
                            "www.yahoo.com",
                            ""))
                        appendChild(aux2,
                            generateDocEntry(1,
                            "Lycos",
                            "www.lycos.com",
                            ""))

                    aux2 = appendChild(aux1,
                        folderNode("Readings"))
                        aux3 = appendChild(aux2,
                            leafNode
                            ("Cartoons"))
                            appendChild(aux3,
                            generate
                            ocEntry(1, "The
                            Dilbert Zone",
                            "www.
                            unitedmedia.com/
                            comics/
                            dilbert/", ""))
                        appendChild(aux3,
                        generateDocEntry(1,
                        "TODAYS CARTOON by
                        Randy Glasbergen",
                        "www.borg.com/
                        ~rjgtoons/
                        toon.html", ""))

                        appendChild(aux3,
                        generateDocEntry(1,
```

```
                                                   "Cravo e
                                                   Ferradura",
                                                   "www.dn.pt/
                                                   imagens/
                                                   cartoon.htm", ""))

               aux3 = appendChild(aux2,
                    leafNode("Computers"))
                      appendChild(aux3,generateDocEntry(1,
                          "Byte", "www.byte.com/", ""))
                      appendChild(aux3,generateDocEntry(1,
                          "DBMS Magazine",
                          "www.dbmsmag.com/", ""))

                      appendChild(aux3,generateDocEntry(1,
                          "Dr. Dobb's Journal",
                          "www.ddj.com/", ""))

                      appendChild(aux3,generateDocEntry(1,
                          "PCworld", "www.pcworld.com/
                          welcome.html", ""))

                      appendChild(aux3,generateDocEntry(1,
                          "Python", "www.python.org/", ""))
                      appendChild(aux3,generateDocEntry(1,
                          "ZDNet", "www.zdnet.com", ""))

    }


// Auxiliary function to build the node
function folderNode(name)
{
var arrayAux
        arrayAux = new Array
        arrayAux[0] = 0
        arrayAux[1] = 0
        arrayAux[2] = 0
        arrayAux[3] = name
        return arrayAux
}


// Auxiliary function to build the node
// The entries in arrayAux[4]..array[length-1] are strings
//     built in generate doc entry
function leafNode(name)
{
var arrayAux
        arrayAux = new Array
        arrayAux[0] = 0
        arrayAux[1] = 0
        arrayAux[2] = 1
        arrayAux[3] = name
        return arrayAux
}
```

```
//this way the generate tree function becomes simpler and
    less error prone
function appendChild(parent, child)
{
        parent[parent.length] = child
        return child
}


//these are the last entries in the hierarchy, the local
    and remote links to html documents
function generateDocEntry(icon, docDescription, link)

{
var retString =""
        if (icon==0)
                retString = "<A href='"+link+"'
                    target=folderFrame><img
                    src='doc.gif' alt='Opens in right
                    frame'"
        else
                retString = "<A href='http://"+link+"'
                    target=_blank><img src='link.gif'
                    alt='Opens in new window'"

        retString = retString + " border=0></a><td
            nowrap><font size=-1 face='Arial,
            Helvetica'>" + docDescription + "</font>"
        return retString
}
// ********************
// display functions
//redraws the left frame
function redrawTree()
{
var doc = top.treeFrame.window.document
        doc.clear()
        doc.write("<body bgcolor='white'>")
        redrawNode(foldersTree, doc, 0, 1, "")
        doc.close()
}

//recursive function over the tree structure called by
    redrawTree
function redrawNode(foldersNode, doc, level, lastNode,
    leftSide)
{
var j=0
var i=0
        doc.write("<table border=0 cellspacing=0
            cellpadding=0>")
        doc.write("<tr><td valign = middle nowrap>")
        doc.write(leftSide)
        if (level>0)
                if (lastNode) //the last 'brother' in the
```

```
                    children array
            {
                    doc.write("<img
                            src='lastnode.gif' width=16
                            height=22>")
                    leftSide = leftSide + "<img
                            src='blank.gif' width=16
                            height=22>"
            }
            else
            {
                    doc.write("<img src='node.gif'
                            width=16 height=22>")
                    leftSide = leftSide + "<img
                            src='vertline.gif' width=16
                            height=22>"
            }
    displayIconAndLabel(foldersNode, doc)
    doc.write("</table>")
    if (foldersNode.length > 4 && foldersNode[0])
//there are sub-nodes and the folder is open
    {
            if (!foldersNode[2]) //for folders with
                    folders
            {
                    level=level+1
                    for (i=4;
                            i<foldersNode.length;i++)
                            if (i==foldersNode.
                                    length-1)
                                    redrawNode(fold-
ersNode[i], doc, level, 1, leftSide)
                            else
                                    redrawNode
                                    (foldersNode[i],
                                    doc, level, 0,
                                    leftSide)
            }
            else //for folders with documents
            {
                    for (i=4; i<foldersNode.
                            length;i++)
                    {
                            doc.write("<table
                                    border=0 cell
                                    spacing=0
                                    cellpadding=0
                                    valign=center>")
                            doc.write("<tr><td
                                    nowrap>")
                            doc.write(leftSide)
                            if (i==foldersNode.
                                    length - 1)
                                    doc.write("<img
```

```
                                                              src='lastnode
                                                              .gif' width=16
                                                              height=22>")
                                              else

                                                     doc.write("<img
                                                     src='node.gif'
                                                     width=16
                                                     height=22>")
                                       doc.write
                                              (foldersNode[i])
                                       doc.write("</table>")
                              }
                     }
          }
}
//builds the html code to display a folder and its label
function displayIconAndLabel(foldersNode, doc)
{
          doc.write("<A href='javascript:top.openBranch(\"" +
                 foldersNode[3] + "\")'><img src=")
          if (foldersNode[1])
                     doc.write("openfolder.gif width=24
                              height=22 border=noborder></a>")
          else
                     doc.write("closedfolder.gif width=24
          height=22 border=noborder></a>")
          doc.write("<td valign=middle align=left nowrap>")
          doc.write("<font size=-1 face='Arial, Hel-
          vetica'>"+foldersNode[3]+"</font>")
}
//*********************+
// Recursive functions
//when a parent is closed all children also are
function closeFolders(foldersNode)
{
var i=0
          if (!foldersNode[2])
          {
                     for (i=4; i< foldersNode.length; i++)
                              closeFolders(foldersNode[i])
          }
          foldersNode[0] = 0
          foldersNode[1] = 0
}
//recursive over the tree structure
//called by openbranch
function clickOnFolderRec(foldersNode, folderName)
{
var i=0
```

```
            if (foldersNode[3] == folderName)
            {
                    if (foldersNode[0])
                            closeFolders(foldersNode)
                    else
                    {
                            foldersNode[0] = 1
                            foldersNode[1] = 1
                    }
            }
            else
            {
                    if (!foldersNode[2])
                            for (i=4; i< foldersNode.length;
                                    i++)
                                    clickOnFolderRec
                                            (foldersNode[i],
                                            folderName)
            }
}
// ********************
// Event handlers
//called when the user clicks on a folder
function openBranch(branchName)
{
        clickOnFolderRec(foldersTree, branchName)
        if (branchName=="Start folder" &&
            foldersTree[0]==0)
                top.folderFrame.location="basefolder.htm"
        timeOutId = setTimeout("redrawTree()",100)
}
//called after this html file is loaded
function initializeTree()
{
        generateTree()
        redrawTree()
}
var foldersTree = 0
var timeOutId = 0
generateTree() //sometimes when the user reloads the
      document Netscape 3.01 does not trigger the onLoad
      event (!!)
// end hiding contents from old browsers  ->
</script>
</HEAD>
<FRAMESET cols="200,*"  onLoad='initializeTree()'>
        <FRAME src="basetree.htm" name="treeFrame">
        <FRAME SRC="basefolder.htm" name="folderFrame">
</FRAMESET>
</HTML>
```

CONCLUSION

JavaScript uses multiple methods to open windows and display text or images. Frames may be created and controlled by using JavaScript. (Check the `http://www.netscape` site for specific help in building frames by using JavaScript). JavaScript can also be used with many different data input validation techniques, some of which have been shown in this chapter.

21

Using Frames with Cold Fusion

- Designing Integrated Frame Layouts
- Creating Master, Top, and Content Frames
- Using Button-Driven Frames
- Creating Cold Fusion-Powered Frames with Database Lookups

Frames make possible fast Web page selection and data retrieval. In a three-frame Web page, the top frame can contain a company logo, navigation buttons, and a corporate message, and because these entities do not change, they can be left in view while the viewer changes the main content-bearing frames using the left-hand frame hypertext links, buttons, or clickable images. This chapter shows how to develop a frame structure that incorporates automated information lookup. Because frames allow quick perusal of Web pages, endusers stay interested in your Web page offerings as they visit your Web site. This chapter develops a frame-based HTML application that integrates frames with button-driven Cold Fusion templates to create versatile Web pages.

Designing Frame Layouts

There are many possible frame layout configurations to choose from when building frame-based Web page layouts. One format is to have the top frame contain a banner and a message. With this layout, approximately 20 percent of the Web page displays a corporate logo or welcome message, animated GIF, and/or navigation buttons. The left navigation frame uses hypertext links to company products, services, or free offers (it's always good to give away something on a Web site, even if you only are offering discounted product or service). The right frame—the remaining area— functions as the content frame. Viewers select links in the left frame to bring up content pages. (You may also include hot buttons to start up Cold Fusion database retrievals in the destination frame —the right frame— as shown later in the chapter.)

Selecting Frame Elements

Web pages succeed in proportion to the amount of planning put into the screen display. Your first key to Web site design is color balancing. No matter what else is done, effort must be spent coordinating images, text, and background colors. If you need to educate your eye about color, walk through a warehouse, supermarket, or retail store and notice which color combinations are used. Color combinations such as blue, green, orange, and gray don't come together very well, so why should they fight against each other on a Web page?

Use complementary colors across all frames of a frame-loaded Web page. I am always surprised when I see individual frames fully color coordinated, but then notice that when moving from one level to another, every page has a different color plan. Pick a color layout (consisting of complementary colors), and then you can interject surprise colors—in small amounts—to give your site a little visual "startle appeal." You can use "startle colors" to highlight important parts of your Web site, but use small dabs. One of the worst things you can do is use large blocks of solid red or black backgrounds; also, Web site visitors will not stay around to read iridescent purple text on a black backgrounds or other similar color combinations.

Offer products, services, and discounts in your navigation frame (the left side) using fast-paced advertising-type language. (In your hypertext links, deliberately omit words such as "the," "and," "a," and most adjectives.) When creating your navigation frame, start out by using hypertext links; you can add small GIF thumbnail-sized images later after the page design begins to mature. Avoid stringing navigation links below the bottom of the Web page if you can. If you have to, reduce the font size of your navigation aids and eliminate superfluous information so that your main navigation aids or hypertext links are all visible all of the time. Design for fourteen-inch monitors, especially if you are going "overseas" with your Web site. Build frames that load in less than a half a minute (test at 14.4 K/sec) to attract a maximum number of Web site visitors. Always remember that most of your potential customers do not have ISDN or T-1 lines. Some overseas sites transfer at a rate of .3K or less, so consider reducing the size of images; some net surfers turn off images while surfing anyway.

The next section shows how to create the top, left, and right frames using HTML documents. Later in the chapter, Cold Fusion templates are used to retrieve information from database tables.

Creating the Master Control Frame

The following code shows how to build the "master" HTML file, which points to each of the individual frames. The master HTML document is shown in Figure 21-1. By using frames, you can build Web pages that will be loaded independently of the navigation frame and that can also contain buttons to start up Cold Fusion templates.

Figure 21-1
A three-window
frame design with
buttons.

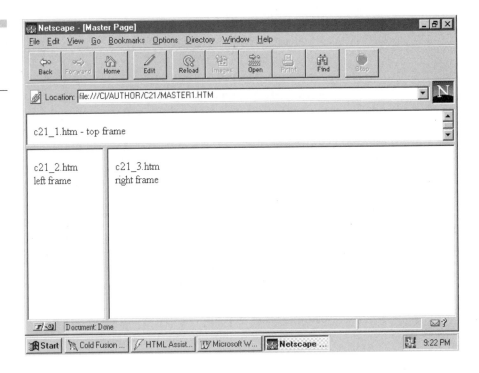

```
<HTML>
<HEAD>
<TITLE>Master Page</TITLE>
</HEAD>
<FRAMESET ROWS="26%, 74%">
          <FRAME NAME="TOP" SRC="C21_1.HTM">
     <FRAMESET COLS="25%,75%">
               <FRAME NAME="TOC"    SRC="c21_2.htm">
               <FRAME NAME="PAGE"  SRC="c21_3.htm">
     </FRAMESET>
</FRAMESET>
</HTML>
```

NOTE: *To avoid opening new "instances" of your browser while using Windows 95, use the following line to always reload the top frame on top, in case you have several layers of Web pages below your main page.*

```
<a target = _top ="YourTopUrl.htm"> </a>
```

Without it, your browser will reload as a second browser "instance" (a whole other browser window will open) when you try to go to your top frame from the lowest-level frame page.

Constructing the Top Frame

The text code <FRAME NAME="TOP" SRC="C21_1.HTM"> in the Master1.htm HTML document controls the HTML document displayed in the top frame window. This top frame window is restricted to 20 percent of the total screen "real estate" by setting the FRAMESET ROWS command to 20 percent. (The remaining 80 percent is split between the left navigation frame and the right content frame).

Frame names can be named from top to bottom; in this case, the SRC HTML document c21.HTM contains a small company logo repeated several times in a row for maximum effect. You could also put an animated GIF in this area. (If you do, please consider letting it "run out" after the first minute or so).

The FRAMESET COLS tag is placed inside the FRAMESET ROWS tag. In the preceding code section, the bolded text <FRAME SRC="c21_1.htm"> controls the top frame.

```
<html>
<body bgcolor="#D9D919">
<center><img src=world2.gif valign=top>
    <img src="wrldcorp.gif" valign=top></center>
<center><b><I>The Multi-national Export
    Company</I></b></center>
c21_1.htm -
</html>
```

The key to this frame is careful design and placement of a company logo in order not to use up too much valuable screen real estate. The left navigation frame will be used to initiate action for the rest of the Web site.

Building the Navigation Frame

In the English language, the eye reads from left to right, but often first focuses to the middle of the page before moving to the starting scanning position at the top left. The left frame must therefore be written like the opening paragraph of a news story—it must grab and keep the first-time visitor's attention. Put some of your most distinctive and commercially important Web site link information in this frame. For an example of how to set up this frame, see Figure 21-2 for the WorldCorp, Inc., company.

Figure 21-2
WorldCorp, Incorporated's left navigation frame offers convenient links.

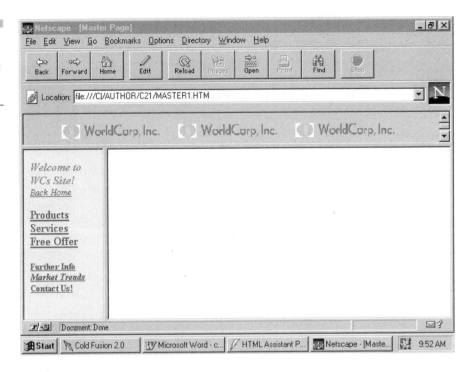

Figure 21-2
WorldCorp, Incorporated's left navigation frame offers convenient links.

```
<html>
<body bgcolor="#FFFF00">
<!-c21_2.htm->
<b><font color=red><i>Welcome to W-Cs
    Site!</i></b></font><P>
<b><a href="c21_3.htm" TARGET="PAGE"> New
    Products</a></b><BR>
<b><a href="services.htm" TARGET="PAGE">New
    Services</a></b><BR>
<b><a href=offer.htm TARGET="PAGE">Free Offer</a></b><P>
<i><a href=president.htm>Industry Trends</a></i><br>
<a href="webmaster.htm">Contact Us!</A><P>
<html>
```

Begin this frame with a welcome from you—the host. You are inviting the first-time visitor to take a tour of your site. The welcome serves as a "virtual handshake." Putting a short welcome message at the top of the Navigation frame is recommended. The welcome message can be in a contrasting color for greater emphasis. As visitors scan the left frame, use subtle font changes—go from bold to italic and back to bold, for example. Each variation helps to keep hypertext links more interesting and eye-catching, as well as helping each item stand out from its neighbors. Use a linespace between groups of similar items.

How the Navigation Frame Ties to the Content Frame

The following line contains the code that connects individual hypertext elements in the Navigation frame to the Content Frame:

```
<b><a href="c21_3.htm" TARGET="PAGE"> New
     Products</a></b><BR>
```

The word TARGET activates the Web page c21_3.htm and causes it to be displayed in the content frame (on the right side). The word PAGE is the general name for the right frame in the master1.htm document and must be used for each hypertext link in the navigation frame.

Frames enable your visitor to switch quickly from one Content page to another—all they do is click on the next hypertext link in the navigation frame to display the new content page. Surveys show that 35 to 40 percent of site visitors leave without going to a second level. Thus, using frames enables visitors to stay on the top level but still get more information even if they do just stay on the first level. Also, exercise "byte" discipline when creating pages for the content frame. Many site visitors give up on waiting for pages to load. Small images such as 2K thumbnails (with hypertext links pointing to big GIFs or JPGs) will load quickly and make visitors feel like staying and viewing all the pages on your Web site. Net surfers like Web pages that are "with it"—that show that the Web designer is sensitive to the needs of the surfer—and the use of thumbnails is one way to show you are one such Web designer.

Interestingly enough, sites such as Netscape's (two million visitors a day) and Microsoft's have become the worst offenders in overloading opening pages with unsolicited image-based information. Too much information slows a Web page from loading and irritates people.

To gain more screen real estate, design the top frame so that the top line contains only the logo on a single line. You can use the height parameter to reduce the size of the logo if you built it a little too tall; try a height of 20 and readjust the top frame to a 20 to 80 percent proportional page size with the tag <FRAMESET ROWS="20%, 80%"> (see Figure 21-3). A current trend is to put a rotating banner in the top frame. In this case notice that a smaller logo is repeated three times across the top frame for increased visual interest. Also, the navigation page now has additional hypertext links shown on the top page.

```
<html>
<body bgcolor="#FFFF00">
```

Figure 21-3
The WorldCorp logo
with increased screen
real estate.

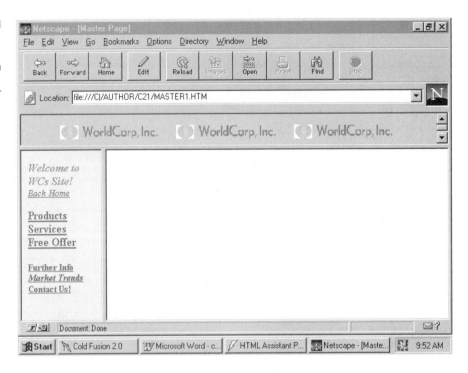

```
<!-c21_2.htm->
<b><font color=red><i>Welcome to WCs
     Site!</i></b></font><BR>
<a href="welcome.htm" TARGET="PAGE"><i><font size="-1">Back
     Home</i></font></a><p>
<b><a href="c21_3.htm" TARGET="PAGE"> Products</a></b><BR>
<b><a href="services.htm"
     TARGET="PAGE">Services</a></b><BR>
<b><a href=offer.htm TARGET="PAGE">Free Offer</a></b><P>
<b><a href=info.htm><font size="-1">Further
     Info</font></a><BR>
<i><a href=presidnt.htm TARGET="PAGE"><font
     size="-1">Market Trends</a></i></font><br>
<a href="webmaster.htm"><font size="-1">Contact
     Us!</font></A><P>
<html>
```

Will people scroll down the navigation icons of a frames page? I haven't
seen any studies, but my initial reaction is, yes, if they have real interest
in the overall contents of the Web site. It is therefore wise to put *everything* you really need people to see in the initial display area on the opening page and not in the below-the-screen area.

Creating the Content Frame (Including Buttons)

Your biggest challenge is building exciting, fast-loading content pages. But great opportunities await you! You can offer button-driven content pages. Who can resist pushing at least one button out of a row of buttons? Label buttons with text across the button's face and use buttons to bring up Cold Fusion database query forms. Place the buttons on the second level page where detailed product information is offered. This is better than having "teaser" pages at the second level that require you to go to a third level before you get the information you need.

Always give real content at the second page level, and remember that nonintrusive but well-thought-out navigation helps visitors get around on your page, if any given page extends deeper than two pages in length. If you spend all your attention on navigation aids, however, your site may be entertaining but won't generate business. In terms of how your Web site works, think about how stores display their products: Products for sale are displayed with prices. In the same manner, you must display something interesting about your on-line products, services, or information.

Building Content Frames

Use buttons to show detailed content. One way to find a button site on the WWW is to use a search engine to search on the word "button." Most button creators tell you whether you can use their buttons on your site (most buttons are freeware). You can also make buttons yourself by using CorelDraw 7, PhotoShop 3, or a button-making software program. A plain gray business-style button (`button.gif`) is included on the CD ROM. Use LVIEW Pro software (also shareware) to lengthen or shrink the button as needed, as described next.

NOTE: *To increase the length of the button.gif, open LVIEW Pro, open* `button.gif`, *click Edit, and then Resize. Next, click your cursor in the New Size box and type a number greater than the displayed number (for example, 150 if the displayed number is 119) to increase the length of the button and a smaller number to decrease it. When you have changed the number, click the cursor into the box to the right, and LVIEW Pro automatically proportionally adjusts the size of the image to the number that you just entered in the New Size box.*

Click OK and then File, Save As, and give the GIF a new name (if you want to save the basic `button.gif` *file for another use in the future). Next, open Paint Shop Pro. Use Paint Shop Pro (PSP) to put a colored font on the button. Open Paint Shop Pro and then the* `button.gif` *file. Paint Shop Pro displays the file in a small window. Click the text tool and then click your cursor anywhere on the face of the displayed button. Paint Shop Pro opens a "type-text" window where you can enter the text you want on the button. When you finish typing, click OK and place your cursor over the face of the button and drag and drop the text where you want it. Right-click on the button's face, and PSP anchors the button. Use File, Save As and save the button with a name of your choice. Depending on your goal, the button can made very ornate or be business gray, with colored lettering across the face. The Courier font works well.*

Figure 21-4 shows some buttons for an on-line music business. The buttons are used to retrieve data from a products table.

```
<html>
<!-OFFER.HTM->
<body bgcolor="#D9D919">
<center><b>Collectors Paradise!</b></center>
<table>
```

Figure 21-4

Buttons are simple to use and help the visitor know exactly what can be found on the site.

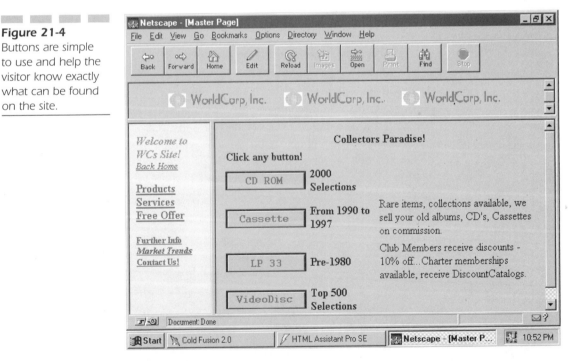

```
<tr><th>Click any button!</th></tr>
<tr><td><a href="http://127.0.0.1/music.cfm"><img
    src="cdrom.gif"></a></td><td><b>2000 Selections</b>
    </td><td></td></tr>

<tr><td><img src="cassett.gif"></td><td><b>From 1990 to
    1997</b></td><td> Rare items, collections available,
    we sell your old albums, CD's, Cassettes on
    commission. </td></tr>
<tr><td><img src="lp33.gif"></td><td><b>Pre-
    1980</b></td><td>Club Members receive discounts - 10%
    off...Charter memberships available, receive Discount
    Catalogs.</td></tr>
<tr><td><img src="Videod.gif"></td><td><b>Top 500 S
    elections</b></td>
</table>
</html>
```

Using Buttons to Start Up Cold Fusion

The text shows the server address and button — cdrom.gif — used to start up a Cold Fusion template. The template retrieves music table data and displays it in the content frame. A server address is used to tell the browser to process the template music.cfm as a template. The CD-ROM button is active in this example.

At this point you can see that Cold Fusion fits very easily into the content frame on the second level. Each button is connected to a different template. A template is activated each time a button is pressed. When a button is pressed, for example, a database query retrieves information about music products. The bolded code line shows how to use a Cold Fusion template to query the music database. In addition, you may want to put a hypertext link called "Music DB" on the top Web page to give frequent patrons quick access to the database. (See the following code inserted into the c21_2.htm navigation Web page; notice that the server pathname is used.)

The Cold Fusion template music.cfm retrieves data from the MS Access music table in the ceramic.mdb. The data making up the music table is shown in Table 12-1.

The music table is grouped by media type, but it can also be grouped by composer, by date of composition, or product cost. In order to make effective database queries, certain selling factors about the product must be considered. To give visitors maximum flexibility when searching the database, they should be allowed to enter a media type, a favorite composer, or favorite piece of music and be able to see the works available.

Table 21-1

The MS Access
Music Table

Group1	Product ID	Composer	Product Name	Units In Stock	Unit Price
CD	100	Horowitz	Piano Concertos	3	$15.00
CD	101	Rubenstein	Rubenstein Piano Concertos	2	$16.00
CD	102	Debussy	La Mer	4	$14.00
CD	103	Alpert	Herb Alpert Brass	2	$10.00
CD	104	Chopin	Nocturnes	3	$14.00
CD	105	Mantovani	Mantovani Strings	1	$7.00
Cassette	106	Rachmaninoff	Rachmaninoff Piano Concerto	3	$12.00
Cassette	107	Tchaikovsky	Tchaikovsky Selections	2	$10.00
Cassette	108	Debussy	Nocturnes	3	$13.00
Cassette	109	Beethoven	Sonatas	4	$13.00
Cassette	110	Barber	Symphony #1	2	$14.00
LP33	111	Beethoven	Moonlight Sonata	5	$17.00
LP33	112	Bach	Goldberg Variations	3	$14.00
LP33	113	Brahms	Symphony #1	2	$15.00
LP33	114	Dvorjak	Selections	4	$16.00
LP33	115	Bach	Harpsichord Variations	5	$15.00
VideoDisk	116	Verdi	Selections	2	$18.00
VideoDisk	117	Gershwin	Porgy and Bess	4	$17.00
VideoDisk	118	Schoenberg	Les Miserables	2	$19.00
VideoDisk	119	Gershwin	Rhapsody in Blue	1	$18.00
VideoDisk	120	Haydn	Chamber Music	4	$19.00

The buttons, therefore, should have some already created queries that allow searches by composer name, as well as by piece name. These types of queries are not difficult to write. The following Cold Fusion template retrieves all of the available data from the music table on CDs (see Figure 21-5). (It can be quickly modified to show different types of media, such as LP33, videodisc and cassette, by composer, or by name of work.)

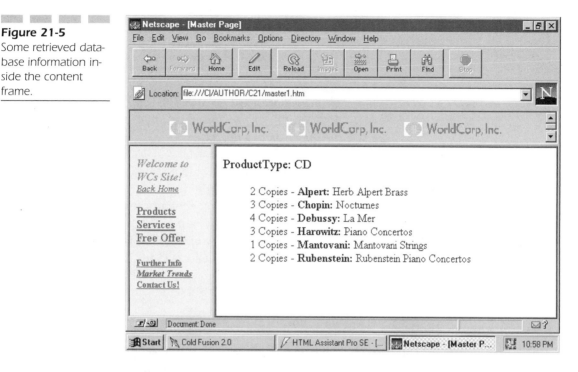

Figure 21-5
Some retrieved database information inside the content frame.

```
<!—music.cfm uses museprod.mdb —>
<CFQUERY NAME="ACCESS21Q" DATASOURCE="CERAMIC  DB">
 SELECT * From museprod
    WHERE Group1='CD'
    Order by Composer
</CFQUERY>
<HTML>
<CFOUTPUT QUERY="ACCESS21Q" GROUP = "Group1" >
<font size="+1">ProductType: #Group1# </font>
<UL>
<CFOUTPUT>
#UnitsInStock# Copies - <b>#Composer#:</b> #ProductName#
      <BR>
</CFOUTPUT>
</UL>
</CFOUTPUT>
</HTML>


<  — Output —  >

ProductType: CD

    2 Copies - Alpert: Herb Alpert Brass
    3 Copies - Chopin: Nocturnes
```

```
4 Copies - Debussy: La Mer
3 Copies - Horowitz: Piano Concertos
1 Copies - Mantovani: Mantovani Strings
2 Copies - Rubenstein: Rubenstein Piano Concertos
```

NOTE: *The column "Group1" could not be called "Group" in the database because Cold Fusion uses "Group" (or any lower- or uppercase variation) as a reserved word, and so the query would not run.*

The output from the previous code could be highly formatted; if you are interested in other ways of displaying data to customers—if you need to select specific values in a field, such as a given composer or the title of a given work, for example-please read Chapter 13, "Using Advanced SQL with Cold Fusion." It is not the purpose of this chapter to show all of SQL's conditional statements that are demonstrated in Chapter 13. In order to choose by different composers, for example, the WHERE statement must say the following:

```
WHERE Composer='Horowitz'.
```

Chapter 13 shows how to make HTML front-end forms that enable en-dusers to search the "museprod" table for all the works of a given composer.

CONCLUSION

This chapter showed how to integrate Cold Fusion into frames. In some applications, the use of frames will be the most effective way to present information. Using button-activated Cold Fusion templates represents a user-friendly way to retrieve table information. You can also include Java-Script-driven help screens and information screens inside of individual frames as needed.

Appendix A

Selected Internet Sites Using Cold Fusion

Electronic Commerce

Wickes Lumber

WICKESNET   As one of the nation's largest building materials suppliers, Wickes wanted to offer customers more than just an on-line store. To satisfy that need, Wickes used Cold Fusion and Cold Fusion components to develop WickesNet, a system that allows builders to do everything from checking on accounts and paying bills to checking inventory at the nearest Wickes Lumber Store.

R.R. Donnelley Financial

MUNICIPAL.COM – WWW.MUNICIPAL.COM   An SEC Nationally Recognized Municipal Securities Information Repository (NRMSIR), Donnelley is the first to bring to the Internet a library of over 50,000 documents including official statements, annual financial information and notices of material events for use by bond traders, financial service companies, and municipal governments. Their Cold Fusion application allows users to search databases for the documents they need and then pay for specific documents using a credit card, or subscribe to the service for unlimited access in a specific time period.

Collaborative Computing

Macroview Communications

SIXDEGREES – WWW.SIXDEGREES.COM   Based on the idea that "it's all about who you know," Sixdegrees offers a free networking service to registered users of almost 50,000 contacts. Created with Cold Fusion, Sixdegrees lets users create interlocking networks of people they know.

The Hazelden Foundation

DAYBREAK   The Hazelden Foundation, a nationally recognized substance abuse recovery center, keeps in touch with its alumni through the Web. Since continued contact with the institution is a crucial part of the recovery process, Hazelden developed an entire Web resource center that includes discussion forums, events schedules, and a bookstore – all driven by Cold Fusion. Computer World named this site one of the top 100 in the U.S.

Interactive Publishing

FARM JOURNAL – WWW.FARMJOURNAL.COM   The Farm Journal, the largest farming magazine in the United States, reaches tens of thousands of readers through an on-line version driven entirely by Cold Fusion. By leveraging dynamic-pages the journal is able offer constantly updated news and information and deliver highly targeted advertising.

Business Systems

Rapid Response

RAPID TRACK   Rapid Response is an integrated marketing service provider offering everything from collateral fulfillment to seminar management. Rapid Track, their extranet created with Cold Fusion, gives customers a comprehensive Web interface to their Rapid Response account for ordering, reporting, and management.

Aveda Corporation

With its extranet, Aveda Corporation, a global leader in the manufacture of environmental lifestyle products, can communicate with field sales and distributors about inventory and orders. Using Cold Fusion, the extranet allows the distributor to easily query the orders in the database.

INDEX

ABOUT THE AUTHORS

John Burke worked as an Associate Engineer in the Intranet Knowledge Base Group of Seagate Technology, San Jose. He helped create the currently used on-line Technical Support Intranet for Seagate's hard-drive and tape storage products. Previously, while at Varian Associates, Inc., he worked as part of Varian's Intranet team in developing a company-wide Intranet. He has worked at Intel, Borland International, The Santa Cruz Operation, FMC, Westinghouse, the Santa Clara Unified Water District, United Technologies Chemical Systems, and Tymshare during the past 15 years. John was a contributing author in the recently published bestseller *Running a Perfect Website*, Second Edition, by Que. He is currently an adjunct faculty member at Bethany College, Scotts Valley, CA. John also writes and performs 12-string-guitar-based Christian ballads and jogs in the redwoods; he and his wife Barbara and their three children live in Felton, CA.

Don Brenneman was a full-time freelance technical and magazine writer for six years and a vice president of corporate communications in international marketing for six years. In all of this, some programming was continuously necessary—writing an ink jet printer driver in BASIC for a Radio Shack 100, writing a financial package in DBase II, writing complex macros to automate the company office, etc. Eventually, it was no longer possible for him to deny that he loved programming, and he decided to learn Visual Basic to write several *computer-based training modules* (CBTs) that were beyond the scope of existing CBT authoring systems at the time. Since then, he uses Visual Basic to create tools for his own use: for analysis, problem-solving, meditation, and self-awareness.

Robert J. Neilsen has been a software engineer for more than 30 years. He has worked on computer operating systems ranging from the largest super-computers to the smallest embedded control systems. He has authored several operating systems for embedded control systems. His most successful operating system, first developed in the late 70's, is still at the heart of many of the semiconductor industry's most successful manufacturing systems.Bob currently writes network device drivers for the Windows NT and Windows 95 operating systems to support wireless LANs.

Bob's interests range from singing in his church choir to creating car rallies to writing for a popular Internet Episodic. He lives at the summit of Battle Mountain in Bonny Doon, California with his wife, Joan, and their three dogs.

ABOUT THE CD

The CD-ROM contains HTML code listings, SQL and Cold Fusion programming examples, and database programs and databases—especially for the MicroSoftAccess database. Code listings and SQL and Cold Fusion program examples are found in their corresponding chapter directories; database examples are found in separate subdirectories. An extended JavaScript example is contained in a subdirectory of Chapter 20.